Egyptian Mythology

W. Max Müller

DOVER PUBLICATIONS, INC.
Mineola, New York

Bibliographical Note

This Dover edition, first published in 2004, is an unabridged republication of the Egyptian section of *The Mythology of All Races, Volume XII: Egyptian, Indo-Chinese,* originally published by Marshall Jones Company, Boston, in 1918.

Library of Congress Cataloging-in-Publication Data

Müller, W. Max (Wilhelm Max), 1862–1919.
    Egyptian mythology / W. Max Müller.
        p. cm.
    "This Dover edition, first published in 2004, is an unabridged republication of the Egyptian section of The mythology of all races, volume XII: Egyptian, Indo-Chinese, originally published by Marshall Jones Company, Boston, in 1918"—Verso t.p.
    Includes bibliographical references.
    ISBN-13: 978-0-486-43674-6 (pbk.)
    ISBN-10: 0-486-43674-8 (pbk.)
    1. Mythology, Egyptian. I. Müller, W. Max (Wilhelm Max), 1862–1919. Egyptian [mythology]. 2004 II. Title.

BL2441.M85 2004
299'.31—dc22

                                                        2004056146

Manufactured in the United States by Courier Corporation
43674803
www.doverpublications.com

CONTENTS

EGYPTIAN

ILLUSTRATIONS IN THE TEXT

ILLUSTRATIONS

ILLUSTRATIONS xi

ILLUSTRATIONS

FULL PAGE ILLUSTRATIONS

Egyptian
Mythology

TO

MORRIS, JASTROW, JR., PH.D.
OF THE UNIVERSITY OF PENNSYLVANIA

AND TO

ALBERT TOBIAS CLAY, PH.D., LL.D.
AND
CHARLES CUTLER TORREY, PH.D., D.D.
OF YALE UNIVERSITY

AUTHOR'S PREFACE

THIS study can hope to give only a sketch of a vast theme which, because of its endless and difficult material, has thus far received but superficial investigation even from the best of scholars; its complete elaboration would require several volumes of space and a lifetime of preparation.

The principal difficulty is to make it clear to the modern mind that a religion can exist without any definite system of doctrine, being composed merely of countless speculations that are widely divergent and often conflicting. This doctrinal uncertainty is increased by the way in which the traditions have been transmitted. Only rarely is a piece of mythology complete. For the most part we have nothing but many scattered allusions which must be united for a hazardous restoration of one of these theories. In other respects, likewise, the enormous epigraphic material presents such difficulties and is so confusing in nature that everything hitherto done on the religion of Egypt is, as we have just implied, merely pioneer work. As yet an exhaustive description of this religion could scarcely be written.

A minor problem is the question of transliterating Egyptian words and names, most of which are written in so abbreviated a fashion that their pronunciation, especially in the case of the vowels, always remains dubious unless we have a good later tradition of their sound. It is quite as though the abbreviation "st." (= "street") were well known to persons having no acquaintance with English to mean something like "road," but without any indication as to its pronunciation. Foreigners would be compelled to guess whether the sound of the word

were *set, sat, seta, sota,* etc., or *este, usot,* etc., since there is absolutely nothing to suggest the true pronunciation "street." A
great part of the Egyptian vocabulary is known only in this
way, and in many instances we must make the words pro-
nounceable by arbitrarily assigning vowel sounds, etc., to them.
Accordingly I have thought it better to follow popular mispronunciations like Nut than to try Newet, Neyewet, and other
unsafe attempts, and even elsewhere I have sacrificed correctness to simplicity where difficulty might be experienced by a
reader unfamiliar with some Oriental systems of writing. It
should be borne in mind that Sekhauit and Uzoit, for example,
might more correctly be written S(e)kh}ewyet, Wezoyet, and
that *e* is often used as a mere filler where the true vowel is quite
unknown.

Sometimes we can prove that the later Egyptians themselves
misread the imperfect hieroglyphs, but for the most part we
must retain these mispronunciations, even though we are conscious of their slight value. All this will explain why any two
Egyptologists so rarely agree in their transcriptions. Returning
in despair to old-fashioned methods of conventionalizing transcription, I have sought to escape these difficulties rather than
to solve them.

In the transliteration *kh* has the value of the Scottish or
German *ch*; *ḥ* is a voiceless laryngeal spirant — a rough, wheez-
ing, guttural sound; *q* is an emphatic *k*, formed deep in the
throat (Hebrew ‏ק‎); ʿ is a strange, voiced laryngeal explosive
(Hebrew ‏ע‎); *ṭ* is an assibilated *t* (German *z*); *z* is used here
as a rather inexact substitute for the peculiar Egyptian pronunciation of the emphatic Semitic *ṣ* (Hebrew ‏צ‎, in Egyptian
sounding like *ṭṣ*, for which no single type can be made).

For those who may be unfamiliar with the history of Egypt
it will here be sufficient to say that its principal divisions (dis-
regarding the intermediate periods) are: the Old Empire (First
to Sixth Dynasties), about 3400 to 2500 B. C.; the Middle
Empire (Eleventh to Thirteenth Dynasties), about 2200 to

1700 B. C.; the New Empire (Eighteenth to Twenty-Sixth Dynasties), about 1600 to 525 B. C.

Pictures which could not be photographed directly from books have been drawn by my daughter; Figs. 13, 65 (*b*) are taken from scarabs in my possession.

Since space does not permit full references to the monuments, I have omitted these wherever I follow the present general knowledge and where the student can verify these views from the indexes of the more modern literature which I quote. References have been limited, so far as possible, to observations which are new or less well known. Although I have sought to be brief and simple in my presentation of Egyptian mythology, my study contains a large amount of original research. I have sought to emphasize two principles more than has been done hitherto: (*a*) the comparative view — Egyptian religion had by no means so isolated a growth as has generally been assumed; (*b*) as in many other religions, its doctrines often found a greater degree of expression in religious art than in religious literature, so that modern interpreters should make more use of the Egyptian pictures. Thus I trust not only that this book will fill an urgent demand for a reliable popular treatise on this subject, but that for scholars also it will mark a step in advance toward a better understanding of Egypt's most interesting bequest to posterity.

W. MAX MÜLLER.

UNIVERSITY OF PENNSYLVANIA,
    September, 1917.

INTRODUCTION

FOR almost two millenniums the religion of ancient Egypt has claimed the interest of the nations of the West. When the Classical peoples had lost faith in the credence of their forefathers, they turned to the "wise priests" of Egypt, and a certain reverence for the "wisdom of Egypt" survived even the downfall of all pagan religions. This admiration received a considerable impetus when Napoleon's expedition revealed the greatness of that remarkable civilization which once had flourished on the banks of the Nile. Thus today an Egyptian temple seems to many a peculiarly appropriate shrine for religious mysticism, and the profoundest thoughts of the human mind and the finest morality are believed to be hidden in the grotesque hieroglyphs on obelisks and sphinxes.

Yet the only bases of this popular impression are two arguments which are quite fallacious. The first has been implied — the religious thought of a nation which produced such a wonderful and many-sided civilization ought, one would naturally suppose, to offer an achievement parallel to what it accomplished in architecture, art, etc. The principal reason for this excessive regard, however, has been the unwarranted prejudice of Classical paganism. Modern readers must be warned against following this overestimation blindly, for it is largely founded on the very unintelligibility of the Egyptian religion, which, in its hyperconservatism, absolutely refused to be adapted to reason. Even the anxiety of dying heathenism could not force the endless number of gods and their contradictory functions into a rational system or explain away the crudity of such aspects of the Egyptian faith as the worship of animals; and the missionaries of Christianity selected these very features as the most palpable illustrations of the folly or the diabolical madness of heathen creeds. Yet the unintelligible always wields a strong attraction for the religious mind, and the appeals of the early Christian apologists to reason alone would scarcely have annihilated all faith in Isis and Osiris even outside the Nile valley, where that belief was not supported by the national traditions of many thousand years. The fact that the Egyptians themselves were so utterly unable to reduce their religion to a reasonable system seemed the best proof of its mystic depth to the Romans of post-Christian times and may still impress some persons similarly. Even after the science of the history of religion had developed, scholars did not examine the religion of Egypt with sufficient impartiality, but constantly sought to overrate it. Of course, the modern student will scarcely be inclined to treat all absurdities as wonderful mystic depths and to place the Egyptian religion at the acme of all religious systems simply because of its many obscurities. Yet scholars have hesitated to treat its crudities as real and have often tried to find more hidden meaning in them than was seen by the Egyptians themselves, so that considerable time elapsed before science dared to examine the religious "wisdom of Egypt" critically and to treat it as what it really was — a bequest of most primitive ages and in great part a remnant of the barbarism from which the Egyptians had gradually emerged.

The earliest Egyptologists dared not venture to explain the Egyptian religion, whose hieroglyphic texts they understood only incompletely. The first decipherers, J. F. Champollion and Sir J. G. Wilkinson, did little more than collect the pictures of the gods. R. Lepsius made the first feeble attempts at the investigation of special chapters of the texts. The earlier school of French Egyptologists, J. J. Champollion-Figeac, E. de Rougé, and P. Pierret, sought to explain the religion of the Pharaohs as a kind of monotheism, drawing this inference, strangely enough, from such epithets as "the Great One," "the Unique," or "the Eternal," even though these titles were given to so many different gods. To their minds a pure monotheism was disguised under the outward appearance of a symbolic polytheism, which had at its root the belief that all the different gods were in reality only diverse manifestations of the same supreme being. It is quite true that such views are found on some monuments,[1] but it is utterly erroneous to regard them as the general opinion or as the original religion of the Egyptians. As additional religious texts were discovered in course of time, the religion revealed itself to be increasingly crude and polytheistic in direct proportion to the earliness of the date of the documents concerned: the older the texts, the ruder and lower are the religious views which they set forth. All pantheistic or supposedly monotheistic passages represent only the development of Egyptian thought from a comparatively recent period. Furthermore, they were isolated attempts of a few advanced thinkers and poets and did not affect the religion of the masses; and finally, they are still far removed from a real monotheism or a systematic pantheism.

Among the apologists for Egyptian religion in an earlier generation of scholars H. K. Brugsch endeavoured with special zeal, but in a way which was far from convincing, to demonstrate that Egyptian religion was originally pantheistic; to maintain his theory he was compelled to analyse the divine principle into eight or nine cosmic forces by means of bolder identifications of the various divinities than even the later Egyptians ever attempted. Previous to him Le Page Renouf had emphasized the cosmic features of the pantheon in a manner which was not confirmed by the discovery of the earliest religious texts; and still earlier Lepsius had tried to interpret Egyptian polytheism as a degeneration of a solar monotheism or henotheism, thus taking a position intermediate between that of the earlier French scholars and that of later investigators. In like fashion, though assuming a more complicated hypothetical development, J. Lieblein also stressed an alleged degeneration from original simplicity; and certain similar theories, holding that Egyptian polytheism was partially (or even largely) developed from monotheism or henotheism by local differentiation, or evincing an erroneous tendency to discover a cosmic origin for all gods, continue to influence more than one of the most modern writers. But, we repeat, even if some elements of higher thought may be gleaned from the texts, these scattered traces did not touch the earliest form of Egyptian belief as it can now be read from texts anterior to 3000 B.C., nor did they affect the religion of the masses even during the latest periods of history. The further back we go, the more primitive are the ideas which we find, with absolutely no trace of monotheism; and those rude concepts always predominated in the religion of the people to such an extent that they represented the real Egyptian creed.

The first step toward an understanding of the fundamental crudity of the Egyptian religion was in 1878, when R. Pietschmann[2] proposed to regard its beginnings as precisely parallel to the pure animism and fetishism of Central Africa, showing at the same time that such a religion must everywhere assume in large part a magic character. The effect of this step has been very great; and although it encountered much opposition and is still denied by some prejudiced scholars and many laymen, it has done much to develop the theory on this subject which now prevails among students of religion. The writer who has been most energetic in the promulgation of this theory has been G. Maspero, whose numerous essays have been the chief factors in establishing a fuller knowledge and understanding of Egyptian religion, although he never wrote an exhaustive presentation of these beliefs.

The stereotyped objection against such a low view of Egyptian religion is its extreme contrast to the whole civilization of the Egyptian nation. Can it be possible that, as Maspero boldly stated, the most highly developed people of the ancient Orient, a nation inferior only to the Greeks in its accomplishments, held in religion a place no higher than that which is occupied by some barbarous negro tribes? Yet the development of civilization rarely runs quite parallel to that of religious thought. The wonderful civilization of the Chinese, for example, is quite incongruous with the very primitive character of their indigenous religion; and, on the other hand, Israel, the source of the greatest religious progress, took a very modest place in art and science before it was dispersed among the Gentiles. Above all, religion is everywhere more or less controlled by the traditions of the past and seeks its basis in the beliefs and customs of early days. According to the usual reasoning of man, his forefathers appear as more and more happy and wise in direct proportion as history is traced further and further back, until at last they are portrayed as living with the gods, who still walked on earth. The ultra-conservative Egyptians were especially anxious to tread in the ways of the blessed forefathers, to adore the same gods to whom their ancestors had bowed down in time immemorial, and to worship them in exactly the same forms; so that the religion of the later, highly developed Egyptians after 3000 B.C. remained deplorably similar to that of their barbarous forefathers. Our present knowledge of the state of Egyptian civilization about and before 4000 B.C. is sufficient to show that some development had already been made, including the first steps toward the evolution of the hieroglyphic system of writing; but the crude artistic attempts of that age, its burials of the dead in miserable holes or in large jars, its buildings in straw and in mud bricks, and its temples of wicker-work and mats still form such a contrast to the period of the Second and Third Dynasties, when Egyptian architecture and art made the first strides toward the perfection of the Pyramid Age, that we do not hesitate to place the religious development of the Egyptians of the fifth millennium on the level of ordinary

African paganism. The rude carvings of that time show that most, if not all, of the later gods, with their names, symbols, and artistic types, existed then and that they had already been transmitted by ancient tradition from ancestral days. Thus we may assume that the Egyptian pantheon had its origin in the most remote and obscure neolithic (or, perhaps, even palæolithic) age, and we may safely consider it a product of a most primitive barbarism. It may seem a little strange that the swift development of Egyptian civilization somewhat before 3000 B.C. should not have led to a better systematization of the religious traditions. Until we know what political conditions produced that rapid evolution,[3] we must rest content with the explanation which we have already advanced, i. e. that everywhere conservatism is one of the most important factors in religion, and that the mind of the ancient Egyptians was peculiarly conservative throughout their history. This conservatism is strikingly illustrated by Egyptian art, which, even in the time of its highest development, could not free itself from the fetters of traditionalism, but tenaciously kept the childish perspective of primitive days, although as early as the Pyramid Age artists were able to draw quite correctly, and occasionally did so. In the religious art this adherence to tradition constituted an especially grave barrier to artistic development; accordingly the figures of the gods always preserved, more or less, the stiff and — in some details — childishly imperfect style of the early period. For example, all the pictures of Ptaḥ, one of the oldest gods, point back to a clumsy type betraying an age when the artists were not yet able to separate arms and legs from the body. The savage simplicity of the age which created the Egyptian religion and indelibly stamped its subsequent evolution is clearly evidenced likewise in the barbarous head-dresses of the divinities,[4] which consist of feathers, horns, and rush-plaited crowns, as well as in the simple emblems held in their hands. These insignia, in the case of male deities, are generally staves terminating in the head of the Sêth animal, while the goddesses usually hold a flowering lotus stalk; the appearance of weapons as insignia is comparatively rare. In this same way the animal shapes of most Egyptian divinities and the genesis of the animal cult itself, such fetish-like receptacles as the one worshipped at This, the strange local divine symbols which remind us of totemistic emblems, etc., all become easily intelligible when considered as a survival from the barbaric age, which we shall endeavour to reconstruct in the next chapter.

EGYPTIAN MYTHOLOGY

CHAPTER I

THE LOCAL GODS

ANIMISM is a very wide-spread form of primitive religion. It has no gods in the sense of the advanced pagan religions; it only believes that earth and heaven are filled by countless spirits, either sedentary or wandering. These spirits can make their earthly abode in men, animals, or plants, or any object that may be remarkable for size or form. As soon as man, in his fear of these primitive deities, tries to placate them by sacrifices, they develop into tutelary spirits and fetishes, and then into gods. Some scholars claim that all religions have sprung from a primitive animism. Whether this be true or not, such an origin fits the primitive Egyptian religion especially well and explains its endless and confused pantheon. The Egyptians of the historical period tell us that every part of the world is filled by gods, an assertion which in our days has often been misinterpreted as if those gods were cosmic, and as though a primitive kind of pantheism underlay these statements. Yet the gods who lived, for instance, in the water, like the crocodile Sobk, the hippopotamus-deity Êpet, etc., did not represent this element; for the most part they merely inhabited a stretch of water. We find that in general the great majority of the old local gods defy all cosmic explanation: they still betray that once they were nothing but local spirits whose realm must primarily have been extremely limited. In the beginning there may have been a tendency to assume tutelary spirits for every tree

or rock of unusual size or form or for every house and field,
such spirits being worshipped in the first case in the form of
the sacred object itself in which they abode, and in the latter
case being embodied in some striking object in the locality or
in some remarkable animal which chanced to frequent the
place. Many of these tutelary spirits never developed into
real gods, i. e. they never received a regular cult. The transi-
tional stage appears in such instances as when, according to
certain Theban wall-paintings, the harvesters working in a
field deposited a small part of their food as an offering to a
tree which dominated that field, i. e. for the genius inhabiting
the tree; or when they fed a serpent discovered on the field,
supposing it to be more than an ordinary creature.[1] This serpent might disappear and yet be remembered in the place,
which might in consequence remain sacred forever; perhaps
the picture of its feeding may thus be interpreted as meaning
that even then the offering was merely in recollection of the
former appearance of a local spirit in serpent form.

Another clear illustration of primitive animism surviving in
historic times is furnished by an old fragment of a tale in a
papyrus of the museum of Berlin. Shepherds discover "a
goddess" hiding herself in a thicket along the river-bank.
They flee in fright and call the wise old chief shepherd, who
by magic formulae expels her from her lair. Unfortunately
the papyrus breaks off when the goddess "came forth with
terrible appearance," but we can again see how low the term
"god" remained in the Pyramid Age and later.

Such rudimentary gods, however, did not play any part
in the religion of the historic age. Only those of them
that attracted wider attention than usual and whose worship expanded from the family to the village would later
be called gods. We must, nevertheless, bear in mind that a
theoretical distinction could scarcely be drawn between such
spirits or "souls" (*baiu*) which enjoyed no formal or regular
cult and the gods recognized by regular offerings, just as there

was no real difference between the small village deity whose shrine was a little hut of straw and the "great god" who had a stately temple, numerous priests, and rich sacrifices. If we had full information about Egyptian life, we certainly should be able to trace the development by which a spirit or fetish which originally protected only the property of a single peasant gradually advanced to the position of the village god, and consequently, by the growth of that village or by its political success, became at length a "great god" who ruled first over a city and next over the whole county dominated by that city, and who then was finally worshipped throughout Egypt. As we shall see, the latter step can be observed repeatedly; but the first progress of a "spirit" or "soul" toward regular worship as a full god [2] can never be traced in the inscriptions. Indeed, this process of deification must have been quite infrequent in historic times, since, as we have already seen, only the deities dating from the days of the ancestors could find sufficient recognition. In a simpler age this development from a spirit to a god may have been much easier. In the historic period we see, rather, the opposite process; the great divinities draw all worship and sacrifices to their shrines and thus cause many a local god to be neglected, so that he survives only in magic, etc., or sinks into complete oblivion. In some instances the cult of such a divinity and the existence of its priesthood were saved by association with a powerful deity, who would receive his humbler colleague into his temple as his wife or child; but in many instances even a god of the highest rank would tolerate an insignificant rival cult in the same city, sometimes as the protector of a special quarter or suburb.

Originally the capital of each of the forty-two nomes, or counties, of Egypt seems to have been the seat of a special great divinity or of a group of gods, who were the masters and the patrons of that county; and many of these nomes maintained the worship of their original deity until the latest period. The priests in his local temple used to extol their pa-

tron as though he was the only god or was at least the supreme
divinity; later they often attributed to him the government of
all nature and even the creation of the whole world, as well
as the most important cosmic functions, especially, in every
possible instance, those of a solar character; and they were
not at all disturbed by the fact that a neighbouring nome
claimed exactly the same position for its own patron. To us
it must seem strange that under these conditions no rivalry
between the gods or their priests is manifest in the inscriptions. To explain this strange isolation of local religion it is
generally assumed that in prehistoric times each of these
nomes was a tribal organization or petty kingdom, and that
the later prominence given to their divine patron or patrons
was a survival of that primitive political independence, since
every ancient Oriental state possessed its national god and
worshipped him in a way which often approximated henotheism.[3] Yet the quasi-henotheistic worship which was
given to the patron of these forty-two petty capitals recurred
in connexion with the various local gods of other towns in
the same nome, where even the chief patron of the nome in
question was relegated to the second or third rank in favour of
the local idol. This was carried to such an extent that every
Egyptian was expected to render worship primarily to his
"city-god" (or gods), whatever the character of this divinity
might be. Since each of the larger settlements thus worshipped
its local tutelary spirit or deity without determining his precise relation to the gods of other communities, we may with
great probability assume that in the primitive period the
village god preceded the town god, and that the god of the
hamlet and of the family were not unknown. At that early
day the forces of nature appear to have received no worship
whatever. Such conditions are explicable only from the point
of view of animism.[4] This agrees also with the tendency to
seek the gods preferably in animal form, and with the strange,
fetish-like objects in which other divinities were represented.

Numerous as the traces of animistic, local henotheism are, the exclusive worship of its local spirit by each settlement cannot have existed very long. In a country which never was favourable to individualism the family spirit could not compete with the patron of the community; and accordingly, when government on a larger scale was established, in innumerable places the local divinity soon had to yield to the god of a town which was greater in size or in political importance. We can frequently observe how a chief, making himself master of Egypt, or of a major part of it, advanced his city god above all similar divinities of the Egyptian pantheon, as when, for instance, the obscure town of Thebes, suddenly becoming the capital of all Egypt, gained for her local god, Amon, the chief position within the Egyptian pantheon, so that he was called master of the whole world. The respect due to the special patron of the king and his ancestors, the rich cult with which that patron was honoured by the new dynasty, and the officials proceeding from the king's native place and court to other towns soon spread the worship of Pharaoh's special god through the whole kingdom, so that he was not merely given worship at the side of the local deities, but often supplanted them, and was even able to take the place of ancient patrons of the nomes. Thus we find, for instance, Khnûm as god of the first and eleventh nomes; Hat-hôr, whose worship originally spread only in Middle Egypt (the sixth, seventh, and tenth nomes), also in the northernmost of the Upper Egyptian nomes (the twenty-second) and in one Lower Egyptian nome (the third); while Amon of Thebes, who, as we have just seen, had come into prominence only after 2000 B.C., reigned later in no less than four nomes of the Delta. This latter example is due to the exceptional duration of the position of Thebes as the capital, which was uninterrupted from 2000 to 1800 and from 1600 to 1100 B.C.; yet to the mind of the conservative Egyptians even this long predominance of the Theban gods could not effect a thorough codification of religious belief in favour of these gods, nor could it dethrone more than a part of the local deities.

As we have already said, the difficulty of maintaining separate cults, combined with other reasons, led the priests at a very early time to group several divinities together in one temple as a divine family, usually in a triad of father, mother, and son;[5] in rarer instances a god might have two wives (as at Elephantine, and sometimes at Thebes);[6] in the case of a goddess who was too prominent to be satisfied with the second place as wife of a. god, she was associated with a lesser male divinity as her son (as at Denderah). We may assume that all these groups were formed by gods which originally were neighbours. The development of the ennead (perhaps a triple triad in source) is obviously much later (see pp. 215-16).

Fig. 1. The Triad of Elephantine: Khnûm, Satet, and 'Anuqet

As long as no cosmic rôle was attributed to the local gods, little mythology could be attached to their personality; even a deity so widely worshipped as the crocodile Sobk, for example, does not exhibit a single mythological trait. Of most gods we know no myths, an ignorance which is not due to accidental loss of information, as some Egyptologists thought, but to the fact that the deities in question really possessed little or no mythology. The only local divinities capable of mythological life, therefore, were those that were connected with the cycle of the sun or of Osiris.

A possible trace of primitive simplicity may be seen in the fact that some gods have, properly speaking, no names, but are called after their place of worship. Thus, the designation of the cat-shaped goddess Ubastet means only "the One of the City Ubaset," as though she had long been worshipped there without a real name, being called, perhaps, simply "the goddess"; and, again, the god Khent(i)-amentiu ("the One Before the Westerners," i. e. the dead),[7] who was originally a jackal (?), seems to have received his appellation simply from the location of his shrine near the necropolis in the west of This. These instances, however, admit of other explanations — an earlier name may have become obsolete;[8] or a case of local differentiation may be assumed in special places, as when the jackal-god Khent(i)-amentiu seems to be only a local form of Up-uaut (Ophoïs). Names like that of the bird-headed god, "the One Under his Castor Oil[?] Bush" (beq), give us the impression of being very primitive.[9] Differentiation of a divinity into two or more personalities according to his various centres of worship occurs, it is true; but, except for very rare cases like the prehistoric differentiation of Mîn and Amon, it has no radical effect. In instances known from the historic period it is extremely seldom that a form thus discriminated evokes a new divine name; the Horus and Ḥat-ḥôr of a special place usually remain Horus and Ḥat-ḥôr, so that such differentiations cannot have developed the profuse polytheism from a simpler system. On the contrary, it must be questioned whether even as early an identification as, e. g., of the winged disk Beḥdeti ("the One of Beḥdet" [the modern Edfu]) with Horus as a local form was original. In this instance the vague name seems to imply that the identification with Horus was still felt to be secondary.

Thus we are always confronted with the result that, the nearer we approach to the original condition of Egypt, the more we find its religion to be an endless and unsystematic polytheism which betrays an originally animistic basis, as described above. The whole difficulty of understanding the religion of the historic period lies in the fact that it always hovered between that primitive stage and the more advanced type, the cosmic conception of the gods, in a very confusing way, such as we scarcely find in any other national religion. In other words,

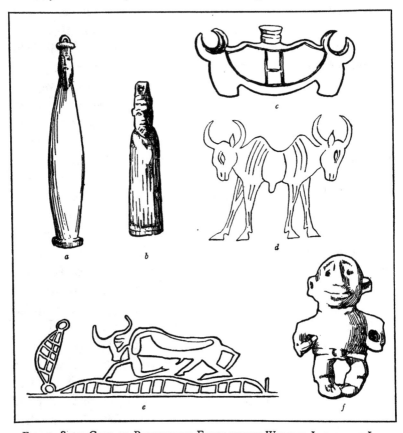

FIG. 2. SOME GODS OF PREHISTORIC EGYPT WHOSE WORSHIP LATER WAS LOST

(*a*), (*b*) A bearded deity much used as an amulet; (*c*), (*d*) a double bull (Khônsu?); (*e*) an unknown bull-god; (*f*) a dwarf divinity(?) similar to Sokari, but found far in the south.

the peculiar value of the ancient Egyptian religion is that it forms the clearest case of transition from the views of the most primitive tribes of mankind to those of the next higher religious development, as represented especially in the religion of Babylonia.

CHAPTER II

THE WORSHIP OF THE SUN

TAKING animism as the basis of the earliest stage of Egyptian religion, we must assume that the principal cosmic forces were easily personified and considered as divine. A nation which discovers divine spirits in every remarkable tree or rock will find them even more readily in the sun, the moon, the stars, and the like. But though the earliest Egyptians may have done this, and perhaps may even have admitted that these cosmic spirits were great gods, at first they seem to have had no more thought of giving them offerings than is entertained by many primitive peoples in the animistic stage of religion who attach few religious thoughts to the great cosmic factors. Was it that these forces, which were beheld every day, appeared to be less mysterious and, therefore, less divine than the tutelary spirits of the town, or did these local spirits seem nearer to man and thus more interested in his welfare than the cosmic gods, who were too great and too remote for the ordinary mortal? At any rate, we can observe that, for instance, in historic times the god of the earth (Qêb) is described as the father of all the gods and as one of the most important personages of the pantheon, but that, despite this, he does not seem to have possessed temples of his own in the New Empire; and the like statement holds true of the god Nuu (the abyss), although he is declared to be the oldest and wisest of all gods, etc. By their very contradictions the later attempts to transform the old local spirits and fetishes into personifications of cosmic powers prove that no such personification was acknowledged in the prehistoric period to which the majority of Egyptian cults are traceable, thus confirming the general absence of homage to cosmic powers. It is even doubtful whether the worship of the sun-god was originally important; while the scanty attention paid to the

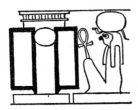

moon in historical times and the confusion of three planets under one name again make it certain that no cult of them had been transmitted from the days of the ancestors.

Fig. 3. The Sun-God Watching the Appearance of his Disk in the Eastern Gate of Heaven

On the other hand, the first attempts at philosophical thought which accompanied the development of Egyptian civilization evidently led to a closer contemplation of nature and to a better appreciation of it. Yet, although we find traces of various attempts to create a system of cosmic gods, no such system was ever carried through satisfactorily, so that a large part of the pantheon either never became cosmic or, as has been said above, was at best only unsuccessfully made cosmic.

The first of all cosmic powers to find general worship was the sun, whose rays dominate Egypt so strongly. The earliest efforts to personify it identified it with an old hawk-god, and thus sought to describe it as a hawk which flew daily across the sky. Therefore, the two most popular forms of the solar deity, Rê' and Horus, have the form of a hawk or of a hawk-headed man (later sometimes also of a lion with a hawk's head). Both divinities had so many temples in

Fig. 4. Pictures of Khepri in Human Form

historical times that we cannot determine their original seats of worship. At the beginning of the dynastic period Horus seems to have been the sun-god who was most generally worshipped in Egypt.[1] Though Rê' does not appear to find official recognition until later, in the Second and Third Dynasties, nevertheless he seems to be the older personification of the sun since his name furnishes the popular designation of the solar disk.

Less popular is the description of the sun as Khepri (Kheprer in the earlier orthography), or "the Scarab-Like," i. e. as a scarab rolling his egg (the sun) across the sky, or as a man who wears a scarab on his head or instead of a head. Later theologians endeavoured to harmonize this idea with the other representations of the sun-god by explaining Khepri as the weaker sun, i. e. as it appears in the morning when the solar egg is formed, or, sometimes, in the evening, or even as the sun

in embryonic condition beneath the horizon at night,[2] when it traverses the regions of the dead and shines on the lower world. When the scarab draws a second egg behind it, or carries two eggs as it flies athwart the sky, it symbolizes the morning and the evening sun.[3]

FIG. 5.
KHEPRI AS
THE INFANT
SUN

FIG. 6.
KHEPRI WITH
THE SUN
IN DOUBLE
APPEAR-
ANCE

At the very earliest period, however, the sun was also described as a man whose face, eye, or head-ornament was the solar body. In the latter instance this was regularly compared to the uraeus, the fiery asp, wound about Pharaoh's brow as a sign of his absolute power over life and death. When, as we shall see, the sun-god is bitten by a serpent as he walks across the sky, on the celestial road, this is merely a later reversion of the myth and blends the interpretations of the sun as an eye (which may be lost) and as an asp. The most popular idea, however, is that in a ship (which has perhaps replaced an earlier double raft)[4] the sun sails over the sky, conceived as a blue river or lake which is a continuation of the sea and of the Nile. At the prow of this solar ship we frequently find a curious detail, sometimes represented as a carpet or mat[5] on which the god is seated, often thus duplicating a second figure of himself in the cabin. This detail still awaits explanation. The deity may either be the only occupant of the boat, which moves by itself or is paddled by him; or he may be accompanied by many

prominent gods, especially the nine gods of the Heliopolitan ennead and the personifications of wisdom, etc. In the latter case the great ship, which one text[6] describes as seven hundred and seventy cubits in length, is rowed by numerous gods and souls of kings and other (originally especially prominent) dead, the "followers of Horus,"

FIG. 7. THE SUN-GOD ROWS A DEPARTED SOUL OVER THE SKY

or "of Rê',"[7] i. e. of the god to whom the ship of the sun belonged. The *Book of the Gates*[8] reverts to an ancient idea by explaining that "the never-vanishing stars" (i. e. again the elect souls) become the rowers of the sun by day. Then the sun may rest in the cabin as a disk in which the god himself may be enthroned, or as the uraeus asp, the symbol of fire; in the latter form he may also twine around the prow, cabin, or any other part of the vessel. In one instance a double asp actually forms the boat which carries the stairs of the sun, i. e. the symbol of its daily way (see below on the double nature of the asp). An extremely ancient idea, which occurs, for instance, as early as the famous ivory tablet of King Menes, is the blending of the human shape of the sun with his hawk form, so that the

FIG. 8. A STAR AS ROWER OF THE SUN IN THE DAY-TIME

FIG. 9. THE SUN-BOAT AS A DOUBLE SERPENT

solar bird sails in the cabin of the huge ship as though it had no wings.

On its daily way the ship of the sun has adventures and

adversaries which apparently symbolize clouds and eclipses; and its perils increase still further at night, when it passes the western mountain ridge, the limit of the earth, and enters hostile darkness. In the morning, however, it always emerges victorious over the eastern mountains; the sun himself and his brave rowers and soldiers have scattered all opponents, sailing successfully through the subterranean course of the Nile or crossing the abysmal ocean into which the sun dips at evening.[9] During the night (or part of it) the sun-god illumines the regions of the dead, who for a time awaken from their sleep when his rays shine upon them, and who are sometimes believed to tow the sun's ship through the dead or windless lower waters or through especially difficult

FIG. 10. THE SUN-GOD AT NIGHT-TIME

With "Wisdom" and "Magic" in his boat, he is drawn by the " spirits of the underworld."

parts of them,[10] or who assist it there against its enemies. At night the sun may also take rest in its special abode in the nether world, in "the island of flames," [11] where the fiery element has its proper centre.

To speak more exactly, the sun-god has two different ships: one — the Me'enzet — for the day, and the other — the Semektet [12] — for the night; sometimes he enters the "evening ship" in the afternoon. This distinction is no more difficult to understand than the later differentiation of the sun into three distinct personalities during the day-time, when he is called Horus (or Ḥar-akhti, "Horus of the Horizon") in the morning, Rê' (his ordinary name) at noon, and Atum(u) toward evening. The latter form, taken from the local god of Heliopolis,[13] is depicted as human, very rarely in the oldest

form of Atum as an ichneumon. The accompanying picture
shows this god of the evening sun in his original animal form
behind the closed western gate of heaven, built on the mountain of the west. We have already seen that the name
Khepri was used for the weaker manifestations; later Rê',
as the oldest name, was also employed more for the weak
and aged sun;[14] while the dying sun of evening and the dead
sun of night were soon identified with Osiris, as we shall see
in the chapter on the Osiris-myth. The representation of the
sun with a ram's head during his nightly journey through
the lower world seems to date from the New Empire only.[15]

FIG. 11. ATUM BE-
HIND THE WESTERN
GATE OF HEAVEN

Its obvious explanation is identification with
Khnûm, the guardian of the waters coming
from the lower world and master of Hades.
The sun at night-time is lost in Khnûm's
dark realm and unites with him. The description of the sun as a fragrant flame of
incense seems to find its explanation in the
fact that it rises in the eastern regions whence
spices and perfumes come.

After 2000 B.C. the worship of the sun, thanks to increasing
official favour, became so dominant that identifications with
the sun or with a phase of it were tried with almost every god
who had not received a clear cosmic function at an earlier
time; and in this way most local divinities were at last explained
as different manifestations of the sun, as the "members" of
Rê' or as his "souls." Attempts to systematize these manifestations tell us that such a great god as the sun has seven or
fourteen souls or doubles.[16] The later solar identifications, of
course, far exceed these numbers.

A slightly more modest place is attributed to the sun-god
when he is parallel with the moon, each of these great lumi-
naries being an eye of the heavenly god, although this celestial
divinity still bears the name of the sun-god as master of the
sky, usually of Horus (whence he is also called "Horus of the

Two Eyes"), more rarely of Rê' or of other identifications with
the sun.[17] The fact that this celestial deity shows only one
eye at a time is explained by the various myths which, as we
shall see later (pp. 85–91) recount how the sun-god lost an eye;
according to the belief which prevailed later, and which was
adapted to the Osirian myth, this occurred in a combat with
Sêth.[18]

The Egyptian word for "eye" being feminine, the disk of
the sun could also be regarded as female. A theory concerning
the sun, reaching the same general conclusion, has already been
mentioned: the solar orb is compared to the fiery asp, the
'ar'et (the uraeus of the Greeks and Romans), which Pharaoh,
the sun-god's representative on earth, wore round his forehead.
Understood as a symbol of fire, this serpent was originally
thought to deck the forehead or to occupy the ship of the
solar or celestial god, as has been described on p. 26, but it
was soon so closely identified with his flaming eye that "eye"
and "asp" became synonymous. Thus both eyes of the celestial
god were identified with asps, regardless of the milder light of
the moon; or two uraei were thought to be worn on the sun's
forehead just as they sometimes adorned Pharaoh. These two
eyes or serpents are often called "the daughters of the sun-
god," [19] and we shall find below the myth of these two rival
daughters. (See also Fig. 9 for a picture of the double asp
as the ship which carries the sun-god's staircase.)

All these expressions furnished methods of solarizing female
divinities. The chief goddesses who were regarded as solar and
described as the daughter, eye, asp, or crown of the sun were
Tefênet, Sekhmet, and Ubastet, whose animal forms (the
lioness with the first and second, and the cat with the third)
also seem to have contributed toward associating them with
the luminary of day, because the sun-god often had a leaning
toward a lion's form (p. 24). Moreover Hat-hôr, Isis, and
other celestial goddesses sometimes betray a tendency to such
a solar interpretation, precisely as male divinities like Horus

hover between solar and celestial functions (pp. 28–29).[20] We must, however, emphasize the fact that all female personifications of the sun had no real hold on the mind of the Egyptians, who were agreed that the sun was a male deity. These solarizations of female gods give us the impression of early transitory attempts whose history is not yet clear. For a myth of the sun's eye as a daughter who wilfully deserts her father see pp. 86 ff. as well as for other legends of the injured (or blind) eye of the sun-god, which is euphemistically called "the sound, intact one," (*uzat, uzait*), because it cannot be damaged permanently.

Religious poetry also calls everything which is good and useful "the eye of the sun," either because all life is due to the rays of the great celestial body, as some hymns graphically declare, or, perhaps, also because the eye, torn out and falling to the earth, created life.

There was much difference of opinion as to the time when the sun came into the world; some held that he proceeded directly from the abyss and created (or at least organized) the whole world, begetting all the gods, and others maintained that, especially in the later solar form of Osiris, he was the result of the first separation of heaven and earth, the two greatest cosmic forces (see pp. 77–78). In any case, the sun is always regarded as the creator of men, who "proceeded from his eye(s)" in a way which was variously interpreted by the Egyptians, and as the god who (alone or through his clerk Thout) organized the world, at least in its present form.

The substance most sacred to the sun-god was the bright metal gold. It played an important part in religious symbolism,[21] and such goddesses as Hat-ḥôr were connected with the sun by epithets like "the golden."

The dominant worship of the sun influenced the whole Egyptian religion and affected all the cults of the local gods, even before it became the fashion to explain most gods as solar. Thus the pair of monolithic red obelisks erected before the gates of the Egyptian temples were originally intended merely to symbolize the limits of the sun's course, and especially its yearly bounds, the equinoxes. We are also told that the sun has two obelisks on earth and two in heaven;[22] again, only one of these pillars may be treated as actually important. An allusion to this conception is doubtless to be found in the huge, single obelisk-like structures on a cubic base which only the kings of the Fifth Dynasty erected to the honour of Rêʻ, because they seem to have claimed him for their ancestor more literally than did the other royal families.[23] Later all obelisks were themselves worshipped as signs of the sun's presence on earth.[24]

On (Un[u?], Eun[u?] in the earliest orthography), the most ancient and the most sacred city of Egypt, the "City of the Sun" — the Heliopolis of the Greeks — was the principal seat of the solar mythology, although the general name of the sun-god, Rêʻ, seems even there gradually to have replaced the old local deity, Atum(u), only after 2000 B.C. Heliopolis contained the earthly proxy of the tree of heaven, the holy *Persea*, and the sacred well which to this day is called "the Sun's Well" ('Ain Shams) and in which the sun was believed either to bathe himself morning and night or to have been born at the beginning of the world, when he arose from the abyss, etc. Thus the pool was not merely a type, but a real remnant of the primeval flood.[25] Such sacred lakes were imitated in many sanctuaries, just as the sacred tree of Heliopolis had local parallels.

In all sanctuaries of the sun the god's presence on earth was indicated by single or double reproductions of the solar ship, which sometimes were enormous constructions of stones or bricks, although generally they were made of wood and were portable, so that the priests could imitate the daily and yearly course of the sun in solemn procession as they carried or dragged the ship around the temple or floated it on the sacred lake near by.

Most closely associated with the sun we find his secretary Thout(i) (the moon), who also heals his eye when it is wounded or torn out. When the gods or "souls" of the prehistoric capitals of divided Egypt, Buto and Hierakonpolis,

FIG. 12.
THOUT AS A
BABOON

who were represented as human figures with the heads of hawks or jackals,[26] and who were also called "the souls of the east,"

a   b

FIG. 13. BABOONS GREET THE SUN

(a) Over the celestial pillar; (b) in the celestial tree.

are described as saluting the sun every morning, some scholars have attempted to see in this allusions to the cries with which the animals of the wilderness seem joyfully to hail the rising sun. However, the cynocephalous baboons who, according to the Egyptian view, likewise welcome the sun thus with prayers and hymns at his rising, also bid him farewell at his setting and even salute, accompany, and aid the nocturnal sun as he voyages through the nether world.[27] Therefore their *rôle* seems to have been developed from the part which Thout played

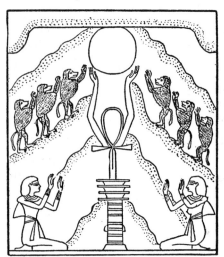

FIG. 14. BABOONS SALUTING THE MORNING SUN

He rises in the eastern mountains from the symbols of the Osirian state and of life.

as assistant to the sun-god, and the hawks and jackals already mentioned likewise rather suggest mythological explanations.

CHAPTER III

OTHER GODS CONNECTED WITH NATURE

IT is remarkable that the moon, which was so important, especially in Babylonia, never rivalled the sun among the Egyptians.[1] At a rather early time it was identified with the white ibis-god Thout(i) (earlier Zhouti, Dhouti), the local divinity of Khmun(u)-Hermopolis, who thus became the deity of reck-
oning and writing and in his capacity as secretary of the company of gods acted as the judge of di-
vinities and of men.[2] The reason is clear: the moon is the easiest regulator of time for primitive man. In like manner when Thout takes care of the injured eye of the solar or celestial god, and heals or replaces it, the underlying idea seems to be that the moon regulates such

FIG. 15. THOUT

FIG. 16. THOUT, THE SCRIBE

disturbances as eclipses; it may, however, equally well imply that the moon, being the second eye of the heavenly god, is simply a weaker reappearance of the sun at night.

Some scholars formerly sought the reason for the ibis-form in the crescent-shaped bill of the bird,

FIG. 17. THOUT IN BABOON FORM AS MOON-GOD AND SCRIBE OF THE GODS

but such explanations fail when we find the cynocephalus regarded as another (somewhat later?) embodiment of the same god of wisdom; so that this species of

baboon appears not only as a special friend of the sun-god (p. 32), but also as the deity of wisdom, the patron of scribes

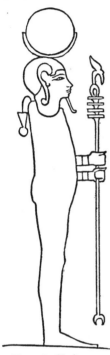

and scholars.[3] Thout is sometimes depicted as sailing, like the sun, across the heavenly ocean in a ship. Originally, like the hawk-gods Rê' and Horus, he was thought to fly over the sky in his old bird-form as a white ibis.

During the period of the Middle Empire[4] also Khôns(u), the least important member of the Theban triad (Ch. I, Note 6), assumed the character of a moon-god because the union of Amen-Rê' as the sun with Mut as the sky led to the theory that the moon was their child.[5] He is usually represented in human form, wearing a side-lock to indicate youth; but later, like Horus, he sometimes has the head of a hawk and also appears very much like Ptaḥ; although he is frequently equated with Thout, an ibis-head for him is rare. A symbol, sometimes identified with him, is thus far unexplained (unless it belongs

FIG. 18. KHÔNS AS MOON-GOD

to another god, see the statements on Dua, p. 132); and it is rather doubtful whether he is represented by the double bull with a single body (Fig. 2 (d)).[6] His name seems to mean "the Roamer, the Wanderer," and it was perhaps for this reason that the Greeks identified him with Herakles.

We have already noted the thought that the sky is water and that it forms a continuation of the Nile or of the ocean, on which the solar barge pursues its way. It is not clear how this was harmonized with the parallel, though rarer, idea that the sky was a metal roof, a belief which may have been derived from observation of meteorites. Sometimes only the centre of heaven, the throne of its master, is thought to be of metal; while other texts speak of "the solar ship sailing over the metal" as though this was under the celestial waters. This conception of a metal dome explains some expressions of later times, such as the name of iron, *be-ni-pet* ("sky-metal"), or the later word for "thunder," *khru-bai* (literally, "sound of the metal"), i. e. thunder was evidently explained as the beating of the great sheets of metal which constituted the sky. This heavenly roof was thought to rest on four huge pillars, which were usually pictured as supports forked

FIG. 19. A PERSONIFIED PILLAR OF THE SKY

above (Υ); more rarely they were inter preted as mountains or (in the latest period) as four women upholding the sky.[7] The sky may also be explained as a great staircase (mostly double) which the sun was supposed to ascend and to descend daily (cf. Fig. 9).

FIG. 20. THE SUN-GOD ON HIS STAIRS

Another early concept describes the sky as a huge tree overshadowing the earth, the stars being the fruits or leaves which hang from its branches. When "the gods perch on its boughs," they are evidently identified with the stars. The celestial tree disappears in the morning, and the sun-god rises from its leaves; in the even-ing he hides himself again in the foliage, and the tree (or its double of evening time) once more spreads over the world,

FIG. 21. THE DEAD WIT-NESSES THE BIRTH OF THE SUN FROM THE CE-LESTIAL TREE

so that three hundred and sixty-five trees symbolize the year, or two typify its turning-points, or night and day.[8] This thought of the celestial or cosmic tree or trees, which is found among so many nations, also underlies the idea of the tree of

life, whose fruit keeps the gods and the chosen souls of the dead in eternal youth and in wisdom in Egypt as elsewhere. The tree of fate, whose leaves or fruits symbolize events or the lives of men, represents the same thought: the past as well as the

FIG. 22. THE SUN-BOAT AND THE TWO CELESTIAL TREES

future is written in the stars. Osiris, as the god of heaven, is frequently identified with the heavenly tree or with some important part of it, or is brought into connexion with its fruit or blossom. Egyptian theology tries to determine the terrestrial analogy of this tree. As the world-tree it is thus compared to the widest branching tree of Egypt, the sycamore; more rarely it is likened to the date-palm or tamarisk, etc.; sometimes it is the willow, which grows so near the water that it may easily be associated with the celestial tree springing from the abyss or the Osirian waters. In connexion with the Osiris-myth, however, the tree is mostly the *Persea* or (perhaps later) the fragrant cedar growing on the remote mountains of Asia, or, again, the vine through whose fruit love and death entered into the world; while as the tree of fate it is once more usually the *Persea* of Osiris. These comparisons may refer to the inevitable attempts to localize or to symbolize the wonderful tree on earth. By a transition of thought it is described as localized in a part of the sky. Thus

FIG. 23. THE DEAD AT THE TREE AND SPRING OF LIFE

"a great island in the Field of Sacrifices on which the great gods rest, the never vanishing stars," [9] holds the tree of life, evidently between the ocean and sky, between the upper and the lower world, where the dead, passing from the one realm to the other, may find it. As we have already seen, the most famous of earthly proxies was the sacred *Persea*-tree of Heliopolis, which we find, e. g. in the accompanying picture, completely identified with the heavenly tree; but the central sanctuary of every nome had a holy tree which, probably, was always claimed to symbolize heaven; even more botanical species were represented in these earthly counterparts than those which we have mentioned (p. 36).

FIG. 24. AMON AS THE SUPREME DIVINITY REGISTERS A ROYAL NAME ON "THE HOLY PERSEA IN THE PALACE OF THE SUN"

When heaven is personified, it is a female being, since the word *pêt* ("heaven") is feminine. Therefore the sky is compared to a woman bending over the earth (Figs. 35, 47), or to a cow whose legs correspond to the four pillars at the cardinal points (Fig. 27).[10] The goddess Ḥat-ḥôr[11] of Denderah, who was originally symbolized by the head or skull of a cow nailed over the door of a temple, or on a pillar, was very early identified with the cow-shaped goddess of heaven; and many other female divinities identified with the sky — especially Isis — indicated their celestial nature in the pictures by wearing the horns or

FIG. 25. SYMBOL OF ḤAT-ḤÔR FROM THE BEGINNING OF THE HISTORIC AGE

even the head of a cow. The popular symbol of Ḥat-ḥôr became a strange mixture of a human and a bovine face, thus

suggesting how long the human
and the animal personification must
have existed side by side. As a symbol of heaven this celestial face may
claim to have the sun and the moon
as eyes (cf. p. 28), although the
goddess more frequently represents
only the principal eye of the celestial god, the sun. In cow-form the
goddess is usually shown as wearing the sun between her horns and
as appearing among flowers and
plants, i. e. in a thicket analogous

FIG. 26. Ḥat-ḥôr at Evening
Entering the Western Mountain and the Green Thicket

to the green leaves of the celestial tree which send forth the
sun in the morning and hide him at evening.[12] These plants
appear at the eastern or western mountain wall, from which
the sun-god arises at dawn or into which he retreats at evening. During the day he may travel under the belly of the cow
or over her back, or may wander only between her horns,
which then symbolize the daily and yearly limits of his course,

in analogy to the two obelisks, or to
the two world-mountains, or to the
two trees, etc. (pp. 31, 35). The sun
may also be thought to hide himself
in the body of the heavenly cow
during the night; so that he enters
her mouth at evening and is born
again from her womb in the morning. Thus, by a conception through
the mouth, the sun-god "begets himself" every night and is called "the

FIG. 27. The Sun-God between
the Horns of the Celestial
Cow

bull of his mother," i. e. his own father, a name which is much
used in hymns. As carrying the sun, Ḥat-ḥôr may herself

OTHER GODS CONNECTED WITH NATURE 39

again be regarded as a solar divinity (see p. 29 on the solarizations of goddesses).

As the mistress of heaven sitting amid green rays, Ḥat-ḥôr
can become seated in or can be identical with the celestial
tree, from which she gives heavenly food and
drink to the souls of the dead (as in Fig. 23),
and thus she is shown as bestowing eternal
life upon them. Her four blue-black tresses
hang across the sky or form it, each tress
marking a cardinal point. Sometimes these
tresses are also attributed to Horus as a
celestial god and the male counterpart of
Ḥat-ḥôr (see pp. 111–13 on the four sons of
Horus). Much mythological fancy seems to
have been attached to this network, beau-
tiful but dangerous, delicate yet strong, which surrounds the
whole world.[13]

Fig. 28. The Dead
Meets Ḥat-ḥôr be-
hind the Celes-
tial Tree

The idea of the sky as a cow is likewise combined with one
which we have already noted, according to which the sky is
the water of a river or a continuation of the ocean; so that the
cow's body may be covered with lines representing water, and
in this form the divinity is sometimes called Meḥ(e)t-uêret
(Greek Μεθυερ), or "the Great Flood." Since this name is
more suggestive than Ḥat-ḥôr, the sun
is usually said to have been born on or
by "the great flood" (Meḥt-uêret), or
to have climbed on her back or between her horns on the day of creation; but the same process may also
take place every morning, for the daily
and the cosmogonic processes are
always parallel. Even when the sun's
primeval or daily birth is described as
being from a blue lotus flower in the celestial or terrestrial
ocean, he can be called "child of Meḥt-uêret." The annual

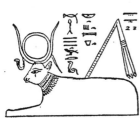

Fig. 29. "Meḥt-uêret, the
Mistress of the Sky and
of Both Countries" (i. e.
Egypt)

parallel in the inundation brought Meḥt-uêret into connexion with the harvest as well. The cosmic cow is likewise called Ahet, Ahit, Ahat, or Ehat, Ehet, principally as the nurse and protector of the new-born sun-god at the creation of the world.

As the goddess of the sky in cow-form Ḥat-ḥôr assumed many of the functions of the Asiatic Queen of Heaven, so that later

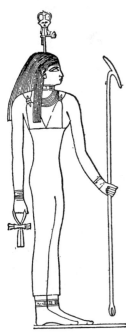

she became the special patroness of women and the deity of love, beauty, joy, music, and ornaments; while, again exactly like the Semitic Astarte, she was sometimes mistress of war. Her husband, as we have seen, is usually Horus, the male ruler of the sky.

This goddess has been multiplied into the group of the "seven Ḥat-ḥôrs" who foretell the future, especially of every child at his birth. The suspicion that these seven fates were originally the Pleiades, which, among certain other nations, were the constellation of human fate (especially of ill-omened fate), and also the foretellers of the harvest,[14] is confirmed when we find the "seven Ḥat-ḥôr cows with their bull"; for the Pleiades are in

FIG. 30. THE GODDESS OF the constellation of Taurus. Since this
DIOSPOLIS PARVA
zodiacal sign is not Egyptian, the New Empire probably borrowed from Asia the connexion of constellations which we have described, although they failed to understand it. Various efforts were made to localize the single forms of these seven Ḥat-ḥôrs in Egyptian cities.[15]

At an early period Ḥat-ḥôr assimilated various other goddesses. The name of Bat (?), the female deity of the city of Diospolis Parva, was written with a similar symbol or with one embodying Ḥat-ḥôr's head; later this symbol was identified with the great goddess Ḥat-ḥôr herself and was explained as a *sistrum*, i. e. a sacred rattle, as it was used especially at the festivals of the joyful goddess.[16]

The representation of the sky in human, feminine form, which Ḥat-ḥôr might also assume, led to the identification with many goddesses who were originally local, but who were often solarized in later times, among these divinities being Isis (sometimes with her sister and rival, Neph-

FIG. 31. NUT RECEIVING THE DEAD

thys), the Theban Mut, and the fiery Tefênet. For the nocturnal sky in particular, the prevalent personification is Nut,[17] who, in conformity with her name, is generally understood to be a celestial counterpart of the abyss Nuu (or Nûn?), i. e. as the heavenly waters which form a continuation of the ocean that flows around and under the earth. We should expect her to be Nuu's consort, but she is seldom associated with him in this capacity; she is, instead, the wife of the earth-god, by whom she gives birth to the sun each morning; and in similar fashion, as "the one who bore (or bears) the gods" (i. e. all the heavenly bodies), she is the mother of all life, or at least of the younger generation of gods who form the transition to mankind, as we shall see on pp. 72, 78. She is often represented as a dark woman covered with stars, bending over the earth-god as he reclines on his back (see Figs. 33, 35, 38, 39). Funerary pictures, especially on coffins, show her receiving the souls of the

FIG. 32. NUT WITH SYMBOLS OF THE SKY IN DAY-TIME

dead into her star-decked bosom, arms, and wings. As the counterpart of the dark abysmal depth she is also explained as the sky of the underworld, where the firmament hangs permanently upside down or whence by night it ascends from the waters, to change place with the bright sky of day. Therefore Nut, the mother of the stars, is united with the

stellar tree of heaven, in which she is hidden, or whose branches are formed by her limbs. She is, however, not always clearly distin-

FIG. 33. QÊB AS BEARER OF VEGETATION

guished from the sky in the day-time, and, correspondingly, all goddesses identified with the vault of heaven may likewise take the place of the nocturnal sky, especially Ḥat-ḥôr in her frequent function of divinity of the West and of the dead.

Nut's husband, by whom she bears the sun-god (and the moon), is Qêb,[18] the god of the earth, who is often depicted as a man resting on his back or his side, and with plants springing from his body. The goose which sometimes adorns his head when he is pictured as standing erect is simply the hieroglyph which forms an abbreviation of his name, but the theologians soon misinterpreted this to mean that the earth-god was a huge gander, "the Great Cack-ler," who laid the solar egg.[19] He also has a ser-pent's head as being the master of snakes, his

FIG. 34. QÊB WITH HIS HIEROGLY-PHIC SYM-BOL

special creatures (p. 104); or on his human head rests the com-

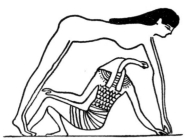

FIG. 35. QÊB AS A SERPENT AND NUT

plicated crown of the Egyptian "crown prince" as he is often called.[20] In all probability Qêb was originally only a local di-vinity (near Heliopolis?) with-out cosmic function, for the earlier traditions know another god of the earth, who is called Aker or Akeru.[21] This deity is

depicted as a double lion with two opposite heads (sometimes human) on one body,[22] the one mouth swallowing the sun at

evening, when he enters the desert mountains in the west;
while from the other he comes forth in the morning, so that

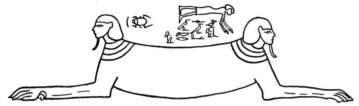

FIG. 36. QÊB WATCHING AKER AND EXTENDED OVER HIM
To the left is seen the sun, as Khepri, in the lower world.

by night the sun-god passes through Aker's body, the earth.
Later theologians sought to reconcile the existence of the
superfluous Aker with that of his successor Qêb
by making the older god the representative
of the lower regions of the earth and depicting
him as black; then Qêb is placed over him as
a guardian,[23] so that some scholars could actually confuse Aker with the Satanic dragon
'Apop, lying in the depths of the earth.[24] Certain later artists and theologians also separated
the composite figure of Aker into two lions

FIG. 37. DISFIGURED
REPRESENTATION
OF AKER, ASSIMI-
LATED TO SHU AND
TEFÊNET

turning their backs to each other and carrying the two mountains between which the sun rises. Subsequently some commentaries called
these mysterious
lions "the morning"
and "yesterday,"
whereas others con-
fused them with the
"two celestial lions,"
Shu and Tefênet, and
accordingly repre-
sented them as seated

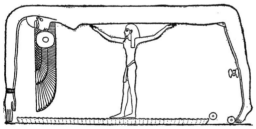

FIG. 38. SHU, STANDING ON THE OCEAN (?), UPHOLDS
NUT, THE SKY

Four phases of the sun are represented.

in bushes (i. e. the horizon; see p. 38) or as sustaining the
sky (see Fig. 37).

The latter two gods, Shu and Tefênet, were mostly understood by the Egyptians as the ethereal space which separates earth and ocean from heaven. This function is especially clear with Shu,[25] who is often represented as a man upraising the

sky on his outstretched hands or holding one of the pillars of heaven; as the supporter of sky and sun he can be pictured with the sundisk on his head or can even be treated as a solar god.[26] Whether he was a son of

FIG. 39. SHU-ḤEKA AND THE FOUR PILLARS SEPARATING HEAVEN AND EARTH

the sun-god (as was the most common acceptation), or was an emanation from the source of the gods, the abyss, which preceded the sun, was a theological problem. At an early date Shu was identified with Ḥeka ("Magic," or "the Magician"), who thus came likewise to be regarded as the sun; but the reason is not so clear as when he is blended with Ḥeḥ ("Infinite Space"), as in Fig. 71, or with Horus.

In pictures of his cosmic function we find an avoidance of his leonine form, although this shape was evidently original, so that his local place of worship was called Leontopolis. Later he was identified with several other deities in human form, e. g. rarely with the lunarized god Khôns at Thebes, more frequently with the warrior An-ḥôret (Greek 'Ονουρις) of This.[27]

FIG. 40. TEFÊNET

How the lioness Tefênet [28] came to be associated with Shu as his twin sister and wife and thus received the function of a goddess of the sky[29] is uncertain; perhaps her lion-form, which never interchanges with human features, furnishes the explanation, or the accidental neighbourhood of the two gods when they were once only local divinities may account for it. Modern com-

parisons of Tefênet to the rain-clouds or the dew are quite
unfounded; if she and Shu are later said to cause the growth
of plants, this refers to other celestial functions than to furnishing moisture, which in Egypt so rarely comes from the
sky.[30] The Egyptian texts speak rather of Tefênet as sending flaming heat (i. e. as solar) and describe her as a true
daughter or eye of the sun-god or as the disk on his head.

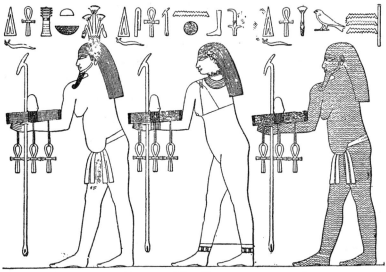

FIG. 41. THE NILE, HIS WIFE NEKHBET, AND THE OCEAN

The pictures likewise always connect her with the sun. As a
female counterpart of Shu she can be identified with such goddesses of the sky as Isis, whence in some places she is called the
mother of the moon; but she is also termed mother of the
sky (in other words, of Nut) and, contrariwise, daughter of the
sky (i. e. of Nut or Ḥat-ḥôr). She and her brother Shu are
likewise named "the two lions"[31] (cf. the explanation of
Fig. 37). The idea of the wicked Sêth as a god of thunder-
storms and clouds, which developed at a fairly early period,
will be discussed on pp. 103–04.

Turning to the element of water, we must first mention its
nearest representative, Ḥaʿpi, the Nile, which is depicted as

a very stout blue or green human figure,[32] wearing a fisherman's girdle around his loins and having aquatic plants on his head.[33] Although much praised by poets, he does not enjoy such general worship as we should expect, this being another proof that the earliest Egyptian theology did not emphasize the cosmic character of the gods (pp. 23–24). From the earliest period it was believed that the source of the Nile was on the frontier of Egypt, between the cataracts of Assuan. There it sprang from the nether world or from the abyss, or sometimes from two distinct sources, and divided into two rivers, one of which flowed northward through Egypt, while the other took a southerly course through Nubia. The Asiatic tradition of four rivers flowing to the four cardinal points [34] has left a trace in the Egyptian idea that the deeper sources of the Nile at Elephantine were four in number,[35] so that the water of life flows from four jars presented by the cataract-goddess Satet, etc. For mythological explanations of the origin and rise of the Nile according to the Osiris-myth, see pp. 94–95, 116, 125, where we find Osiris becoming identical with the Nile.

Two water-goddesses are joined to the Nile,[36] Mu(u)t (or Muit) and Nekhbet. In harmony with her name ("Watery One," "Water-Flood"), in the earliest period the former was sometimes taken to be the wet, primitive principle of the Universe and the mother of all things, though usually she has little prominence. Nekhbet, who is said to stand at the entrance to the abyss,[37] is evidently connected with the prehistoric capital of Upper Egypt, even if she is not directly identical with the vulture-goddess of that city; and the question arises whether the earliest theology did not make the Egyptian course of the Nile begin there instead of at the First Cataract, as was the belief somewhat later. Both wives of Ḥaʿpi sometimes imitate him in being corpulent.

Occasionally the "ocean" (literally "the Great Green") is obese like the Nile, as though he brought fertility; and once his spouse likewise is Mu(u)t, or Mu(i)t. Usually, how-

ever, he is identified with Nuu (or Nûn?),[38] the god of the
abyss. Originally the latter represented not only the dark,
unfathomable waters which flow under the earth and can be
reached in the south,[39] i. e. at the source of the Nile, but
also their continuation which surrounds the world
as the all-encircling ocean; the ends of the ocean,
disappearing in darkness 'and endless space, lead
back to the subterranean waters. These abysmal
floods represent the primeval matter from which
all the deities arose, so that their personification,
Nuu, is called the oldest and wisest god, who existed "when there was no heaven and no earth,"[40]
the possessor of all secrets, and the father of all
gods and of the world. This cosmogonic idea

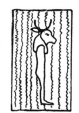

Fig. 42. Nuu
with the
Head of an
Ox

finds its parallel in the sun's daily descent into and rebirth
from the ocean. In Egypt the ocean's representative was the
Nile, which was, accordingly, largely identified with Nuu.[41]
Somewhat later and more mystic conceptions, as we have
already seen, identify Osiris, as the source of the subterranean
waters, with Nuu, and thus connect him with the ocean; still
later Ptaḥ(-Tatunen) also is directly equated with the abyss,
probably after identification with Osiris.

Nuu is ordinarily depicted in human form, though occasionally he has the head
of a frog and once [42] that
of an ox; when he is
shown with two spread-
ing ostrich-feathers on
his head, his later iden-
tification with the wise
Ptaḥ-Tatunen is implied.

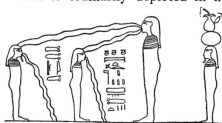

Fig. 43. "Nuu, the Father of the Mysterious
Gods," Sends his Springs to "the Two Mysterious Ones"

One very noteworthy
mythological picture [43] represents "Nuu, the father of the mysterious gods," emitting the two or four sources of all waters
from his mouth while two gods, probably the southern and

northern Nile, each receive a part of these streams and spit them out again.[44] For the ocean in human circular form see Fig. 46 and p. 96; on the late attribution of the ocean to powers hostile to the sun and its identification with 'Apop-Sêth see pp. 104 ff.

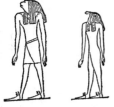

FIG. 44. TWO MEMBERS OF THE PRIMEVAL OGDOAD

The question of the relationship and sequence of the principal parts of the cosmic structure and of the four elements was never solved in a way which met with general acceptation. At first the myth of the creation of the world may have existed in a number of local variants. That Nuu, the abysmal water, was the primary element was, however, one of the first agreements of earliest theology, and the next conclusion was that the creation of the sun was the most important step in the cosmogonic process. In the New Empire the speculations regarding the state of the world before the creation symbolized this chaotic state by four pairs of gods (an ogdoad), the males, as aqueous creatures, being represented with frogs' heads, and the females with the heads of serpents.[45] Their names were Nuu and Nut, the abysmal forces; Ḥeḥ(u) and Ḥeḥet (or Ḥeḥut; "Endless Space"); Kek(u) (or Kekui) and Keket (or Kekut; "Darkness"); Ni(u) and Nit ("Sultry Air").[46] On account of their number these eight parents or ancestors

FIG. 45. ḤEḤ AND ḤEḤET LIFT THE YOUNG SUN (AS KHEPRI) OVER THE EASTERN HORIZON

of the sun-god were connected with Khmun(u), ("the City of Eight") in Middle Egypt (p. 33), and some priests made this (or its "high field") the scene or beginning of creation.

In reality only the first pair, Nuu and Nut, were the parents of the sun-god according to the doctrine just set forth; but it was easy to transfer the cosmic personalities of the ogdoad to the daily birth of the sun, as in Fig. 45, which represents Ḥeḥ and Ḥeḥet, in the function of Shu and Tefênet, lifting

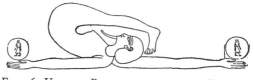

FIG. 46. UNUSUAL REPRESENTATION OF THE HUSBAND OF THE SKY-GODDESS

the infant sun "in the east," i. e. every morning. There seems to have been some uncertainty, however, whether the Nut of the ogdoad was the same divinity as the celestial goddess Nut, who bears the sun every day, or whether she was only the primeval sky or merely an aspect of the watery chaos; but the two personalities were probably identical. According to this theory, then, with Nut as the flood, or with the old water-goddess Mu(u)t, Mu(i)t, Nuu, the father of the gods, begat the sun-god. As a daily event this act of creation once represents Nut as the heaven bending over the ocean, whose circular position seems to distinguish him from the earth-god, who is pictured as lying flat (see Fig. 46).

FIG. 47. THE SKY-GODDESS IN DOUBLE FORM AND HER CONSORT

The later Egyptians do not seem to have understood who this male figure, passing the sun from west to east, was; [47] and the same statement holds true of a very similar representation in the temple of Philae which sought to present the upper and the lower sky as distinct personalities bending over the male principle; it depicts the sun no less than eight times. Very soon the belief became current that the sun, the greatest of all cosmic forces, grew quite by himself out of the abyss as the "god

who begat" or "formed himself";[48] and that he then created
the space of air between heaven and earth (Shu and Tefênet),
after whom heaven and earth (Qêb and Nut) themselves were
brought into being. From these gods came the rest of the
creation, including the new sun as Osiris, or the sun-god continued to create gods and finally produced men from his eyes,
etc. This is the old Heliopolitan doctrine of creation as reflected in the arrangement of the ennead of Heliopolis (see
pp. 215–16). We may thus infer that the doctrine of the ogdoad
rested on the different belief that air preceded the sun and

separated the sky (Nut) and the abyss (Nuu),
from whom the sun was born at the creation, as it
is born anew every day (cf. pp. 47, 49). The double
occurrence of the sun as Atum-Rê' and as Osiris
in the Heliopolitan doctrine, and the very ancient
rôle of Shu as the separator of the two principal
parts of the world, again lead us to suppose that
variants existed according to which the sun-god
took a later place in the creation. In similar

FIG. 48. THE
YOUNG SUN   fashion we read in some texts that after growing
IN HIS LOTUS in the ocean, or in the blue lotus which symbolizes
FLOWER   it, the sun-god climbed directly on the back of the
heavenly cow (see Fig. 27), thus implying the pre-existence of
heaven, air, and other elements, and of the earth as well.

An old variant of this creation of the world from the abyss
seems to be preserved in the tradition which makes the ram-
headed god Khnûm(u) of Elephantine and his wife, the frog-
headed Ḥeqet, "the first gods who were at the beginning, who
built men and made the gods." [49] The underlying idea simply
seeks the origin of all waters, including the ocean, in the
mythological source of the Nile between the rocks of the First
Cataract; so that Khnûm as "the source-god" is treated as a
mere localized variant of Nuu. Even in the Ancient Empire
Khnûm and Ḥeqet were transferred to Abydos for the sake
of fusion with the Osiris-myth, which found there not only the

burial-place of Osiris, but also the spring of life, the entrance
and source of the abyss, etc.

It is doubtful how long the original meaning of Khnûm and
Ḥeqet as the gods of the Cataract region was still understood
correctly after they had been located "at the cradle [more
literally, "at the birth-place," *meskhenet*] of Abydos." [50]

FIG. 49. KHNÛM FORMS CHILDREN, AND ḤEQET GIVES THEM LIFE

In any case later theology no longer comprehended the
abysmal nature of Khnûm when it sought to explain the tradition of his creatorship by an etymology from the root *khonem*,
"to form like a potter," so that he became a "potter-god"
who once had made all beings, from gods to animals, on his
potter's wheel and who still determined the shape of every
new-born child, apparently creating it, or at least its "double,"
in heaven before the infant's birth.[51] In conformity with this

development Khnûm's later consort, Ḥeqet, became a goddess
of birth.

Thus Ḥeqet sometimes is parallel to Meskhenet, a divinity
explained as the "Goddess of the Cradle" (or more literally,
"of the Birth-Seat"), another deity who governs not only
earthly birth, but also the rebirth of the dead for the new life
with Osiris. As her symbol she wears on her head an ornament
resembling two bent antennæ ![antennae symbol] of insects. She can also
be symbolized by a brick (![brick symbol]), or by two of them, alluding to the bricks on which the Egyptian woman bore children, as described in Exodus i. 16. The sun and
Osiris have four different Meskhenets, or birth-
goddesses, a symbolism which admits of various
interpretations (with Osiris preferably of the
four sources of the Nile [p. 46]; with the sun of
the sky, symbolized by the number four [p. 39]).
The name Meskhenet can be explained as "co-
incidence, happening, omen," i. e. as the coin-
cidence of the omens accompanying birth and
thus determining destiny, so that this divinity
becomes a goddess of fate. It is not impossible
that this etymology is the original one, and that the function of birth-goddess was merely derived from it.[52] As we
shall see, Renenutet also is connected with birth and education.

FIG. 50.
MESKHENET

For ordinary people a male principle, Shay ("Fate"),
appears in the New Empire as a male counterpart and companion of the birth-goddess. He is pictured in human form;
later, identified with the Greek Agathodaimon, he takes the
shape of a serpent, sometimes with a human head.

To the cosmic deities we may also reckon, as being apparently
stellar in origin, the very interesting divinity Sekha(u)it
(or possibly Sekha(u)tet),[53] the "goddess of writings," or
Fate, whose pen directs the course of all the world. She is
termed "the one before the divine place of books," i. e. the
librarian of the gods, and in one passage [54] she has the title of

"the one before the book-house of the south," which may suggest a localization in the old capital Nekhbet, or may rather be a hint at her home in the depths of the world, i. e. in the south. A priestly costume (i. e. the leopard's skin) and pen and inkstand (or two inkstands tied together, hanging over her shoulder) characterize her office; while her connexion with the subterranean sky is indicated by two horns, symbolizing her celestial nature (p. 37), but pointing downward.[55] The star between the horns emphasizes this nature; but, contrary to the custom of picturing all stars with five rays, this particular one has seven, a careful indication of a symbolism which we do not yet understand or which may possibly have come from Asia.[56] As a goddess of fate Sekhait sits at the foot of the cosmic tree, or, in other words, in the nethermost (southern) depths of the sky or at the meeting-place of the upper and lower sky; and there she not only

Fig. 51. Sekhait, Thout, and Atum Register a King's Name on the Celestial Tree, Placing the King within it

writes upon this tree or on its leaves all future events, such as length of life (at least for the kings), but also records great events for the knowledge of future generations, since everything, past and future, as we have already seen (p. 36), is written in the stars.[57] Consequently she is sometimes localized at the sacred *Persea* of Heliopolis. She is also identified with the sky, e. g. as Isis, with the heavens by day, or, as Nephthys, with a more remote and less known personification of the (lower?) sky;[58] but not, as we should expect, with Nut. At a comparatively early date the common folk lost the significance of all this symbolism and gave her the meaningless name Sefkhet 'Abui ("the One Who Has Laid Aside her Horns," [59] i. e. from her head).

Although the Egyptian priests claimed to be great astronomers, the planets ("the stars who never rest") did not enjoy

FIG. 52.
THE PLANET SATURN IN A PICTURE OF THE ROMAN PERIOD

the prominence which they possessed in Babylonia. In no place did they receive special worship; and if three (or, originally, four) of them were called manifestations of the same god, Horus, in his capacity of ruler of the sky, it is extremely doubtful whether early times were much concerned to distinguish them. Of course, the morning star (which probably was once differentiated from the evening star) was always the most important of the planets.[60] It was male, being called "the Rising God" (Nuter Dua). Regarded as the nocturnal representative of the hidden sun-god, it symbolized Osiris or his soul, the Phoenix (benu, bin), or the renascent Osiris as Horus-Rê'; while later it was also called "the One Who Ferries Osiris," or "Who Ferries the Phoenix." In the earliest texts the morning star and Orion as the rulers of the sky are often compared. For some gods with a similar name who seem to be confused with the morning star see pp. 132–33 on Dua and Dua-uêr. Clearly viewed as a female principle (an idea which is widespread in Asia, where the concept of Venus as the "Queen of Heaven" early dominated over the older interpretation as a male god 'Athtar or "Lucifer"), we find Venus-Isis only in the latest times in Egypt. In the earlier period the comparison of Sothis and Venus as daughter and wife of the sun-god and mother of Osiris-

FIG. 53. SOTHIS-SIRIUS

Horus is uncertain and can have existed only vaguely.[61] The other planets are less prominent. Jupiter's name was later misread "Horus, the Opener of Secrets" (Up-shetau); the original reading was Upesh ("the Resplendent Star"), or

"Horus, the Resplendent," [62] and also "the Southern Star."
Saturn is "Horus, the Bull"; and Mars is "the Red Horus"
or "Horus of the Horizon" (Ḥar-akhti). It is somewhat surprising that Sebg(u)-Mercury has no connexion
with the wise Thout, as we should expect from
Asiatic and European analogues; and sometimes
this star is actually dedicated to the wicked
god Sêth.[63]

The fixed stars are all gods or "souls," and
particular sanctity attaches to "the never-vanishing ones," i. e. to those stars in the northern
sky which are visible throughout the year. For
these stars as the crew of the solar ship see
supra, p. 26. They also function as the body-
servants of the sun-god, carrying arms in his
service [64] and acting as his messengers. In these
"children of Nut" (p. 41) or their groups the
Egyptians fancied at the same time that they
recognized various fields of heavenly flowers and

FIG. 54.
SOTHIS (CALLED
"ISIS")

plants and that these meadows formed the habitations of the
blessed dead. At the same time they called the heavenly
fields by such
names as "this
field which pro-
duces the gods,
on which the gods
grow according to
their days every
year." [65] Not-
withstanding the
Egyptian belief
that the gods

FIG. 55. SOTHIS AND HORUS-OSIRIS CONNECTED

manifested themselves in the appearance and wanderings of
every star, only the most conspicuous of them played a
part of much importance in religion. First stands the dog-

star, or Sirius, which the Egyptians called Sopdet [66] (Grcck
Σωθις). Since the dog-star is the queen of the fixed stars and
of heaven, Sothis-Sirius was early identified with Ḥat-ḥôr or
Isis. In consequence she is usually pictured as a cow reclining in a ship (like the other heavenly bodies, pp. 26, 34) to symbolize her rule over the heavens (see pp. 37–40 on the cow-shape
of the sky). When portrayed in human form, she usually indicates that she is the companion of her neighbour (and son,
or brother and husband, or father) Orion by lifting one arm
like him. A noteworthy representation also shows her in association with (or rather in opposition to) Horus as the morning

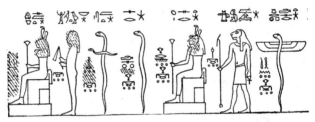

FIG. 56. DECANAL STARS FROM DENDERAH

star, and thus in a strange relation to this leader of the planets and ruler of the sky which we cannot yet explain from
the texts. This same picture further blends her with a (neighbouring and later?) constellation, an archer-goddess, because
she holds a bow and arrows.[67] This most brilliant of the fixed
stars is used as the regulator of the year, whence Sothis is
called "the year (star),"[68] and the astronomical cycle of fourteen hundred and sixty years, in which the ordinary, uninter-
calated year of three hundred and sixty-five days coincides
with the astronomically correct year, is termed the "Sothic
cycle." The identification of Sopdet with Isis gives her an
important part in the Osiris-myth.

Neither do the constellations seem to have been the source
of quite so much religious thinking as in Babylonia. Their
description differed very widely from that of the Babylonian
constellations, so that the Egyptian Lion is not in the least

connected with the Babylonian group of the same name, as
can be seen from the picture given on p. 59; the "Giant"
or "Strong Man" (Nakht) has nothing in common with Orion,
who in Asia is called "the Hero, the Giant," etc. Even the
twelve Asiatic signs of the zodiac are entirely absent from the
sacred astronomy of Egypt before the Greek period. Allusions to them in the more popular mythology, like references
to the bull of the Pleiades (*supra*, p. 40), or the myth of Virgo
holding Spica and Hydra (pp. 84, 153, Ch. VIII, Note 11), are
scanty and do not seem to occur as early as 2000 B.C. To divide the year the Egyptians used,
in place of the zodiacal signs, the
decan-stars, marking on the sky
thirty-six sections of ten days each,
the surplus of five epagomenal days
being counted separately. This belt
of stars began with Sopdet-Sothis,
the dog-star, the "mistress of the
year." In Græco-Roman times the
zodiacal signs became very popular,
and we find them pictured in many
richly developed representations.

FIG. 57. EARLY PICTURE OF ORION

Orion, the most remarkable and most beautiful of all constellations, "fleet of foot, wide of steps, before the southland," [69] represents the hero of the sky, exactly as in the
mythology of Asia.[70] He is early identified with the victorious
sun-god Horus, while his father Osiris (in other words, the dead
or unborn form of Horus himself, who equals Osiris), the deity
in a box or a little boat, is sought chiefly in the constellation
directly below, i. e. the ship Argo or its principal star, Canopus.
Often, however, both gods and their constellations are freely
interchanged as manifestations of the same deity. We can
trace the representation of Orion as a man running away and
looking backward to the time before 2000 B.C. For the most
part he lifts his right arm, usually with the hand empty,

though sometimes he holds a star or the hieroglyph of life.
Later he grasps a spear, in order to connect him with the mili-
tant Horus. As we have seen, he often appears as a companion

of Sothis. In the New Empire we find
also the idea of the two Orions which
is so richly developed in universal mythology as a year-myth; these celestial
twins appear united as in the picture
here given,[71] or are separated.[72] The
Egyptians do not seem to have recognized that this idea corresponded with
their own myth of Osiris-Sêth in many
versions of universal mythology. In
like manner the probable original identity of Orion (or his counterpart or
double, Canopus, the steersman of
the ship Argo?), with the ferryman

FIG. 58. THE DOUBLE ORION

of the lower world "whose face is
backward" or "who looks backward" was forgotten at
an even earlier date.[73]

Among the other decans the most remarkable is the sixteenth, the principal star of the constellation Shesmu (Greek
transcription Σεσμη), an old deity of somewhat violent character who occasionally appears
as the lord of the last hour of
the night.[74] From the hieroglyph of a press which marks
his name, later theologians inferred that he was an oil-presser
and "master of the laboratory,"
a giver of ointment; but earlier
texts describe him rather as a

FIG. 59. THE FERRYMAN OF THE DEAD

butcher or as a cook.[75] He is pictured in human form or with
the head of an ox or of a lion, the latter apparently being the
more original. In other words, Shesmu seems to be the com-

panion of the goddess Shesemtet, who likewise was probably
lion-headed. Her members once were thought to be represented in the tenth, eleventh, twelfth, and thirteenth decans.
At one time, therefore, she was a powerful divinity and was
called mistress of the sky, but she was almost forgotten even
in the Pyramid Period and later disappeared completely; as
early as 2000 B. C. her name [76] is so corrupted in the list of
decans as to be devoid of meaning.[77]

The seven-starred constellation of Ursa Major (Charles's
Wain, popularly called the Great Dipper in the United States)
was only later fully identified with the wicked god Sêth-

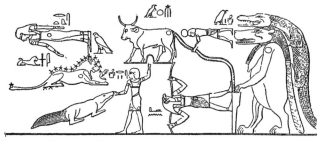

FIG. 60. CONSTELLATIONS AROUND THE OX-LEG

Typhon, the adversary of Osiris, yet even under its old names,
"the Ox-Leg," or "the Club, the Striker" (*Mesekhti*),[78] it was
an ill-omened constellation, although it belonged to the especially venerable "indestructible stars," i. e. those visible during
the whole year in the most remarkable region of the sky near
the North Pole (p. 55).

Following the picture which we here give from the temple
of King Sethos (Setkhuy) I, we can identify a few constellations near the great "Ox-Leg," which here has the form of
an ox. The most prominent among them is the strange goddess Êpet.[79] She is represented as a female hippopotamus
(perhaps pregnant) with human breasts and lion's feet. On
her back she carries a crocodile (which later she sometimes
bears in her paws), and from this association she receives
the head and tail — or only the tail — of a crocodile; later

still she may assume also the head of a lion or of a heavenly goddess in a human form, thus indicating her celestial nature. At one period she must have been worshipped very widely, for the month Epiphi is sacred to her; and accordingly she bears the name of Uêret or, later, T-uêret (Greek Θουηρις), i. e. "the Great One." Originally she seems to have been simply a local divinity, but before the New Empire, as we see in Fig. 60, she was identified with the constellation of Boötes as the guardian of the malevolent "Ox-Leg." Despite her horrible appearance, she is in reality beneficent and is a "mistress of talismans." She affords protection against sickness and is pre-eminently helpful in child-birth, whence she appears not only at the birth

FIG. 61. THREE LATER TYPES OF ÊPET (THE LAST AS QUEEN OF HEAVEN)

of the sun each morning, but, strangely enough, also at its death at evening. Accordingly she is later called "She Who Bears the Sun," and is, therefore, identified with Nut or has the head of Ḥat-ḥôr-Isis.

In this representation of the circumpolar stars we also see the later attempt to discover, as further guardians of the dangerous group of seven stars, the Nubian goddess Selqet (to be discussed on pp. 147, 157), and the "four sons of Horus" (see pp. 111–13). There we likewise find 'An, 'Anen,[80] a god who holds a staff behind his shoulders (hence his name from the verb 'n, "to turn back"?) and who is stellarized as another guardian of the Great Bear, so that sometimes he even be-

comes a manifestation of Horus fighting the monster of the
northern sky.

The strange, ugly, serpent-strangling dwarf (or giant)
Bês [81] may also be considered here,
since, like Êpet, he was placed
among the stars at an early period.
He has the ears, mane, and tail
of some wild animal of the cat-
tribe from which he seems to derive his name, although the artists
are often uncertain whether these
details do not belong rather to a
detachable skin. In the stellar
mythology he appears to correspond to the serpent-strangling

FIG. 62. 'AN-HORUS FIGHTING THE
OX-LEG

constellation Ophiuchos (or Serpentarius) of the Classical
world. It is probable that this Classic localization in the sky
was borrowed from Egypt, although the later Egyptians seem
no longer to have been conscious of any stellar interpretation.

If we may judge from the numerous pictures
of Bês among the amulets, a very rich mythology must have attached to this strange
personality, but since it flourished in oral
tradition only, it is left to our fancy to guess
the stories according to which,
for example, he was so fond
of dancing and music that he
became the patron of these
pleasures, as well as of other
female arts like binding flow-

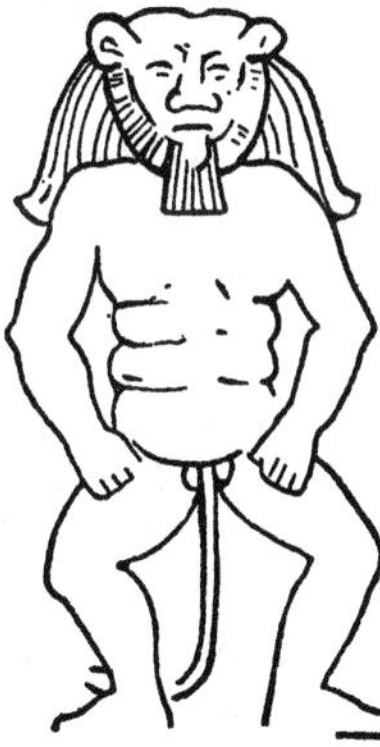

FIG. 63. OLD TYPES OF BÊS FROM THE
TWELFTH AND EIGHTEENTH DYNASTIES

ers, preparing cosmetics, etc.
As a joyous deity he is also
fond of drinking and is represented especially as sucking beer (?)
from large jars through a straw. He appears as amusing in-
fants, principally the new-born sun-god, whom he protects

and nurses, and this explains why he becomes the companion (sometimes the husband) of Uêret-Êpet as a protector of childbirth, etc.[82] He not only strangles or devours serpents, but also

catches boars, lions, and antelopes with his hands. His image on the wooden headrests for sleeping, or over the door, etc., keeps away not merely noxious animals, but also evil spirits. Representations of him in Roman times as brandishing knives or as a warrior in heavy armour (Plate I, 2), seem to show him in this same protective function. As his name cannot be traced beyond 1500 B. C., and as his exact picture is not found with full certainty before 2000, while his

Fig. 64. Bês with Flowers

representation *en face* is rather unusual in Egyptian art,[83] it has often been supposed that he was a foreign god. Nevertheless, passages describing him as "coming from the east, Master of the Orient," or localizing him at Bu-gem (or Bugemet)[84] in eastern Nubia, evidently do not point to his original local worship, but merely to myths concerning him in Nubia or in Arabia; all the gods come, like the stars, from the eastern sky or from the lower world. The long tresses of his beard and hair, and the leopard's(?) skin which he wears (originally, as we have just seen, a part of his body), as well as the feather crown

Fig. 65. Bês Drinking [85]

which adorns him (from the Eighteenth Dynasty?), might, indeed, be considered as analogous to the dress of the red and brown African tribes on the Red Sea; but we ought to know more about myths speaking of dwarfs in the south and about certain dwarf-shaped gods of the earliest period, whose models seem to be unborn or rhachitic children, to understand these and other connexions.[86]

The earliest similar dwarf divinities of both types are usually feminine. The nude female Bês (prob-ably called Bêset) appears not only in the latest period,[87] when we find a male and female deity of this type among gods whose prevailing char-acter is stellar, but also in the magic wands of the Twelfth Dynasty,[88] from which date we here reproduce a statuette of the female Bês, crushing a serpent and wrapped in the skin of some one of the *Felidae*, while her ears likewise are those of that animal.

FIG. 66. THE FEMALE BÊS

· We do not know why the cult of these ancient gods was neglected in the Pyramid Period. It is not until about 2000 b. c. that we find Bês represented on magic objects, and even later he seems to have been a deity worshipped chiefly by the common people and without much official recognition. He became most prominent after 1000 b. c., when his artistic type developed such popularity that not only did many minor gods assume his form,[89] but it very strongly influenced Asia and Europe, so that it can be traced, for example, in Greek art and mythology in the types of the Satyr, Gorgo, Silenus, etc.

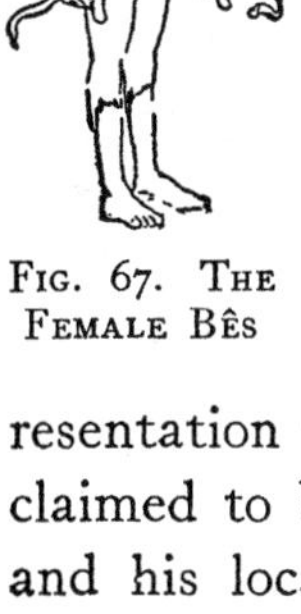

Thus, probably as being one of the oldest divine forms known, Bês and his earlier proto-types or relatives, the bow-legged, undeveloped dwarf gods, furnished the patterns for certain deities in whom the later pantheistic age wished to symbolize the most universal or the most primitive power of nature. This mode of rep-resentation was subsequently applied also to a divinity who claimed to be the oldest of all, Ptah, the god of Memphis, and his local variant, Sokari; and then was fitted to Nuu

FIG. 67. THE FEMALE BÊS

(the abyss) when he was identified with Ptaḥ-Sokari as the primeval god, and with Khepri, the sun while still unformed (p. 25). Herodotus calls the protective amulet figures

of Bês at the prow of Phoenician ships "representations of Hephaistos" (i. e. Ptaḥ) of Memphis, giving their Phoenician name very exactly as *Pataïkoi*, or "little Ptaḥs." [90] The dwarfed, infantile, or even embryo-like representation of these gods then appears to have been understood as symbolizing the beginning of all things. Tearing up and devouring serpents, which probably seemed symbols of primitive hostile powers, they form a transition to Bês.

Fig. 68.
A "Pataïk"

Some of these speculations may also lead back to the idea of Bês as guardian of the young sun, while others seem to have been earlier. The development of these thoughts and pictures needs further investigation (see Fig. 2 (*f*) for a prehistoric statuette of the dwarf type).

We know little about some other divinities who are found in the stars, e. g. Ḥepḥep, who appears in human form and wears royal crowns,[91] or about Ḥeqes,[92] who is once called a god of fishermen and "lord of the mouth of the rivers" (in Lower Egypt?). The meaning and name of many such gods were lost at an early date. Thus a deity called Sunṭ, who is frequently mentioned in the Pyramid Texts [93] as appearing or circulating in the sky, was later forgotten completely. The same fate befell a strange mythological being, a leopard or lion with an enormously long, serpent-like neck which occurs very frequently (often in pairs) on the prehistoric monuments, then appears for a short time on the magic wands of the Middle Empire, and finally vanishes. The special interest of this lost divinity is that it has exact analogies

Fig. 69. Lost Stellar Divinity

in the earliest Babylonian art. Some stellarizations, on the other hand, appear only later. The age and the true estimation of the value of these stellar speculations are often uncertain. They are of special importance in some of the earliest funerary texts which treat of the wanderings of the dead king among the stars, where he himself becomes a star (cf. p. 178). Later even the astronomical meaning of these texts was forgotten, and the conception of the stars as the souls of the dead grew less distinct. New interest in their groups was awakened especially by Greek influence when the twelve signs of the zodiac, which the Greeks had received from the Babylonians, penetrated into the sacred astronomy of Egypt (p. 57).[94]

FIG. 70. THE EAST AND WEST WINDS

The four winds also were considered to be divine. The north wind is a ram or bull with four heads, although variants sometimes occur; the east wind is a hawk, perhaps because the sun-god rises in the east; the south and west winds reveal their burning character by having the head or body of a lion and a serpent respectively. Many of these attributes are quadrupled, four being the celestial number (pp. 39, 52); occasionally they occur in even greater repetitions.[95] Frequently all four winds have the shape or head of a ram as an allusion

FIG. 71. THE AIR-GOD SHU-ḤEḤ WITH THE SOUTH AND NORTH WINDS

to the word *bai* ("soul, breath"). They are usually winged. Their names are known only from very late times.

On the analogy of the four "souls," or rams, of the winds, the Greek period attempted to represent the gods of the four elements also as rams, these deities being Rê' (sun and fire), Shu (air), Qêb (earth), and Osiris (water).[96] Possibly the sun-god with four rams' heads was another basis for this idea, which may have been connected also with the ram of Mendes as representing all nature in Osiris, etc., by theological speculators.

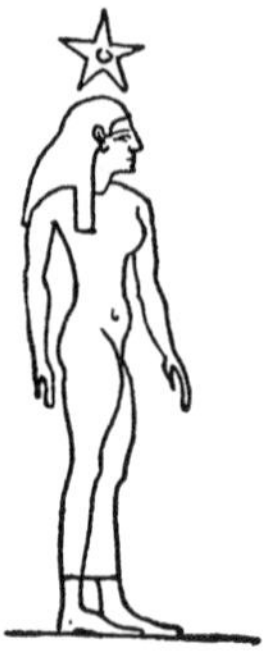

Special gods represented the twenty-four hours of the day.[97] Though the thirty days of the month were not personified, each was placed under the protection of a well-known god, the first, characteristically enough, under that of the moon-god Thout, as the great regulator of time (p. 33).

FIG. 72. AN HOUR

Plant life may be personified in Osiris, so far as it symbolizes the resurrection of the dead. As a more special harvest-goddess the serpent Renenutet (later pronunciation Remute[t]), i. e. "the Raising Goddess," was worshipped, and the eighth month (Pha-rmuthi in later pronunciation) was dedicated to her, evidently because harvest once fell in it.[98] The "God of Grain," Nepri (or, as a female, Nepret, who sometimes is identified with Renenutet), is more of a poetic abstraction like the gods "Abundance" and "Plenty" (Hu, Zefa), etc., all of whom, including Nepri, are often pictured as fat men like the Nile-god (p. 45), with whom they are frequently connected. The "field-goddess" carries a green field on her head. Tenemet seems to have been a patroness of intoxicating drink,[99] and a goddess of baked things was also known.[100]

FIG. 73. NEPRI, THE GRAIN-GOD, MARKED BY EARS OF GRAIN

We may close our enumeration of the gods of nature with the personifications of the four senses, who appear as men bearing on their heads the organ connected with the sense in question and frequently accompanying the sun-god, probably in his capacity of creator of all things. These deities are Hu ("Feeling, Wisdom," frequently confused with Hu, "Abundance"), Sa(u) or Sia(u)

("Taste"), Maa(?) ("Sight"), and Sozem (later Sodem, Sotem, "Hearing"). The first two also symbolize wisdom. Heka ("Magic") is similarly personified,[101] as is Nehes ("Wakefulness [?], Awakening [?]"), both of whom often accompany the sun-god in his ship (cf. Fig. 11). To these male abstractions we some-times [102] find added the female personifications of "Joy" (Aut-[y?]êb) and "Happiness" (Hetpet). On the strange development of Ma'et ("Justice") see p. 100. Countries and cities have female per-sonifications, as is shown by Nekhbet (p. 46). Naturally, however, these abstract deities play little part in Egyptian mythology, and their rôle was quite inferior to that which similar divinities have enjoyed in certain other religious systems.

FIG. 74. THE FIELD-GODDESS

CHAPTER IV

SOME COSMIC AND COSMOGONIC MYTHS

I. THE CREATION OF THE WORLD AND OF MEN

THE fullest text about the creation of the world is a hymn which is preserved only in a papyrus copy written in the reign of Alexander II[1] (310 B. C.), but which seems to go back to originals that are considerably earlier.

THE BOOK OF KNOWING THE GENESIS OF THE SUN-GOD AND OF OVERTHROWING 'APOP

"The Master of Everything saith after his forming:
'I am he who was formed as Khepri.[2]
When I had formed, then (only) the forms were formed.
All the forms were formed after my forming.
Numerous are the forms from that which proceeded from my mouth.[3]

The heaven had not been formed,
The earth had not been formed,
The ground had not been created
(For?) the reptiles in that place.[4]

I raised (myself) among them [variant: there] in the abyss, out
     of (its) inertness.
When I did not find a place where I could stand,
I thought wisely (?) in my heart,
I founded in my soul (?).
I made all forms,[5] I alone.

I had not yet ejected as Shu,
I had not spat out as Tefênet,[6]
None else had arisen who had worked (?) with me.
(Then) I founded in my own heart;[7]

There were formed many (forms?),[8]
The forms of the forms in the forms of the children,
(And) in the forms of their children.

Ego sum qui copulavi pugno meo,
Libidinem sentivi [9] in umbra mea,[10]
Semen cecidit (?) e meo ipsius ore.
  What I ejected was Shu,
What I spat out was Tefênet.
My father, the abyss, sent them.[11]
My eye followed them through ages of ages (?) [12]
As (they) separated from me. After I was formed as the only
  (god),[13]
Three gods were (separated) from me (since?) I was on this earth.
Shu and Tefênet rejoiced in the abyss in which they were.
They brought me my eye (back) (following) after them.
After I had united my members,[14] I wept over them.
  The origin of men was (thus) from my tears which came from my
  eye.
It became angry against me after it had come (back),
When it found that I had made me another (eye) in its place
(And) I had replaced it by a resplendent eye;
I had advanced its place in my face afterward,
(So that) it ruled this whole land.
  Now (?) at its (?) time were their (?) plants (?).[15]
I replaced what she had taken therefrom.
I came forth from the plants (?).
I created all reptiles and all that was in (?) them.[16]
Shu and Tefênet begat [Qêb] and Nut.
Qêb and Nut begat Osiris, Horus (the one before the eyeless) (?),
  Sêth, Isis, and Nephthys from one womb,
One of them after the other;
Their children are many on this earth.'"

Like most ancient Oriental texts concerned with the problem of cosmogony, this is an attempt to use various traditions
of very contradictory character. We see, for example, that it
starts with the assumption that the abyss was occupied by
strange monsters, or "reptiles," among whom the sun-god
grew up; while another theory, evidently much more recent,
regards the solar deity as the very first being that actually
lived and as the creator of all things, so that the sun-god
created, first of all, these primeval monsters.[17] With the formation of the first pair of cosmic gods by the sun the poet loosely
connects the different theory that the creation of ordinary

life or of the present order of the world began by the loss of
the deity's eye. He also alludes to various interpretations
of this myth, of which we shall speak below: (*a*) the lost eye
of the supreme god wanders abroad as the sun; (*b*) it is restored to its former place as the daily sun by Shu and Tefênet,
evidently in their capacity of solar or celestial divinities who
hold the sun in its place; (*c*) the quarrel between the roving
eye and the one which the deity had put in its place, and
the strife with their father, the great cosmic deity, give scope
for various interpretations of this legend by the course of
the sun. The poet does not try to harmonize these interpretations; to him the most important point is the creation
of mankind. The oldest theory, that man originated from
a divine essence flowing from the eye which had been lost
or damaged in some adventure of the creator, is not clearly
set forth; and the hymn emphasizes, rather, the version
which attributes man's creation to a more peaceful emanation from the weeping of the divine eye, a paronomasia
based on the similarity between *remy*, "to weep," and *rômeṭ*,
rôme(*t*), "man," which recurs very often in Egyptian literature
after 2000 B.C. and which admits of a rationalistic interpretation of human and general creation by the rays of the sun.[18]
In its closing lines our text gives yet another theory: men are
descendants of the later divine generations; they are, so to
say, debased gods, connected especially with Osiris, the source
of mortality and ancestor of mortal men. This effort to con-
dense the various cosmogonic theories and traditions into a
few words refers to further myths as well, but we do not consider these here. Our hasty examination of the text sufficiently
shows how impossible it was for the priestly poet to construct
a rational theory of creation from such contradictory material.

This constant incongruity of Egyptian myths is also illustrated by a remarkable series of cosmogonic pictures [19] which
show first "the sun-god growing (in?) members" [20] in a strange
representation which seeks to indicate his embryonic condi-

tion. Near him sit the air-gods Shu and Tefênet as little children. This symbolizes their primeval nature and their precedence of the sun-god, as has been stated on pp. 49–50 (in opposition to the theory set forth in the hymn given on pp. 68–69). Next the sun-god again appears in an embryonic state, floating in an ornamented box which, the explanation says, represents Nut, the heavenly flood, although we should expect the abyss or ocean as the place of the new-born sun (pp.

FIG. 75. THE BIRTH OF THE SUN-GOD

49–50); the chest adapts this idea to the Osiris-Horus myth (p. 57). Then comes the cow "Ehet (p. 40), the development of the members of Khepri," with double emblems of Ḥat-ḥôr and with the symbol of the sky, carrying the sun both on her head and on her body.[21] Before her stands Ḥu, the god of wisdom and the divine word (p. 67), holding an egg, a symbol which may be explained as an allusion to the earth-god Qêb, whose name is sometimes written with the sign of the egg (p. 42), or to the solar egg (?), or to the creation in general. At any rate he represents quite a unique cosmogonic symbolism which would seem to be in conflict with all the other pictures. This is not more strange, however, than "the sun-god (in?) members" (p. 28) in the background as the heavenly face and the half-developed flower, growing from a base which the artist made to be midway between an indication of a

FIG. 76. FURTHER SYMBOLS OF THE BIRTH OF THE SUN-GOD

pool of water and the solar disk. The value of these mystic pictures, claiming to be reproduced according to the earliest traditions, is that they again illustrate the combination of so many different theories about the origin of the sun and of the world; the divergence of these views makes the mystery the more solemn to the Egyptian mind.

In the *Book of the Dead*[22] we find a cosmogonic fragment
which includes allusions to various other disconnected myths.

> "Furthermore I shall ruin all that I have made.
> This earth will appear (?) as an abyss,
> In (or, as) a flood as in its primeval condition.
> I am the one remaining from it together with Osiris.
> My forming is (then) made to me among other (?) serpents
> Which men never knew,
> Which the gods never saw."

The text continues with an account of the distribution of
the world among the gods; the connexion with the preceding
fragment is very unintelligible:

> "What I have done for Osiris is good.
> I have exalted him above all gods;
> I have given him the underworld [variant: as ruler];
> His son Horus (shall be) his heir on his throne in the island of
>   flames (p. 27).
> I have made his throne [variant: his substitute] in the Boat of
>   Eternities."

The text then loses itself in the ordinary Osiris-myth, giving
an interesting description of the fate of Osiris's enemy Sêth:

> "Furthermore I have sent the soul of Sêth to the west,
> Exalted above all gods;
> I have appointed guardians of his soul, being in the boat." [23]

We are here informed that Sêth's soul, after his destruction
on earth, is kept imprisoned in the west, evidently as the ocean-
serpent which lies in darkness, a confusion of Sêth and 'Apop,
which shows that this part of the text, at first unconnected
with the cosmogonic fragment, is subsequent to 1600 B.C.
In like manner we cannot be quite certain that the threat to
return the world to its primeval condition was originally associated with a mythological fragment which precedes it and
which speaks of a rebellion of the gods:

> "O Thout, what is it that hath arisen among the children of Nut? [24]
> They have committed hostilities, they have instigated (?) disorder,
> They have done sin, they have created rebellion,

They have committed murder, they have created destruction,
And they have done (it), the great one against the small
With all which I (?) have done.
Give, O Thout, an order to Atum!"[25]

The compiler seems to have understood this last fragment to refer to the rebellion of Sêth and his companions against Osiris which brought about a reorganization of the world, a parallel to the rebellion of men against the sun-god (p. 74). Whether the first fragment may be interpreted as an allusion to the deluge (as Naville thought) is uncertain; it seems to be only a threat of the sun-god, under his name of Atum. Its interest lies in the fact that it confirms a cosmogonic theory found in the Papyrus of Nesi-Amsu, as recorded in the hymn quoted on pp. 68–69: the sun-god grew among the monsters which filled the abyss and constituted the oldest generation of divine beings, thus possibly affording a parallel to the good gods who dwell in the abyss described in the following myth.

The Asiatizing theory that this older generation opposed the new cosmic power and that the sun-god created the new order of the world in a war against the abysmal powers (or at least against some of them) does not belong to the earlier strata of Egyptian theology, as has been noted above from the mention of 'Apop, the serpent of the abyss, but it forms a transition to the next collection, which is very important.

II. THE DESTRUCTION OF MANKIND

A document of the Middle Empire — probably from the early part of that period — which has been preserved in a much disfigured tradition in two royal tombs of the Nineteenth and Twentieth Dynasties is a compilation of various mythological texts similar to those which we have just considered, full of contradictions and redacted with equal carelessness.[26] There we find an important legend of the destruction of the human race.

"[Once there reigned on earth Rê', the god who[27]] shines,

the god who had formed himself. After he had been ruler of
men and gods together, then men (2) plotted [against him] at
a time when His Majesty — life, welfare, health (to him)! —
had grown old. His bones were of silver, his members of gold,
his hair of genuine lapis lazuli. His Majesty (3) recognized
the plot which the men [had formed] against him and he said
to his followers: 'Call to me my eye and Shu (4) and Tefênet,
Qêb and Nut, together with my fathers and mothers who were
with me when I was in the abyss, and also the god [28] Nuu.
He shall (?) bring his courtiers (5) with himself. Bring [29]
them secretly (?); the men shall not see it, and their heart
shall not run away.[30] Come with them to the palace that they
may speak their opinions respectfully (?), (6) and that I may
go in the abyss to the place where I was born.'

"Those gods were brought [to this god], and those gods
[placed themselves] at his side, touching the ground with their
foreheads (7) before His Majesty (that he should) make his
report before his father, the oldest god (i. e. Nuu), (he) the
maker of men, the king of human beings (?).[31] They said
before His Majesty: 'Speak (8) to us that we may hear it.'
Rê' said to Nuu: 'Thou oldest god, from whom I have arisen,
and ye gods of a former age! behold, the men that have arisen
(9) from my eye, they have plotted against me. Tell me what
ye would do against this. Behold, I am undecided. I would
not slay them before I shall have heard what (10) ye say concerning it.' The Majesty of Nuu said: 'My son Rê', the god
greater than the one who made him and more powerful than
those who created him, stay in thy place! (11) Thy fear is
great; thine eye will be against those who plot against thee.'
Rê' said: 'Behold, in terror of their hearts they have run away
to the (desert) mountains because of what they have said.'
(12) They said before His Majesty: 'Make thy eye go that it
smite for thee those who have plotted wicked things! Let not
the eye be in front of her [32] to smite them for thee!' (13) (So)
it went as Ḥat-ḥôr.[33]

"Then this goddess came (back) when she had slain the men on the mountains. Then the Majesty of this god said: 'Welcome, O Hat-ḥôr, hast thou done that for which I sent thee?' (14) That goddess said: 'By thy life for me, I have been powerful among the men; that was pleasure for my heart.' Said the Majesty of Rê': 'Thou shalt be powerful among them in Herakleopolis (15) by their annihilation.'[34] This was the origin of Sekhmet (i. e. "the Powerful One") and of the mixed drink(?),[35] of the night of passing over their blood, originally (?) in Herakleopolis.[36]

"Rê' said: (16) 'Call me now speedy messengers, swift-running like the shadow of a body.' Such messengers were brought (17) immediately. This god said: 'Go to Elephantine and bring me many mandrake fruits.'[37] Those mandrakes were brought, and [Rê' appointed] (18) the miller (?)[38] who dwells in Heliopolis to (?) grind those mandrakes while slave women brewed (?) grain for beer. Then those mandrakes were put in that mixture, and it was like (19) human blood, and seven thousand jars of beer were made.

"Then came the Majesty of the King of Upper and Lower Egypt, Rê', with those gods to see that beer when the morning broke (20) on which the men were to be killed by the goddess at their [39] (appointed) time of going southward. The Majesty of Rê' said: 'How fine this is! I shall protect (21) the men before her.' Rê' said: 'Bring this now to the place where she said she would kill the men.'

"On that day Rê' [stood up] (22) in the best part (?) of the night [40] for causing this sleeping-draught to be poured out, and the fields were flooded four spans high by [that] liquid through the power of the Majesty of this god. When (23) that goddess came in the morning, she found this causing an inundation. Her face looked beautiful (reflected) therein. She drank from it and liked it and she came (home) drunken without (24) recognizing the men. Rê' said to that goddess: 'Welcome, thou pleasant one!'

"Thus originated the girls in the Pleasant City.⁴¹ Rêʿ
said (25) to that goddess: 'Make sleeping-draughts for her
at the time of the New Year festival! Their number (shall be)
according to (?) that of my (temple) slave-girls.' Thus originated the making of sleeping-draughts for (?) the number of
slave-girls at the festival of Ḥat-ḥôr by all men since that day."

Here we again find the story closed by learned etymologies
of divine names and by explanations of local ceremonies. The
most interesting feature of this myth, however, is the possibility, as Naville first pointed out, of seeing an analogy to
Semitic deluge-traditions in the almost complete destruction
of mankind and the flood of drink which covered the land.
Egyptian fancy would thus have turned the deluge, sent for
destroying the human race, into the means of saving men from
their deserved punishment of extinction; but until we find
further texts, the analogies of the Egyptian story with the
flood-stories of other countries must remain rather problematic. Similar uncertainty attaches to the mythological fragment (p. 72) which presents certain parallel ideas, although it
belongs, rather, to the following myth which tells why the sun-
god departed from earth. Plato's statement ⁴² that the deluge
did not reach Egypt also implies that the Egyptians had no
distinct flood-legend. The only faint Egyptian parallel to the
deluge is the legend of Osiris or Horus, the ancestor of mankind,
floating in a chest at his birth or death, as will be told in the
following chapter. The connexion between the myth just
related and the New Year admits of various interpretations.⁴³

III. WHY THE SUN-GOD WITHDREW FROM EARTH

To the tradition of the destruction of mankind the same
text adds another story which seemed capable of association
with it.

"The Majesty of Rêʿ said to that goddess: 'Is this illness ⁴⁴
the burning of (ordinary?) illness? What, then, hath befallen

(me?) (27) by illness?' The Majesty of Rê' said: 'By my life, my heart hath become very weary to be with them. I have killed them, (but it is) a case as though I was not (?). Is the stretching out of my arm a (28) failure?'[45] The gods who were following him said: 'Do not yield (?) to thy weariness; thou art powerful whenever thou wilt.' The Majesty of that god (29) said to the Majesty of Nuu: 'My limbs are weak for the first time; I shall not come (back that) another (such case?) may reach me.'[46]

"The Majesty of Nuu said: 'My son Shu, the eye (30) of (his?) father [who is wise at?] his consultation, (and?)[47] my daughter Nut, put him [on thy back].' Nut said: 'How so, my father Nuu?' Nut said: ' . . . (31) . . . Nuu.' Nut became [a cow (?)]. [Then] Rê' [placed] himself on her back. When those men had [come] (32) [they sought the sun-god?]. Then they saw him on the back of the [heavenly] cow. Then those (33) men said: '[Return] to us (that?) we may overthrow thine enemies who have plotted [against thee].' [Although they said?] this, His Majesty (34) went to his palace [in the west (?)]. [When he was no longer] with them, the earth was in darkness. When the earth became light in the morning, (35) those men came forth with their bows and their [weapons] for shooting the enemies (of the sun). The Majesty of this god said: 'Your sins are behind you.[48] The murderers (36) are (too) remote (for their) murderous (plans).' Thus originated the (ceremony of) murdering . . . The Majesty of this god said to Nut: 'Put me on thy back to raise me.'"

The next lines are too mutilated for coherent translation, but, as we see, the sun-god establishes his permanent abode in heaven, where he creates the celestial fields "with all shining (or: verdant, growing) stars" (cf. p. 55).

"Then Nut began (41) to tremble in (?) the height" (i. e. under the weight of these new things), and the endless space (Ḥeh) was created for support.[49] Then Rê' said: (42) 'My son Shu, put thyself under my daughter Nut. Take heed for me

of the (sun-bark called) 'Millions of Millions' (which is)
there, and (?) of those who live among (or, of?) the stars (?).
Put her on thy head.'"

Thus heaven and earth were separated, and the sun-god
remained on the back of the heavenly cow. In this way human
sin had driven the gods from this earth, and no repentance
could bring them back to dwell again among mankind. This
legend is obviously a different version of the preceding myth,
though all its allusions are not yet intelligible; the "bows," for
instance, may be an astronomical term. We may also compare

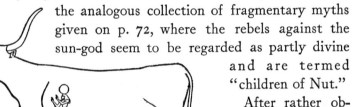

the analogous collection of fragmentary myths
given on p. 72, where the rebels against the
sun-god seem to be regarded as partly divine
and are termed
"children of Nut."

After rather ob-
scure directions how
to depict the new
order of things,[50]
this same collection
gives another very
interesting explana-

FIG. 77. THE HEAVENLY COW, THE SUN-GOD, AND THE
GODS SUPPORTING HER (SHU IN THE CENTRE)

tion of the sun-god's departure from the earth to the sky.

(56) "The Majesty of that god said to Thout: 'Call now for
me to the Majesty of Qêb thus: "Come, hurry immediately!"'"
Then the Majesty of Qêb came. The Majesty of that god (i. e.
Rê') said: 'Take care [51] (57) with thy serpents which are in
thee! Behold, I have feared them as long as I have existed.
Now thou knowest their magic (formulæ).[52] Thou shalt, therefore, go to the place of my father Nuu and shalt say to him:
(58): "Guard against the reptiles inhabiting land and water," [53]
and thou shalt make a (magic) writing for every place [54] of
thy serpents which are there, saying namely: "Guard against
playing any tricks!" They shall know that (59) now I shall
give light for them.[55] But behold, they belong (?) to (thee,

my) father, who is (?) on this earth forever. Beware now of these sorcerers, skilled (60) with their mouth. Behold, the god of magic [56] (himself) is there. Who swallows him (?), behold there is not one who guards (me?) from a great thing (?). It has happened (61) before me. I have destined them for thy son Osiris (who will?) guard against their small ones and make the heart of their great ones forget. Those prosper (?)[57] who do (62) as they like on the whole earth with their magic in their breast.'"

In great part the text is mutilated to a degree which renders it hopelessly obscure, yet we may at least infer that, in the opinion of the compiler of these ancient mythological fragments, we have here another reason why the heavenly gods no longer dwell on earth: serpents or a serpent drove them away. The writer's only doubt is whether this was done by a serpent of the earth-god after the organization of the world or whether it refers to the primeval beings who inhabited the abyss (p. 69) and from whom the sun-god separated himself when he began to build this world. The writer or redactor thus confuses two ages of the world and two theories; and he even seems to allude to a third theory, namely, to that of the great enemy of the gods, the cosmic serpent 'Apop, who constantly threatens to swallow the sun-god and thus forces him to be on his guard and to keep high in the heavens. This combination of theories about serpents which were dangerous to the gods seems then to have been worked into a magic incantation for protection against reptiles, at least so far as we can understand the hopelessly obscure lines 58–61.

IV. THE SUN-GOD, ISIS, AND THE SERPENT

On the basis of the compilation of myths from which we have thus far given four sections it is possible to gain a better understanding of the somewhat later myth of the sun-god and Isis.[58]

LINE
(12) "Chapter of the divine god who arose by himself,
    Who made the heaven, the earth, the air of life, and the fire,
    The gods, the men, the wild animals, and the flocks,
    The reptiles, the birds, and the fish,
    The king of men and of gods together,
(13) (Whose) ages are more than (human?) years,[59]
    Rich in names which people here know not,
    Neither do those yonder know.[60]
        At that time[61] there was Isis, a woman
    Skilful in sorcery (?), whose heart was tired
    Of living forever[62] among men;

(PLATE CXXXII)

(1) She preferred time forever among the gods;
    She esteemed (more highly) living forever among the illuminated
        spirits.
    Was she not able[63] (to be) in heaven and on earth like Rê',
    To become mistress of the land of gods?[64]
    So she thought in her heart
(2) To learn the name of the holy god.
        Now Rê' came every day
    At the head of his followers,[65]
    Established on the throne of both horizons.
    The god had grown old; his mouth dripped,
(3) His spittle flowed to the earth,
    His saliva fell on the ground.

        Isis kneaded this with her hand
    Together with the earth on which it was.[66]
    She formed it as a holy (4) serpent;
    She made it in the form of a dart
    It did not wander alive before her;
    She left it rolled together (?) on (?) the way[67]
    On which the great god wandered
    At his heart's desire over (5) his two countries.[68]

        The holy god — life, welfare, health (to him) — appeared
            (*from*) *his palace*,
    The gods *behind*[69] following him.
    He walked as every day.
    (Then) the holy snake bit[70] him.

        A living flame came forth from (6) himself[71]
    To drive away (?) the one in the cedars.[72]

LINE   The holy god opened [73] his mouth.
The voice of His Majesty — life, welfare, health (to him) —
   reached heaven.
His circle of gods (said), 'What is it?'
His gods (said), 'What is the matter?'
(7) He found not a word [74] to answer to this (question).
His jaws trembled,
All his limbs shook,
The poison took possession of his flesh
As the Nile takes possession [of the land, spreading [75]] over it.

(8) The great god concentrated all his will-power.[76]
He cried to his followers:
'Come to me, ye who have arisen from my members,
Ye gods who have come forth from me,
That I may inform you what hath happened! [77]
(9) Something painful hath pierced me
Which my heart had [not?] noticed,
And mine eyes had not seen,[78]
Which my hand hath not made.
I know not who hath done all this.
I have not (ever) tasted such suffering;
No pain is stronger than this.
(10) I am the prince, the son of a prince,
The issue of a god which became a god;
I am the great one, the son of a great one.
My father hath thought out my name;
I am one with many names, with many forms.
(11) My form is in every god.
I am called Atumu and Ḥar-ḥekenu.[79]
My father and my mother (however) told me my (real) name;
It hath been hidden within me since (?) my birth
(12) In order that power and magic (force) [80] may not arise for one
   who (may desire to) bewitch me.

I had come forth to see that which I (once) made,
I (began to) walk in the two countries which I created,
(13) When something pierced me which I know not.
Neither is it fire,
Nor is it water.[81]
My heart is aglow,
My limbs tremble,
All my members shiver (14) with cold.
The children of the gods [82] should be brought to me,

LINE Those wise of words,
    Skilled with their mouth,
    Who with their knowledge reach the firmament.'

(PLATE CXXXIII)

    (1) There came the children of the god; each one
Was there with his lamentations.
There came (also) Isis with her wisdom,
The place of her mouth (full) of breath of life,
(With) her formulæ expelling suffering,
(With) her words (2) quickening those deprived of breath.
She said: 'What is it? what is it, my divine father?
Hath a serpent spread pain (?) within thee?
Hath one of thy children lifted his head against thee?
Then I shall subject (3) it by excellent magic,
I shall drive it away at (?) the sight of thy rays.'

The majestic god opened his mouth:
'I walked on the road,
I wandered in the two countries and the desert,
(4) (For) my face (?) [83] wished to see what I had created.
(There) I was bitten by a serpent without seeing it.
It is not fire,
Nor is it water.
I feel colder than water,
I feel hotter than fire.
(5) All my limbs are sweating;
Mine eye trembleth and cannot be fixed;
Nor can I look upward.
A flood covereth my face like (the inundation) at the time of
    summer.'

(6) Isis said: 'Tell me thy name, divine father!
The man will keep alive who is worshipped [84] by his (correct)
    name.'
    (The sun-god replied:)
'I am the one who hath made heaven and earth, who hath
    raised [85] the mountains,
And created what is upon it.[86]
(7) I am the one who hath made the water which became the Great
    Flood,[87]
Who made the Bull of his Mother,
Who became the wanderer (?).[88]

LINE I am the one who made heaven as a secret and (its) two hori-
zons,[89]
In which I have placed the soul [90] of the gods.
(8) I am the one who (only) openeth his eyes, and there is light;
When his eyes close, darkness falleth.
The flood of the Nile riseth when he hath ordered it.
(9) The gods know not his name.
I am the one who made the hours so that the days came.
I am he who made the year begin and created the rivers.
I am he who made the living fire
(10) For producing works of smithcraft.[91]
I am Khepri in the morning, Rê' at his standing still,[92]
Atumu at evening time.'

The poison was not stopped as it went on;
The great god did not feel well.
(11) Isis said: 'Thy name is not in the enumeration which thou hast
made.
Tell it to me, and the poison will leave;
The man will live whose name is pronounced.' [93]

(12) The fire burned like a flame;
It became more powerful than a melting stove in flame.
The Majesty of Rê' said:
'I have been searched (too much) by Isis;
My name will come forth from my bosom into thy bosom.'
(13) The god hid himself from his gods;
His place was prepared in the ship (called) 'Millions [of Years].'
In the moment in which (the name) had left (his) heart,
She (Isis) said to her son Horus:
'I have bound him by a holy oath (14) that the [great?] god
give up [to thee] his two eyes.'
[The great god, his name was betrayed to Isis, great in magic,
Leave, O spell; come forth from Rê'!]."

The last two verses do not seem to belong to the original
poem, but to the application of the myth as a conjuration for
a person bitten by a snake. The story, the papyrus explains,
is to be written twice, one copy to be wrapped around the
neck of the patient, and the other to be washed off and drunk
by him in beer or wine, according to a custom to be described
in the chapter on magic (p. 199).

This myth, which is as remarkable for its poetry as for its theology, seems to date from the beginning of the New Empire, since its pantheistic views scarcely admit of a period more remote. The story shows in good logical connexion the ancient Asiatic astral myth associating the constellations Virgo, Hydra, and Orion (= the sun) which we shall find again in our chapter on foreign influences; and it gives another version of the legend which precedes it, answering the question why the gods dwell no more on earth: a serpent caused the sun-god to withdraw to higher spheres. Its relation to the series of myths which we have considered in II and III is not yet clear; the incoherence and the language of that collection give the impression that its legends belong to an older epoch than the papyrus. For an earlier Egyptian idea which prepared the way for the legend of Isis and the sun-god see p. 25 and the myth of the lost eye of the solar deity (pp. 86–88).

V. HOW THE MOON BECAME RULER OF THE NIGHT

The compilation of myths which has told us of the destruction of mankind and why the sun-god withdrew from earth also contains a legend of the way in which the moon was installed as lord of night.

(62) "The Majesty of this god (i. e. Rê') said: 'Call Thout(i) now to me.' He was brought directly. The Majesty (63) of this god said to Thout: 'Behold,[94] I put thee now in the sky (64) in my place while I (65) give light to the luminous spirits (i. e. of the dead) (66) in the underworld and the island of Baba.[95] (67) Write there thy judgement (?) [96] of those who are in them (i. e. those two places) (68) (for) what they have done (?) committing (69) sins. Art not thou [among?] (70) my servants in (?) this shameful act? [97] (71) Thou shalt be in my place, my representative.[98] Now let this be said to thee, Thout, the representative of Rê': I shall let thee send (hab) such as are greater than thou.' (Thus) originated the ibis

(*habi*) of Thout. 'I shall (72) let thee stretch out thy hand against (?) the gods of [my?] circle who are greater than thou. My (?) *khen* is fine.' [99] (Thus) originated the two wings (*tekhenui*) of the ibis of Thout. 'I shall let thee surround (*enh*) (75) the sky with thy beauty and with thy rays.' (Thus) originated the moon (*io'h*) of Thout. 'I shall let thee turn back the barbarians ('*an'an*).'[100] Thus originated the cynocephalus ('*an'an*) of Thout. '[Thou] shalt be (76) judge (while) thou art my representative. The face of those who see thee will be opened in (?) thee. The eyes of all men will thank thee.'"

This installation of a vicegerent instead of the sun for the dark night offers various interesting features. In the first place it is connected with the judgement of the rebels: from the time of their uprising Thout takes a more prominent place, since a judge becomes necessary for the sinful world; but there is only an obscure and passing allusion to the parallel thought that the sun-god must descend to hell where the rebels are instead of shining on earth throughout the twenty-four hours. The most important thing, however, is to explain the origin of the cult of Thout's animals by plays on the words by which the sun installed him. We see here the first attempts to interpret a piece of animal worship — a remarkable proof that this most primitive feature of the ancestral religion began to disturb Egyptian thinkers about 2000 B. C., the period from which this legend would seem to date. Plays on words always had a very deep significance to the ancient Orient, as we can see also from the explanations of ceremonies given on pp. 75–76.

VI. THE LOST EYE OF THE SUN-GOD

We have already had a reference (p. 70) to the myth which tells how the sun-god once lost his eye (the sun) and how it rebelled against him. Fuller information on this legend has

been preserved only in very late texts [101] in which its meaning is much effaced and where it runs, in several variants, as
follows.

The sun's eye, as Tefênet or Ḥat-ḥôr, had retired from
Egypt to Nubia, where it lived as a wild lioness or lynx.
As messengers to bring her back the sun-god sent Tefênet's
brother, the lion-formed Shu (or his local manifestation,
Eri-ḥems-nofer), and the baboon or ibis Thout (or both in
the form of two baboons or two lions). Wandering through
all Nubia, they finally discovered her in the eastern mountain
of sunrise in a place called Bu-gem(et) ("the Place of Finding"),[102] and winning her consent with some difficulty (especially by the wise speech of Thout), they finally brought her
back to Egypt. There she was received with music, dancing,
and banquets, and thus the memory of her return was celebrated in many temples throughout the ages that followed.
The sacred baboons, i. e. the two gods just mentioned, or else
the baboons who greet the sun each morning (p. 32), saluted
and guided the returning goddess; and in Heliopolis she was
reconciled to her father. The theologians then tried to connect this myth with the battle of Rê' and Ḥat-ḥôr, his "eye
and daughter," against rebellious men (pp. 74-75). Thus, for
example, the temple of Ombos boasts of being

"The place of Shu at the beginning,
To which came his father Rê',
Hiding himself from those who plotted against him
When the wicked came to seek him.
Then Shu made his form
(As that) of Horus, the fighter (?) with his spear;[103]
He killed them immediately in this district.
The heart of the sun-god was glad over this,
Over that which his son Shu had done for him." [104]

Later "came Nuu (?), the one without (?) eyes (?),[105] to this
district as a lion great of strength to avenge his father Rê'
again. . . . Then came Tefênet to this place with her brother
Shu when she came from Bu-gem(et?)." This returning god-

dess is then identified with Ḥat-ḥôr and with the terrible Sekh-met, the destructive solar force (p. 75). We have, however, no early connexion of this myth with that revolution of sinful men to which allusion is made in various myths already studied, especially in the tale of the moon's installation as ruler of night; even in the late legend just quoted this asso-ciation looks feeble and secondary.

The old hymn of the creation, which we have considered in

FIG. 78. Ṭḥout in Ibis-Form (Twice), with Shu and Tefênet as the Two Lions

the first section of this chapter, refers to the myth of the lost eye in another way: the eye follows Shu and Tefênet into the abyss to bring them back; but later these air-gods themselves make the eye return from that place (p. 69). In either version Tefênet and the sun's eye are differentiated, although it is difficult to say whether this was the earliest form of the story. The following reference to a myth of two eyes of the sun, the old one which came back from the depth and its (temporary?) substitute, describes the estrangement between the sun-god and his one daughter or eye (pp. 29–30) as a consequence of jealousy between the two eyes (perhaps the solar and the lunar, or the one of day-time and the one invisible at night) and as

subsequent to the return of the single eye.[106] On the other
hand, the texts of the Ptolemaic period make the estrangement of the "angry goddess" from her father the reason for
her departure to Nubia, though they fail to give any explanation for the hostility of the pair. It is remarkable that in all
these traditions we find no connexion with the Osiris-cycle,
and this looks like a trace of the fact that the myth in its original
form was based on a very old tradition, dating from a time
when the Osiris-cult had not yet spread through Egypt.

The ancient Pyramid Texts have, for the most part, only

Fig. 79. Thout Greets Tefênet Returning from Nubia (a Continuation
of the Preceding Cut)

indistinct allusions to the sun's eye, "which is born every
day," [107] as a fiery asp (see p. 29 for this form of the single or
double eye of the sun); although even they begin to connect
it with the struggle between Horus and Sêth. Thus we have
mention of "the asp proceeding from Rê'" and of "the asp
[of the royal crown, which is mentioned previously in the same
passage] proceeding from Sêth [!], which was taken away
and brought back." [108]   This restoration was scarcely to Sêth,
although such an asp was worn "on the head of Sêth," [109]
just as it regularly adorned the forehead of the solar deity;
it would seem rather that Sêth had stolen it for a time, and
that the sun-god had accidentally found it.[110] The most

definite allusion declares that "(the king going to heaven will) take the eye of Horus to him(self?); (the king) is a son of Khnûm." [111] In other words, the lost eye disappeared in the depths of Khnûm's watery realm, in the source of the Nile and the ocean, at the First Cat-aract, where it lives as "the (goddess), great in magic, of the south." [112]

All this enables us to under-

Fig. 80. The Solar Eye in the Watery Depth

stand the mythological picture which accompanies the seventeenth chapter of the *Book of the Dead*. It represents two subterranean lakes or springs which are guarded by two water-gods, one of whom is portrayed as youthful or as less fat than the other. One of them holds the palm-branch which symbolizes time, year, renewal, fresh vegetation; and he stretches his other hand over a hole which contains the eye of a hawk, i. e. the eye of the hawk-shaped (p. 24) sungod which was lost in the underworld. Before long this representation was misunderstood and disfigured, so that two eyes of the sun were depicted. The Papyrus of Ani adds an explanatory inscription to the basin holding the hawk's eye: "The ocean; his name is 'Lake of Purification of Millions'"; and thus indicates a parallel interpretation of the legend as

the daily descent of the sun's eye to the depths of the ocean and its return from it; while the deity to the left, holding the palm branch, is explained

Fig. 81. The Solar Eye Guarded in the Deep

as Ḥeḥ (infinite space), i. e., like Shu, an air-god (p. 44). Thus we understand why parallel representations (see p. 43) substitute for the pictures here given the two lions who carry the sun, i. e. the air-gods Shu and Tefênet, who each day separate the eye of the sun from

its place in the water, and so restore it to the world. Here we
have the origin of the *rôle* of Shu and Tefênet, but we also
see, to our surprise, that their participation in the myth was
secondary and comparatively late (1500 B. C.?), for the Papyrus
of Ani, like other early manuscripts of the *Book of the Dead*,
still depicts the alleged air-god as the deity of the Nile and
covers even his body with lines to represent water.

In other variants [113] we see the source-god Khnûm himself,
sometimes armed like a watchman, and sometimes holding in
one hand the solar eye, while its double (the sorely disfigured
hawk's eye) is in one of Khnûm's two water-holes. The
baboon of the wise divinity Thout likewise appears, evidently
as the healer of the eye. Once Khnûm stands on a lion, in
which we recognize the old earth-god Akeru (p. 43); the
crocodile which here accompanies him cannot be interpreted
with certainty (p. 109). Thus we see once more that the
place where the eye was lost is found in the mythical source
of the Nile, the ocean, and all waters of the whole world, at
the First Cataract or the region south of it.[114]

Next, the Nile's water is itself explained as the lost eye, since
it is an important manifestation of Osiris-Horus, disappearing
or diminishing in winter, but brought back from Nubia in the
summer inundations by Isis, or by her tears, or as Isis herself,
since she is another daughter of the sun. Allusions to this interpretation of the myth will be found in the magic text of the
tears of Isis translated on pp. 125–26. There the wise Thout
also reappears; and this healer, reconciler, and regulator of all
solar manifestations thus leads us back to the connexion of the
lost eye with the Osirian myth. Like the body of Osiris, the
solar eye of the renascent Osiris, the sun-god Horus, is torn
into many parts in the combat with Sêth, so that Thout must
put together its six, or fourteen, or sixty-four pieces. The
fifteenth or sixty-fifth fragment apparently had been completely lost and was restored only by the magic of the divine
physician; hence it is declared that the sixth and fifteenth day

of each month "fill the sacred eye." [115] To this restoration and to the numerical interpretation of "the safe eye," "the intact eye" (*uzait*), the priests alluded when they depicted the solar eye in the peculiar symbol ⟶ which became the most popular amulet of the Egyp- tians. Thus the older solar myths and their sub- sequent tendency toward adaptation to the Osirian cycle, which was partly solar, merged in such various ways that we can no longer separate them.

We may infer that the myth of the eye which went to, or was lost in, the region of darkness and the abysmal depths existed in endless variants, of which some day we may hope to recover many more. The versions which are extant, especially those of the Græco-Roman period, as we have already said, contain little more than a very dim recollection of this wealth. To cite but a single instance, even the cosmic meaning of Nubia as the corridor to the underworld, or as the underworld itself (pp. 46–47, 86, 147), had then been completely forgotten.

Thus far it is unsafe to compare this myth with analogous traditions in stories from other mythologies which tell how the sky-god or the solar deity lost an eye (usually the lunar one) which sank into a pit, etc.[116] The study of such parallels must be reserved for future researches.

All the legends which we have recorded show that the mythology of the ancient Egyptians must have been one of the richest in the world, notwithstanding the deplorable fact that for the most part we are forced to gain our knowledge of this wealth by gathering fragmentary allusions. We might endeavour to reconstruct much more here, but this first necessitates the re-establishment of a group of myths to be set forth in the following chapter.

CHAPTER V

THE OSIRIAN CYCLE

AT a very early time a special group of gods, all local in origin, was brought into a mutual connexion which gave rise to an extremely rich growth of myths that overshadowed all other mythology[1] and thus made those divinities the most popular, not only of Egypt, but, subsequently, of the whole ancient world. Accordingly, they are best treated separately from the other members of the pantheon, although their cosmic functions have been mentioned in great part in the chapters on the cosmic deities. Here we have the most com-

FIG. 82. OSIRIS plete grouping of divine personalities in the whole
AS A BLACK Egyptian religion, and yet in this very connexion
GOD we can notice with especial clearness how little the Egyptians cared for a systematic and logical presentation of their religious beliefs. The only feeble attempt to describe this cycle systematically was made by the Greek Plutarch of Chaeronea (about 120 A. D.) in his famous treatise "On Isis and Osiris." Although he failed, and introduced many non-Egyptian ideas, this little study gives us some valuable information, whereas other Græco-Roman accounts of Egyptian religion con-

FIG. 83.
tain only fragments of truth. We shall often OSIRIS HIDDEN
have occasion to refer to it in our study. IN HIS PILLAR

Osiris[2] was originally the local god of the city of Dêd(u) (also called Dêdet) in the Delta, which the Greeks termed Busiris, i. e. "Home of Osiris," and where a strangely shaped pillar with circular projections separating bands of various

colours was his symbol.³ At a rather early date he became a
cosmic deity, and after oscillating between symbolizing either
the sun or the sky, he finally developed into the god of changing
nature in the widest sense. Thus he could become the divinity
of the most important change, i. e. death, and could be evolved
into the patron of the souls of the departed and king of the

Fig. 84. Osiris in the Celestial Tree

The deity stands between the two obelisks which symbolize time. From a
sarcophagus in the Museum of Cairo.

lower world, being at the same time the lord of resurrection and
of new and eternal life. The latter conception gave him great
pre-eminence over the many earlier deities of necropoles who
had nothing to do with the hope of resurrection and who,
therefore (with the exception of Anubis, an ancient Upper
Egyptian god of the departed, see *infra*, p. 111), remained local
guardians of the dead. This explains his great popularity. As
changing nature, Osiris, according to the views of historic
times, may be seen in the daily and yearly course of the sun,
which dies every evening and revives in the morning, becomes

old and weak in winter and strong again in spring. The dispersion of the god's members originally seems to have involved a belief that the stars are scattered fragments of the dead sun. As ruler of the sky, however, he can actually be identified with the sky; he can sit in the celestial tree, or can be that tree itself, or an important part of it. When he grows forth from the tree, he shows his solar nature (p. 35). As a bull (especially of black colour) he is also celestial.[4] Three hundred and sixty or three hundred and sixty-five lights were burned in his honour, three hundred and sixty-five trees were said to be planted around certain of his temples, etc., thus showing him to be the god of changing time and of the year. As master of the year his festivals were chiefly lunar, so that he could easily assume features of the moon, the regulator of the sky; later he was directly called the moon as "renewing himself." Moreover he can be sought in many important stars or con-

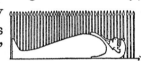

FIG. 85. THE NILE RE-VIVES THE SOUL OF OSI-RIS IN SPROUTING PLANTS

FIG. 86. OSIRIS RISING TO NEW LIFE IN SPROUTING SEEDS

stellations. Thus the morning star was brought into connexion with him, or, rather, with his double, Horus; the parallel queen of the fixed stars and of heaven, Sothis, was then associated with him as sister-wife or as mother (p. 56). He can be found likewise in the planet Jupiter as another ruler of the sky.[5] In the constellation Argo and its chief star, Canopus, he appears as a child or as dead, floating in a chest,[6] while in Orion he is seen as the victorious warrior, i. e. renascent as Horus (for the easy interchange of these constellations see pp. 57–58). The rising Nile likewise reminds the faithful of him because it is an annual calendric phenomenon of reviving nature, side by side with other explanations of this event as Osirian (see below).

By laying the major emphasis on the death of Osiris he

becomes the master of the underworld, the ruler of the dead.
Nevertheless he is not treated as an earth-god,[7] although he is
symbolized in a way quite analogous to that in which the
Asiatic god of plants and springs, Tammuz-Adonis, is typified [8]
by the new life of the vegetation which springs from the ground.
Osiris can also be compared to or identified with the water of
the summer inundation because it enables the crops to grow
again, and both ideas are combined in a picture (Fig. 85)
which shows how the Nile-god awakens to life the soul (i. e.
manifestation) of the "Phoenix-Osiris" in the new plants. The
rebirth of the life-giving river reveals Osiris himself;[9] or the
water flows from his wounded or dismembered body in mysterious depths, or he causes it through the tears of Isis (and
Nephthys) which flow for and over him. The modern Egyptians
still believe that a mysterious drop, falling into the river on a
spring night, causes its sudden swelling, a thought which is only
another version of the tears of Isis. When Osiris thus becomes
identical with the Nile, this applies especially to its mysterious
subterranean portion, so that Osiris is identified with the abyss,
and even with the ocean (p. 46). Even in the late period, which
understands the sea as "Typhonic," i. e. antagonistic to Osiris,
we still find it plainly stated that Osiris is the ocean.[10] Thus
he often represents the whole principle of water as the life-
giving element, whence a magician of Roman days, writing in
Greek, calls Osiris "water," and Isis "dew," because of her
falling tears.[11] As the subterranean Nile Osiris has four birth-
genii, or Meskhenets (p. 52), a symbolism which seems to allude
to the four sources of the Nile (p. 46).[12] As the ocean which
encircles the lower world, the conception of Osiris reverts to the
idea of ruling or representing the dark realm of the dead. In
this connexion particular interest attaches to the famous
picture from the sarcophagus of King Setkhuy (Sethos) I.
This cosmic scene shows Nuu, the god of the abyss, in the
morning, lifting the solar ship from the depths; the inscription
reads, "These arms come from the water; they lift this god."

The sun as a scarab is accompanied by Isis and Nephthys, showing that Rê', Khepri, and Osiris are identified. Strangely enough, the earth god Qêb stands next in the ship, and then Shu, Ḥeka ("Magic"), Ḥu ("Wisdom"), and S(i)a ("Knowledge"), while to the right are three "keepers of the gate," evidently of the lower world. Mother "Nut receives the sun" at nightfall and passes him on to his resting-place in the western deep, where the lowest circle of the water of the abyss is depicted as a god in circular form (cf. Fig. 46), and described as "this is Osiris who encircles the underworld" (*Duat*).[13] See Fig. 87.

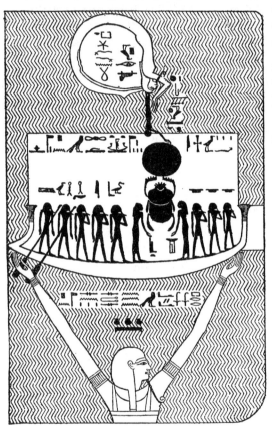

Fig. 87. Birth and Death of the Sun, with Osiris as Master of the Abysmal Depth

Thus there is scarcely any part of changing nature in which Osiris cannot be found, which is in itself a proof that originally he possessed no cosmic function whatever. Because of this universal sway he seems to bear the frequent title of Neb-er-Zer, or "Lord of Everything."

The main function of this god, however, always remained that of ruling over the region of the departed, whence he is frequently pictured as black.[14] He sits on his "throne of metal," [15] or on a platform (sometimes of a shape which resembles a hieroglyph for "justice," ⬜⬜), or on lofty stairs.

The stairs in the accompanying picture, on which the (personified) balance of justice and the gods of the divine circle of Osiris stand, must originally have meant the stairs on which the sun-god ascends and descends (p. 35). The later period, however, seeks Osiris's throne preferably in the depths of the earth or of the sky. From his seat he directs the occupations of the dead, supervising especially — since he is connected with the vegetation

Fig. 88. Osiris as Judge on his Stairs

which comes mysteriously from the deep — the work in the fields of Earu (the "field of sprouts"; p. 55). Under or near his throne he guards the water and the plant of life (with both of which, as we have seen, he is often identified); and since he

Fig. 89. Osiris with the Water and Plant of Life, on Which Stand his Four Sons

decides the fate of the dead in their second life, this kind king of the departed becomes a stern judge of their past moral life. On his divine helpers in this judicial function, see p. 176. With the stars he and his whole kingdom arise at night-time from the depths,[16] and in other respects also his solar and celestial functions mingle with those of the keeper of the lower world. This again shows him as the lord of resurrection and as the prototype of the dead who gain eternal life. For this reason

his name Un(en)-nofer, or Unnofru (Greek 'Ονοφρις), "the Good Being," characterizes him as the mildest and most beneficent of all the gods.

His worship spread from Busiris over all Egypt, but its principal seat soon became Abydos in Middle Egypt, the necropolis of the ancient capital This, where he replaced the old wolf(?)-god Ophoïs (Egyptian Up-uaut) and his variant Khent(i)-amentiu (p. 21). There a hole in the ground at U-peqa (or U-peqer, Re-peqer, "the Place, the Mouth of Peqer") was shown as the entrance to the lower world, a pond was regarded as the celestial "Jackal Lake" or as the source of the abyss (p. 51), a great flight of steps represented the stairway of the sun (pp. 35, 97), etc. Osiris himself had once been buried there; and after the dispersion of his members the head at least had remained behind at Abydos, where it was worshipped as the holiest of all relics of the "good god."[17] The tomb where his body once had lain (or still was preserved) was found later in a royal tomb of the earliest period, whose owner had been forgotten. This nearness of Osiris made all Egyptians wish to find immortality by being buried at Abydos, so that an immense cemetery developed there.

FIG. 90.
Isis

At Memphis he was soon identified with the local god of the necropolis, the hawk Sokari,[18] and then with Ptaḥ and the deities identified or associated with him, such as the local sacred bull Apis (Ḥap). This led to the name Osorḥap ("Osiris-Apis"), the Serapis of the Greeks.[19] His worship at the "City of the Sun," Heliopolis, was less distinct, although the old solar symbols of this earliest of the holy cities (p. 31) later received explanations in great part from the Osirian myth.

At a very early period Isis was associated with Osiris as his wife, probably because she enjoyed a neighbouring cult and also because her name (Êset in Egyptian) was sufficiently like that of Osiris [20] to permit the wide-spread idea of the celestial twins (with different sex) to be seen in this divine pair. We do not know enough about the earliest seats of worship of Isis in the Delta to say with any certainty whether her primitive local cult was, e. g. at Per-ḥebet (the Iseion of the Greeks and the modern Behbeit). It is possible that the strange amulet (a peculiar knot of flax?) which symbolizes Isis may be the hieroglyph for a long-forgotten place in which she had her original local cult. Her most famous temple in the latest times, on the island of Philae in the First Cataract, was not built until near the Greek period (see p. 244).

FIG. 91. THE SYMBOL OF ISIS

Parallel with the solarization of Osiris, Isis had to represent the heaven as wife and mother of the sun, principally in the daytime, though as mother of the stars she also

symbolized the sky of night. She is identified with other celestial goddesses, above all with the heavenly cow Ḥat-ḥôr, etc., and hence she often bears the horns of a cow on her human head, as a symbol of heaven (p. 37). Thus she is even identified with her own mother (Nut),[21] with the tree of heaven and of life (notwithstanding the fact that Osiris also was identified with this; see p. 94), and then likewise with Selqet, the scorpion-goddess from the lower world, etc.

FIG. 92. ISIS-ḤAT-ḤÔR

Later, as consort of the dying god, Isis is often called "Goddess of the West" (i. e. the western sky or the necropoles of Egypt), and thus she is compared with "the West," that mythological personage who wears, as a symbol of the western regions, an ostrich-feather on her head or instead of her missing head, or simply appears as a headless (i. e. lifeless) figure. This personification of the regions of death receives the sun at evening, stretching her arms from the sky. Later we even find similar arms stretched from the sky (or from the ocean, as in Figs. 87, 94) to send the sun forth in the morning, so that they become a symbol of heaven. As a

FIG. 93. THE WEST RECEIVING A DEPARTED SOUL

personification of the region of the dead the headless goddess
is euphemistically called "the good, beautiful west," or "the
good, fine necropolis," or, even more euphemistically, "the
good (goddess)," Nofret. This mysterious fig-
ure receives further strange interpretations.

Since as a hieroglyph the ostrich-feather sig-
nifies both "west" and "justice," she is soon
also called "(the goddess of) justice (or, truth),
the daughter of (the sun-god) Rê'." [22] Thus
"Justice" often stands in the boat of the sun
or near his celestial throne in a function which
is never explained, but which must have meant

FIG. 94. THE CELES-
TIAL ARMS RE-
CEIVING THE SUN-
GOD

more than that the god is righteous. Sometimes this daughter of the sun is connected with
the solar asp as his daughter (p. 29). Her
presence at Osiris's judgement of the dead and at his balance
is more in harmony with this secondary explanation as a personification of righteousness, but it still alternates there with
the original conception of the feather-wearing goddess as "the
West, the beautiful West," who introduces the dead to Osiris
and to their second life. Plutarch still knows that Isis is
identical with "Justice or Nemesis." By a misreading of the word ma'tiu, the "judges" who are
mentioned in the hall of Osiris, the theologians
of the New Empire come to the conclusion that
"the justice" of Osiris is double; and accordingly
the pictures often represent her thus or as differentiated into the headless (i. e. dead) and the complete (i. e. live) form. In the mythologies of other
nations a virgin (often explained as the constellation Virgo) occurs as dying at or after giving
birth to the god or gods, and frequently as being

FIG. 95.
"THE DOUBLE
JUSTICE"

deprived of her head. This conception seems to be traceable
to the Egyptian symbolism which we have just described.
Probably the people of the Nile-land sought thus to have a

dying goddess as parallel to the dying god Osiris.[23] When this doctrine of the "double justice" became popular, Isis and Nephthys [24] were identified with these two feather-wearing goddesses at the judgement of Osiris. Male deities with two feathers were

Fig. 96. The Symbol of the Horus of Edfu

referred to the same function.[25] All this symbolism, mixed with the Osiris-myth, remained very vague.

Isis is early connected with Sothis, the queen of the fixed stars (see the picture on p. 55), and in the latest period she is also associated with the planet Venus [26] as the evening star (daughter of the sun) or the morning star (mother of the sun), all these stellar manifestations of the queen of heaven having Asiatic analogies (see p. 54).

The Osirian celestial triad was completed by the addition of Horus (Egyptian Ḥor, Ḥoru), a solarized deity with the form or, at least, with the head of a hawk (more exactly, perhaps, a falcon) and possessing, as we have said (p. 24), too many temples for us to determine his original localization. His cult at Edfu (Greek Apollinopolis) is very old, and that city is often supposed to have been his original home; but the special symbol of the Horus of Edfu (the winged disk) seems to militate against this hypothesis, since it betrays the blending of several personifications of the sun-god (Fig. 96). The mythology of this temple has been handed down only in very late tradition, but it contains interesting

Fig. 97. One of the Smiths of Horus

features, such as a crowd of valiant "smiths" (*mesniu, mesentiu*) as companions of Horus, the lioness Men'et as nurse, etc. Hierakonpolis ("the City of Hawks"), west of Eileithyiaspolis (the modern el-Kāb), at or near the oldest capital of Upper Egypt, would seem to be a

much more ancient seat of Horus,[27] but a temple in the Delta
would better explain his place in the triad. His worship was,
at the beginning of Egyptian civilization, so general that the
hieroglyph of a hawk or falcon came to serve as the class-sign
for all male divinities, just as a serpent stands for all goddesses.[28] His name seems to mean "the High One," which
would point to an original function as god of the sky, and
even in the latest period he appears as such when sun and moon
are called "the eyes of Horus" (pp. 28–29) or when he is regarded as the morning star (p. 54) or as Orion. He was incor-
porated into the Osirian family by being interpreted as the
young rising sun in opposition to the dying evening sun as Osiris;

a   *b*   *d*

FIG. 98. OLDEST PICTURES OF SÊTH

(*a*) prehistoric; (*b*) and (*c*) from the Second Dynasty; (*d*) from the Third Dynasty.

in other words, since Horus was such an important god that
he could not be subordinate to his father, he was explained
as Osiris reborn in the morning or in the proper season (p. 94).[29]
No excessive stress was laid on this interpretation, however,
for both priests and worshippers still liked to keep the two gods
as distinct and as individual as possible. The wife of Horus
is usually the goddess Ḥat-ḥôr, the mistress of the sky (p. 39).

After the completion of this triad the political contrast
between two dynasties of kings and between their local gods
caused the formation of an adversary to the triad, the divinity
of the older city of Ombos in Upper Egypt (the modern
Naggadah or Naqqadah),[30] the strange deity Sêth.[31] This
god is often called "Lord of the South," and his worship seems
to date from a time even more remote than that of any member
of the Osirian triad.[32] He was represented in the shape of an
animal which perplexed the ancient Egyptians themselves,

so that we feel tempted to explain it as derived from one
which had perhaps become extinct in prehistoric times or
from an archaic statue of so crude a type that it defied all
zoological knowledge of subsequent artists.[33] At all events, the
later Egyptians no longer understood it. In the New Empire
Sêth is sometimes represented in ordinary human form.
Originally the adversary (and brother) of Horus only, Sêth
became the enemy of the whole Osirian triad, the murderer
of his brother Osiris, and the persecutor of Isis and Horus. Al-

FIG. 99. SÊTH TEACHES THE YOUNG KING ARCHERY, AND HORUS INSTRUCTS HIM
IN FIGHTING WITH THE SPEAR

though this made him the villain among the gods,[34] yet he
held full standing as a deity and was especially honoured by
soldiers, who considered this wild, reckless character, "the son
of Nut, great of strength," to be their most suitable patron.[35]
In contrast to Horus, whose chief weapon is the spear, he is
an archer. The cosmic *rôle* ascribed to him is that of the god
of the sky and of thunder in the conception of the nations north
of Egypt, but in a degraded, harmful form, which corresponds
to the fact that thunder-storms in Egypt are rare and unprofit-
able. Thus Sêth manifests himself in the thunder-storm,[36] but
this is explained as a battle between Horus and Sêth, so that

lightning is the spear of Horus, and thunder the voice of his
wounded antagonist, roaring in his pain.[37] A Greek papyrus
addresses Sêth as "hill-shaker, thunderer, hurricane-raiser,
rock-shaker; the destroyer, who disturbs the sea itself."

After 2500 B. C. the Asiatic myth of the combat between the
god of heaven and light (Bêl-Marduk, etc.) and the abysmal
dragon of the ocean (Tiâmat) penetrated into Egypt, where it
gave rise to the story of the gigantic serpent 'Apop (Greek
'Aποφις),[38] the enemy of the sun-god. Only faint traces of the
Asiatic tale of the creation of the world from the carcass of
the primeval monster, the all-covering abyss, are found in

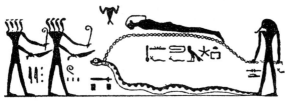

Egypt, perhaps
in the idea that
iron represents
"Typhon's
bone." Better
preserved is the

FIG. 100. 'APOP BOUND IN THE LOWER WORLD

parallel Asiatic
version that the dragon was not killed and annihilated, but
still lies bound in the depths under the earth [39] or in the ocean,
so that an earthquake or the raging of the sea betrays its
vain struggles against its fetters. We find the idea recurring
in many variants that countless hands of gods or of departed
souls (including even those of all foreigners) must hold down
the "wriggling monster" (nuzi) in the depths of the earth.
Here belongs the accompanying picture (Fig. 100) of 'Apop,
"whose voice re-echoes in the lower world." He is bound
with chains of metal, and at his head lies the Nubian goddess Selqet, who appears repeatedly as guarding him (Fig. 60
and p. 60). This suggests that the four-headed watchmen are
an allusion to Khnûm, the master of the four sources of the
Nile and the neighbour of Selqet. A variant shows the earth-
god Qêb (not reproduced in Fig. 101) and the four sons of
Osiris or Horus (pp. 111–13) binding four serpents, while a
fifth rises from the ground; behind them stands "Osiris before

the West." Here also the scene is laid in the Cataract region, and the artist seeks mystically to express the belief that the four sources of the Nile, rising from the lower world, may be considered either (according to older traditions) as part of Osiris (p. 95) or as coming from an abysmal depth hostile to this good god. Another

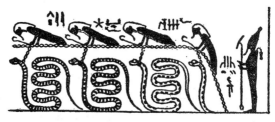

FIG. 101. THE SONS OF OSIRIS GUARD THE FOURFOLD SERPENT OF THE ABYSS BEFORE THEIR FATHER

variant, shown in Fig. 102, misses this symbolism by making the "children of Horus" equal to five chains.[40] There the watchmen (only one of whom is visible here) have the heads of dogs or jackals like Anubis, while the baboons, which carry four hands away, seem to hint

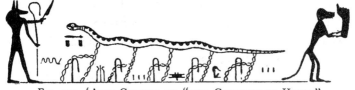

FIG. 102. 'APOP CHAINED BY "THE CHILDREN OF HORUS"

at Thout's wisdom as instrumental in depriving the monster of his limbs. Although he appears in a useful and worshipful function, we may still recognize the serpent of the abyss in another picture where he wraps himself around the infant sun-god Khepri, thus alluding to Osiris as the ocean and the Nile, or as hidden in them [41] (see Fig. 115 for a

FIG. 103. THE UNBORN SUN HELD BY THE WATER DRAGON

parallel representation of "the many-headed serpent," whose four heads [42] symbolize the four sources of the Nile); while, as encircling the unborn sun, it becomes another expression of the chest holding this god (pp. 71, 94). There

are numerous variants of such pictures, of which later artists
had scant comprehension.[43] Side by side with these applica-
tions of the myth to the Nile or to its source (i. e. the local

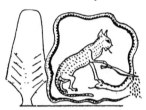

ocean of the Egyptians, who were little
given to sea-faring), we find the recollection that in reality the wide ocean
represents 'Apop in captivity, girding
the earth in bonds and keeping it together, but at the same time threatening to break his fetters and to destroy
the world. Accordingly the sea becomes
"Typhonic," or anti-Osirian, in contrast

FIG. 104. THE CAT-GOD KILL-
ING THE SERPENT AT THE
FOOT OF THE HEAVENLY
TREE

to its early Osirian character (p. 95). That 'Apop "is thrown
into the ocean at the new year's day" is a reminiscence of the
Babylonian doctrine that the struggle of creation is typologi-
cally repeated at the beginning of the new year in spring. At
an early time, however, the Egyptians began to interpret the
combat between light and darkness, between the sun-god and
his gigantic adversary, as a daily phenomenon. The sun is
swallowed up by 'Apop at evening when it sinks into the
ocean, or has, at least, to battle with the dragon as it journeys
by night through the underworld. There, from the dark river
or behind the mountain of sunrise, the monster raises himself
against the solar bark; but in the morning he has been cut
to pieces, and the sun reappears victorious, or at least the
monster must disgorge it (p. 27).

We also find pictures [44] of a serpent at the foot
of the celestial tree (i. e. in the watery deep), where
it is cut into fragments by a divine cat which is
explained as symbolizing the sun. Unfortunately
we have no text which gives a full description of
this myth, so that we are unable to say with cer-
FIG. 105. "THE
CAT-LIKE GOD"
tainty whether the cat is connected with Mafdet, "the Lynx-
Goddess," who is sometimes described as fighting on behalf of
the sun. A male deity, called "the cat-god," or, more literally,

"the one like a she-cat," and holding a serpent,[45] may allude to the same myth, which seems to represent no more than another version of the story of 'Apop. A knife-bearing cat is also depicted at the side of the stellar divinities mentioned on p. 63, so that it may once have been explained as a constellation.

This battle may likewise be found in the sky by day when storm-clouds darken the face of the sun, so that the myth of the serpent and the solar deity Rê' merges into the old story of the conflict between Horus and Sêth. Thus the serpent becomes more and more identical with Sêth as being an additional manifestation of the wicked god who later is said to have fought against Horus in the form of other water monsters as well, such as the hippopotamus and the crocodile. This confusion of 'Apop and Sêth, however, does not take place until after the Eighteenth Dynasty. Monuments of that dynasty still not only

FIG. 106. THE DEAD AIDING THE ASS AGAINST THE DRAGON

distinguish the warrior Sêth from the great serpent, but make him fight against it in company with the gods, while in one chapter of the *Book of the Dead*[46] the serpent even attacks the ass of Sêth (Fig. 106). In like manner the *Harris Magic Papyrus* says of the dragon:

"The god of Ombos (i. e. Sêth) sharpeneth (?) his arrows in (!) him;
He shaketh sky and earth by his thunder-storms;
His magic powers are mighty, conquering his enemy;
His battle-axe (?) [47] cutteth up the wide-mouthed dragon."

Similarly "the god of Ombos (pierceth?) the serpent with his arrows";[48] and in the *Vatican Magic Papyrus*[49] we find a curious passage which, somewhat parallel to the one which we have already quoted on p. 72, seeks to rehabilitate Sêth:

"Stand up, O Sêth, beloved of Rê'!
Stand at thy place in the ship of Rê'!
He hath received his heart in justification;
Thou hast thrown down [the enemies] of thy father Rê'
Every day."

This text tries to associate the warlike Sêth with the beneficent Rê', and begins to intermingle the Osirian myth. Here, as has been shown on p. 103, the Asiatic idea, according to which the thunder-storm is a revelation of the good god of light and of heaven against the power of darkness and inert matter below, conflicts with the Egyptian conception of this phenomenon. In

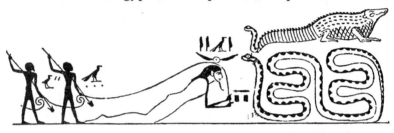

FIG. 107. THE GOD WITH ASS'S EARS IN THE FIGHT AGAINST 'APOP

Egypt, therefore, the storm-clouds are Sêth, but in contradiction to this the rain which falls from them is often called another manifestation of the good god (Osiris), as in Asia. Thus we have conflicting views on storms quite similar to those which we have previously found to exist regarding the ocean as beneficent and representing Osiris, or as opposed to him and to the whole order of the world (pp. 95, 105–06).

The beginning of the confusion of Sêth and 'Apop can be traced in the scene (Fig. 107) in which the latter attacks the sun-god, whose head, united legs, and falling position indicate his Osirian character. The ornament at the side of his solar disk is here indistinct, so that we might think of the winged disk of Horus, but doubtless it developed into the ears of an ass in such variants as the one given in Fig. 108;[50] and thus it has been supposed that the strange name of the sun-god in this scene, Eay, Ay, meant (or was later interpreted to mean) "ass" (io').

If this be true, a strange confusion of Sêth (in the solar-bark?) and Osiris must be assumed. At all events the Egyptians were puzzled by this old picture, as its two accompanying descriptions show. The "harpoon-bearers" seemingly either drag the god along or uphold him with their rope, but the text reads, "They guard the ropes of Ay, not permitting this serpent to rise against the ship of the great god." The meaning of the strange crocodile Shes-shes above the dragon is obscure (cf. the crocodile in the depth, with Khnûm, p. 90), like several other details of this picture;[51] but it is possible that the rope originally represented a net. The Asiatic idea that the dragon was caught alive or was killed in a net seems to be alluded to elsewhere in the representation of a huge net for catching the enemies of the sun-god.[52] Good spirits fighting against the monster often swing above their heads what later looks like a rope, but originally appears distinctly as a net. The spear of Horus, like various other details, again betrays the Asiatic origin of this whole dragon-myth (see Note 101).

FIG. 108. THE GOD WITH ASS'S EARS

The confusion of the older tradition of Sêth and the later legend of 'Apop soon becomes complete, so that subsequently we find Sêth called "the serpent that is cut in pieces, the obscene (?) serpent" (*nik, neyek*), etc.[53] This contributes most toward making the old thunder-god at last the representative of all evil ("all red things"), a real Satan, whose name it is best not to pronounce, but to replace by a contemptuous "that one" (*pefi*), or by a curse, or by spitting, so that Sêth is invoked only in forbidden black art.[54]

FIG. 109. GENII FIGHTING WITH NETS OR SNARES

The identification of Sêth with the seven stars in the constellation of the Great Bear (Charles's Wain)[55] runs practically parallel to the equation of the deity with 'Apop. This constellation, called "the Ox-Leg" in ancient Egypt (p. 59), is then occasionally explained as being, for example, a foot of Sêth, which must be kept chained and watched by guards.

The confusion began by identifying the "Ox-Leg" with the water-dragon (possibly on the basis of Asiatic theories), so that the scholars of the New Empire sought to find the four sons of Horus, the guardian Selqet, etc., in stars near the northern monster, as is

FIG. 110. HORUS-ORION, ASSISTED BY ÊPET, FIGHTS THE OX-LEG (CF. FIG. 62)

shown by the representation given in Fig. 60.

The reasons why the obscure goddess Nephthys (Egyptian Nebt-ḥôt, "Mistress of the Temple") [56] was associated with Sêth as his wife are unknown, and the Egyptians themselves were quite uncertain as to what cosmic *rôle* was to be attributed to her. Horns and the disk sometimes symbolized her as mistress of the sunny sky.[57] When called "Mistress of the West," she became queen of the night and of the dead, like Isis-Ḥat-ḥôr (p. 99), so that several times she is identified with the "Book-Goddess," or Fate (pp. 52–53), and with the headless queen of the west, the so-called "Justice" (p. 100). Thus, as the sky of the underworld, she forms — as Plutarch also knew — a counterpart of Isis when the latter is understood as the sky of day.[58] Nephthys is never described as hostile to her brother Osiris; notwithstanding her union with Sêth, she bewailed Osiris and cared for his body together with Isis, and she nursed the infant Horus,[59] while according to some traditions she even bore Anubis to Osiris, perhaps another connexion of Nephthys with the lower world.

FIG. 111. NEPHTHYS

Anubis (Egyptian Anupu) was originally a black jackal (or possibly a dog; often the wolf, jackal, and dog cannot easily

be distinguished), usually pictured in a recumbent position.
"On his mountain" he ruled over some local necropolis, perhaps
at Kynopolis in the seventeenth
nome [60] or in the Delta or at
the site of the modern Turrah
near Memphis. Then, at least
for Upper Egypt, he seems to
have become the general god
of the dead, guiding their souls
on the dark ways to the lower
world.[61] This function devel-

FIG. 112. ANUBIS AS EMBALMER

oped even before he was associated with the Osirian cycle;
after this incorporation he was called the son (or, more rarely,
the brother) of Osiris or of the (identical) sun-god or
of Sêth, and was said to have aided Isis in burying
Osiris and to have given him the embalmment which
ensured freedom from destruction, whence all the departed pray that Anubis may care for their bodies.

FIG. 113.
DIVINE
SYMBOL
LATER
ATTRIB-
UTED TO
ANUBIS

He assists also at the examination of the dead before
Osiris; evidently in earlier times he was their only
judge (p. 93). It is quite uncertain how his emblem,
apparently from the Middle Empire onward, came to
be the skin of a newly killed ox, spotted black and
white, hanging from a pole, and sometimes dripping blood into a vessel placed
beneath it.[62] Originally this symbol
seems to have represented an entirely
different god.

In magic an evil spirit called Maga,
or Mega(y), pictured as a crocodile,
appears as a "son of Sêth" or is represented as his double.

FIG. 114. THE SONS OF HORUS

Four genii termed "the sons of
Horus" or "of Osiris" [63] often follow Osiris, watching his corpse
and assisting him in his judgement; accordingly they become

guardians of the embalmment of all dead, whose viscera are placed under their protection in "canopic vases," which are ornamented with their likenesses, i. e. a man, a baboon, a

jackal, and a hawk. The regular order of their names was Emesti, Ḥepi, Dua-mut-f ("Honouring

FIG. 115. THE FOUR SONS OF OSIRIS-HORUS UNITED WITH THE SERPENT OF THE DEEP GUARDING LIFE

his Mother"), and Qebḥ-snêu-f ("Refreshing his Brothers"). Their interpretation as the four sources of the Nile, which we have already noted (pp. 104–05), appears at an early date, when they are connected with the cataract-god Khnûmu or with the extreme south, "the door of the water region, the water of Nubia," [64] or when they grow from a flower (the flower of life, parallel to or synonymous with the water of life) which springs from the throne of Osiris (cf. Fig. 89), or swim in the water, whence the crocodile Sobk fishes them out.[65] As coming from the abyss (i. e. Osiris) they are symbolized in later times (Figs. 103, 115) as four heads growing from a serpent who holds the hieroglyphic symbol of life (again a confusion of their father Osiris, as the life-giving Nile, with the later dragon of the abyss).[66] On the other hand, a very old parallel interpretation considers them to be celestial; in other words it identifies them with the four Horuses dwelling at the four cardinal points or in the east or south of the sky (see Note 67), or with "the four tresses of Horus" at the four cardinal points (p. 39),[67] whence they "send the four winds." [68] Attempts were made to localize them in the constellations, and in one picture they seem to be found in the sky no less than five times.[69] They are sought es-

FIG. 116. THE SONS OF HORUS-OSIRIS IN THE SKY NEAR THEIR FATHER ORION (CALLED "OSIRIS")

pecially near their father, Orion, among the decanal stars, or close to the celestial counterpart of the dragon of the abyss, the dangerous "Ox-Leg," whom they guard, as they hold ʿApop in Figs. 100–02. They also have an (immovable?) place in the eastern horizon as patrons of the first four hours of the day. Their original meaning remains uncertain after all.

By combining the most important of the various fragmentary and widely divergent views about the group of gods who form the Osirian circle we can obtain the following connected myth, using Plutarch's sketch as a basis wherever possible and marking the most important variants by brackets.

Osiris, who was especially "fine of face" and tall, was a child of the earth-god, Qêb, and the sky, Nut (p. 41), as a new impersonation of the sun. He was born on the first of the five epagomenal days which closed the year and which were regarded as particularly sacred.[70] With him his twin sister, Isis, saw the light

FIG. 117. OSIRIS UNDER THE VINE

[some sources, however, state that she was born on the fourth epagomenal day]. When his birth is described as from the ocean, like his son and double, the solar deity Horus,[71] this is merely another interpretation of his mother, Nut, since there is little distinction between the ocean and its continuation, the sky. Osiris created all life, especially mankind, and ruled over it. [Others later declared that he established civilization, teaching men religion and agriculture, particularly the cultivation of his special plant, the vine (p. 36), etc.,[72] and abolish-

ing barbarism; his reign was usually limited to Egypt, since
the countries outside aroused little interest.][73] He provoked
the jealousy of his [older] brother, Sêth. According to the
earliest tradition, Sêth waylaid Osiris when he hunted gazelles
in the desert and slew him.[74] [Later sources declare that Sêth
acted with a band of seventy-two confederates[75] or, according
to Plutarch, also with an Ethiopian queen named Aso;[76] and
the conspirators placed Osiris, either murdered or alive, in a
coffin which they threw into the river.] His faithful wife, Isis
[who, Plutarch tells us, received her first information from the
"Pans and Satyrs" of Chemmis, i. e. from the spirits who accom-

FIG. 118. ISIS (AS SOTHIS OR
THE MORNING STAR?) AND
SELQET-NEPHTHYS GATHER-
ING BLOOD FROM THE
MUTILATED CORPSE OF
OSIRIS

panied the birth of the sun],[77] hunted
for him, and finding him in the desert
or river, she revived him with some kind
of magic. [According to other versions,
she discovered that Sêth had hacked
him into fourteen [78] pieces, which she
put together with great care with the as-
sistance of Anubis or of the wise Thout.]
In the belief of later times, when all
gods were represented as winged,[79] she fanned life [for a time
only] into him with her wings. According to another (later)
version, Isis did not unite the fragments, but buried them
wherever she discovered them — a rationalistic attempt to explain the relics of Osiris which were found all over Egypt[80] in
the principal temples or special burial-places of Osiris, the so-
called Serapeums. [Where the reuniting of these members is
emphasized, the spot only is considered to be hallowed by the
finding of one of them.][81] According to another (later) version,
she followed the body in the coffin to the Phoenician coast,
whither it had drifted. At Byblos, Plutarch tells us, it had been
taken into the house of the royal couple, Melqart and Astarte
(i. e. the two Byblian city-gods as Asiatic doublets of Osiris
and Isis), as a beam [having been overgrown by an erica or
tamarisk, or having become such a shrub or tree; other myths

imply a reminiscence of a cedar containing Osiris or his heart or head[82]. On account of her sweet smell the ladies of the court engaged Isis as nurse to the infant prince, and she nursed him by putting her finger in his mouth,[83] while at night she laid him aside in a "purifying fire"[84] and in the form of a swallow flew wailing around the wooden column which contained the body of Osiris. The queen surprised her one night, cried out when she saw the child amid the flames, and thus deprived it of immortality.[85] Revealing her divine nature, Isis obtained from the king the coveted column and cut the sarcophagus or the body out of the stem of the tree; the column itself, wrapped in linen like a mummy and sprinkled with myrrh (cf. Fig. 83 ?), remained as an object of worship at Byblos.[86] Accompanied by her sister, Nephthys, Isis took the body, either alone or in the coffin, back to Egypt to bewail it; as mourners both sisters were often represented in the form of birds. [Plutarch makes Sêth, hunting by moonlight,[87] again find the body and cut it in pieces, which Isis is obliged to reunite.]

According to some versions, Horus had been born [or conceived] before his father's death [others maintained, however, that he was begotten while Osiris and Isis were yet in the womb of their mother, i. e. the sky]; but the prevalent theory was that from the corpse of Osiris, [temporarily] revived [without opening the coffin completely, or from the reunited body, or even from mere pieces of it], Isis conceived him, either in a human way, as when she is often represented as sitting on the coffin and usually reassuming the form of a bird, or from blood oozing from the body, or from its pieces (Fig. 118). [Earlier ideas are that she conceived from the fruit of the cosmic or fatal tree (usually the vine [88]) or from another part of this tree; these views are, however, applied also to the birth of Osiris, who is after all, as we have so often observed, identical with his son, though he tends to represent the pessimistic side of the myth.]

With her son Horus [still unborn, or new-born, or very young]
Isis fled [from prison] to the marshes of Lower Egypt and [in
the form of a cow (cf. pp. 37, 99)] hid herself from the persecu-
tions of Sêth in the green bushes of the jungles on an island
[or on a floating island, whose name the Greeks rendered by
Chemmis], where Horus, like other solar divinities, was born
in green thickets.[89] Various gods and goddesses, especially her
sister, Nephthys, and the wise Thout,[90] helped to protect and
nurse her and the infant god (see p. 114 on the "Pans and
Satyrs ").

Some taught that to hide the child Isis placed it in a chest

or basket, which she let float down the Nile.
This conception permits the blending of the
birth, death, and revivification of the two
identified deities, Osiris and Horus, in the chest
which swims in the abyss, or in the ocean, or

FIG. 119.
ISIS NURSING
HORUS IN THE
MARSHES

in its Egyptian counterpart, the Nile, representing Osiris-Horus. This chest could also
be found in the sky in the constellation Argo
(p. 58), symbolizing the dead or infant deity floating in the
ocean; and the principal star of this group, Canopus, could
be regarded as the god himself.[91] According to Plutarch,
Horus was found in the river and was educated [at the bidding
of Kronos, i. e. the old sun or the old year[92]] by a water-
carrier [called Pamyles at Thebes, who was told to announce
to the world the birth of the great divinity].[93] Another
version seems to hold that the divine nurse Renenutet (Greek
Θερμουθις; cf. p. 66) took care of him in the lower regions of
the sky until he could reveal himself to the world.[94] The
birth and education of Horus are localized at or near Buto,
the earliest capital of the marshy Delta (see *supra* on the
island of Chemmis). Some adventures embellish this period
of his life, telling, for example, how the infant Horus was
once stung by a scorpion[95] and healed by his mother, the
great magician, or by Thout; or narrating how, on the

1

2

PLATE I

3

1. GREEK TERRA-COTTA OF THE YOUNG HORUS FLOATING IN HIS BOAT. The infant god has his finger raised to his lips as a conventional sign of childhood, though later this was mis-interpreted as an admonition to maintain silence before divine mysteries. Cf. pp. 94, 243.

2. BÊS IN THE ARMOUR OF A ROMAN SOLDIER. The divinity here appears in an apotropaic function. A primitive god, and long obscure, he finally rose to such popularity that rep-resentations of him even influenced Classical conceptions of Silenus and the Satyrs. See pp. 61–64.

3. ZEUS-SERAPIS. From a local divinity at Dêd, in the Delta, Osiris became a god of changing nature in the widest sense. Among his many identifications was that with the bull Apis, called Hap in Egyptian; and hence arose Osor-hap, the Serapis of the Greeks. When the cult of Serapis became popular in the declining days of Classical religion, Serapis was naturally equated with the Greek Zeus as all-god and was represented in Classical style. Cf. pp. 92–93, 98, 239–40, 242–43.

contrary, he enjoyed the protection of seven scorpions (cf. p. 147), etc.

In later times two forms of the young Horus were distinguished: Ḥar-uêr (Greek ᾽Αρουηρις, "Great [i. e. adult, or elder?] Horus") and Ḥar-pe-khrad (Greek ᾽Αρποκρατης, "Horus the Child, Young Horus"). [The latter, who was the most popular form of Horus, especially in the Roman period, was confused by Plutarch with the dwarf gods (pp. 63–64), since he alleged that the deity had been prematurely born.] Some regarded these two forms of Horus as two distinct personalities born at different times, or distinguished the elder Horus [96] from Ḥar-si-êset (Greek ᾽Αρσιησις, "Horus, son of Isis"), but the oldest mythology knows only one Horus, who is the reincarnation of his father Osiris.

According to some sources, Isis also took care of Anubis, her sister's child [by Osiris, who begat him through confusing Isis and Nephthys [97]], and by

FIG. 120. OSIRIS IN THE BASKET AND IN THE BOAT, AND ISIS

rearing him she gained a faithful companion, this legend being a reversion of the older variant that Anubis or Nephthys [or both] took care of the infant Horus in the underworld.[98]

When Horus attained manhood, "putting on his girdle (i. e. the sign of manhood) in the jungle" [99] and resolving to be "his father's avenger" [100] [being exhorted by his father's spirit], he ascended the Nile with a host [of smiths (cf. p. 101)] and "conquered his heritage." [He fought in the form of the winged disk of Edfu, or for the struggle he and Sêth changed themselves into men or hippopotami.[101]] At the great battle [which lasted three days, or even longer] Sêth hurt or put out an eye of Horus, but he lost his virility and finally was conquered. According to most later texts, he [together with his

followers in the form of wild animals [102]] was annihilated by
being burned or cut in pieces, or he was flayed [alive].[103] Others
explain the repetition of the combat as due to the fact that,
being merely wounded and chained [or caught in a net (pp.
106, 109)], he broke loose again. [Isis set him free; or at least,
according to another version which will be set forth below,
she protected him against the death-blow; Horus decapitated
his mother for this act — an explanation of the headless woman
(p. 99) as Isis. Later her human body and cow's head in some
pictures were interpreted as the result of the healing of that
wound by the god Thout, who also cured the eye of Horus
when it was injured by Sêth (pp. 33, 90).] The confusion with
the dragon 'Apop in the ocean or the lower world (p. 106) made
the renewal of the struggle easily intelligible; thus it could be
understood, as we have already seen, of tempests and clouds,
of the stormy sea and the night, of the changes in the course
of the sun or .moon, and (very dimly)[104] of the world's beginning; while in various ways it could be read in the stars
(p. 110).

Rather early the struggle between Horus and Sêth was made
a legal contest, an idea which evidently had its origin in the
conception of Osiris as the great judge [and Isis as Justice
(p. 100)], although the judgement is usually transferred to the
wise Thout, who not only heals the wounds of the two con-
testants, but also reconciles them after deciding their claims.
Both Osiris and Horus are called "the one just of voice,"
i. e. justified, victorious in court, an expression which is
likewise applied to the human dead to designate them as
blessed souls, vindicated by Osiris, the judge. According to
later theories, the legitimacy of the posthumous child Horus,
contested by Sêth, was proved, or his claim to the throne
of Osiris was vindicated [or Thout or the earth-god Qêb
decided that Egypt should be divided between Horus and
Sêth, so that the former inherited the north and the latter
became the heir of the south].

Since Osiris was the type of righteousness, and thus was worthy to initiate resurrection and eternal life, whether directly in the lower world or indirectly in his son, the young solar deity, the question seems sometimes to have been asked, especially in the New Empire, Why had he to die? Why did death come on all humanity through him? This pessimistic conception of Osiris had to be explained by some wrong deed. Wedlock with one's sister was a general and ancient custom; therefore it was not clear what guilt he contracted by his marriage, except in some variants which made Isis his daughter or mother[105] (or, perhaps, inviolable as being "Justice"). In these variants the fault was

FIG. 121. HORUS EXE-
CUTES SÊTH (IN THE
FORM OF AN ASS) BE-
FORE OSIRIS

usually laid on his wife [or daughter, or mother], who caused his death by her love, but the numerous divergent forms of this pessimistic speculation are only faintly preserved in more popular sources like fairy stories and magic texts[106] and are obscured in the official religion, so that we can understand them solely by comparison with the Asiatic myths of the Queen of Heaven, the mistress of love and life, who nevertheless brings death and misery to her lovers and all humanity. Traces of such thoughts about Osiris's death are, however, hinted at in the very earliest religious texts of Egypt and are, therefore, at any rate something more than late loans from Asia.

FIG. 122. HORUS
KILLS SÊTH AS A
CROCODILE

Though all the gods once lived and reigned on earth,[107] Osiris is often regarded as the first ruler of Egypt and thus as analogous to the Pharaohs. The idea is that he, who brought death among the gods, and whose tomb can be

worshipped in this world (pp. 98, 114), is the ancestor of mankind, although several gods ought to have reigned again on
earth after him.[108] Accordingly the later Egyptians celebrated
the jubilee of the reign of Osiris, thus treating him quite like
a human king.[109]

From 1500 B. c. onward the Egyptians themselves appeared
to be fully conscious of the similarity of the myths of Osiris
and of Adonis-Tammuz and even liked to connect the story
with romantic Asia, especially with the ancient holy city of
Byblos.[110] Quite a number of evident reciprocal borrowings
connect Osiris and the Asiatic dying god, Tammuz-Adonis
(the Babylonian Dumûzu-Dûzu), and make it difficult to
decide the priority of Asia or Egypt.[111] It is probable that
the worship of Osiris and Isis remained local in the Delta
for a long time; it is even questionable whether it was officially
recognized in Upper Egypt before the Second Dynasty, although
the power with which it soon afterward spread through all
Egypt and influenced its whole mythology makes us suspect
that it played an important *rôle* at an earlier period, at least
in popular religion. Until we know more completely the
Babylonian form of the legend of Tammuz,[112] it is unsafe to
derive the Osiris-myth wholly from Asia. It is quite probable
that its primitive ideas came from Asia; but if this be so,
they had an early, rich, and rather independent development
in Egypt, whence a portion of them wandered back to
Asia. It is particularly noteworthy that it was only in
Egypt that Osiris fully developed into a judge of the dead.
Isis, on the other hand, is a rather meaningless and colourless character compared with her original, the Asiatic goddess
of love.

When the Egyptian religion spread through the whole
Classical world in the Roman period, it was almost entirely
the Osirian circle which found so much interest and worship,
and the richly varied mythology which we have just sketched
proved one of the strongest reasons for this success. This

subject and the very un-Egyptian character which those Egyptian gods finally assumed in Europe will be discussed in the concluding chapter of our study. This superficial adoption of Egyptian divinities was, in reality, only a desperate attempt to bolster up Classical paganism in its declining days; but the spirits of Egypt and of Greece and Rome were too unlike for any true blending. The "Isiac mysteries" could never possess the deep influence over the Classical mind which was exercised by the other two great religious importations — the "Great Mother" of Asia Minor and the Mithra of Iran.

CHAPTER VI

SOME TEXTS REFERRING TO OSIRIS-MYTHS

I. THE DIRGE OF ISIS AND NEPHTHYS

"Hymn sung by the two divine sisters in the house of Osiris, the one before the west,[1] the great god, lord of Abydos, in the month of Choiak,[2] the twenty-fifth day."

"Isis saith:
'Come to thy home, come to thy home,
Thou pillar-god (?),[3] come to thy home!
Thy foes are not (longer in existence);
Thou good king, come to thy home,
That thou mayest see me!
I am thy sister who loveth thee.
Mayest thou not separate thyself from me (again),
 O beautiful youth!
 Come to thy home immediately, immediately!
 (When) I see thee no (more),
 My heart bewaileth thee,
 Mine eyes seek thee;
 I search for thee to behold thee.

 'How good it is to see thee, to see thee!
 O pillar-god (?), how good to see thee!
 Come to thy love, come to thy love!
 O Un-nofer,[4] thou blessed one!
 Come to thy sister,
 Come to thy wife, come to thy wife,
 Thou god whose heart standeth still, come to the mistress of
  thy house!
 I am thy sister of thy mother,
 Separate not thyself from me!
Gods and men, their faces are on thee,
Beweeping thee all together when (they) see me.
 I cry for thee with weeping
 To the height of heaven,

(But) thou doest not hear my voice.
I am thy sister who hath loved thee on earth.
None loveth thee more than I,
The sister, the sister!'

Nephthys saith:
  'O good king, come to thy home!
  Make glad thy heart; all thy foes are not (longer in existence).'
  Thy two sisters are beside thee
  Protecting thy funeral bed,
  Calling thee in tears.
  Thou art prostrate on thy funeral bed.
  Thou seest (our) tenderness;
  Speak with us, O king, our lord!
  Expel all grief which is in our hearts!
  Thy courtiers among gods and men,
  When they see thee, (exclaim):
  "Give to us thy face,
  O king, our lord!
  It is life for us when we behold thy face.
  May thy face not turn from us!
  Joyful are our hearts when we behold thee,
  O good king, [joyful are] our hearts when we behold thee."
    I am Nephthys, thy sister who loveth thee.
  Thine enemy is overthrown,
  He is no more.
  I am with thee
  Protecting thy members for ever and in eternity.'"

The hymn goes on in endless repetitions from which we select
the following:[5]

          "Shine [6] for us in the sky, every day,
            We cease not to behold thy rays;
            Thout is thy protection;
            He establisheth thy soul in the bark of night
            In this thy name, 'Divine Moon.'"

Thus Osiris is here called both sun (like Rê' and Atum) and
moon, the latter being merely another manifestation of the
ruler of the day. Accordingly he is termed "master of the sixth
day" (p. 90), and of him it is said not only that "thou comest
to us as a little child every month" (i. e. as the crescent moon),

but also that "thy picture (?) is glorious in Orion (and?) the stars in the sky," i. e. all heavenly bodies are his manifestation. He represents all good in nature and appears principally in vegetation and in the Nile (p. 95).

> "Thy glorious emanation proceeding from thee
> Keepeth alive gods and men.
> Reptiles and (four-footed) animals
> Live from it.
> Thou approachest us from thy (dark) cave at thy season,
> Pouring out the water of thy soul-force [7]
> To increase sacrifices for thy double (i. e. soul),
> To nourish gods and men alike.
>   Hail to (our) lord!
> There is not a god like thee;
> Heaven holdeth thy soul,
> The earth thy figure;
> The underworld is fitted out with thy mysteries." [8]

II. THE PIG IN THE SUN'S EYE

The myth which tells how a black pig penetrated into the eye of Horus, temporarily making him half blind, is the earliest trace of the identification of the pig with Sêth (Ch. V, Note 33). Otherwise it is only a new version of the myth of the lost solar eye (p. 90), although the writer tries to distinguish both ideas. So far as we can understand the very corrupt text of this remarkable story,[9] it runs thus:

"Rê' said to Horus: 'Let me look at what is in thine eye [today].' He looked at it. Rê' said to Horus: 'Look, pray, at that black pig yonder.' He looked [at it]; behold, his eye was hurt with a great disturbance.

"Horus said to Rê': 'Behold, mine eye (feeleth) like that stroke which Sêth hath done against mine eye.' Behold, he felt grieved. Rê' said to the gods: 'Put him on his bed; may he become well again! It is Sêth who hath changed his form into a black pig. Behold, the wound in his eye burneth him.' Rê' said to the gods: 'The pig is an abomination to Horus.'"

The text then becomes confused, but it would seem that

advice is given to cure (?) Horus by "a sacrifice of his oxen, his small cattle, his sheep." The name of "Horus on his green (plant)" [10] arose, according to line 13 of this same chapter, because Horus expressed the wish, "Let the earth be green, and let the heavenly disturbances (i. e. the thunder-storms) be quenched"; in other words, the old interpretation of Sêth as the storm-clouds obscuring the sun is clearly applied here to a myth which originally, in all probability, referred to eclipses.

III. THE TEARS OF ISIS

Reference has already been made (p. 90) to a magic formula which describes the result of the tears of Isis when they fall in the Nile. The text itself runs as follows: [11]

"Isis struck with her wing,
She closed the mouth of the river,
She made the fish lie still on the surface (?); [12]
Not a wave moistened it.
(Thus) the water stood still, (but) it rose
When her tear fell on [13] the water.

Behold, Horus violated his mother-
Her tear fell into the water,
A cubit among the *uz*-fish
(And?) in the mouth of the baboon;
A cubit of shrubs reported (?) [14] in the mouth of Qêb (?). [15]
It is Isis who demanded it.
No crocodile doth (anything?).
Magic protection is coming, protection!"

The meaning seems to be that water and vegetation rise in a parallel way through the tears of Isis, exactly as Osiris is visible in both forces of nature (p. 95). The *uz*- or *woz*-fish, to which a curse is attached, according to the Osiris-myth allude to the sin for which Horus-Osiris had to die (p. 119), and the baboon Thout seems to be a reference to the flight of Isis (as the lost solar eye) to Nubia (p. 90), whence the wise god brought her back, another explanation of the rising of the Nile

after the season of low water. The last three lines seek to turn
these blended myths into a magic spell for safe travel on the
river.

IV. ISIS IN THE COMBAT OF HORUS AND SÊTH [16]

"The thirteenth day of the month Thout,[17] a very bad day. Thou
shalt not do anything (7) on this day. It is the day of the combat
which Horus waged with Sêth.

  Behold, they struck each other, standing on their soles together,
(8) Making their shape that of two hippopotami,
(At?) the temple (?) of the masters of Khar-'aḥaut.[18]
Then they spent three days and three nights thus.

Then Isis let fall (9) their [19] metal on them.
It fell toward (?) Horus.
He cried aloud, 'I am thy son Horus.'
  Isis called to the metal thus,
'Break away! break away (iii. 1) from my son Horus!'
She let another fall toward (?) her brother Sêth.
He cried aloud, 'Have pity (?)!'

(2) She called to the metal thus, ['Stop!'].[20]
He said to her many times,
'Have I [not] [21] loved and honoured the son of my mother?'
  Her heart was filled with compassion for her elder brother.
She called to the metal thus, 'Break away, break away,
Because he is my elder brother!'

The metal loosened itself from him;
They stood there as two persons who would not speak [22] to each other
The Majesty of Horus grew wroth with his mother Isis like a
        panther from the south;
She fled (?) before him.
This is the ordering (?) of a combat of (?) a storm.[23]

He struck off the head of Isis;
Then Thout gave (it) its form by magic,
Fixing it upon a cow.[24]
Let a sacrifice be brought to her name and to that of Thout on this
        day."

  We may note here that Plutarch [25] also knew the story of how
Horus tore off his mother's head because she had released

Sêth (p. 118), a legend which was very offensive to the Greek writer.

V. THE DESTRUCTION OF THE DRAGON 'APOP [26]

"The god [27] great of magic saith:
  'My soul (*ka*) is magic.
  I sent them [28] forth to annihilate my enemies with the best (words)
    on their lips.
  I sent those who arose from [29] my limbs
  To conquer that wicked enemy.'"

After this lame attempt to connect the text with the creation-myth which has been translated on pp. 68–69, the hymn begins:

"He hath fallen by (?) the flame;
  A knife is in his head;
  His ear is cut off (?);
  His name is not (any longer) on this earth.
  I ordered him stricken with wounds;
  I annihilated (?) his bones;
  I destroy his soul every day;
  I cut the vertebrae of his neck asunder,
  Opening with (my) knife,
  (And) separating his flesh,
  Cutting off (?) [30] his hide.
  He was given to the flame,
  Which overpowered him in her name, 'the Powerful One'; [31]
  She hath lit on him in her name of 'the Lighting One.'
  (I?) have burned the enemy;
  I have [32] annihilated (?) his soul,
  I have incinerated his bones;
  His members passed into the fire.

  Then I commanded Horus, the one great of strength,
  At the prow of the boat of Rê';
  He fettered him,
  He fettered him with metal;
  He made his members
  So that he could not struggle at his time after his malice.
  He forced him to vomit what was in his stomach.[33]
  He is guarded, fettered, bound;
  Aker took his strength away.[34]

I separated his members from his bones;
I cut (?) his feet;
I cut off his hands;
I shut his mouth and his lips;
I blunted (?) [35] his teeth;
I cut his tongue from his throat;
(Thus) I took away his speech.
I blinded his eyes;
I took his hearing from him;
I cut his heart from its place.

I made him as though he never had been.
His name is not any more (in existence);
His children are not;
He existeth no more,
Nor his kindred.[36]
He existeth not, nor his record;[37]
He existeth not, nor his heir.
His egg cannot grow,
Nor is his seed (?) raised;
His soul or body is not (longer in existence),
Nor his spirit, nor his shadow, nor his magic (power)."

The hymn, which was to be repeated during the rite of burning a wax or papyrus figure of 'Apop,[38] after trampling it and
spitting on it, wanders along in endless, jejune repetitions.
It evidently dates from a much later time than the creation-
myth (pp. 68–69), because the legend is here so lifeless. That
the most contradictory views on the fate of the dragon are
mentioned side by side, is, however, a phenomenon which is
neither late nor unusual (see pp. 69, 71, etc.).

An interesting fragment referring to Osiris and Sêth has
already been translated on p. 72.

CHAPTER VII

THE OTHER PRINCIPAL GODS

BESIDES the Egyptian divinities who have been considered in the preceding chapters, there were many others,
whose names and characteristics are here given in alphabetic
order.[1]

Aḥi: see Eḥi.

Aḥu (?), Aḥuti (?): see Note 40 on Khasti.

Amon (earliest pronunciation Amonu, Amanu; in the Middle
Empire rarely Amoni[2]) was the chief god of Thebes. When he
is represented in human form, he has blue skin
and wears two very high feathers on his head.
He was also called "Master of the Head-Band"
from the fillet which holds these feathers straight
and hangs down his back. Numerous pictures
show that his earliest statues exactly imitated
those of Mîn, being blue-black and ithyphallic,
having one arm upraised, and with the same
chapel and tree (or trees) behind him, etc.; his
very name shows that he was a local dissimilation of the latter ancient god.[3] At first his
sacred animal was a goose, but after 1600 B. C.
it became a ram, whence Amon himself is often
represented in the shape of that animal or with

FIG. 123. AMON

its head.[4] He was then associated with Mut and Khônsu; and
his early consort, Amonet, became a very obscure personality.
Amon is an especially clear instance of solarization; and as a
sun-god he became the highest divinity of the Egyptian pantheon in the New Empire (p. 19), so that the Greeks called

him Zeus, which caused him to be misinterpreted as the god of air.[5] His temporary persecution will be considered in our last chapter (pp. 224–26).

Amonet (Amenet), the earlier consort of Amon, was, as we have just seen, almost forgotten in the days of her husband's

greatness. Her name seems to mean merely "the One of Amon, Amon's Wife." Curiously enough, she always wears the crown of Lower Egypt.[6] She is also called Nebt-taui, or "Mistress of Both Countries."[7]

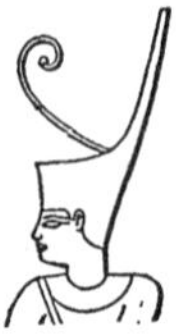

FIG. 124. AMONET

'Anezti, an ancient god wearing two ostrich-feathers on his head and carrying a royal *flagellum* and a crooked staff in his hands, was called "the one before the eastern districts" and (because of his insignia?) was identified with Osiris at an early date.[8]

An-ḥôret: see Onuris.

Anit (Enit), the spouse of Monṭu, was represented in human form, often wearing a symbol like the "antennae" of Meskhenet (p. 52).

Antaeus (Antaios) is known only by this classical name, though he can scarcely have shown much similarity to the wrestling giant of the Greek myth of Herakles. He was worshipped at Antaiopolis in Middle Egypt, where he was associated with Nephthys and sometimes compared with Horus.[9] Our only pictures of him date from the Roman period, when he was represented as a warrior or hunter of gazelles (reminding us of the Syrian god Reshpu, for whom see p. 155), with high feathers on his head and clad in very modern armour. For a remarkable picture of him see the Classical concept in Fig. 218.[10]

FIG. 125. ANTAEUS

'Anti was identified with Osiris at the temple on the site of the modern Gurna.

Anupet, once termed "the female greyhound," was the consort or female form of Anubis at Kynopolis (cf. the parallel instance of Amon-Amonet).

'Anuqet, a goddess of the Cataract region, and thus associated with Khnûm(u) (see Fig. 1), is characterized by a feather crown of unusual shape and on rare occasions appears as a vulture.[11] Why the Greeks compared her with Hestia, their divinity of the hearth, is obscure.

Ari-ḥems-nofer: see Eri-ḥems-nofer.

Asbet ("the Flaming One") was a goddess, perhaps in serpent-shape,[12] and possibly was the same as Sebit.

Ash was a god in human form who was worshipped in the west of the Delta (?).[13]

Babi (Babai, Bebi, Bibi[?]) must have been worshipped extensively in Upper Egypt from the earliest times, since his name is sometimes written with the white crown and the royal whip, symbols of dominion over the whole southern country. Accordingly his name still seems to have been used extensively as a proper name in the Middle Empire. The Pyramid Texts [14] term him "master of darkness" and compare him to a bull, as though he had once been a rival of Osiris or had been understood as another name for Osiris or Bati. Thus the *Book of the Dead* mentions him as "the first-born son of Osiris," [15] though it usually describes him as a terrible persecutor and butcher of souls who guards the entrance to the lower world.[16] A later passage of the same book already makes him a fiend somewhat parallel to Sêth; and in the Greek period Bebon (or Babys) becomes synonymous with Sêth. For the confusion between Babi and Bati see the paragraph on the latter.

Bast(et): see Ubastet, which is the correct reading.

Bati, another deity of the earliest period, was later worshipped only in the obscure town of Saka, where he received honour beside Anubis (Ch. V, Note 60) and Ubastet. The author of the *Tale of the Two Brothers*, therefore, regards

Bati (not to be read Bata or Batau) as a celestial and solar divinity synonymous with Osiris. Manetho seems to refer to him as a mythical king Bytes.[17] He appears to have been confused to a considerable extent with Babi.[18]

Behdet, i. e. "the goddess of Edfu," as the consort of the Horus of that city (pp. 21, 101) was necessarily, according to later theology, like Hat-hôr (pp. 39, 102).

Bi-n-dêd(u): see Mendes (p. 164).

Breith: see Note 55 on Merui.

Buto (Egyptian Uazit, Uzoit) was the serpent-shaped goddess of Pe(r)-uzoit, the Buto of the Greeks and the earliest capital of Lower Egypt. Accordingly, whether represented in serpent-form or as a woman, she usually wears the crown and holds the sceptre of that region. She and the vulture-goddess Nekhbet, as two serpents (cf. pp. 26, 29), frequently symbolize Lower and Upper Egypt.[19]

Dêdet, "the One of Busiris," was worshipped at Busiris and at Mendes (at Sebennytos as well?) and was later regarded as a celestial goddess like Isis-Hat-hôr, though originally she was probably distinct from Isis.[20]

Depet: see Note 19.

Dua(u) ("the Worshipper," or "Rising One" [?]) was a deity whose name was written with a symbol closely resembling the one for Khôns which has been discussed on p. 34, except that in the old passages the piece of meat which it seems to represent hangs down behind from the standard. If this god was adored at Herakleopolis, we have an inexplicable Greek comparison with Herakles, as in the case of Khôns.[21]

Dua[-uêr] ("the [Great] Worshipper" [?]) was called, because of his hieroglyph, a bearded chin,[22] "the barber of the gods" or "the washer of their faces." [23] When termed "husband of the Sothis star," [24] he seems to be confused, because of the similarity of names, with the morning star ("the Divine Worshipper") and with

Orion-Horus. (The accompanying symbol of a full face with a long beard[25] appears to refer to a different deity.)

Ehi (Ahi) was associated with the Hat-hôr of Denderah as her little son (p. 20), whence he was represented like Horus; he often bears musical instruments.

Ekhutet ("the Resplendent"[?]), an ancient goddess, was a deity of whom little was known.[26]

Emesti: see p. 112.

Enit: see Anit.

Eri-hems-nofer (Ari-hems-nofer, Greek 'Αρενσ-νουφις; "the Companion Good to Dwell With") was the local deity of a small cataract island near Philae and was compared especially with the lion-shaped Shu.[27]

Esdes: see Ch. III, Note 3.

Ha (?): see Note 40 on Khasti.

Hat-mehit[28] was the goddess of the nome of Mendes and, therefore, wore its hieroglyph, a fish, on her head. Associated with the (Osiris-) ram of Mendes, she became like Isis and was called the mother of Harpokrates ("the young Horus"). Later she was also associated with Horus as his wife.

FIG. 127. EHI

Heka (late form Heke) was identified with Shu, as in Fig. 39. It is a question whether he is another deity than the divinity Heka ("Magic"; Fig. 10).

Heken was a hawk-god (identical with Har-heken [Ch. V, Note 28]?).[29]

Heknet ("the Praiseworthy"; earlier form Heknutet[30]) was a little-known goddess who was pictured in various forms, principally with the head of a vulture.

FIG. 128. HAT-MEHIT

Hemen, a hawk-god[31] of Tuphion (?) in Upper Egypt, was widely known only in the Twelfth Dynasty.

Hem(?)-hor ("Servant of Horus") was a lion-headed god.[32]

Heqet,[33] a goddess with the shape or head of a frog, was worshipped at the city of Her-uret near Edfu and later at

Abydos as well (p. 50). At an early date she was associated with her neighbour Khnûm as the creator, whence she became

FIG. 129. HESAT

a protector of birth (p. 52). Her cult was politically important in the Pyramid Period.

Her-shef ("the Ram-Faced," Greek ʿΑρσαφης, i. e. evidently a wrong etymology, based on a pronunciation which compared him with Horus) was worshipped at Herakleopolis.

Hesat was early explained as a celestial divinity like Hat-hôr or Isis, being a cow-goddess.[34] Her local cult seems to have been on the site of the modern Atfiyeh.[35]

Hetmet (or Hetmit, "the Destroyer"[?]) is once depicted like Êpet, but with a lion's head.[36]

Hu ("Taste, Feeling, Wisdom") was a god in the form of a man or of a sphinx. He often accompanied the solar deity in his boat (cf. Fig. 87). Hu, the divinity of plenty, cannot well be separated from him (pp. 66–67).

Iu-s-ʿa-s ("She Who Comes is Great") was a goddess of northern Heliopolis [37] and the wife of Har-akhti. She was, therefore, treated as a celestial goddess like Hat-hôr, etc.

Kenemtef(i) ("the One Who Wears His Leopard's Skin") is usually reckoned among the four sons of Horus (p. 112), though he is sometimes identified with Horus himself.[38] The picture here given depicts him like a priest of the class called "Wearers of the Leopard's Skin." It is a question whether he may not be the same as the lost divinity Kenemt(i), who fills the first three decanal stations.[39]

FIG. 130. KENEMTEFI

Kenemt(i): see Kenemtef(i).

Khasti (?),[40] "the lord of the west," was adored in the city of Sheta (in the Delta?). Because of his symbol (three mountains, the sign of foreign lands) he was also termed "lord of all foreign countries," whence his representations as a warrior arose. At an early date he was identified with Horus.

Khenset (Khensit), the wife of Sopd, being treated like the celestial goddesses, was pictured in the human shape of Hat-ḥôr-Isis, or wearing a feather on her head as "Justice" (p. 100), or as a cow.

Khnemtet was usually understood to mean "the Nurse," whence her name was applied to the nursing goddesses Isis and Nephthys.[41] Later she was also explained as a divinity of bread and cakes (p. 66).[42]

Khnûm(u) (Greek Xνουβις)[43] was the deity of Elephantine, the Cataract region ("Lord of the Cool Water"), and some other places in Upper Egypt, such as Esneh, Shas-ḥetep, Herakleopo-lis, etc. He is represented as a ram or as ram-headed, and later he sometimes receives four rams' heads, probably symbolizing the four sources of the Nile. See pp. 28, 50–51, 89.

Ma'et, the goddess of justice, was char-acterized by an ostrich-feather (p. 100).

Mafdet ("Lynx") was a warlike goddess widely known in the early dynastic period.[44]

FIG. 131. OLD SYMBOL OF MAFDET

Ma-ḥos: see Mi-ḥos.

Mandulis: see Note 55 on Merui.

Maṭet, "the portress of the sky," was a goddess who later was nearly forgotten, but who was connected with a tree or shrub.[45]

Matit ("the One Like a Lioness" [?]), a goddess adored under the form of a lioness in the twelfth (and fifth?) nome of Upper Egypt, was later compared with Hat-ḥôr.

Ma(t)-si-s ("the One Who Sees Her Son"), worshipped in the fifth and eleventh nomes of Upper Egypt, was later called, like so many other goddesses, a form or an epithet of Hat-ḥôr.

Meḥen (?) (Meḥnet, Meḥenit [?]; see also under Meneḥtet, infra) was a name for the mythological serpent which wound about the sun-god or about his head (p. 25). In later times "uraeus gods" (i. e. deities wearing the uraeus on their heads), both male and female, were called "followers of Meḥen."[46]

Mehet was a lioness who was worshipped in the old city of This.[47]

Mehi (Mehui?[48]) was a deity of whom little was known and who was perhaps identified with Thout.

Meht-uêret ("Great Flood") was a name of the celestial cow (p. 39) and was perhaps localized in the fifteenth nome of Upper Egypt.

Menehtet (Menhet, Menhit), a leontocephalous goddess, sometimes, like Sekhmet and other solarized divinities, wore the solar disk. She was worshipped at or near Heliopolis (?) and was also identified with Neith and confused with the solar serpent Mehen, mentioned above.

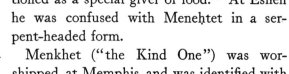

Men'et, the lion-headed "Nurse," is mentioned at Edfu and compared with Hat-hôr as the wife of Horus (p. 101).

Menhu(i), a god in human form, is mentioned as a special giver of food.[49] At Esneh he was confused with Menehtet in a serpent-headed form.

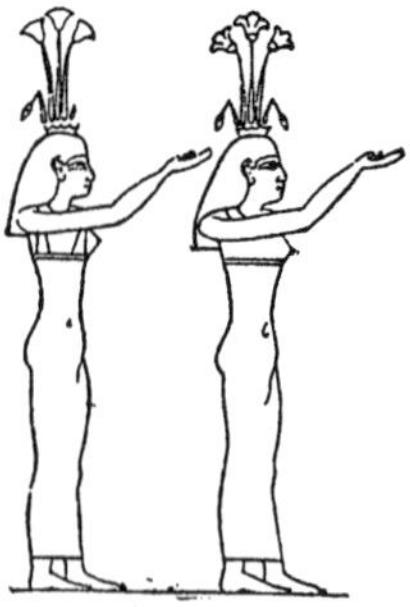

FIG. 132. MERET IN DOUBLE FORM

Menkhet ("the Kind One") was worshipped at Memphis and was identified with Isis (sometimes with Nephthys as well [Ch. V, Note 59]). The "linen-goddess" Menkhet is probably a different divinity.

Menqet, a goddess mentioned as producing vegetation and orthographically connected with a tree, is later pictured as a woman holding two pots and is often described as making beer and other drinks.[50] It is uncertain whether she was thus compared to Hat-hôr, who gives food and drink from the celestial tree (pp. 36, 39).

Meret wore a bush of aquatic plants on her head, like the Nile, and was, therefore, explained as a water-goddess.[51] Her name usually occurs in the dual number as Merti ("the two Merets"), or these are divided into "Meret of the South" and "Meret of the North," whence the pair are compared to the two Niles (p. 46) or the two divine representatives of the two kingdoms of Buto and Nekhbet. One of them sometimes has a lion's head,[52] and both are described as musicians.[53] The query arises whether they are "the two daughters of the Nile who split (?) the dragon" (i. e. divide the water of the abyss and the Nile into an upper and a lower course?) [54] Such a conflict with the older Osirian theology, however, would not be unusual (pp. 95, 106).

FIG. 133. MI-ḤOS, IDENTIFIED WITH NEFER-TÊM

Merḥi, a divinity with the shape or the head of a bull, was worshipped in Lower Egypt.

Mert-seger ("the One Who Loves Silence") was patroness of a portion of the Theban necropolis and was usually pictured in the guise of a serpent, though in rare instances she was represented also in human form like the great goddess Ḥat-ḥôr.

Merui (?), a deity in human form, though probably originally in the shape of a lion, was called "son of Horus" and was worshipped at Kalabsheh in Nubia, near the First Cataract.[55]

Meskhenet was the goddess of fate and birth (p. 52) and was sometimes identified with Isis and similar deities, especially with Tefênet (as coming from the deep? cf. p. 90).

Mi-ḥos (inferior reading Ma-ḥos; Greek Μιυσις; "the Grim-Looking Lion") was usually represented as a lion rising up in the act of devouring a captive. He was worshipped in the tenth nome of Upper Egypt, and being regarded as the son of the solar deity Rê' and the cat or lioness Ubastet, he was identified with the lion-god Shu (p. 44) or with Nefer-têm, as in Fig. 133.

FIG. 134. HIEROGLYPHIC SYMBOLS OF MÎN FROM PREHISTORIC OBJECTS

Mîn(u),[56] one of the oldest Egyptian gods, was worshipped at many places in Upper Egypt, where his hieroglyphic symbols, looking somewhat like a thunderbolt or a double harpoon, were wide-spread in prehistoric times; but the special sites of his cult were at Chemmis (i. e. Khem-mîn, or "Sanctuary of Mîn," the modern Akhmîm) and at Koptos, where the

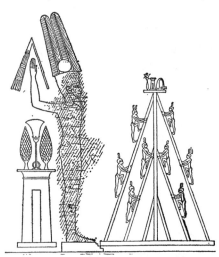

most important road to the Red Sea branches off to the desert. Hence he was called the patron of the wild inhabitants of the eastern desert, the Antiu tribes (the Troglodytes, or Trogodytes, of the Greeks), and even of regions farther to the south, such as the incense coast of Punt. These barbarians assembled at his festivals for a strange ceremony — a contest in climbing poles.[57]   Mîn's oldest prehistoric statues[58]

Fig. 135. Barbarians of the Desert Climbing Poles before Mîn

show him standing erect, grasping his immense phallus with his left hand, and in his hanging right holding a *flagellum*, while the back of his body is decorated with animals of the sea and of the desert. Later pictures make this ithyphallic god, whose colour was originally black,[59] lift his whip in his right hand; his head is ornamented with high feathers; and a fillet with a long pendant behind serves to keep these feathers upright, exactly like Amon of Thebes, who seems to be merely an old localized and slightly differentiated form of Mîn (pp. 21, 129). Behind him is pictured his chapel in various peculiar forms, or a

Fig. 136. The Earliest Sanctuaries of Mîn, Decorated with a Peculiar Standard

grove is indicated by a group of tall trees (generally three in number) within an enclosure, or the grove and chapel are combined. He is subsequently identified with Osiris, as being likewise phallic,[60] and thus is called a god of the harvest,[61] whence "Mîn, fair of face," is associated still later with the Asiatic goddess of love (see p. 156). Tradition also regards him as son of the sun (or of Osiris and Isis, or of Shu) and thus identifies him either with the young sun or with the moon. The Greek identification with the Hellenic shepherd-god, Pan, seems to depend on his pillar-like archaic statues. His sacred animal was a (white?) bull.

Mont(u) (Greek Μωνθ), the deity of Hermonthis (Egyptian An-montu, the modern Erment) and other places south of Thebes, was also adored at Thebes in the earliest times and regained worship there in the latest period, when this city and its god, Amon, had lost their importance. He is usually pictured as a hawk or as a man with a hawk's head, wearing two high feathers (like Mîn and Amon?); he is frequently adorned

FIG. 137. MÎN BEFORE HIS GROVE

with the solar disk, since he was identified with the sun-god at a very early date, so that he is also called Montu-Rê'. His original form, however, which was later preserved at Zeret (perhaps to be identified with the modern Taud), had the head of a bull; and even at Her-monthis his sacred animal remained a black bull, called Buchis in the Roman period (see p. 163). His hawk's head was borrowed from the solar deity, Rê'-Horus, and later Montu's bull was actually called "the soul of Rê'" (or of Osiris).[62] All texts agree in describing Montu as terrible and warlike, alluding, evidently, to the weapons which he holds. At different places various goddesses were associated with him as his wife, such as Ra't-taui (Ch. II, Note 20), Enit, and Ḥat-ḥôr.

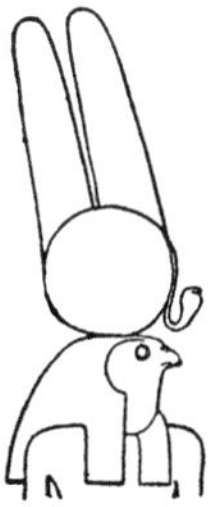

FIG. 138. MONTU

Mut ("Mother"), the later wife of Amon (pp. 129–30), was represented either as a vulture or in human form. She is

to be distinguished from Mu(u)t "the Water-Flood" (p. 46).

Nebet (Nebit?), i. e. "the Golden One," was the name of a local form of Ḥat-ḥôr (cf. p. 30 on gold as solar).

Neb-taui (modernized as P-neb-taui), i. e. "the Lord of Both Countries," a local deity of Ombos, was treated as the son of Horus and Sonet-nofret (or T-sonet-nofret) and was depicted like the young Horus (with a human head) or like Khôns (cf. Fig. 18).

FIG. 139. OLDEST TYPE OF MONṬU

Nebt-ḥotep ("Mistress of Peace" or "Mistress of the Lake of Peace") was later explained as a form of the goddess Ḥat-ḥôr.

Nebt-taui: see Amonet.

Nebt-uu ("Mistress of the Territory") was regarded as another form of Ḥat-ḥôr and received adoration at Esneh.

FIG. 140. MUT WITH A HEAD-DRESS ASSIMILATING HER TO AMON

Nefer-ḥo(r) ("Fair of Face") was a special form of Ptaḥ at Memphis, besides being an epithet of various other divinities, especially of Osiris (pp. 113, 139).

Nefer-ḥotep ("Fine of Peace," i. e. "the Peaceful") was a local form of the Theban deity Khôns(u), although an independent divinity of this name also occurs in the seventh nome of Upper Egypt.

FIG. 141. NEFER-TÊM

Nefer-têm, adored at Memphis, was grouped with Ptaḥ and Sekhmet as their son, while as the offspring of Ubastet, the cat-headed variant of Sehkmet, he was also connected with Heliopolis. His emblem is very unusual, being an open lotus flower from which two tall feathers and other ornaments project. The god, in the form either of a man or of a lion (cf. under Mi-hos, with whom he is identified), holds this symbol on a staff in his hand or wears it on his head. We know nothing about his functions, except that allusions ascribe a cosmic *rôle* to his fragrant and beautiful flower "before the nose of Rê'" (possibly implying the cosmic flower, i. e. the ocean; pp. 39, 50), he is, accordingly, identified with Horus.⁶³

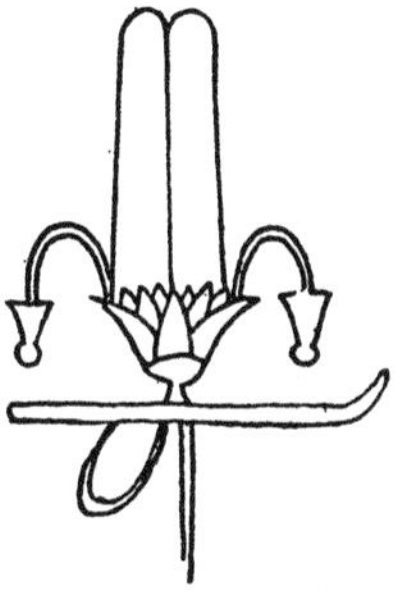

Fig. 142. Emblem of Nefer-têm

Neha-ho(r): see the following paragraph.

Neheb-kau ("the Overturner of Doubles") was originally an evil spirit in the form of a serpent ("with numerous windings")⁶⁴ who attacked and devoured the souls of the deceased in the underworld or on the way thither, south of the Cataracts (cf. under Selqet, *infra*). Later, however, he was honoured by being made one of the forty-two assessors in the law-court of Osiris, exactly like a similar serpent named Neha-ho(r) ("the One Turning the Face"), who subsequently was sometimes confused with the satanic dragon 'Apop.⁶⁵

Nehem(t)-'auit ("the One Who Removes Violence, Delivers [from] Violence"[?]; Greek Νεμανους [?]), a goddess associated with Thout, the divinity of wisdom, especially at Hermopolis (and at Ba'h in Lower Egypt?), is pictured in human form, wearing the *sistrum* or pillar or other emblems of Hat-hôr on her head. She must have been identified with this goddess at an early date, for she is also called "the one who is fond of music" (cf. p. 40),⁶⁶ "daughter of the sun," and the like.

Fig. 143. Nehem(t)-'auit

Nehes ("Awake, Awakening"): see p. 67 on this abstraction as companion of the sun-god. A similar epithet later applied to Sêth seems to characterize him as the "watchful" dragon, lurking in the lower world (p. 106).

Neith (Greek pronunciation;⁶⁷ Egyptian orthography N[i]t,

once Nrt) was a very ancient goddess who was known throughout Egypt even in the prehistoric period, when she extended
her influence from Saïs, her centre of worship, over the entire

western frontier of the Delta and up to the
Fayûm. Accordingly the local deity of the
latter region, Sobk, was called her son
(whence she is represented as giving the
breast to crocodiles); and she is even
termed patroness of all Libyans. She is
represented as a woman with the ordinary
yellow (sometimes light green?) skin which
characterizes her sex in Egyptian art and
she wears the red crown of Lower Egypt;
yet she often appears also as a cow, i. e. as
a celestial divinity (p. 37). Because of her
hieroglyph, two crossed arrows, she frequently bears bow and arrows;[68] but later
this sign was misunderstood as a weaver's
shuttle,[69] so that she was connected with
the art of weaving[70] and of tying magic

FIG. 144. NEITH

knots as "a great sorceress" like Isis.

Nekhbet was the vulture-goddess of the earliest capital of
Upper Egypt, the Eileithyiaspolis of the Greeks and the
modern el-Kāb, and was, conse-
quently, the oldest patroness of
that portion of the land, the
counterpart of Buto (p. 132).
Accordingly she is regularly represented as flying above the king
and holding a ring or other royal
emblems. She likewise appears
as a woman (sometimes with a

FIG. 145. NEKHBET PROTECTING THE
KING

vulture's head), and since she wears the white crown of Upper
Egypt, she is termed "the white one,"[71] and her cities Nekhbet
and Nekhen (cf. p. 101) are called "the white city." In later

days she, as "daughter and eye of the sun-god," was compared
with the celestial divinities. The Greeks and Romans identified her with Eileithyia-Lucina, the lunar goddess who protected birth, possibly because she later watched over Osiris
and his resurrection; but distinct connexion of this deity with
the moon cannot be proved from Egyp-
tian sources. Her *rôle* as wife of the
Nile-god (p. 46) is evidently in accord
with a very old tradition which made
the Egyptian course of that river begin
at the capital, situated very near the
southern frontier, since the two southern-
most nomes must at that time have
been populated by Nubian tribes. This
seems again to explain her connexion
with the birth of Osiris as the Nile.
Whether a Greek transcription Σμιθις
referred to the name Nekhbet is open
to question (see under Semtet).

Nemanus: see Neḥem(t)-ʿauit.

Nesret ("the Flaming, Fiery [Ser-
pent]"; p. 26) was a deity whose localization is doubtful, but who was later
identified with the serpent-goddess Buto.

Onuris (Egyptian An-ḥôret, "Guiding
[on] the Highway") was localized in

Fɪɢ. 146. Lᴀᴛᴇ Tʏᴘᴇ ᴏғ
Oɴᴜʀɪs

This, Sebennytos, and elsewhere, and was usually represented
as a man in a standing posture, holding a spear in his raised
hand (or in both hands), and wearing four high feathers on
his head. Since he was regarded as a warrior (whence the
Greeks identified him with Ares) who aided the sun-god in his
struggle, his picture later protected the house against noxious
animals and other evils. Thus he was regarded as the same as
Horus and was likewise represented occasionally with the head
of a hawk. The prevalent identification, however, was with

Shu, the god of the air (p. 44), because of the similar headdress of four feathers, so that it is possible that, like those feathers, "the highway" was interpreted celestially.

Fig. 147. Ophoïs

Ophoïs (Egyptian Up-ua(u)t, "Opener of the Way"), the wolf-god of Lykopolis (Assiut), This, and Saïs, was frequently confused with Anubis (pp. 110–11). The Egyptians of the Greek period explained his animal as a wolf, perhaps because it was represented standing, whereas the jackal (?) of Anubis was recumbent. The warlike features of Ophoïs may be derived from his worship at the capital This, or from the weapons which decorate the bases of his pictures, or from celestial interpretations of his name. The Ophoïs of Saïs "follows the King of Lower Egypt,"[72] as the older form is the "jackal of the South."

Opet (?) (Greek 'Ωφις) was the goddess of a quarter of eastern Thebes, whose hieroglyph she bears in the accompanying picture, together with celestial symbols.

Pekhet (Pakhet, once erroneously Pekhet?) was a lioness who was worshipped in Middle Egypt in the desert valley near Speos Artemidos, a name which shows that the Greeks identified her with Artemis, probably because she was a huntress and roved in the desert.[73]

Peyet: see Note 19.

Ptaḥ (Greek Φθα), the god of Memphis (Egyptian Ḥat-ka-Ptaḥ, "Place of the Soul of Ptaḥ"), was pictured as a bearded man of unusually light (yellow)[74] colour and as clad in white, close-fitting garments, a tassel from his neck holding his collar in position. His head is usually bare, though later various royal crowns are worn by him, and a sceptre is generally held in both his hands.

Fig. 148. Opet

The feet, ordinarily united as though the deity were mummified, reveal the very primitive antiquity of the artistic tradition (cf. Figs. 136–37 for equally primitive, pillar-like statues of

Mîn, and the archaic divine types, p. 12). His cult is, indeed,
declared to be the oldest in Egypt, and he is called "the
Ancient,"[75] while "the age of Ptaḥ" and "the years of Ptaḥ"
are proverbial phrases. The divinity stands on a peculiar
pedestal which was later explained as the hieroglyph of justice,[76] and this pedestal is generally represented within a small
chapel. Coming into prominence when the pyramid-builders
moved their residence near his temple, he was called "the
first of the gods," "the creator of the gods and of the world."
He was the divine artist "who formed works of art" and was
skilful in all material, especially in metal, so that
the Greeks compared him to Hephaistos, and his
high-priest had the title of "chief artificer."[77]
Therefore on a potter's wheel Ptaḥ turned the
solar and the lunar eggs (or, according to others,
the cosmic egg, though this is doubtful). In his
special capacity of creator he bears the name Ptaḥ-
Taṭunen, being identified with a local deity Taṭunen, who appears in human form, wearing feathers
and a ram's horn (cf. pp. 47, 150); and later he

FIG. 149. PTAḤ

is equated with the abyss (Ptaḥ-Nuu) or with the Nile,[78] but
also with the sun (Ptaḥ-Aten, "Ptaḥ the Solar Disk"), or with
the air (Ptaḥ-Shu), so that he becomes a god of all nature.
When plants are said to grow on his back, this may come
quite as well from his identification with Sokari, and from the
subsequent blending of Ptaḥ-Sokari with Osiris (p. 98), as from
comparison with Qêb (p. 42). Sokhmet and Nefer-têm were
associated with him as wife and son.[79]

Qebḥet (Qebḥut) was a serpent-goddess, and as "the
daughter of Anubis" was localized near that divinity in the
tenth nome. Her name ("the Cool One") gives rise at an
early date to myths which connect her with sky or water.[80]

Qed was a deity with the head of an ox [81] (cf. the decanal
constellation Qed(u?), which, however, has no human representation elsewhere).

Qerḥet, a serpent-goddess, protected the eighth nome of Lower Egypt, the later land of Goshen.

Rê'et: see Ch. II, Note 20.

Renenutet (Remenutet, Remutet): see pp. 66, 116.

Repit (Greek Τριφις; "Youthful One," "Maiden") was a very popular goddess in the latest period. She is often represented as wearing on her head the hieroglyphic sign of a palm-branch, symbolizing fresh vegetation and youth (p. 89), which renders it difficult to separate her from the personification of time and the year (Ronpet?), who has a similar symbol.[82]

Ronpet: see the preceding paragraph. For the Sothis-star, called "the year-goddess" as the regulator of time, cf. p. 56.

Rururi: see Ch. III, Note 31.

Satet[83] (Greek Σατις) was worshipped at the First Cataract and was associated with Khnûm. She is represented in human form and wears a high conical crown with the horns of a cow (cf. the picture given on p. 20); later she was occasionally compared with such celestial divinities as Isis and Hat-ḥôr. Her name denotes "the Thrower, the Shooter," and hence she carries bow and arrows, although the original meaning referred, rather, to the falling waters of the Cataract.

Seb (?) was a little-known deity who was worshipped in the form of a flying hawk.

Sebit (Sebait) was a goddess of whom little is known[84] (identical with Asbet?).

Sekha(i)t-ḥor ("the One Who Thinks of Horus") was depicted as a recumbent cow and was worshipped in the third nome of Lower Egypt.[85] On account of her name, she was often identified with Isis.

Sekhmet[86] ("the Powerful"), a leontocephalous goddess, was adored at Memphis (cf. *supra* on Ptaḥ and Nefer-têm as her associates) and at some other places, chiefly in the Delta, as well as in the thirteenth nome of Upper Egypt. Generally she wears the solar disk on her head, and the texts speak of her as a warlike manifestation of the sun, a solar eye (p. 29), "the fiery one, emitting flames against the enemies" of the gods (cf. p. 75). She is often compared with the neighbouring cat, Ubastet, who is termed her friendly manifestation.

Selqet (Greek Σελχις) was symbolized by a scorpion, although in later times she was usually represented in human form (see p. 60 and Fig. 60). Her name is abbreviated from Selqet Ehut ("Who Cools Throats"),[87] one of the four goddesses who assist Nuu, the deity of the abyss, and protect or represent the four sources which he sends to the upper world. This confirms the tradition that Pselchis, in northern Nubia near the mythological sources of the Nile, was her original home.[88] With her sting she later protects the dead Osiris and the nursing Isis (with whom she is occasionally identified), so that some of the entrails of the embalmed, etc., are placed under her guardianship. As the patroness of magic power she is also called "mistress of the house of books," so that she seems to have been felt to be analogous to the goddess of fate (p. 53) as dwelling, like her, in the extreme south, i. e. in the underworld. Accordingly she is associated with the subterranean serpent Neheb-kau.[89] Later she is sometimes termed the wife of Horus, a fact which corresponds with her occasional celestial and solar insignia.[90]

Fig. 150. SEKHMET

Sema-uêr ("Great Wild Ox") was an old name of the celestial bull (Ch. III, Note 10).

Semtet is a goddess who reminds us of Smithis, but her name cannot be read with certainty.[91]

Sepa: see Sop.

Seqbet: see Note 100.

Ser ("Prince") was usually explained in later times as Osiris [92] and was localized at Heliopolis.

Shemtet, a goddess mentioned only on rare occasions, had the head of a lioness.[93]

Shenet, whose name likewise seldom occurs, was pictured

in human form, with long tresses like a child.[94] She was probably identical with the following divinity.

Shenṭet (later forms Shentit, Shentait) was a goddess whose

earliest representation seems to have been a long-haired girl (holding a child?). Later she is treated as a variant of such celestial goddesses as Isis, and also appears in the form of a cow.[95] Her seat of worship was Heliopolis or Abydos (?). Cf. the preceding paragraph.

FIG. 151. SOKARI HIDDEN IN HIS BOAT OR SLEDGE

Shut (Shuet; "the One of Shu") is a rare name for the lioness Tefênet.[96] Cf. names like Amonet, Anupet, etc.

Smentet was a little-known goddess who was treated as parallel to Isis.[97]

Smithis: see under Nekhbet and Semtet.

Sobk (Greek Σουχος),[98] a crocodile-god, seems originally to have ruled over the lake and the country of the Fayûm in the western part of Middle Egypt, whose capital was Shedet(i)-Krokodilopolis. He was also the lord of some other places along the western frontier of the Delta (see p. 142 for his association with Neith) and likewise enjoyed worship at an early period in Upper Egypt at Ombos (where he was associated with Ḥat-ḥôr), Ptolemaïs, Her-monthis, etc. Later he became, especially at Ombos, a form of the solar deity Sobk-Rê',[99] and at other places still more strange attempts were made to identify him with Osiris, perhaps because crocodiles dwell in the darkest depths of the water.[100]

FIG. 152. SOPD AS AN ASIATIC WARRIOR

Sobket: see Note 100.

Sokar(i) (Greek Σοχαρις), a deity of a place near Memphis

(whence the modern name Saqqarah may perhaps be derived) "at the bend (*pezut*) of the lake," [101] was at first regarded as a manifestation of Horus, the sun, and thus was represented as a hawk or falcon sitting in a strange bark on a sledge (*henu*) which was drawn around his temple at festivals as a solar bark.[102] When this place became the necropolis of the great city of Memphis, "Sokari in his crypt (*shetait*)" was made a god of the dead and was identified with Ptaḥ and Osiris, so that his temple Ro-setau ("Gate of Corridors") was explained as the entrance to the passages which led to the underworld. Thus, as the revived Osiris,[103] "Sokar, the lord of the ground"(!), became the earth-god as well (cf. p. 98 and above on the deity Ptaḥ).

Sonet-nofret (modernized form T-sonet-nofret; "the Fine Sister"), a deity at Ombos, was identified with Tefênet, whence she was sometimes represented with the head of a lioness, though she usually appeared as human, resembling Ḥat-ḥôr. Her husband was the Horus of Ombos, and her son was (P)-neb-taui (p. 140).

Fig. 153. Archaic Type of Sopd

Sop (earlier Sepa), a god who was worshipped in and near Heliopolis, was later identified with Osiris. This and the later pronunciation are shown by Osarsyph, the alleged Egyptian name which Manetho ascribes to Moses.[104]

Sopd(u), "the lord of the east, the one who smites the Asiatics," was the deity of the twentieth nome of the Delta (later termed "the Arabian Nome") at the western entrance to the valley of Goshen, with the capital Pe(r)-sopd(u) ("House of Sopd"; also called "House of the Sycamore"), the modern Saft el-Ḥene. This warlike divinity is usually represented as a man wearing two high feathers on his head, and sometimes, as master of the Asiatics, he appears in an Asiatic type and bearded. He is also shown as a falcon in the archaic type (cf. Ch. V, Note 27), a fact which results in comparing him with Horus. Later he is also pictured like a winged Bês (p. 61).[105] Khenset is his wife.

Tait ("Mistress of Linen") was the goddess of weaving, perhaps in Busiris, although this may be an artificial connexion with Osiris, the divinity swathed in linen, whence she is also called Isis-Tait.[106]

Tatunen (Tetenen, etc., perhaps also Tanen, Tenen) was usually identified with Ptaḥ, and then also with Nuu (pp. 47, 145). He had human form and wore two ostrich-feathers and two ram's horns on his head.

Tebi was a name of a solarized god.[107]

Tekhi, a goddess in human form, wore a pair of high feathers

FIG. 154. TAIT CARRYING CHESTS OF LINEN

(like Amon) and was patroness of the first month instead of Thout, with whom she was likewise interchanged elsewhere.[108] This identification seems to be based principally on the vague similarity of the name and does not appear to be ancient.

Temhit ("the Libyan") was a goddess who was worshipped in Heliopolis (?).

Tenenet (later Tanenet) received adoration at Her-monthis, where she was identified with Isis and Anit. Like the latter, she wears two royal crowns or bending antennae (p. 130) on her head.

Triphis: see Repit.

Ubastet [109] ("the One of the City of Ubaset" [p. 21]) was the cat-goddess of Bubastos, the Pi-beseth of Ezekiel xxx. 17, but she also had an ancient sanctuary at Thebes on the Asheru Lake near Karnak which was later appropriated by Mut. She is often identified with Sekhmet (see, e. g., under Nefer-têm), whence her head is frequently that of a lioness, as in the accompanying cut, where the asp characterizes her as a "daughter of the sun-god" (p. 29). As an alleged huntress, the Greeks called her Artemis, like the lioness Pekhet (p. 144).

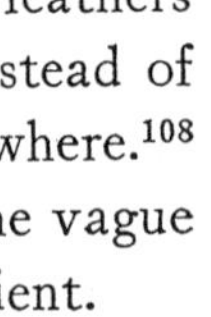

FIG. 155. UBASTET

Ung (Ungi; "Sprout" [?]), a "son of the solar deity" or his messenger,[110] treated like Shu, was later identified with Osiris.

Unut (Unet) was a goddess said to have been worshipped at Unut (?), Hermopolis ("Hare-City"), Menḥet, and Denderah; she is not to be confused with "the hour-goddess" Unut (p. 66). A picture shows "the Unet of the South" in human form and lying on a bed as though dead, and "the Unet of the North" like Isis suckling Horus.[111] The later Egyptians inferred from her name that she was a female hare, but we suspect that originally the name meant simply "the Heliopolitan" (see p. 31 on On-Heliopolis and cf. Note 37).

Upset was identified with Tefênet, Isis, and similar solar and celestial goddesses at Philae, etc.

Ur-ḥeka ("Great in Magic") was a god in the form of a man (or of a serpent?).

Urt-ḥekau, a leontocephalous goddess, was called "wife of the sun-god," possibly because she was compared with Isis as a sorceress (p. 82). She is also represented with a serpent's head, and is then not easily distinguished from a male divinity of the same name. Urt-ḥekau is likewise an epithet of Isis, Neith, Nephthys, Êpet, etc., so that this goddess is often confused with them.

Fig. 156.
Unut

Usret ("Mighty One") was applied as an epithet to many goddesses, but in its special sense it was the name of a very popular divinity of the earlier period, who was, perhaps, in the shape of a serpent. She is described as "residing on the western height,"[112] in the fifth nome of the Delta. Later she was little known, although once[113] she is called, curiously enough, "mother of Mîn."

Utet was a deity who possibly had the form of a heron.[114]

Uzoit: see Buto.

Zedet (Zedut): see Note 20.

Zend(u) (Zendr(u); "the Powerful One," "the Violent One") was a very ancient deity who, like Sokari, sat in a sacred sledge-ship and, again like him, was compared with Osiris at an early date.[115]

The ambiguity of hieroglyphic letters makes the reading of some names especially doubtful, as in the following examples.

Igay (Egay) was the leading god of the Theban nome in earliest times.[116]

Iaḥes (Eaḥes), "the patron of the South," must have been worshipped near the southern frontier.[117]

Iamet (Eamet) was a goddess who is described as nursing young divinities.[118]

Ukhukh(?), a god worshipped near the site of the modern Meïr, was symbolized by a staff decorated with two feathers and two serpents.[119]

CHAPTER VIII
FOREIGN GODS

THE Egyptians of the earlier period did not feel it necessary to bring foreign gods to their country; when they went to Syria and Nubia, they temporarily worshipped the local divinities of those lands, without abandoning their own deities.[1] It is true that concepts of Asiatic mythology constantly passed freely into the religion of Egypt,[2] and, in particular, the fairy stories of the New Empire not only employed Asiatic *motifs* very liberally, but often placed their scenes in Asia, thus frankly confessing their dependence on Asiatic material. Accordingly the *Story of the Two Brothers* (Ch. V, Note 106) is laid largely on the "cedar mountain" of the Syrian coast; and the *Story of the Haunted Prince* makes the hero wander as a hunter to the remote East, the country of Naharina (corresponding approximately to Mesopotamia), to win the princess there. This prince, who is doomed to be killed by his dog (a non-Egyptian explanation of Sirius) or by a serpent (Hydra), represents a northern idea of the hunter Orion; and his wife, whom he gains in a jumping-match, is clearly Astarte-Venus-Virgo, who rescues him by restraining Hydra.[3] From folk-lore and magic sooner or later such ideas finally passed into the official theology; and future scholars will ultimately recognize that a very considerable part of Egyptian religious thought was derived from or influenced by the mythology of Asia. Tracing such *motifs* to the Pyramid Period certainly does not prove that they were autochthonous. The earliest centre of Egyptian religion, the ancient city of On-Heliopolis (p. 31), was situated at the entrance of the great

caravan route from the East, and there we must assume a
constant interchange of ideas even in the most remote periods.
In the present state of our knowledge, however, we cannot
pass very positive judgement on the many prehistoric loans of
this nature,[4] and these borrowings, moreover,
consist of religious *motifs* alone. The actual
gods of Asia, or at least their names, could
not well be appropriated by a nation which
leaned so strongly on ancient local traditions
as did the Egyptian in the more primitive
stages of its history.

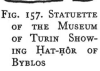

The only early exception was the goddess
of the holiest city of Phoenicia, the famous
Baʿalath of Gebal-Byblos, who became known
and venerated in Egypt soon after 2000 B. C.,
when she was identified with Ḥat-ḥôr, the
Egyptian divinity most similar to the Asiatic
type of heavenly goddesses (p. 40), or was
worshipped simply as "the Mistress of
Byblos," a remarkable acknowledgement of
the fame of her city. Thus a statuette of
the New Empire in the museum of Turin
represents an Egyptian holding a pillar of
"Ḥat-ḥôr, the mistress of peace, the mistress
of Kup [ordinarily Kupni, i. e. Byblos] and
of Wawa [a part of Nubia]." Thus far the
admission of the connexion of that city with
the worship of Osiris (p. 120 and Ch. V, Note 110) cannot be
traced to quite so early a date, but it may be much more
ancient; the period of the Old and Middle Empires was still
reluctant to confess loans from Asia.

Fig. 157. Statuette
of the Museum
of Turin Show-
ing Ḥat-ḥôr of
Byblos

In the New Empire, however, after 1600 B. C., when Egypt
underwent great changes and wished to appear as a military
state and a conquering empire on Asiatic models, and when
the customs and the language of Canaan thus spread through-

out the Nile-land, the worship of Asiatic deities became fashionable, being propagated by many immigrants, mercenaries, merchants, etc., from Syria. The warlike character of the gods of Asia and the rich mythology attached to them made them especially attractive to the Egyptian mind.[5]

Ba'al (Semitic "Lord") is described as the god of thunder, dwelling on mountains or in the sky, and terrible in battle, so that the Egyptians often identified him with their warlike god Sêth (see the next divinity).

FIG. 158. RESHPU

Resheph, or Reshpu (Semitic "Lightning") was represented as a man wearing a high, conical cap (sometimes resembling the crown of Upper Egypt),[6] often tied with a long ribbon falling over his back[7] and ornamented above the forehead with the head of a gazelle, probably to indicate that he was a hunter. He carries shield, spear, and club, and sometimes has a quiver on his back. Once he is called Reshpu Sharamana, i. e. he is identified with another Syrian god, Shalman or Shalmon.[8] As we shall see, he was associated with

Astarte-Qedesh. One form, marked by a long tassel hanging from the top of the cap, which we here reproduce after a monument of the museum of Berlin, is there identified with Sêth, "the one great of strength." Thus Sêth, as the general patron of Asiatics and of warriors (p. 103), was considered to manifest himself in all the male deities of Asia.

Some female divinities from Asia were even more popular.

FIG. 159. RESHEPH-SÊTH

Astarte ('Astart) had her chief temple in Memphis,[9] although she was also worshipped in the city of Ramses and elsewhere. This "mistress of heaven" was scarcely known as a goddess of love in Egypt, where she was, rather, the deity of war, "the mistress of horses and of the chariot." [10] She usually wears the conical crown of all Asiatic divinities, with two feathers as an Egyptian addition. The two following deities evidently constitute mere manifesta-

FIG. 160.
"ASTARTE, MISTRESS OF HORSES AND OF THE CHARIOT"

tions of Astarte. In Asiatizing art she seems to be represented also by the non-Egyptian female sphinx, whose head is marked by long tresses and a peculiar kerchief, such as was worn by Syrian women.

Qedesh (Semitic "the Holy, Awful One") is pictured like the nude goddesses of Babylonian art, standing on a lion and holding flowers and a serpent which often degenerates into another flower; [11] in keeping with her title, "mistress of heaven," she wears the sun and moon on her head. Her two lovers, the youthful Tammuz-Adonis and his warlike rival, appear on either side of her, the latter as Resheph-Reshpu, and the former as the Egyptian god Mîn, who thus again shows himself to be like Osiris (p. 139).

FIG. 161. ASTARTE

'Asît always rides on horseback. The name may be nothing more than a popular form of Astarte when pronounced 'As[t]eyt, but in any case 'Asît was treated as a separate divinity.

FIG. 162. ASTARTE AS A SPHINX

'Anat has a similar dress and equipment, but is not found with the horse. Like Astarte she is warlike and sensual, yet eternally virgin.

Ba'alt ("Mistress"; see p. 154 on the identical name Ba'alath) was the feminine counterpart of Ba'al, and we also find a Ba'alt Zapuna ("Ba'alt of the North").

Rarer goddesses of this kind were Atum(a), who seems to have been the female form of the Canaanitish god Edom; Nukara, or Nugara, i. e. the Babylonian Ningal, the deity of the underworld; Amait, who was worshipped in Memphis; etc. See pp. 207–09 for the numerous names of deities borrowed from Asia by the sorcerers. We are, however, uncertain how far those divinities really found worship in popular circles.

FIG. 163. QEDESH

The African neighbours of Egypt to the west scarcely influenced the pantheon in the historic period; after 1000 B. C. only one goddess, Shahdidi, seems to have come from Libya. It is, however, a fact which has not yet been observed by Egyptologists that the Egyptians of the earliest times worshipped some Nubian gods. This was due less to Egyptian conquests of Nubia in prehistoric days, like those of the Fourth, Sixth, Twelfth, and Eighteenth Dynasties, than to the strong cultural (and perhaps ethnological) connexions which existed between the prehistoric Egyptians and

FIG. 164. ʻAsîr

the tribes to the south of them, as excavations in Nubia have recently shown. It is likewise probable that as mercenaries the Nubians played the same important part in the history of pre-dynastic Egypt that they had later, when several dynasties of the Pyramid Period appear to have been of Nubian descent. Thus the goddess Selqet (p. 147) had her local worship south of the Cataract region, and yet was a very important Egyptian divinity, connected with the Osiris-myth. In like fashion Dedun, a god in human form,

FIG. 165. ʻANAT

originally pictured as a bird on a crescent-shaped twig, was worshipped at remote Semneh in Nubia, near the Second

Cataract, as "the youth of the south who came forth from Nubia," and yet it seems that kings of the Sixth Dynasty still called themselves after this foreign god.[12] The hieroglyphs of Dedun and Selqet appear combined on remarkable vessels of

the earliest dynastic period.[13] Thus we see that the frontier of Egypt could once be drawn rather far north of the First Cataract, or else at this Cataract (as was usually the case in historical times), or it could be extended far south of it, even to the Second Cataract, according to varying political conditions and the personal opinions of the ancient scholars.[14]

FIG. 166. HIEROGLYPHS OF DEDUN AND SELQET

After Alexander the Great the Greek gods of the ruling classes replaced the Egyptian divinities in some Hellenized places, but made little impression on the Egyptian pantheon where it was still maintained (see pp. 239–40, and for Serapis cf. p. 98).

CHAPTER IX

WORSHIP OF ANIMALS AND MEN

FROM ancient times no feature of Egyptian religion has attracted so much attention as the wide-spread cult of animals.[1] A few of the Classical writers viewed it with mystic awe, but the majority of them expressed dislike or sarcasm even before the Christians began to prove the diabolical nature of paganism by this worst madness of the Egyptians (pp. 7–8). Until very recently modern scholars themselves have found this curious element inexplicable. Some of them, over-zealous admirers of Egypt, attempted to excuse it as a later degeneration of a symbolism which the alleged "pure religion" of earliest Egypt might have understood in a less materialistic sense. The precise opposite is true, for animal worship constitutes a most prominent part of the primitive Egyptian beliefs. If we start from the theory that animism was the basis of the beginnings of Egyptian religion, we have no difficulty in understanding the *rôle* which animals played in it. When the majority of spirits worshipped by the rude, prehistoric Egyptians were clad with animal form, this agrees with the view of the brute creation which is held by primitive man in general. It is not the superior strength or swiftness of some creatures which causes them to be regarded with religious awe, and still less is it gratitude for the usefulness of the domestic animals; it is the fear that the seemingly dumb beasts possess reason and a language of their own which man cannot fathom and which consequently connect them with the mysterious, supernatural world. It is true that the lion, the hawk, and the poisonous serpent predominate in the Egyptian pantheon, but the form

of the crocodile is limited to one or two gods; and the most
terrible of wild animals, the leopard, and perhaps the hippopotamus,[2] are, possibly accidentally, wholly lacking, while,
on the other hand, the little shrew-mouse appears. We have
already explained the frequency of black bulls as belonging, in
all probability, to the advanced stage of cosmic gods (Ch. III,
Note 10), and the hawk may, likewise, indicate the same age in
which the hawk-shaped sun-god was dominant. Hence we must
be careful not to use these forms for explaining the primitive
meaning of that phenomenon. Where the cult of an animal
has survived in later times, it is repeatedly stated in clear words
that the spirit of some god has taken possession of it (see p. 164,
for instance, on the designation of the Mendes "ram" as the
"soul" of a deity). That the later Egyptians thought at the
same time of such divinities as residing in heaven presented
no difficulty to them, for gods were not limited to one soul;
a deity had several souls (or, rather, "forces")[3] and might,
therefore, live contemporaneously both in heaven and on earth,
or might even appear in a number of earthly incarnations
simultaneously. The inconsistencies of these theories of the
incarnation of celestial beings show, however, that they were,
after all, a secondary development. We see this with especial
clearness in instances where the god, though said to be incarnate in an animal, is never actually represented in that
form, as is the case with Ptaḥ, Osiris, Rê', Mîn, etc.; or when,
as we shall see, the later Egyptians no longer understood the
connexion between the solarized god Montu and his original
bull-form, the Buchis, but tried, on the analogy of the Apis,
etc., to explain the latter animal as the embodiment of other,
more obviously celestial divinities.

The earliest Egyptians, who scarcely sought their gods outside the earth, must have worshipped such an animal, supposed to be possessed by an extraordinary spirit, as divine in
itself. It was only the tendency of a more advanced age to
invest the gods with some higher (i. e. cosmic) power and to

remove them from the earthly sphere that compelled the theologians to resort to these theories of the incarnation of celestial divinities. A similar attempt to break away from the crudest conceptions of animal worship betrays itself likewise in the numerous mixed representations of the old animal-gods, i. e. with a human body and the head of an animal. Evidently the underlying idea was that these deities were in reality not animals, that they merely appeared (or had once appeared) on earth in such guise, but that as a matter of fact they lived in heaven in the form most becoming to gods, i. e. in an idealized human shape. This modification of the old animistic religion can be traced to a date far anterior to the Pyramid Period.[4] The prehistoric Egyptians, as we have said above, must have had the opposite view, namely, that the worthiest form for the gods was that of animals.

We have no information as to how the earliest period treated the succession of the divine animals which were adored in the temples. The later theory that reincarnations came from heaven in regular order, as we shall see when we consider the Apis bull, does not seem plausible for the original local cults of prehistoric times, since their means were so extremely limited that it must have been very difficult for them to find another animal with the requisite physical characteristics. It is possible that some sacred animals did not have such a succession. Some, like the crocodiles of Sobk, seem to have bred in the temples. It is possible that in later times certain of the sacred animals may primarily have been kept at the sanctuaries merely as symbols to remind men of the god who now dwelt in heaven after having once shown himself on earth as an animal in the days of the pious ancestors when divinities still walked in this world. The popular mind, however, anxious to have a palpable sign of the god's existence, could not draw the line between sacredness and real divinity, and soon regarded the symbolic animal as a supernatural being in itself, thus returning to the original conception of sacred animals.

The great difficulty in the problem under consideration is that we know very little about the majority of the sacred animals; only the most prominent cults, which were observed throughout Egypt, have left relatively full information. Here we are largely dependent on the Græco-Roman writers, to whom this feature of Egyptian religion seemed especially remarkable; unfortunately, the data which these more or less superficial observers record are not always trustworthy. The hieroglyphic inscriptions do not have much to say concerning the cult of animals, which is in itself a proof that the learned

priests could do little with this bequest of the ancestors. It remained a mystery to the generations that had outgrown the animistic stage. This very obscurity, however, seemed only a proof that such cults were peculiarly venerable as transcending human understanding and intellect.

FIG. 167. STATUETTE OF THE APIS SHOWING HIS SACRED MARKS

The most popular sacred animal was the Apis (Egyptian Ḥp, pronounced Ḥap, Ḥop; "the Runner") of Memphis, a black bull with certain special white marks, "resembling an eagle's wings," on his forehead and back, a "scarab-like" knot under (?) his tongue, and other signs. According to later belief, he was conceived by a ray of light descending on a cow, i. e. he was an incarnation of the sun. His discovery, his solemn escorting to Memphis, and his pompous installation as "the holy god, the living Apis," at the temple called the "Apiaeum" were celebrated throughout Egypt. He was kept in great luxury and gave oracles by the path which he chose, the food which he accepted or refused, etc. He was usually regarded as the embodiment of Ptaḥ, the chief local god, being called "Ptaḥ renewing himself" or "son of Ptaḥ," but later he was considered more as an incarnation of Osiris-Sokari, especially after his death.[5] He is depicted wearing the solar disk between

his horns and is thus connected not only with the sun (Rê'
or Atum) but also with the moon, whence it is obvious that,
as we have noted above, he was originally a god himself
without any connexion with nature. The fact that he was
allowed to drink only from a well, not from the Nile, shows
that he was compared likewise — though very secondarily
— with Ha'pi, the Nile (or with Osiris in the same function?).
The anniversary of his birth was celebrated for seven (?) days
every year; when he died,[6] great mourning was observed in the

whole land, and he was
sumptuously interred at
Saqqarah, where the tombs
of the Apis bulls and of
their mothers, who had become sacred through the
divine birth, were found by
A. Mariette in 1851. Soon
after the seventy days[7] of
mourning over the loss of
the god, a new Apis calf was
discovered by the priests
with suspicious promptness.[8]

FIG. 168. BUCHIS

Next in reputation was the Mnevis (Egyptian Nem-uêr,
"Great Wanderer"), the sacred animal of Heliop-olis, who was
explained as "the living sun-god Rê'" or "the (living) reproduction of Rê'" and also of Osiris. His name reveals the
early comparison with celestial phenomena. He was a black
and white bull, somewhat similar to Apis. In later times the
black sacred bull of Montu, which was called Bekh or Bokh
(the Βαχις, Βακχις, or, better, Βουχις, of the Greeks) at Her-
monthis,[9] was likewise called "the living soul of Rê'" or of
Osiris (whence he also took the name Osorbuchis); he is pictured much like Apis. Regarding the (white?) bull of Mîn
(p. 139), the cow of Momemphis, the bull (perhaps of Osiris-
Horus) at Pharbaethos,[10] etc., we know little.[11]

A very curious problem is presented by the sacred ram (?) of the city of Mendes in the Delta, called Bi-neb-dêd(u) (muti-

lated in Greek as Μενδης), i. e. "Soul of the Lord of Busiris." Thus he was understood to embody the soul of the god Osiris of the neighbouring city Busiris;[12] occasionally he was also called "soul of Rê'."[13] The divine incarnation in him likewise was manifested by bodily marks "as described in the sacred books," which the priests "recognized according to the holy writings." He seems to have been worshipped as a god of fecundity like Osiris; and accordingly his

FIG. 169. THE MENDES RAM AND HIS PLANT SYMBOL

emblem also was an ear of grain. The Classical stories about sexual intercourse of these sacred animals with women are probably due to misunderstandings of the interpretation of Mendes as a symbol of fertility or to errors regarding ceremonies relating to such symbolism. Strangely enough, all Græco-Roman sources agree in describing Mendes as a he-goat. This contradiction to every

FIG. 170. AMON AS A RAM

Egyptian representation has not yet been explained in a satisfactory way.[14] The ram of other gods, e. g. of Khnûm(u), does not enjoy any prominence; and although in later times Amon had a ram instead of his earlier goose (p. 129), its worship was not very marked.

A lion was kept, we are told, at Leontopolis for Shu (p. 44); a she-cat was probably honoured at Bubastos (cf. p. 150); and a baboon, in all likelihood, represented Thout at some place (pp. 33–34). Accordingly we may assume the

FIG. 171. ATUM OF HELIOPOLIS

existence of many other sacred animals, arguing from the representations of gods in animal form or with the heads of animals.

None of these creatures, however, gained a prominence comparable with the importance of the animal gods which have
been mentioned above. At Denderah we find,
not a single cow of Ḥat-ḥôr, but a whole herd of
kine, the Ṭentet.

FIG. 172. "ATUM,
THE SPIRIT OF
HELIOPOLIS"

Among rarer mammals of smaller size the
most interesting is the ichneumon, which once
embodied the god Atum of Heliopolis. This
deity, who so very quickly assumed solar functions and a human form (p. 27), nevertheless
appears in animal guise in some pictures from
which we see that the later artists were in doubt
as to what this creature was; e. g. one statue, carrying weapons, has a weasel-like head, or he is shown as an enigmatic

FIG. 173. SHEDETI

animal in the interesting picture of the evening
sun, reproduced in Fig. 11. "Atum, the spirit
(*ka*) of Heliopolis," is clearly an ichneumon.[15]
The like statements apply to a god Shed (more
probably to be pronounced Shedeti, "the One
from the City of Shedet" in the Fayûm); i. e.,
analogously, we later find incorrect pictures of
him like Fig. 174 besides the ichneumon type (Fig. 173), which
was probably original. After 2000 B. C., curiously enough,
this deity bears a Semitic name, Khaturi, or Khatuli ("the
Weasel [?]-Like").[16] Mummies of ichneumons
have also been found at various places in the
Delta, and in later times the whole species
seems to have been sacred.

FIG. 175. THE
PHOENIX

The shrew-mouse is said
to have been dedicated to
the Horus of Chemmis.
Among sacred birds the

FIG. 174.
KHATULI-SHEDETI

most important apparently was the phoe-
nix (*benu;* read *bin, boin*) [17] of Heliopolis, a species of heron
with long crest feathers. It symbolized the sun-god under the

names of Rê' and Osiris (p. 95) and in later times was also their embodiment in the planet Venus (p. 54). In the morning, according to Egyptian belief, the heron, "creating himself,"

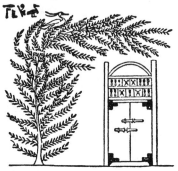

rises in a fragrant flame (p. 28) over the celestial sycamore (or its local representative, the *Persea* of Heliopolis), or as "the soul of Osiris" it rests (at night?) on this tree above the sarcophagus of Osiris, as in the accompanying picture. This forms the transition to the fanciful Greek stories [18] that the phoenix came from Arabia (i. e. the region of sunrise) to the temple of Heliopolis, em-

FIG. 176. "THE SOUL OF OSIRIS" IN A SACRED TREE OVERSHADOWING HIS SARCOPHAGUS-LIKE SHRINE

balmed his father (i. e. Osiris) in an egg (the sun?), and then burned himself. The Greek misunderstanding of his appearance in Egypt only at the end of a long calendric period — variously given as 500, 540, 654, 1000, or 1461 years — seems to show that no heron was kept at Heliopolis in Classical times; but this proves nothing whatever for the earliest period, which was more materialistic in outlook.[19]

The tame crocodile of Sobk-Suchos which was honoured at Arsinoë has become especially famous through the graphic description which Strabo [20] gives of its feeding by pious visitors. According to this author, "it is called Suchos," so that it was regarded, at least by the laity of Roman times, as a real in-carnation of the local deity Sobk.

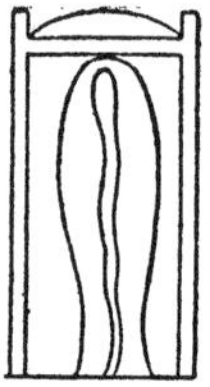

FIG. 177. STATUE OF A GUAR-DIAN SER-PENT IN A CHAPEL

Serpents, which are considered demoniac creatures in so many countries, were objects of especial awe in Egypt as well. Numerous goddesses were worshipped in the form of snakes, or could at least assume this shape, and the serpent was even used as the general hieroglyph for "goddess." It was probably for this reason that pictures of "erect serpents," standing free or in chapels, protected the entrance to the temples, and the geographical lists give the names of the principal "erect snake" kept alive, perhaps in a cage, at each important shrine of the nome, evidently because a tutelary spirit of this form was thought to be necessary for every sacred place, exactly as each had to have a sacred tree. The temple of Denderah even had eight sacred serpents with carefully specified names, although it is not clear whether these were living reptiles or mere images.[21] Mummified frogs, fish, and scarabs may be due rather to the sacredness of an entire species, on which we shall speak below.

Granting that the Egyptians of the historic period had little understanding of the fragments of primitive religion preserved in these remnants of animal worship, we may nevertheless assume that their explanation of this phenomenon by incarnation of gods contains an idea which is partly correct, if stripped of cosmic theories. The unsatisfactory material at our command, however, renders it difficult to determine why we cannot prove a worship of a living incarnation for every deity who is represented on the monuments in a form either wholly or partially animal. We must wonder why, for example, the sacred hawk or hawks of Horus at Edfu (who never has human form) are scarcely mentioned. We might try to explain this by the cosmic *rôle* which this important god assumed at a very early time, so that he accordingly withdrew from earth; and thus we might suppose that the dog of Anubis and the wolf of Ophoïs lost some of their dignity when these deities were attached to the cosmic ideas of the Osirian circle. On the other hand, Nekhbet and Ḥeqet, for example, never became cosmic divinities to a degree which would enable us to explain why we hear nothing positive concerning the cult of their incarnation in a vulture and in a frog. Thus it is difficult to say why numerous local animal cults left only half-effaced traces, while others survived in rather primitive form. It would be wrong to distinguish between such modernized or half-forgotten cults and the few sacred animals which, through the greater importance of their cities, attained high prominence and later enjoyed worship throughout Egypt; this would be a repetition of the error of Strabo,[22] who regarded the obscurer animals as merely sacred, not divine. We have already seen (p. 161) that a distinction between sacred, symbolic animals and those which claimed to be real incarnations of a divinity was too subtle for the Egyptian mind. Neither do the cosmic interpretations of the prominent animals constitute a general difference. These explanations, as we have seen above, are suspiciously uniform and thus betray the influence of the more advanced period.[23] This epoch, seeking the gods in nature and in heaven, must have allowed many places to lose their animal cults, though the old pictures and names still revealed the barbarous origin of the local gods. It was only here and there, it would seem, that local tradition proved strong enough to maintain the ancestral cult without too much modernization.

A different problem presents itself when we consider the sacredness of a whole species of animals as contrasted with the individual sanctity of which we have thus far spoken. It may be either local or universal. The Classical writers describe with sarcasm how a species of animal — the crocodile, for example — was venerated in one nome, while in the one adjoining it was even cursed and persecuted. In most instances of this character we can see that the original sacredness of an individual animal had been extended to the species; a god's relatives also seemed to deserve worship. This explains the case of some creatures, whether wild or domesticated as pets, which were treated with more or less veneration throughout the whole country. Thus, for instance, the Greeks state that the ibis (of Thout), the hawk (of Horus), and the cat (of Bubastis) were everywhere so inviolable that even unintentional killing of them was punished by death (the mob usually lynching the offender), that they were fed by the population or by official keepers, and that after death they were embalmed and buried in collective tombs,[24] some being laid in central tombs at the capital of the nome, while the mummies of others were sent from the whole country to the most important place of worship. Cats, for example, were usually interred in an immense cemetery devoted especially to them at Bubastos. It is quite true that these animals were considered to be merely sacred, and not divine, so that they could not receive prayers and offerings, but the popular mind often failed to observe this subtle distinction and actually termed such sacred creatures "gods." This cult of whole species attained this degree of prominence only in the latest period and seems to have developed gradually from a local veneration of less intense character; on the other hand, it again marks a reversion to some primitive ideas. In like manner, when the snakes inhabiting a house are fed by the owner, the wish to gain protection through such demoniac beings rests on a most primitive animistic conception. When we learn, however, that various kinds of fish might not be eaten, it is not always clear whether this prohibition was based on their sacredness or on a curse.[25] Mummified species of fish prove their sacredness only for later times.

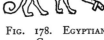

FIG. 178. EGYPTIAN CHIMERA

Fabulous beings which were believed to populate the desert belonged, of course, to the realm of the supernatural and formed the transition to the endless number of strangely mixed forms which more obviously were part of the divine world, inhabiting the sky or the lower regions. We may suppose, moreover, that earthly creatures which fanciful hunters imagined that they had seen in the desert or in the mountains,[26] such as the griffin, the chimera (a winged leopard with a human head projecting from its back), and the lion or leopard with a serpent's neck, which was so popular in the prehistoric period (pp. 64–65), were indistinct recollections of representations which were once worshipped, as well as the double-faced bull (Fig. 2 (d)) and the double lion (p. 43). Indeed, we find all these fabulous beings pictured by magicians side by side with real gods, whether because the sorcerers kept up old traditions, or because

FIG. 179. THE BIRTH OF A KING PROTECTED BY GODS

they returned to forgotten divinities. The sphinx, originally a picture of Ḥu, the god of wisdom (p. 67), survived as an emblem of royalty and in its strictly Egyptian form was always represented as male (for the foreign female sphinx see p. 156 and cf. Fig. 162).

This brings us to the question how far men were worshipped. The most prominent examples of the adoration of human beings were the kings.[27] Every Pharaoh claimed to be a divine incarnation; according to the prevailing official theory he was a "form," or "double," or "soul," or "living representation," etc., of the sun-god, the many souls of this deity (pp. 28, 160) facilitating such a belief. As the living image of the sun the king might also claim to have himself many souls or "doubles" (ka), the number of these being as high as fourteen.[28] Accordingly we find such royal names as "Firm is the Form of the Sun-God" (Men-kheper-rê‘, i. e. Thutmosis III), or "Finest of the Forms of the Sun-God" (Nefr-khepru-rê‘, i.e. Amen-ḥotep IV before his heresy),

FIG. 180. THE KA OF A KING, BEARING HIS NAME AND A STAFF - SYMBOL INDICATING LIFE

etc. The pompous titles of the monarchs as "the good god," etc., were no mere poetic licence, but were meant to be taken

1   2

3

PLATE II

1. AMEN-ḤOTEP. The divinization of men is by no means restricted to Egyptian mythology.

2. I-M-ḤOTEP. This scholar became so famous that ultimately he was believed to be of divine ancestry and was regarded as a son of the god Ptaḥ.

3. THE ZODIACAL SIGNS. This picture, dating from the Roman period, shows the blending of Egyptian and Classical conceptions. See pp. 57, 65.

quite literally. "Birth-temples" were erected to commemorate the birth of each new king and to describe and glorify in
inscription and in picture the conception and advent of the
new divinity sent from the skies to be the terrestrial representative of the gods and to rule that land which reproduced
heaven on earth.[29] The full divinity of the Pharaoh was manifested, however, only at his coronation, which was accordingly
commemorated similarly in memorial temples. We also find
kings sacrificing and praying to the divine spirit resident in
themselves, or to their own *ka* ("double," or "soul"), which
was distinguished from their earthly personality and which
was thought to follow them as a kind of guardian spirit.
After death the Pharaoh was held to be a new manifestation
of Osiris, and in some cases the worship of the dead ruler
sought to excel the honour which had been paid him while
he was alive. This was the case, e. g., with the short-lived
Amen-ḥotep I, who became the divine ruler of a part of the
Theban necropolis, for which his burial probably opened a new
tract of land. In similar fashion great builders might receive
divine honours near their monuments, as did "Pramarres"
(Amen-em-ḥêt III, of the Twelfth Dynasty) in the Fayûm,
which he seems to have reclaimed from the lake.[30] Even
private citizens of extraordinary ability might receive worship
as saints and subsequently rise to the rank of gods. The
princely scholar I-m-ḥotep of the Fourth Dynasty became so
famous for his learning that in the latest period he was the
patron of all scholars, and especially of physicians, whence
the Greeks explained "Imuthes" as the Egyptian Asklepios.
He is represented as a seated priest with shaven head, holding a book on his knees. Here royal blood may have contributed somewhat, but we also find Amen-ḥotep, the son of
Ḥap(u), the prime minister of Amen-ḥotep III, worshipped as
a famous scholar at his memorial sanctuary at Dêr el-Medi-
neh;[31] and there were some similar minor saints, such as two
at Dandur in Nubia who were called "the genius" (*shay;* cf.

p. 52 for this expression) of the locality and "Osiris, much praised in the underworld."[32]

Generally speaking, all the dead might be worshipped on the theory that as blessed spirits they lived with the gods in a state of illumination and sanctification. Their chapels were, however, places to pray for them rather than to pray to them; and the sacrifices offered there were not to win their intercession, but served merely to maintain their hungry souls (p. 177). Contrary to the usual belief, therefore, the worship of ancestors, as we shall see in the following chapter, was not so clearly and strongly developed in ancient Egypt as among some other peoples.

CHAPTER X

LIFE AFTER DEATH

THE doctrine of life after death [1] was so richly developed in ancient Egypt that here we can sketch only a few of its most remarkable features. It would require an entire volume to do justice to this chapter, for no people ever showed so much care for the dead as the Egyptians, or so much imagination about the life hereafter.

Even in the earliest prehistoric times the soul was believed to be immortal, as is shown by the gifts of food, drink, and ornaments found in all graves of that period. There only a large tray or pot placed over the bodies, which were interred in a crouching position, or a few stones or mud bricks show gradual efforts to guard the dead against the animals of the desert; but the large tombs of the kings at the beginning of the Dynastic Period commence to betray precisely the same care for the existence of the departed as was manifested in later times. In the Pyramid Period embalmment begins with the kings, increasing care is given to the tombs of private citizens, and rich inscriptions reveal to us most of the views about life after death which the later Egyptians kept so faithfully. We see from them that in the earliest period as well as in the latest the most contradictory views reigned concerning life after death, in harmony with the general character of Egyptian religion, which desired to preserve all ancestral opinions as equally sacred without examining them too closely and without systematizing them.

We may infer that the most primitive period held that the spirits of the dead haunted the wide desert where the graves were situated, filling the stony mountains of this inhospitable region by night. In consequence of their miserable abode and hard existence such spirits were not very safe company for the

wanderer in the desert. The best wish for the soul of one's relatives may have been that it might become the most dangerous among all those demons, feared and respected by the rest. The custom of placing all

FIG. 181.
THE SOUL-
BIRD

kinds of weapons beside the dead to protect him in this life of danger, in which he is hunted by the terrible demons of the desert or of the underworld, also looks like a remnant of such primitive ideas, although it survived until the New Empire.[2]

The soul of man is usually depicted as a human-headed bird fluttering from his mouth at death. An earlier term for "soul," *ka* (or *kai* ?),[3] the hieroglyphic symbol of which is two uplifted arms, as in Fig. 180, seems to imply that the soul continues to live in the form of a shadowy double of the body. In the New Empire especially the defunct soul is distinctly identified with the shadow, which is symbolized by the silhouette of the body or by the hieroglyph of a parasol (cf. Fig. 189). Some very late theologians sought to distinguish the three synonyms, "double," "soul," and "shadow," as different parts of the soul and occasionally even added as a fourth element the "illuminated soul," or *ikh(u)*. No decision was ever reached as to whether the soul continued to live in the corpse, returning, some believed, from the realm of the dead after its purification (i. e. mummification), either forever or from time to time; or whether it stayed in or near the grave, or roamed in the

FIG. 182.
THE SOUL RETURN-
ING TO THE BODY

desert, or went far hence to the place of Osiris. The funerary texts and burial preparations of the wealthier classes tried to take all these different views into account, although they gave preference to the last theory, as being the most advanced. For the first possibility all care is

taken to protect and preserve the corpse;[4] if, nevertheless, the
body should decay, the soul may settle in one or more portrait
statues placed in the grave. There food is prepared, either
actually (meat being sometimes embalmed), or
in imitations in stone, clay, or wood, or in pictures and written magic formulae, these material offerings being renewed on festival days.
Prayers also express the wish that the dead may
be able to leave his tomb and to appear not
merely by night, when all spirits are freed to
haunt the earth, but also by day, taking whatever form it may choose. For this the shape of

Fig. 183. The
Soul Returns
to the Grave

several birds is preferred, although even the crocodile, the
snake, the grasshopper, and the flower are considered.[5] The
spirit desires to visit his home — a belief which is not always
pleasant for the superstitious inmates[6] — or if it roams in
the desert, the tomb ought to open itself to house it again.
A little ladder assists the dead to ascend to heaven, or a small
model of a ship enables him to sail to or over it, or prayer and
magic help his soul to fly up to the stars. The way to the remote realm of Osiris is indeed blocked by many difficulties.
Evil spirits threaten to devour the soul; dozens of gates are
watched by monstrous guardians armed with knives (the
"knife-bearers") or with sharp teeth and claws; broad rivers

Fig. 184. The Dead Visits
his House

and steep mountains must be passed,
etc. Magic formulae and pictures for
overcoming all these obstacles are placed
on the walls of the tomb or on the sarcophagus, are later included in books
laid near the mummy or inside it (e. g.
in its arm-pit), and finally are even
written on the wrappings round the
mummy. Thus the rich literature of semi-magic illustrated
guide-books for the dead developed, above all the great collection which we call the *Book of the Dead*.[7]

These texts and other magic aids assisted the dead to over-
come all obstacles, to be carried by strange ferries across the
Stygian river or the ocean, to fly to heaven in the form of a bird
or of an insect or to be transported thither on the wings of gods
or of their messengers, to climb to the celestial heights by the
heavenly tree or by a ladder or to walk to them over the mountains of the west, to open the door of heaven or to descend the
long subterranean roads leading to the underworld. The last
and most serious difficulty awaited the departed when finally
he approached the judgement hall or court of Osiris for examination of his life on earth. There he expected to be brought

before the throne of this god and his as-
sembly of forty-two assessors,[8] most of whom
were monsters of horrible aspect and terrible names, such as "Blood-Drinker,"
"Bone-Breaker," or "Shadow-Swallower." [9]
His heart was weighed by Thout and his
cynocephalous baboon (p. 33)[10] and by
Anubis (p. 111); and he himself read from his
guide-book the "Negative Confession," enumerating forty-two sins of which he declared

FIG. 185. THE DEAD
WANDERS OVER A
MOUNTAIN TO THE
SEAT OF OSIRIS

himself guiltless, triumphantly exclaiming at the end, "I am
pure, I am pure." He was then admitted to the realm of
Osiris, which is described as situated in heaven or in a deep
hole (tephet) under the earth, or between sky and earth; according to the earliest theory, it ascended and descended in the stars
(p. 97) which form the "divine fields." In the oldest texts the
ferry to that land is usually described as sailing on the dark
waters which come from the realm of Khnûm (the lower
world), i. e. on the subterranean Nile and the abyss (p. 89);
the latter, however, leads to the great terrestrial ocean and its
continuation in the sky, which likewise receive description as
being the way to Osiris (p. 95). For the strange ferryman
"who looks backward, whose face is backward," see p. 58.

In company with the gods the departed lead a life of luxury, clad in fine linen and eating especially grapes and figs "from the divine garden," [11] bread from the granary of the deities, or even more miraculous food, as from the tree of life or similar wonderful plants which grow in the various "meadows" or "fields";[12] sometimes they are even expected to drink milk from the breasts of the goddesses or water from the fountain of life (Fig. 89), which was often identified with the source of the Nile (p. 95). Such food gives eternal life and divine nature. More modest is the expectation of a farmer's life in prolific fields which the dead plough, sow, and reap under the direction of Osiris. Since this still remains a laborious existence, subsequently little proxies of wood or earthenware, the *ushebtiu* ("answerers"),[13] are expected to answer for the departed when Osiris calls his name, bidding him work and wield the wooden hoe in the heavenly fields. While the peasants will be glad to toil for Osiris as they did in their earthly existence, the nobles desire a new life of greater leisure. Various pastimes are considered in the other world, as when the dead wishes to play at draughts (sometimes, according to later texts, with his own soul).[14] In the belief of the period from 3000 to 1800 B.C. the figures of bakers, butchers, and other servants which were put into the grave provided for the food and comfort of the dead, saving him from toil; and the human sacrifices described below may have had the same purpose of furnishing servants for the departed.

This brings us back to the fact that, after all, man dares not depend entirely on celestial nourishment. Do not the gods themselves, though surrounded by all kinds of miraculous food and drink, need the sacrifices of man? From such beliefs arise the many preparations which we have described for feeding the soul in or near the grave, or for providing food even for its life in the more remote other-world. Precautions for all contingencies are advisable, since no fate of a soul is more sad for it than to be compelled, in its ravenous hunger and thirst, to live on offal and even to swallow its own excreta. Accord-

ingly it was the anxious wish of every Egyptian to have children to provide sacrifices for his soul; and the first duty of each
man, according to the moral maxims of Ani, was, "Pour libations of water for thy father and thy mother, who rest in the
valley. . . . Thy son shall do the same for thee." Wretched
indeed is the soul of the childless, who has none to remember
him!

This care for the feeding of the departed seems to us, of
course, in flagrant contradiction to the condition which the
dead ought to enjoy according to the higher views. They are
not merely with the gods, but they completely share their life
of luxury. They sit on thrones in the circumpolar region of the
sky, where the highest divinities dwell (p. 55); or they perch
like birds on the branches of the celestial tree, i. e. they become
stars (p. 35), even some very prominent stellar bodies which
are usually identified with the greatest deities. As rowers or
soldiers they take a place in the ship in which the sun-god
sails over the celestial ocean,[15] or they sit in the cabin as honoured guests and are rowed by the god, as in Fig. 7. They
actually become like Osiris, the personification of resurrection,
to such an extent that they are kings and judges of the departed, wherefore each one who has passed away, whether
male or female, is addressed as "Osiris N. N." Deceased
women are later styled also "Ḥat-ḥôr N. N." With Osiris
the dead may assume a solar, lunar, or stellar character and
may appear as this same deity in the other manifestations of
nature. The *Book of the Dead*, however, prays also that the
deceased may become in general a god and that he may be
identified with Ptaḥ, etc.[16]

Many of these expectations were originally suitable only for
the kings, who, being divine in their lifetime, claimed an exalted
position after death; yet just as the costly burial customs were
gradually extended from the Pharaohs to the nobles and thence
to the common folk, those high hopes of future life were soon
appropriated by the nobility and finally by the ordinary popu-

lace. Thus "followers of Horus" (or of Rê' or Osiris)[17] quickly
came to mean simply "the blessed dead," although primarily
it seems to have been restricted to the kings, who alone had
a right to be ad-
mitted to the
solar bark. On
the other hand,
side by side with
these extrava-
gant desires we
are told that the
hopes of some
of the wealthy

Fig. 186. The Dead before Osiris, the Balance of Justice, the Lake of Fire, and "the Swallower"

would be satisfied if their souls might dwell in their spacious
and comfortable tombs, sit on the green trees without, and
drink from the artificial lake that lay there; nor were the very
modest expectations of the peasants forgotten whose highest
longing was to dig the grounds in the fields of Osiris (p. 177).
The *Book of the Dead* describes all these hopes and desires that
each and every one of them may be realized.

These pleasant promises are only for the worthy. The souls
of the wicked are soon annihilated by the multitude of demons
who inhabit the underworld or by the stern guardians who
watch the roads and gates to the kingdom of Osiris. If they
reach his tribunal, they are condemned to a second death.

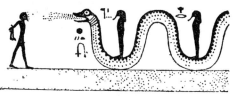

Fig. 187. The Condemned before the Dragon

The forty-two terrible
judges themselves may
tear them to pieces im-
mediately; or the mon-
strous watch-dog of
Osiris,"the swallower,"[18]
or "swallower of the
west" — a mixture of crocodile, lion, and hippopotamus — may
devour them; or they may be cast before a fire-breathing dragon
who seems to be none other than the dragon 'Apop; or Anubis

or the baboon of Thout will lead them, sometimes in the degrading form of a pig (apparently usually female), to the place of punishment, "the place of slaughter." The doom of these

sinners is a hell filled with flames and biting serpents, or the depths of the abyss in which they will be drowned,[19] or lakes of flames (or of flames in the form of fiery serpents) or of boiling water, or ovens in which we see the burning of heads (as the seats of life)

FIG. 188. SHADES SWIMMING IN
THE ABYSS

or of the shades (as in the accompanying picture; cf. p. 174); or swarms of evil spirits, armed with knives (p. 175) to behead or dissect the souls, will execute the wicked. At the place of torture Thout, as the god of justice, has his four baboons [20] who watch the lake of fire or catch the souls of the condemned in a net to deliver them to torment (for the net cf. p. 109). These punishments mean instantaneous annihilation or long agony, as does also life with one's head hanging downward, although eternal torture is nowhere so clearly stated as eternal bliss.[21]

The view that only virtue and piety toward the gods free man from such an evil fate and secure him bliss can be traced in its beginnings to the Pyramid Period, and officially it predominates in general after the Middle Empire. Even kings are subject to it and expect to recite the "Negative Confession" before the tribunal of Osi-

FIG. 189. A FEMALE GUARDIAN WITH FIERY BREATH
WATCHES SOULS, SYMBOLIZED BY SHADES AND HEADS,
IN THE OVENS OF HELL

ris, although in our chapter on magic we shall find some strange passages which place the Pharaoh beyond all justice and above the gods themselves, thus forming a marked contrast to the general teaching. This ethical theory, however, was never able entirely to displace the more primitive view that bliss for the dead could be mechanically secured after death by sacrifices, prayers, and religious ceremonies which might be considered magical from the point of view of a more advanced religion. The equipment of the dead with endless amulets and with writings and pictures of a semi-magic character, such as we have described on p. 175, is likewise quite essential for every one. In later times embalmment also was counted among these mechanical means (p. 111), for it had been forgotten that the only object of the mummification of the body and the preservation of the most important viscera in canopic vases (p. 112) was to keep an abode for the soul. It was then believed that Osiris was the first to be mummified, and that embalmment by the fingers of Anubis had secured for him eternal life. This seems likewise to have been the purpose of a strange and diametrically opposite custom which was ir-

FIG. 190. 'THOUT'S BABOONS FISHING SOULS

regularly applied to the dead from prehistoric times to the Pyramid Period and according to which the corpse was cut into a larger or smaller number of pieces. The idea seems to have been that if Osiris met such a fate, and if the fragments of his body were afterward put together for a blessed life (pp. 114–15), it was wise to imitate this feature of the Osiris-tradition and thus to provide perfect identity with the king of the dead.[22] At the funeral the priest and the sacred scribe may have appeared to the popular mind mostly as sorcerers whose paid services were more important for the future of the departed than his past virtues. Thus when with a strange hook the priest touched the mouth of the dead "to open it," it was wrong to doubt that he gave the mummy power to speak in the other world, etc. It is quite possible that all these mechanical

means were even considered capable of cheating the divine
judges of the dead, although their omniscience was affirmed
with sufficient clearness. Such a conflict of ideas can, however,
be found in many other religions as well.

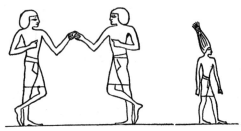

FIG. 191. DANCERS AND A BUFFOON AT A FUNERAL

The details of the
cult of the dead cannot
be described here. The
ceremonies at the burial
were endless and were
very complicated in
character, frequently
representing the thought and the customs of very different
ages. Thus at funerals of the wealthy in the sixteenth century B. C. companies of wailing women, beating their breasts
and filling the air with their cries, accompanied the funeral procession, together with male dancers, tumblers, and buffoons,
some of them in strange costume. Equally endless were the
preparations for the comfort of the dead in their tombs or in
the other world. As we have already said (p. 172), however,
the leading idea of the entire cult of the dead was merely
the feeding and com-
fort of the souls, not
worship of the ances-
tors as divine. This
also accounts for the
heartless neglect of
the dead who did not
belong to the family.
Households of wealth
could not do enough
for their members,

FIG. 192. LARGE SACRIFICE BROUGHT BEFORE A
SEPULCHRAL CHAPEL IN THE PYRAMID PERIOD

e. g. by sumptuous burial and by the erection of costly tombs
decorated by the best efforts of painters and sculptors, and
filled with furniture, ornaments, etc., for the use of the de-

parted;[23] at certain festivals the altars of the memorial chapels seem to have been heaped with food, and for the maintenance of these cults large foundations of fields, money, and slaves were often established. Yet when all had died who took a personal interest in these particular departed, no one was ashamed to appropriate the unprotected tomb for his own dead, to replace the name of the first proprietor by new inscriptions, and to use certain parts of the funerary outfit a second time. It is less surprising that most tombs containing valuables were plundered in antiquity and that even great numbers of police were unable constantly to protect the jewellery in royal tombs; there was too much poverty in the ancient Orient. Even kings showed piety only toward the buildings of their nearest ancestors and were not ashamed to efface the names of earlier monarchs from their ancient monuments to replace them by their own titles, or to pull down the older buildings and to use the stones, though they thus abandoned the victims of their recklessness to oblivion, a most dreadful fate which entailed neglect and hunger for their souls (p. 177). Sooner or later sequestration was the fate of foundations for sacrifices to souls, even those of the Pharaohs of past dynasties. This proves that there was no really serious fear of the dead and that the deification of the departed to which we have repeatedly alluded must not be overestimated. In this also we again recognize the crude animism from which the religion had developed.

CHAPTER XI

ETHICS AND CULT

THIS chapter may be connected with the preceding by a hymn which, according to the *Book of the Dead*,[1] the departed is supposed to address to Osiris and his tribunal when he is brought before them.

"Hail to thee, O great god, lord of the judges!
I have come to thee, my lord;
I have been brought to see thy beauty.
I know thee and the names of the forty-two gods
Who are with thee in the court of judges,
Who live cutting the sinful in pieces,[2]
Who fill themselves with their blood
On that day of taking account of words before Unen-nofer (p. 97)
Near his [variant: thy] two daughters, (his) two eyes.[3]
Lord of Justice is thy name.
I have come to thee,
I have brought justice to thee,
I have removed wickedness away for thee.
I have not done wrong to men,
I did not oppress [variant: kill] relatives,
I did not commit deceit in the place of justice,
I did not know transgression [variant: worthless things]."

The text then rambles on in an enumeration of special sins which the deceased declares that he has not committed, one of the so-called "Negative Confessions" (see p. 176 and below).

It is very difficult to judge the morality of a nation from a distance of several thousand years and from scanty material derived chiefly from cemeteries. Such inscriptions create an exaggerated impression of piety by which we must not be deceived, just as we must not permit ourselves to be misled by the elaborate preparations for life after death. This latter

feature did not make the Egyptians a nation of stern philos-
ophers, as modern people so often believe. On the contrary,
their manners were gay to the point of frivolity, and their many
superstitions were but a feeble barrier to their light-hearted-
ness. The most popular song at banquets[4] was an exhortation
to use every day for pleasure and to enjoy life "until the day
shall come to depart for the land whence none returns." It is
better to use one's means for luxuries than for the grave; even
the tombs of the greatest and wisest, like the deified I-m-ḥotep
(p. 171), are now deserted and forgotten. This contradiction of
the dominant view of the value of care for the dead is no more
flagrant than the conflict between the rules for the conduct of
life, as laid down in the books of the wise,[5] and the actual ob-
servance of these rules. All the sages, for example, warn against
drunkenness from a practical point of view, yet drunkenness
seems to have been the most common vice in ancient Egypt;[6]
and similar conditions may be proved to have existed in many
things forbidden by the moral as well as by the religious books.

On the other hand, the code of morals of these sources is
theoretically of the very highest type. Thus the "Negative
Confessions" of the Book of the Dead [7] include among cardinal
sins even falsehood, slander, gossip, (excessive?) grief, cursing,
boasting, unkindness to animals (even to harmless wild ones),
extinguishing the fire (when needed by others?), damming
water (for private use), polluting the river, etc. Other texts
inform us that it was considered (by some?) sinful to destroy
life even in the egg. Formal restrictions about clean and
unclean things seem to have been numerous, although we
know little about them. When, for instance, we read in
Genesis xliii. 32 that "the Egyptians might not eat bread with
the Hebrews; for that is an abomination unto the Egyptians,"
this probably means that all foreigners were held to be cere-
monially unclean. It is strange that the prohibition of pork
does not seem to have developed until later, probably after
1600 B. C. (for the reasons see Ch. V, Note 33); but subsequently

the pig was the most unclean animal imaginable, completely defiling whatever it touched. Greek writers state that cows were not killed, evidently because of the celestial cow (p. 37) and the goddesses identified with her. Many kinds of fish were forbidden (p. 169) — in some localities all fish — and then (in most places?) the heads of killed animals were prohibited, not because they were unclean, but because, as the seat of life, they belonged to the gods, so that the head was regularly offered at sacrifices. Blood was, perhaps, only locally unclean for the Egyptians. At present it is difficult to decide which of these rules for clean and unclean were really local in origin, and which sprang from tabus of holiness rather than from tabus of abhorrence (see Ch. I, Note 3). Special laws of clean and unclean existed for the sacrificial animals. Some rules, e. g. for the uncleanness of women at certain times, are general. Circumcision existed in Egypt from time immemorial, but had no religious character and was merely a preparation for marriage; it applied to girls as well as to boys. Restrictions of marriage because of kinship seem scarcely to have existed. Marriage with a sister was a very common custom (p. 119), and Ramses II appears to have taken his own daughter, Bent-'anat, to wife. Polygamy was unlimited in theory, though not very extensive in practice.

If we may believe the epitaphs, charity to the needy — "giving bread to the hungry, water to the thirsty, clothing to the naked, a ship to the stranded" — protection of the weak, honesty, etc., were observed in a manner which would satisfy even the highest moral demands.[8] Unfortunately, however, we also read of many crimes, especially of wicked and oppressive officials; and among the nations the reputation of the Egyptians was never brilliant. Practically they appear, as we have already stated (p. 185), to have been of rather lax morality in many respects.

One of the reasons for this may be found in the dry formalism of the religion. Being too strongly fettered to the imperfect beliefs of crude ancestors by the bonds of traditionalism, religion could not attain sufficient spiritual development, and thus failed to emphasize the ethical side as seriously as some other pagan faiths. It is quite true that, as we have already seen (p. 180), the belief that the soul's salvation depends principally on a moral life is old, and that after 2000 B.C. it was formulated with increasing clearness. Yet

FIG. 193. TEMPLES OF THE EARLIEST PERIOD

the earliest forerunner of the "Negative Confession," a passage in the Pyramid Texts, which claims that a man's soul can ascend to heaven because of his morality, still rests on a purely formal righteousness.

> "He hath not cursed the King;
> He hath not mocked (?) the goddess Ubastet;
> He hath not danced at the tomb of Osiris (?)." [9]

When, therefore, we learn that the ferryman of the gods will transport to heaven only the "just dead," we must not think of justice in the sense of the New Testament (for the funerary formalism which conflicts with the idea of ethical justice see p. 181). Some development toward higher ethical ideals and a more personal piety may, however, be traced after 1500 B.C., as we shall see in our concluding chapter.

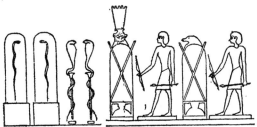

FIG. 194. GUARDIAN STATUES AND GUARDIAN SERPENTS OF A TEMPLE

The temples of prehistoric times were mere huts of primitive form and light material (mats, wicker-work, or straw) enclosing an idol. A fence and, perhaps, a small court protected the entrance, which one of our pictures represents decorated with horns above and with poles at the sides. Later

the wonderful development of architecture made the temples
large buildings of stone; only the outer courts usually had
walls of mud bricks. The road leading to the temple was generally spacious, well kept for processions, and lined with statues
(principally sphinxes and other sacred animals) to guard the
entrance against evil powers (cf. pp. 166–67 on the guardian
serpents). The front wall formed two high, tower-like buildings,

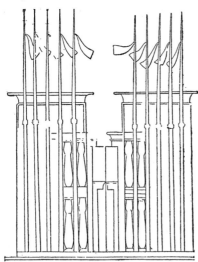

the so-called pylons, which,
decorated with flagstaffs and
pictures of large dimensions,
flanked the entrance. Before
them usually stood two obelisks of granite, whose most
important part was the py-
ramidal point, the *benben,* or
pyramidion, which was sometimes made of metal (for the
cosmic signification of the obelisk, which was probably repeated in the pylon, see p. 31).
Behind the pylons generally
came a large court where the
laity might assemble and wit-

FIG. 195. FRONT OF A TEMPLE ACCORDING
TO AN EGYPTIAN PICTURE

ness sacrifices, next there was a dimly lighted, columned hall in
which the priests gathered, and finally the holiest place of all,
a dark chamber (the adytum), accessible to the higher priesthood alone. Here the principal idol or the sacred animal
dwelt, often housed in a chapel-like shrine, or *naos,* which, if
possible, was cut from a single stone. Round the adytum
were small magazines in which some of the divine outfit and
ceremonial utensils and books were kept. In larger temples
the number of rooms might be greater, but those which we
have just mentioned were the essential parts. Where several
gods were worshipped in one temple, each divinity might have
a special adytum, so that practically several parallel shrines

were combined, though not always under the same roof; the idols of a triad (p. 20), at least, were generally united in a single adytum. Larger temples had kitchens for the offerings and festal meals, laboratories for the preparation of the sacred perfumes and cakes, shops for the manufacture of the amulets which were sold to pilgrims, etc.; and round them were houses for the priests and granaries for their food, so that they even formed large sacred cities.

In place of the divine statues, to whose simplicity we have already alluded (p. 12), we sometimes find pillars with the head of the divinity, like the Greek herms,[10] or with divine emblems. Such "sceptres" or "columns," occasionally as tall as obelisks, are mentioned as objects of worship, and (Fig. 196) we find the king bringing sacrifices to them as "gods." [11] Their more original meaning is unknown, so that we cannot say to what extent they were analogous to the sacred pillars of the Semites.

The decoration of the temples was very uniform in so far as the ceiling was always painted blue to represent the sky (usually with indication of the stars and sometimes with elaborate pictures of the constellations), while the ground is green and blue like meadows or the Nile, so that each temple is a reproduction of the world, a microcosm. The outer walls represent the deeds of the royal builder, often his wars, for the laity; the inner walls depict the worship of the gods for the priests.

This description of the normal temple does not apply to all religious buildings. The funerary shrines for the cult of the souls of deceased kings present peculiarities,[12] as do those which commemorate exclusively the birth or enthronement of a king (p. 171) or the more extensive constructions which were erected when a Pharaoh celebrated the so-called "jubilee of thirty years," etc.[13] Some large sanctuaries built by the kings of the Fifth Dynasty are quite unique: on a large base, surrounded by courts with altars, stands a single obelisk, whose proportions are too huge to be monolithic. These were erected in honour of the sun-god, whose ship, constructed of bricks,

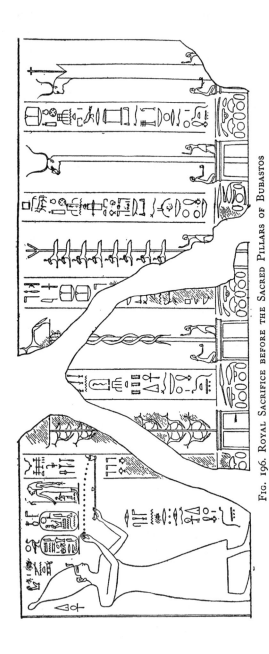

Fig. 196. Royal Sacrifice before the Sacred Pillars of Bubastos

was in the immediate vicinity, or as his resting-place. The
mural decorations of these sanctuaries are also unusual and
depict very worldly scenes.

The priests were divided into various classes:[14] some officiated regularly,
while others had secular employment
and came to the temple only from
time to time, the so-called "priests for
hours"; or their priesthood was purely
nominal, as in the case of many nobles.
In the earlier period the priesthood
and the laity were not distinctly separated. The king's position as the
highest priest of the nation was due
to his divinity (p. 170). He was the

Fig. 197. The King Offering
Incense and Keeping a
Meat-Offering Warm

proper intercessor with the gods, and from time immemorial
a "sacrifice offered by the king" was desired for every one
who died, since it was sure to please the deities and to secure
eternal life. Before long, however, this high-priesthood of the
Pharaoh became merely a fiction, and in the New Empire we
find sharp conflicts between the royal power and the hierarchy,
while in later times the priests formed almost as distinct a class
as was the case in ancient Israel.

Priestesses were permitted only for
female divinities, the greater number
of these women being found in the
earlier period; and their rank was inferior to that of male priests of the
same cult. In the worship of male
divinities women ordinarily formed
only the choir which sang before the

Fig. 198. Temple Choir in Unusual Costume

god, rattled *sistra* and peculiar chains, and danced; in later
times noble women were fond of calling themselves "musicians
of the god N. N." Herodotus correctly observes [15] that women
did not enjoy full priestly standing, and we must not be misled

by the later Greek usage of applying the name of "priestesses" to those who performed the services which we have
noted.[16] A semi-priestly position was also held by the "twin

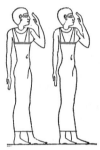

sisters" in temples of Osiris, where they probably represented the twins Isis and Nephthys.
The exact status of other women, called "the
harem of the god, the women bound" (i. e. to
the temple), is not clear. Were they temple
slaves? When the kings of later days dedicated one of their daughters to Amon under
the title of "wife" or "worshipper of the god,"
this seems to be nothing more than a pious
form for the sequestration of the excessive
amount of land held by the Theban temple of
Amon; and thus the princess had a pleasant
sinecure for occasionally "playing the *sistrum*"

FIG. 199.
TWO WOMEN REP-
RESENTING ISIS
AND NEPHTHYS AS
MOURNERS AT
PROCESSIONS

before the god as his "wife." The position held in the earlier
period in the temple of Amon by the solitary, female personage called "the worshipper of the god"
is uncertain.

Peculiar symbolic names were attached to the more
important priestly offices, as when the high-priest of
Heliopolis was called "the great seer" (i. e., probably, astronomer; cf. p. 54), or the high-priest of
Ptaḥ was "the chief artificer" (p. 145). Even the
lower orders of the priesthood sometimes received
a wealth of such names, which were intelligible only
to the local scholars; and dress and insignia likewise
had endless local variations. The incomes of the
sanctuaries varied from princely wealth, derived

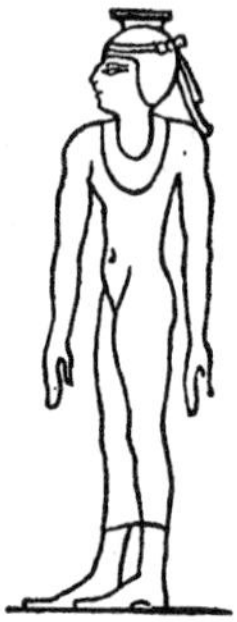

FIG. 200.
"THE WOR-
SHIPPER
OF THE
GOD"

from hundreds of villages of serfs with their fields, to meagre
stipends for the one or two priests who constituted the
whole staff of a little temple.

All priests were obliged to be scrupulously clean, especially
for the sacrifices. Their shaven heads and beards, their white

linen clothing, their special lustrations, and their abstention
from certain foods, etc., were intended to prevent any defile-
ment of the sacred places and ceremonies. Besides
the washable garments, the leopard's skin played
an important part in the ritual, being the regular
vestment of some priestly classes, the "wearers of
the leopard's skin" (p. 134), evidently as a remnant of the primitive times when wild animals
abounded in Egypt. Other details of priestly
dress also date from a very early period, such as

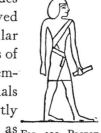

FIG. 201. PRIEST
WITH THE BOOK
OF RITUAL

the strange side-locks of some orders which the
Egyptians of historic times retained only for small
boys, and later for royal sons. On the other hand,
the shaving of the head and beard seems, in general,
to be lacking in the Pyramid Age for priests. Ceremonial cleanness, however, appears at all times to
have been almost more important than moral sanctity. Even the layman might not enter the temples
without carefully purifying himself; but in later times

FIG. 202.
ARCHAISTIC
PRIESTLY
ADORNMENT

this cleansing became a per-
functory ceremony of sprink-
ling with holy water from
vessels at the entrance to the temple,
or turning a brass wheel from which
(originally?) water ran, or merely pulling a brass ring at the gate.[17]

In the temples the priests performed
endless rites from early morning, when
they broke the seals of clay which had
protected the sacred rooms during the
night, till evening fell; sometimes the
night also was celebrated with lighted
lamps, as on the eve of major festivals.

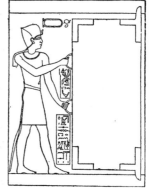

FIG. 203. A KING PULLING
THE RING AT THE TEMPLE
DOOR

Adoration of the deities by bowing, prostration, recitation of
hymns, burning of incense, libations, etc., was practically con-

tinuous, and groups of priests took these services by turns. At
certain times the idols had to be washed, anointed, and per-
fumed with oil and in-
cense; their eyes were
painted,[18] and their
clothing and golden
decorations were
changed. Sometimes
they were taken out in
procession to encircle
the temple (p. 31) or
to traverse the city, or
even to visit a neigh-
bouring divinity. On

FIG. 204. A GOD CARRIED IN PROCESSION

such excursions the god generally was carried on the shoulders
of the priests; and usually the portable shrine
had the form of a ship, not so much because
travelling was done chiefly on the Nile as because all the gods ought to sail on the heavenly ocean (p. 34). The sacred lake near the
temple (p. 31) often symbolized this ocean,
the source of life, etc.; the god sailed on it or
was bathed in it. Thus there were endless
reproductions of mythological scenes, whether

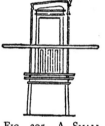

FIG. 205. A SMALL
PORTABLE SHRINE

quiet ceremonies in the adytum of the shrine, or long spec-
tacular performances (especially of the Osiris-myth) for the

FIG. 206. MYTHOLOGICAL SCENES FROM A PROCESSION [19]

public, frequently embellished with music, dancers, and acro-
bats. Sometimes the general public might take part in these
"miracle plays" and reproduce, for example, mythological

battles by a combat between two sides. Numerous festivals, occasionally lasting for several days, gave the populace an opportunity to eat and drink to excess in honour of the gods. Sometimes the sanctuary distributed bread to the multitude for this purpose, but the principal banquets to the glory of the divinity were held in the temple by the priests and some guests, either from the income of the shrine or from special donations.

FIG. 207. AN ACROBAT FOLLOWING A SACRIFI-CIAL ANIMAL

The festival days varied, of course, according to the local cults. It would seem, however, that the great calendric feasts were observed in all, or almost all, sanctuaries, such as the five epagomenal days (p. 113), the New Year, the first, sixth, and middle (fifteenth) day of every month (pp. 90–91), etc., even when the deity worshipped in the temple was not associated with sun, moon, or sky.

The many and richly varied sacrifices of food which the monuments depict were evidently used for the maintenance of

FIG. 208. SMALL HOLOCAUSTIC SACRIFICE ON AN OVEN

the priesthood after they had been spread before the gods. Sending them to heaven by burning was always known, but was not so popular as in Asia, since the deities were almost invariably thought to be present.[20] The original theory of the sacrifices seems to have been a simple feeding of the divinities; e. g. nò oracles appear to have been sought from them. Nevertheless much symbolism attached to them. Thus far we do not know why a sacrifice of the highest type consisted of four bullocks of different colour (spotted, red, white, and black), or of four different sorts of game; and we are equally ignorant as to why at certain festivals a pig was offered at a time when this animal had already come to be considered very unclean, etc. Sometimes, as in foundation sacrifices,

images of pottery, etc., were substituted for the expensive
sacrificial animals (cf. p. 175 for this custom of substitution,
and see *infra* for its use instead of human victims). In the

FIG. 209. HUMAN SACRIFICE AT
A ROYAL TOMB OF THE FIRST
DYNASTY

symbolism dominant in the Græco-
Roman period [21] the sacrificial animals represent the enemies of the
gods; red or brown animals or reptiles in particular symbolize Sêth.
Accordingly the object in killing and
burning them was simply to please
the gods; the use of the meat as food
is scarcely mentioned. Evidently this
is a late development of the holocaustic offerings, dependent
principally on the transformation of Sêth into a Satan (p. 109);
and it may also transfer to the animal victims a subsequent
theory of human sacrifice. Concerning the latter type of offerings we possess almost no information. Nevertheless we may
infer that it was employed in earlier times, since in the latest
period cakes in the shape of men and animals were given to
the gods as an avowed substitute for human sacrifices. We
learn, moreover, that human victims were still burned at

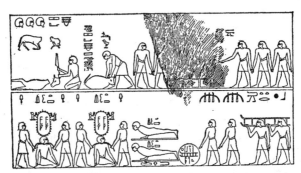

FIG. 210. NUBIAN SLAVES STRANGLED AND BURNED AT A FUNERAL

Eileithyiaspolis even in the time of Plutarch.[22] The former importance of the offering of men is also manifest from certain
pictures which show that once upon a time slaves were killed

and buried near their defunct owner or were burned at the
entrance to his tomb, not merely at the funeral of a king, but
even at the burial of wealthy private citizens, as in Fig. 210.[23]
It is possible that we have a trace of such occasional sacrifices in some corpses found in the royal tombs of the Eighteenth Dynasty, and this permits us to infer parallel usages in
the divine cults.

The way in which oracles were given is likewise very obscure.
For a long time they seem to have played a very minor part, at
least politically. One of the earliest instances is a text in which
Ramses II describes how he nominated the high-priest of Amon
by consulting the god himself.[24] The King enumerated before
Amon the names of all officials capable of filling the post and
asked the deity's assent; but "the god was not satisfied with
one of them, except when I told him the name" (of the nom-
inee). In the twelfth century B. C., however, when the priesthood gained greater power than ever, the priests brought before
the deity, either orally or in writing, all political questions and
many legal cases, sometimes of very minor importance. He
decided these problems, as we have just indicated, by saying
"yes" or "no"; but how he did this is not described. Later
we hear little of such direct consultations. Some prophetic
and oracular writings have been preserved; their language is,
naturally, very obscure.[25] The gods also communicated their
will to men by dreams. For the knowledge of lucky and unlucky days and for other practical wisdom of the theologians
see the following chapter.

CHAPTER XII

MAGIC

MAGIC played an important *rôle* in ancient Egypt, where it was perhaps an even more vital factor than in Babylonia.[1] It is, however, very difficult to state where religion ends and magic begins; and to the Egyptian mind magic was merely applied religion. The man who best knew the gods and understood how to please them could obtain from them what he desired. Great theologians were always believed to be sorcerers as well; e.g. the famous scholar Amenhotep, son of Ḥapu,[2] is reported to have been not only a prophet, but also the author of a magical book filled with especially unintelligible *galimatias;* and the great magicians of popular stories are always "ritual priests." This theory of the identity of witchcraft, scholarship, and theology is not specifically Egyptian, but has its parallels in many other religious systems as well.

FIG. 211.
A RITUAL
PRIEST

The very *naïve* Egyptian spirit, which was so unable to distinguish between the material and the supernatural, and the excessive formalism of the worship give us the impression that the whole religion of the Nile-land had a strongly magic character. This is true of most religions which are based on animism (p. 10), yet we may easily go too far, as when, for example, some scholars brand as magic all the customs intended to secure eternal life for the dead or to improve their state (p. 181). It is quite true that the assertion of a funerary text that the dead goes to heaven [3] may be understood as a prayer; but a prayer which is sure to be efficacious, and a wish passing into reality in vivid imagination, indeed border on magic, a statement which is equally true of the numerous ceremonies and amulets which mechanically benefit the soul of the dead. The *Book of the Dead*, with its directions how to find the way to Osiris, what to say before him, what words to recite, and what mysterious names to give to the guardians of his realm, presents a close approximation to magic; yet, after all, it is no secret knowledge, but is open to all who can read, and, therefore, does not fall under the modern definition of sorcery; neither did the Egyptians themselves consider it magical.

In similar fashion the healing art is inseparably connected with magic and religion. No medicine will have full effect without certain ceremonies and an incantation, which is usually repeated four times.[4] The incantation may also be written down, washed off into the medicine, and drunk (p. 83), as is still done so commonly in the modern Orient. Ceremonies and incantations accompanying the healing usually have a religious character, and the man to apply them is the general scholar, the priest. He summons the gods to come and to cure the disease, or he speaks in their name, threatening or coaxing the evil spirits which are always believed to have caused the illness, as in every strongly animistic religion. He often recites a story in which an analogous trouble was healed by the deities, and much of our mythological material is derived from such texts. Sometimes the divinities in person (i. e. their images) are brought to exorcize the demons, and we even hear of idols being sent to or brought from foreign countries to heal the illness of princes.[5] Frequently, however, the medical incantations also assume a character which seems to us purely magical, and frequently they degenerate into mere gibberish; likewise many of the amulets, such as' cords with magic knots,[6] used for expelling or preventing disease have no religious meaning whatever. Nevertheless everything employed for controlling the supernatural world (i. e. the demons in the present connexion) becomes religious in the hands of the proper individual, the theologian, and is considered accordingly.

The calendars of lucky and unlucky days[7] plainly belong
to the category of useful religious knowledge even more than to
that of witchcraft. They set forth which days are propitious
and which are so unlucky that on them it is advisable for one
not to leave his house at all, or on which certain occupations
should be avoided, e. g. the making of a new fire, which always remains an especially important action.[8] Often the
mythological reasons are given. Children born on certain unlucky days will die a violent death; birth on one specified day,
for example, condemns the individual in question to be killed
by a crocodile. Lucky dates of birth bring long life and luxury,
the most enviable death predicted being one in intoxication.
Astrological oracles and horoscopes, on the other hand, are
known only in the latest period and follow Babylonian models.[9]

Considering the usefulness of magic in so many respects and
bearing in mind its religious character, it is no cause for wonder
that the gods also rule the world by magic, i. e. by hidden
wisdom (see pp. 44, 151 for some of these deities who are called
"magicians" or "great in magic"). The master of sorcery
among the male divinities is Thout. Among the goddesses
his counterpart is not the stern "book-goddess" Sekha(u)it
(pp. 52–53), whom we should expect, but rather Isis, who even,
according to a myth which we have translated on pp. 80–83,
wrested the secret name, and thus omniscience (which practically means supreme power), from the aged and infirm sun-god
by a cruel ruse which shows that honesty was not an essential
characteristic of the divinities.

If the deities themselves were not particularly scrupulous
in the acquisition and use of such power, we need not wonder
that the Egyptian theologians were not content to learn the
will of the gods or to implore their aid, but that they often
sought to force the divinities to lend their power to the magician. From promises of sacrifices the sorcerer goes on to threaten
that the offerings will be withdrawn, so that the gods will be
hungry.[10] If the magician speaks in the name of a certain deity,

or claims to be identical with him, then the other gods cannot
refuse his request without endangering the whole divine order
of things. Thus the incantation may warn them that the entire
course of nature will stop. The sun and the moon will be darkened, and the Nile will dry up; heaven will be turned into
Hades; and the divinities will lose all their power and existence. When the magician can speak in the name of a higher
god, the lower pantheon must obey, and hence the sorcerer
constantly desires to learn the hidden, real names of the very
highest gods. This secret is so profound that none has ever
heard it; the owner of the name alone knows it, and even his
mother may be ignorant of it. When the deity has revealed
this wonderful name, it means power over the whole universe
for him who can pronounce the marvellous word. Thus in the
story of Isis and the old ruler of the universe, the sun-god
(pp. 80–83), we see how the betrayal of the name divests the
formerly mysterious deity of his power and subjects him to the
will of the sorcerer. Generally speaking, the name is the essence
of everything. Many materials or objects in ordinary life have a
hidden force which comes under the control of him who can
call them by their true name, unknown to the ordinary man.
Accordingly it is the highest aim of the scholars to know the
real name of everything in the whole world, first of each supernatural being, and then of all forces of nature. The endeavour
to accomplish this brings the sage in touch with every depart-
ment of science. Thus the word and the thought of man can
rule the universe and can accomplish more than some gods
can do, possibly transcending even the power of the greatest
divinities.

Such a desire to surpass the deities themselves is not impiety,
and if a scholar acquires such wonderful knowledge, he feels no
scruples in applying it. The very gods rule the world by their
power rather than by their holiness, as we have already seen;
although emphasis is often laid on the opposite conception of
the divinities as representing absolute morality.

A section of the Pyramid Texts [11] describes the apotheosis of the king and his advancement to the highest power among the gods in the following fanciful hymn which is very instructive for the light which it casts on the low Egyptian view of the gods and of religion (cf. also p. 16).

"The sky is darkened by clouds,
  The stars by rain (?); [12]
  The constellations become disordered,
  The bones of the earth-god [13] tremble.
  The carriers (?) shut their mouth
  When they see King N. N.,
  When (his) [14] soul ariseth as a god,
  Living on his fathers,
  Feasting on his mothers.

  N. N. is a lord of wisdom
  Whose mother (even) knoweth not his name;
  His glory is in the sky,
  His might is in the horizon,
  Like Atumu, his father who begat him.
  After he had begotten N. N.,
  N. N. was stronger than he.

  N. N. is the bull of the sky,
  Fierce in his heart,
  Living on the essence of every god
  And eating their intestines,
  When they come, having filled their bellies
  With magic from the island of flames. [15]

  He judgeth the word together with the one whose name is hidden
  On the day of slaughtering the eldest ones.
  N. N. is a master of sacrifices
  Whose offerings are prepared (?) by himself.
  N. N. is one who eateth men and liveth on gods,
  A master of tribute
  Who graspeth (?) presents sent by messengers.

  The 'Grasper of Locks' [16] in Keḥau,
  He lassoeth them for N. N.
  The serpent 'Wide (Reaching) Head' it is
  Who watcheth them and driveth them back (into the fold) for him.

The 'One on the Willows' (?) [17] bindeth them for N. N.
The 'One Hunting All Knife-Bearing (Spirits)' [18] strangleth (?)
    them for N. N.;
He taketh out their entrails,
He is the messenger whom N. N. sendeth for punishment (?).
Shesmu [19] cutteth them up for N. N.,
He cooketh a part of them
In his kettles as supper [or, in his supper-kettles].

N. N. eateth their magic qualities
And devoureth their illuminated souls.
Their great ones are for (his) morning portion,
Their middling ones for his evening meal,
Their little ones for his night meal,
Their old ones, male and female, for his burning.
At the north pole of the sky the great ones [20]
Put fire to kettles full of them
With the legs of their oldest ones.[21]
Those that are in the sky run around (?) [22] for N. N.;
With the legs of their women the kettles are filled for him.

N. N. hath encircled the two skies together,
He hath gone around the two regions (i. e. Egypt).
N. N. is the great, the mighty one
Who is powerful among the powerful [or, overpowereth the power-
    ful];
N. N. is the great, the strong one.

Whomsoever he findeth on his way
He eateth up immediately (?).
His safe place is before all the noble (dead)
Who are in the horizon.

N. N. is a god, older than the oldest.
Thousands (of sacrifices) come for N. N.;
Hundreds are offered to him (as sacrifices).
A position as 'the great, the mighty one'
Is given him by Orion, the father of the gods.
N. N. ariseth again in the sky,
He shineth like a star (?), as master of the horizon.

He hath counted the joints (?) of . . .,
He hath taken away the hearts of the gods;
He hath eaten the red (blood);
He hath swallowed the fresh (juice?);
He hath feasted on lungs (?);

The sacrifice of N. N. to his satisfaction
Meaneth living on hearts and their magic power.
Their magic is in his belly.
His wisdom [23] is not taken away from him.
He hath swallowed the knowledge of every god.

The lifetime of N. N. is eternity,
His end is everlasting time in this his dignity
Of the one who doth what he will,
And doth not what he will not,
Who liveth in the limits of the horizon
Forever and for eternity.

Their (soul-) force (is) in his belly,
Their souls are with him;
More abundant is his portion than that of the gods.
His fuel is of their bones;
Their (soul-) force is with N. N.,
Their shadows are with their companions."

This strange hymn seems to betray its great antiquity by the
difficulties which it apparently presented to the scholars of the
Fifth Dynasty and by its many repetitious accretions. It harks
back again and again to the crude fancy of a new divinity who
will show his power over the old pantheon in a barbarous fashion, recklessly depriving the gods of their magic potencies. It
looks, indeed, like a survival from the most primitive age, from
the purely animistic religion whose deities were lurking spirits
rather than gods (p. 16), and which held very pessimistic views
concerning the souls of the dead.[24] On the other hand, it is remarkable that this old text still appealed to the Egyptian mind
after 3000 B. C., a fact which again shows the lack of a moral
basis for the divinities of the Egyptians and is significant of
their inclination toward a magic conception of religion, as we
have said on p. 198. Other passages of these ancient funeral
texts in the Pyramids (p. 180) are somewhat parallel, such as
the one which wishes the king to have unlimited power in
heaven "so that at his heart's desire he may take any woman
away from her husband." The Pharaoh's royal power on

earth may have been despotic enough, but the inscriptions would scarcely boast of this particular ability; when such wishes were reduced to writing, they were preferably hidden in the obscure burial chamber and may be regarded as approximating magic.

Here we enter the realm of true black art, i. e. forbidden magic. We must remember that sorcery in itself was not held to be wrong. Even the most ordinary Egyptian layman was expected to wear a number of amulets for his health and good fortune, to protect his home against dangerous animals and spirits by other charms, and to do many more things which often cannot well be termed religious ceremonies, although, as we have said on p. 199, the Egyptians may still have felt them to be such. Spells of this character came under a ban only when they were used to injure others. The wicked brought disease and death on their enemies by torturing and killing them in effigy, a custom which is traceable throughout the world. Thus we read of a terrible criminal who wished to murder his benign sovereign, the Pharaoh, by making wax figures which represented the King, and then piercing them; to increase the heinousness of this offence he had stolen from the royal library itself a magic book. This book evidently contained awful formulae to accomplish the end at which he aimed, but in the divine hands of the king their use meant no wrong. Evil effects could be obtained by merely cursing one's adversary, whence such maledictions were considered sinful, especially if they were directed against the gods or the king. The "evil eye" was much dreaded, and "He Who Averts (*seta*) the Evil Eye" was a popular personal name.

Though cruel punishment was meted out for all such abuses of magic, we may be sure that they were extremely common. Above all, love-charms and love-philtres were not treated with as much severity by public opinion as by strict theology.[25] The extant magic papyri prove that the sorcerers collected useful knowledge of all kinds without drawing a line between

medicine and magic, between the forbidden and the beneficent.
The largest of all these papyri,[26] e. g., contains the most harmless medical prescriptions, like the treatment of warts, gout,
dog bites, etc., and notes about medicinal plants and minerals,
mixed with subjects of a forbidden character, e.g. numerous
erotic charms and prescriptions (with their antidotes), advice
for separating man and wife, and even more dangerous matters,
such as sending madness on an enemy, as well as many
methods of divination for consulting gods or spirits, for dis-
covering a thief, etc.   Again we see that in ancient times all
sciences formed a unity and centred in religion (p. 201).

It was, of course, believed that magic could accomplish
practically everything. Thus some famous sages, according to
a popular story, once made a living crocodile of wax which
caught an evil-doer, kept him living seven days under water,
set him free, and became wax again; a lake was rolled up like
a blanket; a head was cut off and replaced, etc.[27] Such
scholars possess books written by the gods themselves. According to another Egyptian tale, one of these volumes was
discovered in the Nile, enclosed in six boxes of metal and
defended by monsters. He who read it "enchanted heaven,
earth, the underworld, the mountains, the seas; he understood all that the birds of the heaven, the fishes of the sea,
and the wild animals spoke; he saw the sun manifesting himself in heaven with his cycle of gods, the moon appearing,
and the stars in their forms," etc.[28] The extant magic papyri
do not, of course, furnish quite such miraculous knowledge.
Their most serious portions reveal the beginnings of hypno-
tism, as when oracles are obtained by the sorcerer gazing,
either directly or through a medium (usually an innocent boy),
into a vessel filled with some fluid (especially oil) or into the
flame of a lamp, as is still done in the Orient.[29] That the beginnings of natural science can be traced to such books has
been mentioned above.

The language of the magic formulae is, as we should natu-

rally expect, one of stilted obscurity. Accordingly it likes to
borrow from foreign languages and names, and especially from
Asiatic sources. It plays on such words and sacred names by
endlessly repeating, inverting, varying, and mutilating them
(Note 32), and thus often degenerates into mere *galimatias*, yet
for the most part we can still recognize invocations of deities
in this seeming nonsense. There are no
special gods for the sorcerers; it is only
in the later period, when Sêth is becoming a kind of Satan (p. 109), that his name
readily lends itself to forbidden magic.
As we have noted above, Asiatic deities
were very popular in this black art, e. g.
such Babylonian goddesses of the lower
world as Ningal and Ereskigal, while in
the latest period the highest rank as a
divinity of this nature was taken by the
strange and mysterious God of the Jews,
who jealously allowed no god beside Him.
Ethiopic deities do not seem to have been
popular, although the Southland held
mystic attractions (p. 91). The principal
divine assistants of the magician were

FIG. 212. A SECTION OF
THE METTERNICH STELE

the forgotten and neglected divinities of whom there were
so many. Such a god, whose temples have disappeared, and
who has not received a sacrifice for a thousand years, must be
more grateful for a cup of milk and a cake than a popular
divinity may be for a holocaust of a hundred oxen; the forgotten deity is, after all, a god and able to be useful. It was,
therefore, considered wise, especially after 700 B. C., to collect
all possible divine names and pictures from earlier monuments
and to unite their reproductions; they might as a body prove a
powerful aid for the man who had such a gallery of gods, or a
single one of their number might show himself to be especially
potent and grateful for having his forgotten picture reproduced.

Such a monument is the famous Metternich Stele, a small section of which is here shown; this stone, covered with hundreds of minute divine figures and magic incantations, must have protected some very rich house against all evil influences (Fig. 214). Thus magic again returns to the purely religious basis from which it once started.

A great many features of this complicated and difficult subject still require further examination. We do not know, for example, the mode of use of the magic wands of bone which date from the period subsequent to 2000 B. C. and which are covered with many pictures of gods, sometimes unusual and frequently astral in origin.[30] Yet they, too, show once more how all magic has a religious foundation to which it ever reverts.

FIG. 213. FRAGMENT OF A MAGIC WAND

To illustrate the character of Egyptian magic we give here a few specimens of texts of this nature, beginning with a

"SPELL FOR BRINGING A BONE FORTH FROM THE THROAT."[31]

"I am he whose head reacheth the sky,
And whose feet reach the abyss,
Who hath awakened the crocodile of wax (?) in Pe-zême of Thebes;
For I am So, Sime, Tamaho,[32]
This is my correct name.
Anuk, anuk![33]
For a hawk's egg is what is in my mouth,
An ibis's egg is what is in my belly.[34]
Therefore, bone of god,
Bone of man,
Bone of bird,
Bone of fish,
Bone of animal,
Bone of anything,
None being excepted;
Therefore, that which is in thy belly,
Let it come to thy chest!

That which is in thy chest,
Let it come to thy mouth!
That which is in thy mouth,
Let it come to my hand now!
For I am he who is in the seven heavens,
Who standeth in the seven sanctuaries,
For I am the son of the living god."

This must be said seven times over a cup of water; and when the patient drinks it, the bone will come out.

Still more gibberish appears in a

"SPELL UTTERED OVER THE BITE OF A DOG."[35]

"The spell of Amon and Triphis thus:
I am this strong messenger (?),[36]
Shlamala, Malet,
The mysterious one who hath reached the most mysterious one,[37]
Greshei, Greshei,
The lord of Rent, Tahne, Bahne.[38]
This dog, this black one,
The dog, the mysterious one,
This dog of the four (bitch?) pups, [39]
The wild dog, son of Ophoïs,
Son of Anubis,
Relax [40] thy tooth,
Stop [41] thy spittle!
Thou actest as the face of Sêth against Osiris,
Thou actest as the face of 'Apop against Rê'.
Horus, the son of Osiris, born by Isis,
Is he with whom thou didst fill thy mouth; [42]
N. N., son of N. N.,
Is he with whom thou didst fill thy mouth.
Listen to this speech,
Horus, who healed burning,[43]
Who went to the abyss,
Who founded the earth;
Listen, O Yaho-Sabaho,
Abiaho [44] by name!"

The reader will recognize in the closing lines an especially clear invocation of "Jehovah of Hosts" (Hebrew *YHVH* S*e*bhāôth), the God of the Jews (cf. Note 32).

As an example of a longer mythological story narrated by
the magician to form an analogy to the magic effect which he
desires we give

THE LEGEND OF ISIS AND THE SCORPION.[45]

"I, Isis, left the mansion in which my brother Sêth had placed me.
Thout, the great one, commander of justice in heaven and earth,
    spake to me:
'Come, O Isis, O goddess, for it is good to listen,
And one liveth when another acteth as guide.
Hide thyself with thy little son!
He will come to us when his limbs have grown,
And his full strength (hath developed?).
Make him take his place then on the throne of his father,
Hand over to him the dignity of the ruler of both countries!'

I went forth at the time of evening.
Seven scorpions were my followers and furnished me aid;
Tefen and Ben were behind me;
Mestet and Mest-(yo?)tef were near me;
Petet, Tetet, and Matet prepared the way for me.

I gave orders to them aloud, my voice found access to their ears thus:
'Know that obedience in worship . . .
Distinguisheth a son of somebody from a subject.[46]
Let your face be below on the road
As companions and guides seeking for me.'

We reached the city of Psoïs [47] and the City of the Two Sisters
At the beginning of the (Delta) marshes as far as (?) the city of Deb.
I approached the houses of the most respectable women.[48]
The noblest saw me on my way;
She closed her door to me,
Suspicious of my companions.
These, therefore, took counsel,
They placed their poison all together on the tail of Tefen.
A poor woman opened her door for me,
I entered into her house.
Tefen secretly (?) entered under the wings of the door,
She stung the son of the rich woman.
[Fire broke forth in the house of the rich woman;
There was no water to quench it,
Neither was there rain against it in the house of the rich woman;
It was not the season for this.] [49]
This was because she had not opened to me.

Her heart was in grief,
She knew not (how to save) his life;
She roamed around (?) in her city lamenting;
There was not one who came at her voice.

Therefore my heart was grieved for the sake of the child;
(Wishing) to restore the innocent being to life,
I called her: 'To me! Come to me! Come to me!
Behold, my mouth holdeth life;
I am a daughter well known in her city,
Through whose word the bite (?) is stilled.
(The word) which my father taught me,
That should be known;
I am his true daughter.'

Isis put her hands on the child
To revive that which had no more breath (?):

'O poison, O Tefen, come!
Come forth on the ground! Go not on!
The poison shall not penetrate!

O Befnet, come!
Come forth on the ground!
I am Isis the goddess,
The mistress of magic who doth magic,
The best one to speak (?) words.

Listen to me, ye reptiles of all kinds that bite!
Fall down, thou poison of Mestet!
The poison of Mest-(yo?)tef shall run no farther,
The poison of Petet and Tetet shall not rise!
Thou shalt not enter, Matet!
Fall down, do not bite!'"

After this "Isis the goddess, greatest in magic among the
gods" (cf. pp. 82, 200), begins another address to the scorpions. The terms of this are very obscure,[50] but the lines
which we have quoted are sufficient to show that the magician merely narrates the story to keep all scorpions away
from the house or to render their bites harmless.[51]

CHAPTER XIII

DEVELOPMENT AND PROPAGATION OF EGYPTIAN RELIGION

AT first glance it would seem that the religion of ancient Egypt had been successfully stereotyped in prehistoric times, and that the priests had completely realized their aims of following the same ideas, worshipping the same gods, and using the same forms of adoration as the blessed ancestors of that incredibly remote age from which the bulk of their religious beliefs must date. It is perhaps true that the Egyptians present the most extreme case of religious conservatism that we know; yet on closer examination we observe that even they could not entirely resist the various influences which, in course of time, are common to religion. We may thus observe many gradual changes in religious thought and may watch the growth or decay of creeds and forms of worship both in smaller and in larger circles of the ancient Egyptians. Here, however, we can sketch only the most salient features of such developments.

The representations of the gods in sacred art are, indeed, the most remarkable instance of conservatism. The majority of artistic types dated from the prehistoric period and underwent very little alteration; it was only in Roman days that slight adaptations to Græco-Roman types of the divinities, were to be found (see Fig. 218).[1] Beginning with the New Empire many (or even most) gods receive wings (Ch. V, Note 58), or at least have indications of them, wrapped like shawls around the body; or some parts of the dress have feather patterns as an indication of celestial nature (cf. the type of Onuris-An-ḥôret as pictured in Fig. 146). The more archaic and primitive a statue was, the

more venerable it appeared (see p. 139, on Mîn, and p. 144, on
Ptaḥ). In many instances, of course, the later artists did not
understand old models, but misinterpreted them to a considerable degree.²

The greater part of the religious development of Egypt lies
long before historic times, as is shown by the conflicting views
which meet us in the Pyramid Texts of the Fifth and Sixth
Dynasties. These texts were taken from books which, in part,
evidently were understood only imperfectly by the Egyptians
of 2800 B.C., and they are, consequently, the most ancient
religious texts of the whole world. At the same time a warning
must be uttered against the tendency, which is now prevalent,
to overrate too strongly their general antiquity. Some portions may, it is true, date even from predynastic times, but the
bulk of the texts, according to the Osirian theology which is
dominant in them (p. 120), was written in the early Pyramid
Age, about 3000 B. c. The contradictory teachings of these
texts, especially in regard to cosmic forces and the life after
death, seem, as we have just said, to imply previous millenniums
of religious thought; but thus far it would be very hazardous
to date such views from these documents according to any
impressions of crude or advanced ideas which we may receive
from them. Are we quite certain, for example, that one of the
most primitive specimens of religious fancy, that the king's
soul lives by cannibalism on other souls, even those of the gods
(p. 202), goes back to the time before 5000 B. c., when the
dwellers in the valley of the Nile may well have been real can-
nibals? Could not a loyal magician's fancy wander thus far
even in the age of highest civilization? On the other hand, it is
not safe to assume that some isolated and remarkable advances
of thought in these texts, e.g. a certain moral standard demanded even for the king if he is to be admitted to the realm
of the gods (p. 180), could not be much earlier than the great
development of Egyptian civilization which begins about
3000 B. c. The Egyptians themselves could not classify the

traditions. Wherever we find the theologians wrestling with the problem of reconciling the worst contradictions among the religious traditions of the ancients, their thought, fettered by the fear of losing anything derived from antiquity, could move only in strange circles, increasing the number of inconsistencies by awkward attempts to harmonize them and invariably ending in what appears to us to be utter confusion (see, for example, the myth of the lost eye of the sun, pp. 29, 90, or the conflicting views on the ocean, pp. 47, 106). This helpless attitude toward the traditions remains characteristic of Egyptian theology in all periods.

It is clear that the purely animistic stage which we presuppose as the very earliest stratum of religious thought (p. 15) was far prior to the historic period. Even in the remote days when the first attempts were made to reduce religious poetry to writing (i. e., probably, before 4000 B. C.) the Egyptians must have outgrown this primitive stage of pure animism. Nevertheless that system of thought left strong traces in the religion of all the millenniums which followed, and its expression in so many small isolated local cults actually remained the most characteristic feature of Egyptian religion throughout its history (p. 18). We may suppose that the next step, probably some time before the historic period, was marked by a tendency which sought to remove all the old local spirits and fetishes from this earth and to place them in heaven.[3] It would seem, therefore, that the tendency to make the gods cosmic (i. e. to distribute the forces of nature among them) must be dated somewhat later still, since it implies the initial steps toward a philosophic conception of the universe.

Before any real system had developed from these attempts at primitive philosophy, they were crippled by the exaggerated position given to the sun in the cosmic pantheon (p. 24). No cosmic function seemed desirable for any local deity except that of the sun, the lord of heaven. The solarization of the pantheon is traceable at least as early as the First Dynasty (see p. 26 for the blending of different ideas regarding the sun-god which we find at that period). Rê' appears to have become solar at an earlier period than Horus, whose cosmic explanation hovered even later between the celestial and the solar interpretation (p. 28). The increasing emphasis laid on the official *rôle* of these two blended solar deities as protector, type, ancestor, and even soul of the king (p. 170) did not stop the free transference of this kind of cosmic conception, and later it proceeded more rapidly (see e. g. p. 149 for Sokari's solarization in the Pyramid Texts). In the Middle and New Empires few deities escaped some degree of assimilation to it. In particular Amon of Thebes, advancing to the position of lord of the pantheon, became an imitation of Horus-Rê' which was called Amen-Rê' (p. 129); and most goddesses were solarized as the "daughter" or "eye" or "diadem" of the sun (p. 29). Lunarization of divinities, on the other hand, remained a rare process (p. 34). The other cosmic functions were distributed only in very incomplete and unsuccessful fashion, as has been shown in Ch. III. Repetitions of such functions, therefore, never caused serious difficulty to the Egyptian theologians.

It is not easy to estimate the enormous number of divinities in the Egyptian pantheon at the beginning of history. Fortunately many deities whose popularity decreased in comparison with the "great gods" fell into oblivion; and this diminution, which continued in the historic period, must have made considerable progress long before the days of the pyramid-builders. The priests never hastened this process of reduction violently; all that they could do to bring the bewildering mass of divine names into some degree of system was to endeavour to form at least approximate groupings of the deities and to place them in mutual relation on the model of a human genealogy. The numerous triads (p. 20) may represent the beginning of this classification and may have satisfied the smaller local centres for a long time. At the place which was the most important for the theological history of Egypt, Heliopolis (p. 31), a wider-reaching grouping of the nine most important divinities of all Egypt was undertaken, possibly somewhat before the beginning of the Pyramid Period. This "ennead" (perhaps a triple triad in origin) consisted of the following genealogy: [4]

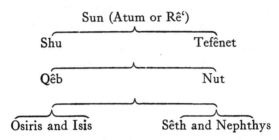

Imperfect as this system was, it was felt to be a great step forward. Parallel with this "great ennead," therefore, a "little ennead" was later formed in which the other gods of the Osirian cycle and Thout found a place, together with various minor divinities. Sometimes the double ennead of eighteen gods was expanded into a triple one of twenty-seven. The ennead of Heliopolis and its duplication became known and mentioned everywhere, but the priests could not follow it strictly if it did not include the local divinity, or if it failed to give this deity his proper eminence. Accordingly local imitations sprang up, as when, for example, at Memphis one began with Ptaḥ as the earliest and the foremost god. Everywhere the priests tended to ascribe nine followers to their principal deity or to make him the chief of eight other gods. Thus the term "ennead" finally lost its numerical meaning and became synonymous with "circle of associated gods." The unsystematic character of the Egyptian mind clearly revealed itself in these attempts at some methodical arrangement.[5]

As for the kaleidoscopic character of the mythology, there never was a rationalizing wish to change it. We children of an over-rationalistic age too easily forget that most mythologies once had this indistinctness of character and that to the ancient mind it was not a disadvantage, but a beauty. In like manner the Egyptians, proud of the wealth of fanciful variants which distinguished their mythology above those of all the neighbouring countries were careful not to correct this mystic confusion, which we find so bewildering. Even in Plutarch's systematizing account of the Osiris-myth we see how seldom the necessity of harmonizing contradictory variants was felt.

The next mode of adapting the incoherent cults of the ancestors to the mind of a more advanced age was always the comparison and identification (syncretism) of similar gods. The assimilation of deities must have been in progress even before the time when cosmic ideas were made to underlie the old names. It was impossible not to compare and identify divinities with the same animal form or with similar symbols or dress. Thus the lionesses Sekhmet, Tefênet, and Pekhet, for example, were treated as manifestations of one and the same personality at an early date, and soon the cat Ubastet joined them. Next, identical functions led to identification. When almost all female divinities assumed the character of personifications of the sky (Ch. VIII, Note 2), it was natural to ask whether they were not merely different forms or names of one great goddess. The male pantheon did not lend itself to identifications quite so easily, for more individuality was exhibited in it; nevertheless it could be reduced to a very limited number of types. When the solarization which we have just described was applied to almost any of these types, it became possible to fuse them all into one god of the universe. As the first steps rather bold instances occur as early as the Pyramid Texts, where several divinities not too similar in character are declared to differ only in name.[6] This contradiction of the theory that the name is the most essential thing in a deity was reconciled with it by the doctrine that all names and personifications are not alike; some are greater, and one is the greatest, most true, original, and essential (p. 201). This permitted the full preservation of local names and cults; the priests of each local divinity or the worshippers of a special patron could claim that their deity

was the oldest and best of all "names" or manifestations of
that god whom the king officially recognized as the leader or
father of the pantheon. Side by side with such religious par-
ticularism, however, the process of assimilation and identification went on unhindered until, after 1600 B. C., it ended in
the most radical syncretism, in a pantheistic approach to
monotheism which will be described below.

It must not be forgotten, however, that all such speculations
remained the property of a few priests of the highest rank of
education who had mastered the whole realm of traditional
theology with so much success that they were able to reach
beyond it. Ordinary people said their prayers and deposited
their offerings at the local temple without speculations on the
nature of the deity whom they thus worshipped. His adoration had continued from time immemorial, and this was reason
enough for following the trodden path, leaving the interpretation of the venerable traditions to the theologians. Yet, contrary to the opinion often held by modern writers, the teachings of these learned priests were not mysteries withheld from
the laity. There was no secrecy about them; they were generally inscribed on temple walls where they might be read by all
who could do so; and they were repeated in places which were
even more easily accessible. The limited number of those who
could read difficult texts and the conservatism of the masses
sufficed to prevent the spread of ideas which might sometimes
have become dangerous to traditionalism. It was only some
funerary texts of a semi-magic character which pretended to be
"a book great in secrecy," as when we read in one later
chapter of the *Book of the Dead*,[7] "Allow no human eye to see
it; a forbidden thing it is to know it; hide it." Yet ultimately
any one might buy this mysterious literature for his dead
(cf. p. 199).

These speculations of learned priests, furthermore, ordinarily moved along strange lines, as we have stated on p. 214. It is
only in rare instances that they are philosophical, and for the

most part they show the priests quite as fettered by traditionalism as were the people. The best illustration is the strange
commentary and supercommentary contained in the seventeenth chapter of the *Book of the Dead*, which seems to have
been considered a masterpiece of theological thought. Sometimes it seems reasonable enough, as when the departed says,[8]
"I am the great god who became by himself," on which the
commentary remarks, "What does this mean? It is the water
[according to other manuscripts, "the abyss, the father of the
gods"]; another interpretation: it is the sun-god" (see pp. 44,
48, on the question who was the oldest god). We can at least
follow the thought when the words, "I know the yesterday and
the tomorrow," are glossed, "What is this? The yesterday is
Osiris, and the tomorrow is Rê'," thus distinguishing the dead
sun-god from the one who is reborn every day. Then, however,
we find the text declaring, "I am Mîn at his appearance, my
two feathers are given me on my head." These simple words
the commentators endeavour to render more profound by the
gloss: "Mîn is Horus, who avenged his father [cf. p. 117]; his
appearances are his birth; his two feathers on his head are Isis
and Nephthys, who went and placed themselves on his head
when they were two birds [cf. p. 115], at the time when his head
ached. Another interpretation: the two uraeus serpents [p. 29]
are they before his father. Another interpretation: his two
eyes were the feathers on his head." We perceive how difficult
it was for such minds to rise above a very shallow symbolism,
and we are not surprised that wisdom of this type moved in a
circle for several thousand years. Nevertheless here also we
see the constant tendency toward a syncretistic comparison
and identification of divinities. Thus we read again in a similar
commentary:[9] "The soul of Shu is Khnûm, the soul of endless space [Ḥeḥ, p. 44] is Shu (?), the soul of (primeval) darkness is night, the soul of Nuu is Rê', that of Osiris is the
Mendes, the souls of the Sobks are the crocodiles, the soul
of every god is in the serpents [cf. p. 166], that of 'Apop is

in (the land of) Bekh,[10] that of Rê' is over the whole earth."
Here once more we note the endeavour, which gained ground
in the New Empire, to identify the abyss (Nuu) with the sun
(Rê') and thus to explain the latter as "self-begotten" (p. 50)
and as the essence of the whole world, in opposition to earlier
doctrines (p. 50). We likewise observe that "soul" or "force"
approximates the sense of "manifestation" or "antitype."

More detailed in its syncretistic speculations is a document
which claims to have been found on a worm-eaten and partially
illegible papyrus about 720 B. C. and which was then incised on
a block of stone as a very wonderful specimen of ancestral
thought.[11] It daringly reconciles the Memphitic and Heliopolitan doctrine. Ptaḥ, the local deity of Memphis, was the
earliest of all gods. He existed in eight forms, the oldest of
which were Ptaḥ-Nuu as the father and Ptaḥ-Nekhbet as the
mother (!) of Atum.[12] When this sun-god Atum propagated
the rest of the ennead, as described on p. 216, these divinities
were not only descendants of Ptaḥ, but were in fact mere
manifestations of him. In other words, as our text explains,
Ptaḥ, "the Great One," is the heart and tongue of the ennead,
and thought and speech (on whose mutual relations some
speculations are added) represent the activity of every god.
Consequently Ptaḥ is the universal power. Then the "little
ennead" of Heliopolis is considered. Horus and Thout — the
latter the organizer of the present pantheon — likewise "came
from Ptaḥ" both directly and indirectly, and thus the whole
universe has emanated from him and is ruled by him.[13]

Such pantheistic tendencies are elsewhere attached to Rê',
to his parallels, Amen-Rê' and Osiris, "the master of all things"
(p. 96),[14] etc., but especially, from the Nineteenth Dynasty
onward, to the Memphitic deity Ptaḥ-Taṭunen (whom we
have mentioned above) and to his variant, Sokari-Osiris. When
Ptaḥ is called "he who standeth on the earth and toucheth
the sky with his head, he whose upper half is the sky and whose
lower half is the underworld," etc.,[15] or when Osiris-Sokari

(= Ptaḥ) is described not merely as the earth-god who gives
life to plants, etc., or as ruler of the lower world, and at the
same time producer of the air, but even as possessing solar
faculties,[16] we have the development of a conception of deity
as the cosmic universe which cannot but end in a pantheistic
belief in one god, though he manifests himself in a hundred
forms and names. A clear expression of this doctrine is found
in a late hymn [17] in which the supreme god Amen-Rêʻ is treated
as the sun and thus is identified with such solar manifestations
as Mîn, Atum, Khepri, Monṭu, and Ḥar-shaf, perhaps even
with androgynous combinations like Shu-Tefênet and Mut-
Khônsu (line 37), and repeatedly with the universalized Ptaḥ-
Taṭunen-Sokari. Consequently

"Thy forms are Nile and Earth,
  Thou art the eldest, greater than the gods.
  Thou art the abyss when it stretched itself over the ground;
  Thou didst return in thy ripples (?).
  Thou art the sky, thou art the earth, thou art the underworld,
  Thou art the water, thou art the air between them."

It would be a mistake to see Iranian influence in this text
merely because it chances to be preserved in a temple dating
from the reign of Darius I; it was evidently written several
centuries before, and its thoughts can be traced to a time even
more remote. As early as the Nineteenth Dynasty the *Litany
of the Sun* [18] declares that the solar deity Rêʻ-Ḥor manifests
himself in practically all gods. Not only are all divinities who
admit of solarization identical with him as his "power," but
he is one with Nuu (the abyss), Qêb (the earth), Shay ("Destiny," see p. 52), the new "furnace-deity" (Ketuiti) which
represents hell and the lower world (Ch. X, Note 21), and
even with such female forces as Isis and Nephthys.

All this enables us to understand a hymn to a mysterious
cosmic god in which a magician wishes to express his idea of
an unknown god greater than anyone had hitherto been able
to imagine.[19]

"O thou dwarf of heaven (?),[20]
Thou big-faced dwarf
With high back,
With weakly legs,
The great pillar which (reacheth) from heaven (to) the lower world!
O lord of the corpse which resteth in Heliopolis,
O great lord of life who resteth in Dêdet! [21]
N. N., son of N. N., guard him by day,
Watch him by night;
Protect him as thou hast protected Osiris against [Sêth?] [22]
On that day of (his) burial in Heliopolis! [23]

I am the lion in the ship (?) [24] of the Phoenix.
Thy form is that of a monkey [25]
With the face of an old man.
There were (?) witnesses when thou didst send (a message) to me,
(When?) a resting-place was taken in the wall (i.e. of Memphis?).
Thus: may a chapel of one cubit be made for me!

'Art thou not a giant of seven cubits?'
I said to thee, 'Thou canst not enter into this chapel of one cubit;
Art thou not a giant of seven cubits?'
(But) thou didst enter it and rest in it.

[Fall (?), O flames which know (!) not the abyss! [26]
Thou chapel, open, open thyself!
Thou who art in it with thy monkey face,
Woe! Woe! Fire! Fire!
Thou child of the maiden (?),[27]
Thou baboon!"]

The last strophe seems to have no connexion with what
precedes, and it has the appearance of an incongruous magic
addition like the one translated on p. 83. Yet in the first part
of the hymn we find the idea of a god who, like Osiris-Rê' (i. e.
the Heliopolitan god), represents the entire universe and has
the outward form partly of the dwarf or giant Bês, and in
greater degree that of his Memphitic variant, Ptaḥ-Nuu-
Sokari, as a dwarf (p. 64). Obviously the magician again regards the latter as the god of all nature, both infant and old
man, the beginning and the end, the smallest and the greatest
principle of nature, etc. Osiris, elsewhere the deity of universal

nature, is here merely subordinate to this all-god and is, it would seem, only one of his manifestations.

Thus we can also understand the origin and meaning of magic representations, dating from the latest period, of a mysterious, nameless deity. His pictures unite the portrayals

FIG. 214. LATE NAMELESS GOD OF THE UNIVERSE

of the hawk Horus, and sometimes of the crocodile Sobk, the phallic divinity Mîn, and the similar picture of the "self-begotten" Amen-Rê', etc.; but the principal source is Bês, who, as above, is the same as Sokari, who in turn equals Nuu-Ptaḥ. The representation with innumerable eyes covering his body, somewhat like the Greek Argos,[28] has a forerunner in a deity who is described [29] as having seventy-seven eyes and as many ears. The shoes are those of the primeval ogdoad (p. 48); the feet tread the abyss (in serpent-form; p. 104) and his helpers;

the surrounding flames shield this mysterious being from the profane world.[30] It is an amalgamation of the greatest cosmic powers, as being all identical, into one new god of the universe.

The hymn which we have translated above, with its striving after a mysterious, nameless, all-embracing divinity of the entire universe, is found in a papyrus of the Twentieth Dynasty (twelfth century B. C.), but the text has been copied from earlier sources. As we have repeatedly stated, the clear doctrinal formulation of pantheism, as in the· texts which we have quoted, seems to appear about the beginning of the New Empire, in the Eighteenth Dynasty.

If the growth of pantheistic ideas in this epoch, the time after 1600 B. C., betrays a struggle against traditionalism, a groping for a new and larger conception of the godhead, and a tendency toward a solar explanation of the origin of all nature, we can understand how, not much later, an effort could be made violently to reform the religion of Egypt — the famous revolution of Pharaoh Amen-ḥotep (Amenophis) IV, about 1400 B. C. The pantheistic striving of scholars had at least prepared the way for the revolution. At all events this very interesting movement, the only violent religious reform of which we know, not only in Egypt, but in the entire pre-Christian Orient outside Israel, must not be explained as due to Asiatic influences. Neither can it be understood as coming from the old Heliopolitan theology, as some scholars have supposed; contrary to Egyptian traditionalism, it did not seek to support itself by that most venerable school of tradition, but desired to be an entirely new doctrine.

Like so many other religious revolutions, this also seems to have had a political basis. The King, being the son of a woman who was not of royal blood (Teye, the daughter of an ordinary priest), probably encountered opposition from the Theban hierarchy as not being quite legitimate, and he punished the priests by deposing Amon from his position as the official chief god. Wishing to suppress entirely the worship of Amon, the

Pharaoh tried to bring oblivion on the divinity by erasing the deity's name and that of his consort Mut from all earlier monuments, even those of a private nature, such as old tombs. He himself moved from Amon's city of Thebes to a place in Middle Egypt near the site of the modern Tell Amarna, where he built a new capital. Thus breaking with all tradition and finding ready to hand the concept that the sun-god was the master or, in reality, the only deity of the whole universe, the King was unwilling to employ any of the old names and representations for this supreme divinity, but rationalistically called him simply Aten ("the Disk") and portrayed him in an entirely new manner as a plain disk with rays ending in hands (a symbolism indicative of activity?). To this new god he built a magnificent

FIG. 215. AMEN-ḤOTEP IV AND HIS WIFE SACRIFIC-
ING TO THE SOLAR DISK

temple in the new capital, which he called "Horizon of the Disk" in Aten's honour (see Fig. 195 for a picture of the front of this sanctuary), and he even changed his own name from Amen-ḥotep ("Amon is Satisfied") to Akh-en-aten ("Splendour of the Disk").[31] Parallel with these innovations free scope was given to a certain realistic modernism in art, etc. These violent reforms met with much opposition, and after the King's death so strong a reaction set in that his successors were constrained to return hurriedly to the old faith and to re-establish the worship of the Theban triad. The memory of the heretic and of his god was persecuted as mercilessly as he had repressed the religion of Amon, and in particular the schismatic temple of the sun was razed to the ground. Thus we know little about Amen-hotep's new "doctrine" to which his inscriptions proudly allude; few texts have survived concerning it, and these documents are only hymns which vaguely extol the sun as the benefactor of all animate nature.

The revolution does not seem to have been quite so radical a solar monotheism as modern writers often state. We have no evidence that any cults outside the divine triad of Thebes were persecuted. Some old names and forms of solar deities were still retained in the new royal worship (especially Horus and Har-akhti), or at least were tolerated (Atum). Thus the system may have been henotheistic or monolatristic rather than monotheistic. Neither was it iconoclastic to the extent of strict avoidance of the human or animal types of the deities who were retained or tolerated. Nevertheless it remains a very remarkable rationalistic attempt, and it reveals independence of thought by refusing the support of the pantheistic amalgamations of old names and forms which we have described above.[32]

FIG. 216. PROFILE OF AMEN-HOTEP IV

It is quite true that the only motive of Amen-hotep in avoiding this pantheism seems to have been, not philosophical thought, but simply the fear that he might be compelled to retain all the traditional names and cults, and thus to admit Amon also as a manifestation of the universal god of the free-thinkers. Yet we must give him credit for breaking away from the crude old beliefs which, after theoretically removing the deities to heaven, had in reality kept them on earth within the touch of man and in the human and animal forms of primitive tradition. Although the thought was far from new, nevertheless it was a radical step actually to remove the supreme divinity to the sky and to worship him only in the form in which the sun appears daily to every eye. This break with traditionalism, however, was the fatal difficulty. The conservative mind of the masses was unable to abandon the time-hallowed names and cults of the forefathers. We may admire the great boldness of the King's step, may view it with sympathy, and may regret its failure, yet Amen-ḥotep IV must not be overrated and compared with the great thinkers and reformers in the world's history.

As an illustration of his doctrine and of the literature developed at his court we here quote his famous hymn to the sun.[33]

"The praise of the sun-god [by the King N. N.]:
Thou appearest beautiful in the horizon of the sky,
O living Disk, beginning of life!
When thou risest in the eastern horizon,
Thou fillest every land with thy beauty.
Thou art beautiful, great,
Resplendent and exalted over every land.
Thy rays encompass the lands
To the extent of all things which thou hast made;
(Since) thou art Rê', thou bringest them all,
Thou subjectest them to thy beloved son (i. e. to the Pharaoh).
(Though) thou art afar, thy rays are on earth;
Thou art on their faces [and thus they feel?] thy steps.

(When) thou goest to rest in the western horizon,
The earth is in darkness, in the condition of death.
(Men) lie in their chambers with their heads wrapped up;
One eye seeth not the other.
Their belongings are stolen (even when) lying under their heads,
And they notice it not.
Every lion cometh from his den,
All serpents bite,
Darkness [is their protection?],
The earth (resteth) in silence
(While) he who made them is in his horizon.

The earth is bright when thou risest on the horizon,
Resplendent as the sun-disk in day-time.

Thou removest darkness
(When) thou sendest thy rays.
Both lands (i. e. Egypt) are in festival joy,
Awakening and standing on (their) feet;
Thou hast raised them up.
Their limbs being bathed, they take (their) clothing;
Their arms are (lifted) in worship at thy rising;
(Thereupon) all the land perform their toil.

All cattle rejoice in their grass;
Trees and herbs are greening; [34]
The birds are flying from their nests (seshu),
Their wings are (lifted) in worship to thy being;
All (wild) animals skip on their feet;
The birds and all things fluttering
(Feel) alive when thou hast arisen for them.
The ships sail (on) the stream up and down alike;
Every way is open when thou arisest.
The fish in the rivers leap (?) before thee;
Thy rays are (even) in the innermost of the great ocean.

Creator of issue in women,
Maker of seed in men,
Who preserveth alive the son in his mother's womb
And keepeth him quiet that he weep not,
A nurse (for him even) in the (maternal) womb.
Who giveth breath to keep alive all that he maketh;
(When) it descendeth from the womb, [thou showest care for it?] on
        the day of its birth;
Thou openest its mouth, giving it voice;
Thou makest what it doth need.

The young bird crieth in the shell
(Because) thou givest it breath within to preserve its life.
When thou hast given it strength [35] to open [36] the egg,
It cometh from the egg
To cry with full strength.
It runneth on its feet
When it cometh forth from it.

How manifold are (the things) which thou hast made!
They are mysteries before [us?].
Thou only god,
Whose place none else can take!

Thou hast created the earth according to thy heart —
Thou being alone —
Men, flocks, and all animals,
Whatsoever is on earth,
Going on feet,
Whatsoever is high in the air, flying with its wings,
The foreign lands, Syria and Ethiopia,
(And) the land of Egypt.

Thou assignest every man to his place,
Thou makest what they need.
Each one hath his food,
And his lifetime is counted.[37]
The tongues are distinguished in speech;
Their forms and also their skins [38] are differentiated;
(Thus) thou didst distinguish the strange nations.

Thou madest the Nile in the lower world,
Thou bringest him according to thy liking.
For furnishing life to mankind,
As thou hast made them for thyself,
Thou, their lord, (lord) of them all,
Resting among them,[39]
Thou lord of every land
Who ariseth for them,
O sun-disk of the day, great of power!

All foreign countries, the remote,
Thou makest life for them;
(Because) thou hast placed a Nile in the sky,
It descendeth for them,
It maketh waves on the mountain like the great ocean,
Irrigating [40] their fields in their towns.

How excellent are thy plans, O lord of eternity!
Thou [hast established] [41] the Nile in the sky for the foreign lands
And for the wild beasts of every mountain country wandering on [42]
    their feet;
(But) the Nile cometh from the underworld for Egypt.

Thy rays nourish [43] every green spot;
(When) thou risest, they live
And they grow for thee.

Thou hast made the seasons
To produce all that thou makest;
The winter to cool them,
The (season of) heat (when) they (really) taste thee.
Thou didst make the sky far away to rise in it
And to behold all that thou makest.

Thou art alone, rising in thy forms as a living disk,
Appearing, shining, departing, and (again) drawing nigh.
Thou makest millions of forms from thyself alone,
Cities, villages, and tribes,
Highways and rivers;
Every eye beholdeth thee before them
(When) thou art the disk of day-time above [them]."

The text, apparently becoming corrupt after this strophe, has some very obscure sentences whose approximate meaning seems to be: "Thou hast not (?) gone away since (?) thine eye hath existed (which?) thou hast created for (?) them that thou shouldst not see joy (?)"; and it then continues in a more personal prayer.

"Thou art in my heart (i. e. understanding);
None other is there who knoweth thee
Except thy son, Akh-en-aten;
Thou hast made him wise in thy plans and in thy power.[44]

The (whole) earth is at thy command
As thou hast made them.
When thou hast risen, they (feel) alive;
When thou hast set, they (feel) dead.
(Thus) in thyself [45] thou art lifetime;
People live from thee;
(All) eyes (are fixed) on thy beauty until thou settest;
All work is stopped (when) thou settest in the west.

Arising, thou makest [everything good?] grow for the king
[Who hath been a servant following thee?],[46]
For thou hast founded the earth
And raised it [47] up for thy son,
The one who came forth from thy limbs,
The king of Upper and Lower Egypt,
Living in [48] truth, lord of both countries,

Nefer-khepru-rê' [" the Best of the Forms of the Sun "; cf. p. 170],
   Ua'-n-rê' [" the Only One of the Sun "],
Son of the sun, living in [48] truth,
The lord of diadems, Akh-en-aten.
Long (be) his life,
And the chief royal wife, beloved of him,
The mistress of both countries,
Nefer-nefru-aten, Nefert-iti,
Who liveth and flourisheth for ever and for eternity."

There are some shorter hymns and prayers of this same
period, usually abridged from the long hymn which we have
just quoted.[49] All of them have the same character: they follow a modern, lyric style of poetic description, depicting nature
with a minute observation of small details, but they present
scarcely a religious thought which cannot be found in earlier
literature. They might almost as well have been written of the
solar deities of preceding generations.

The reaction which set in after the death of Amen-ḥotep IV
re-established the old forms and names of the deities everywhere and even sought to emphasize them more than before.
It was easy to destroy the heresies of the schismatic Pharaoh
since his short-lived reform had nowhere penetrated the masses.
If the reformation left any trace, we might find it in the fact
that the style of religious literature did not return to the dry
formalism which had reigned before the New Empire; the
warmer, pietistic tone was maintained, and this could be done
with impunity since the heretical movement did not, strictly
speaking, inaugurate this style, which had had forerunners
before the time of Amen-ḥotep IV. This lyric, personal tone [50]
seems to deepen even in the Nineteenth and Twentieth
Dynasties, so that the worship of the ancient deities was,
after all, not quite the same as in the days of the ancestors,
and this wholly apart from the pantheistic syncretism of
scholars. The texts reveal an increasing tendency to break
away from formalism in worship and to inculcate a personal
devotion to the deity. They emphasize that the divinity loves

man, not merely the human race, but each individual, even the most humble; the very animals are objects of his fatherly care. Where earlier poetry praised the divine power exclusively and regarded it with awe alone, now the kindness of the gods toward the poor and needy is described. The sick, the orphan and the widow, and the unjustly accused will not pray in vain for deliverance from their misery (cf. p. 237). Such fatherly love must be reciprocated by a manifestation of man's love toward the deity and by devotion to him and to his worship. We nowhere find it stated in plain words that sacrifices or ritual alone cannot save; yet the wise Ani,[51] who seems to have lived at the end of the Eighteenth Dynasty, at least denounces the belief that loud, formal, and lengthy prayers can compel the deity to do his worshipper's bidding.

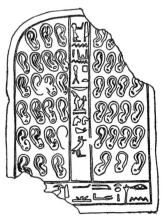

FIG. 217. PRAYER-STELE WITH SYMBOLS OF HEARING

"The sanctuary of the god,[52] shouting is its abhorrence;
Pray for thyself with a loving heart!
All his (?) words [53] are in secret;
He performeth thy cause;
He heareth thy saying;
He receiveth thy sacrifice."

With this lofty view of prayer we may contrast the contemporary stelae which pilgrims erected and on which they depicted first one pair of ears to express the invocation, "May the god hear my supplication!" and then multiplied these symbols to show how intensely they desired to compel the deity to hearken, as in the accompanying cut, whose inscription reads, "Praise to the soul (*ka*) of Ptaḥ, the lord of justice, great in might, (who) heareth prayer!"

Other advanced thinkers departed even further from formalism by urging the silent, humble prayer of the contrite heart, as when we read:[54]

"Thou savest the silent, O Thout,
 Thou sweet well of water for him who is athirst in the desert!
 It is closed for the eloquent; [55]
 It is open for the silent.
 When the silent cometh, he findeth the well;
 The one that burneth with heat, him dost thou refresh."

This does not mean that it is not man's duty to honour the gods by praise, for he must extol them constantly before men.

"I make praises for his name,
 I praise him to the height of heaven;
 As wide as the ground (of the earth) is
 I describe his power to them that go southward and northward." [56]

The wise Ani certainly would not destroy all formalism, for in his *Maxims* we read:[57]

"Celebrate the feasts of thy god!
 Observe [58] his (sacred) seasons!
 The god is wroth when he experienceth trespassing."

See also p. 178 for his admonition to sacrifice for the dead in the traditional way.

The deities expect not only loving worship, but also obedience to their moral demands; if these be broken, affliction will follow as a speedy punishment.

"Beware of him!
 Tell it to (thy) son and to (thy) daughter,
 To the great and to the small!
 Report it to the (present) generation
 And to the generation which hath not yet come!
 Report it to the fish in the deep,
 To the birds in the sky!
 Repeat it to him who doth not yet know it,
 And to him who knoweth it!
 Beware of him!" [59]

In remorse a man who seems to have sworn a false oath by the moon-god erects a stele to confess his sin:[60]

"I am a man who had wrongly said,
 '(As) he remaineth' to the moon concerning (?) the barrier (?). [61]
 Then before the whole country he made me see how great his might is.
 I report thy power to the fish in the river
 And to the birds in the sky.
 They (i. e. mankind) shall say to the children of their children,
 'Beware of the moon, who can turn this (away) when he is appeased.'"

A similar case is described more pathetically.[62] A man grew blind, attributed his affliction to perjury which he had committed, and implored the god's forgiveness in the following words:

"I am one who swore falsely by Ptaḥ, the Lord of Justice;
 He made me see darkness in day-time.
 I shall tell his power to the one who knoweth him[63] not, as well as
   to the one who knoweth,
 To the small and to the great.
 Beware of Ptaḥ, the Lord of Justice!
 Behold, he doth not overlook a (wrong) deed of any man.
 Abstain from pronouncing Ptaḥ's name wrongly!
 Lo, he who pronounceth it wrongly,
 Behold, he goeth to destruction.

 He made me to be like a dog on the street;
 I was in his hand.
 He made me to be a spectacle for men and for gods
 Since I have been a man who wrought abomination against his
   master.

 Ptaḥ, the Lord of Justice, is just to me;
 He hath afflicted me with punishment.
 Be merciful unto me!
 I have seen that thou art merciful."

Another man excuses himself before the deity in a more general way:[64] "I am an ignorant, heartless (i. e. stupid, brainless) man who knoweth not the difference between good and evil." Others declare that mankind as a whole is weak and helpless

before the gods. Even when no specific sin burdens the conscience, it is well to confess this human weakness before the
divinities and to assume that they might easily discover faults
if they were not so gracious and forgiving. This is the tone of
the following hymn:[65]

> "Thou (art) the only one, O Har-akhti!
> There is none indeed like unto him,
> (Able to) protect millions
> And to shield hundreds of thousands,
> Thou protector of him who calleth for him!
>
> O Lord of Heliopolis, reproach me not for my many sins!
> I am one who knoweth not (anything),[66]
> Whose breast [67] is ignorant;
> I am a man without heart; [68]
> I spend the whole time walking after my own mouth
> As an ox (goeth) after the grass.
> If I forget (?) my time, . . .
> I walk . . . " [69]

This pietistic tone penetrates even the official inscriptions.
We find Pharaohs who humbly pray to the gods for divine
guidance and illumination where, according to the traditional
theory of Egyptian kingship (p. 170), they should have spoken
haughtily as being themselves incarnate divinities and masters
of all wisdom. Thus one royal prayer runs: [70] "Suffer me not
to do that which thou hatest; save me from that which is
wicked!" Nevertheless such humble confessions of royal
fallibility and weakness are not so numerous as the parallel
assertions of the older view, according to which the Pharaoh
was too far above the level of ignorant and feeble humanity
to commit sin. After 1000 B.C. the old formalism, generally
speaking, stifled the pietistic tone more and more, especially
after 750, when mechanical copying of the earliest forms was
the prevailing tendency, and when Egyptian conservatism celebrated its greatest triumph. In increasing measure it became
the highest ambition of the theologians to search the ruins of
temples and tombs for inscriptions and papyri, and to gather

from them old and imperfectly known texts, as well as names
and pictures of the gods whom the ancestors had worshipped,
thus bringing to light many forgotten divinities. This archaiz-
ing tendency begins with the Ethiopian kings of the eighth
century B. C. and culminates in the fourth century with the
reign of Nectanebo, a pious monarch famous in later tradition
also as a scholar and magician, who has left a surprising number of monuments illustrative of the pantheon and of the
doctrines of the remote past (see p. 207).

To demonstrate the great contrast between the pietistic style
in the religious poetry of the New Empire and the old poetic
vein we quote a specimen from a long hymn to Amen-Rê'
which is preserved in a papyrus of the museum at Cairo.[71]
This hymn is composed of poetic fragments of various ages
and thus exhibits the old formalism side by side with the more
lyrical style. In it, accordingly, we find examples of the most
stilted and archaic tone:

"Awake in health, Min-Amon,[72]
  Lord of eternity,
  Who hath made endless time!
  Lord of adoration,
  The one before . . .[73]

  Firm of horns,
  Fair of face,
  Lord of the crown,
  With high feathers!
  Fine with the ribbon on his head,[74]
  (Wearing) the white crown.
  The serpent diadem and the two serpents of Buto [75] belong to his
      face,
  The ornaments (?) of the one in the palace,[76]
  The double crown, the royal cap, and the helmet!
  Fine of face when he hath received the fourfold crown!
  Who loveth the Southern as well as the Northern crown!
  Master of the double crown who hath received the sceptre!
  Master of the club, holding the whip,
  The good ruler who appeareth with the white crown!"

Thus far the hymn merely describes the incredibly old statue of the god Mîn of Koptos (p. 139), of whose mythological character the poet could say little, since he was obviously unwilling to follow the deity's later identification with Osiris (pp. 139, 156). At this point the style becomes slightly more vivid and modern, and passes over into a hymn to the sun.

"Lord of rays, maker of light,
To whom the gods give praises,
Who sendeth forth his arms as he will!
His enemies fall by his flame,
It is his eye which overthrew the wicked.
It sent its spear to be swallowed by the abyss,
It forced the impious dragon to spit forth what he had swallowed.[77]

Hail to thee, O Rê', lord of truth,
Whose shrine is mysterious, master of the gods!
Khepri in his ship,
Who uttered the command, and the gods were made!
Atumu, the creator of men,
Who distinguished their forms and made their life,
Distinguishing the form [78] of one from (that of) the other!"

Now follows a section in the most modern, lyric vein:

"Who hearkeneth to the prayer of him that is in prison,
Kind of heart when one crieth unto him!
Who delivereth the timid from him that is violent of heart,
Who judgeth the oppressed, the oppressed and the needy!

Lord of knowledge, on whose lips is wisdom,[79]
At whose pleasure the Nile cometh!
Lord of pleasantness, great of love,
Who giveth [80] life to men,
Who openeth every eye!
O thou (that wert) made in the abyss,
Who created pleasure and light!
The gods rejoice at the signs of his goodness,[81]
Their hearts revive when they behold him."

The next section of the hymn reverts to a jejune style which celebrates the deity, as worshipped in Thebes and Heliopolis, "for whom the sixth day and the middle day of the month are honoured" (cf. p. 90). With endless repetitions it describes his crowns and emblems. After a time, however, the account of his activity as creator and sustainer resumes a modern, pietistic tone.

> "The only one who made what is,
> Creator of all men, who made what doth exist!
> Men proceeded from his eyes,
> The gods sprang from his lips.
> Who maketh grass for the herds,
> The life-bearing trees for men;
> Who permitteth the fish to live in the river,
> The birds to touch (?) the sky.
> He giveth breath to that which is in the egg;
> He sustaineth the grasshopper
> And keepeth alive (even) the gnat,[82]
> The creeping and the flying things alike;
> Who maketh food for the mice in their holes
> And feedeth the flying (creatures) on every tree.
>
> Hail to thee for all these things!
> The one, the only one, with many hands,[83]
> Who lieth awake for all men when they sleep,
> Seeking what is best for his animals!"

It is clear that the Egyptian conception of the gods in the New Empire meant a great advance beyond the low, primitive ideas which we have described on pp. 16, 202–04, etc. The deities of these later religious hymns have not only gained unlimited power over all nature, but appear as great moral forces, as the principles of love, thought, and justice — at least in the figure of the supreme divinity whom the religious thinkers and poets seek. If we could cleanse these Egyptian descriptions from polytheistic and pantheistic traits, their conception of a fatherly and omnipotent deity would seem at times to approach the Biblical idea of God.

On the other hand, we must constantly query how far the masses could follow so lofty an advance. Not even the priests had that ability, for they were unable to free the mythology from the old objectionable traditions which described the gods as very weak and imperfect beings, both in morality and in power.[84] In the magic of all periods the deities appear still more fallible. The late sorcerers are even particularly fond of preserving and emphasizing the traditional weaknesses of the divinities, as in the retention of objectionable myths in magic rites (p. 80). Sometimes they actually endeavour by threats to draw the gods from their celestial abodes (p. 201). Nevertheless they never completely return to the conception of the local spirits which was current in the primitive age, and similar conflicts between higher and lower ideals of the gods can be found to continue in other religions than that of the Nile-land.

Foreign influences cannot be discovered in any of the developments which we have thus far considered. The borrowing of Asiatic *motifs* by Egyptian mythology (p. 153) could never revolutionize Egyptian thought, nor could this be done by a few Asiatic deities which enjoyed worship in Egypt at one period (pp. 154–57). These foreign cults existed side by side with the ancient Egyptian worships, neither mingling with them nor affecting them. In later times the intrusion of many inassimilable elements of this kind only made Egyptian religion more conservative. This is equally true of the Greek period, when even the official Serapis cult (p. 98) advanced very slowly among the native Egyptians. It was only magic that was always open to foreign influence (p. 207). In the Roman period, when the religion of Greece and Rome had been strangely Egyptianized, and when the spread of Christianity threatened every type of paganism alike, we perceive a certain amount of intermingling of the Egyptian and Græco-Roman systems in the popular mind. This influence, however, was less strong in the temple cults, which still endeavoured, as best they could, to copy the most ancient models. The sun-god, once pictured at Philae as an archer, is one of the rare adaptations to Greek mythology;[85] and the same statement holds true of a curious change of the old type of the god Antaeus (p. 130) to that of Serapis with a non-Egyptian halo, the dress and armour of a Roman soldier, etc. Anubis and Ophoïs, guarding a tomb near Alexandria, are represented in similar fashion; one of them, with the lower part of his body in the form of a serpent, may possibly be

explained as a curious reminiscence of the serpent in the underworld (p. 105); it is again quite a new liberty. The strange degeneration of the sacred uraeus serpent on the same tomb is equally non-Egyptian. Still bolder innovations can be found among the terra-cotta figures which adorned private houses of this period (see Plate I, 1, 2 for specimens), but we know little about the meaning of such strange fancies.

FIG. 218. ANTAEUS-SERAPIS

The influence of the Egyptian religion on neighbouring countries was strongest in Nubia, where such Egyptian divinities as were recognized throughout Egypt (i. e. the Theban and Osirian circles) were rendered popular by conquest, colonization, and the imposition of the official cults on the dark-skinned subject races. Amon especially, as being the highest divinity in the state cult, became the official god of Napata and Meroë, and of all the great Ethiopian Empire as well when it won its independence. The Egyptian priests of the Greek period actually looked southward with envy and described the Ethiopians as the best, most pious, and, consequently, happiest men on earth.[86] In particular the employment of oracles to direct politics and even to choose kings continued in Ethiopia until the Persian period, as it had in Egypt in days gone by

(p. 197). As the supreme official divinity of the conquering Egyptian empire between the Eighteenth and Twentieth Dynasties, the ram-headed Amon also became known as the highest god in Libya, west of Egypt, as is shown by the name of the "Oasis of Amon" and its famous oracle in the Libyan Desert. The influence as manifested in Asia and earlier Europe was less direct, although Egyptian art imported many Nilotic *motifs* thither. Since Phoenician art was always much more strongly influenced by the Egyptian style than by that of Babylonia, we may assume that the

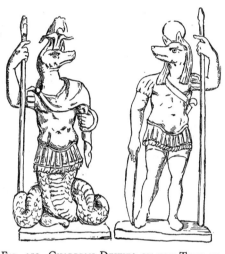

FIG. 219. GUARDIAN DEITIES ON THE TOMB OF KÔM-ESH-SHUGAFA NEAR ALEXANDRIA

religion of Phoenicia likewise borrowed liberally from Egypt. Thus Tammuz-Adonis was worshipped at Byblos like Osiris with Egyptianizing forms of cult (Ch. V, Note 84), the Phoenicians gave the name of Taaut to the inventor of writing (Ch. III, Note 2), etc. In like manner we find, for example, the sacred musical instrument of Egypt, the *sistrum*, or rattle (p. 41), used in religious ceremonies in Crete as early as Minoan times, when it is pictured on the famous vase of Phaistos. Thus we are not surprised that distinctly Egyptian traits are numerous in Greek mythology, and some seem to have wandered even to northern Europe.

FIG. 220. GUARDIAN SYMBOL FROM THE SAME TOMB

Despite all this, the Egyptians never propagated their religion abroad by missionaries. After the time of Alexander

the Greeks, who had always been somewhat attracted by the
mysterious worship of the Nile-land, began to imitate some
of its cults in their entirety, even outside Egypt itself; in the
Roman period these cults spread to Italy, and thence through
the whole Roman Empire as far as Brittany. As we have already seen (p. 121), this propagation of the Egyptian religion
was almost exclusively restricted to the deities of the Osirian
cycle, the most popular of the Egyptian divinities, and to the
Græco-Egyptian Serapis. In the dispersion the cults sought
to imitate as closely as possible — though not always with
success — the ancient traditions of the Nile-land. The architecture and the hieroglyphs of the temples, the obelisks and
sphinxes before the shrines, the strange linen vestments of the
priests with their shaven heads and faces, the endless and
obscure ritual, and the animal forms of some of the idols everywhere filled the Classical world with peculiar awe, and
wonderful mysteries were believed to be hidden under these
incomprehensibilities. It mattered not that some free-thinkers
always scoffed at the animal worship and other strange features
of this barbarous cult; the proselytes only clung to its mysteries
with the greater zeal, and the "Isiac" religion proved a formi-
dable competitor of rising Christianity.[87]

The principal reason for this success must have been the
strong impression which the tenacious conservatism of Egypt
made on that skeptical age. While the ancient Græco-Roman
religion had lost all hold on the people and could be mocked
with impunity, while the deities of old had become meaningless names or shadowy philosophical abstractions, the Egyptians, in childlike faith, showed all the miraculous trees, lakes,
rocks, etc., of mythology, the abode of the gods in their temples
on this very earth, and the divinities themselves actually embodied in statues and in sacred animals. This staunch faith,
combined with the mysterious forms of worship, gave strangers
the conviction that Egypt was the holiest country in the world
and that "in truth the gods dwelt there." A pilgrimage to the

Nile was always thought to bring marvellous revelations and spiritual blessings, and the pilgrims, returning with freshened zeal, spread at home the conviction that the profoundest religious knowledge had its home in the gloom of those gigantic temples which, in their largely intact condition, impressed the Roman traveller even more than their ruins now affect the tourist from the West.

Nevertheless the Classical world, though longing for new religious thought, was unable to copy that same conservatism which it admired in the Egyptians. Even in Egypt the more popular divinities, especially of the Osirian cycle, had been invested, as we have already noted, with some non-Egyptian ideas in the cities with a larger Greek population; and in Europe amalgamation with Greek and Asiatic names and mythologies, and with philosophic speculations, reduced them to vague, pantheistic personalities. At last Isis and Osiris-Serapis, as they were worshipped abroad in the mystic cult of secret "Isiac societies," retained little more of their Egyptian origin than their names and forms of worship. Strange new myths were also invented. The picture of Harpokrates, or "Horus the Child" (p. 117), putting his finger to his lips as a conventional sign of childhood (cf. Figs. 45, 48, and Plate I), was misinterpreted as commanding the faithful to be silent concerning the deep religious mysteries of Egypt, an interpretation which strongly appealed to proselytes to that faith. The so-called "Hermetic literature" blended Greek and Egyptian religion with great freedom.[88] Even the speculations which Plutarch, in his treatise "On Isis and Osiris" (p. 92), sought to read into the names of the divinities of the Nile-land are Egyptian only in part. On the other hand, the masses, especially the women of the Roman world, clung, as we have said, at least to the outer forms of the Egyptian religion to the best of their ability, as when, for instance, the representation of the great mother Isis always retained the type which we can trace to the Pyramid Period.

In Egypt itself, for the first three centuries of the Christian era, the temples saw the old creed, the old cults, and the pious throngs of worshippers without revolutionary change. After that time Christianity spread far more rapidly, and when, near the end of the fourth century, the famous edict of Theodosius ordered the closing of the pagan shrines, the masses had abandoned the ancient faith so thoroughly that the populace even turned against the heathen priests and their few followers. The scanty remnants of Egyptian and Greek religion, much disfigured by amalgamation during this bitter period, as we have repeatedly stated, died in wild riots during the fifth century. It was only on the beautiful little island of Philae (p. 99) that the cult of Isis and her associates continued undisturbed and uncorrupted. The wild, brown, nomadic tribes of the Blemmyans and Nobadians, east and south of Egypt, still refused to accept Christianity, and by clinging to the old faith they forced the Roman government, which feared the raids of these barbarians and even paid tribute to keep them quiet, to tolerate a few priests of Isis in the temple at Philae, at the southern frontier. In the beginning of the sixth century, however, the powerful Emperor Justinian suppressed these remnants of paganism, closed the temple, imprisoned the priests, and propagated the preaching of the Christian religion among the Nubians. With the death of the last priest who could read and interpret the "writings of the words of the gods," as the hieroglyphs were called, the old faith sank into oblivion. It was only in popular magic that some superstitious practices lingered on as feeble and sporadic traces of what had been, a couple of centuries before, a faith which bade fair to become the universal religion; or a statue of Isis and Horus, which had escaped destruction, was interpreted as a representation of the Madonna and Child. A vague sentiment of admiration and of awe for this strangest of all pagan religions still survived, but from the very incomplete information given by the Classical writers no clear idea of the vanished faith could be constructed, and when the thunder of Napoleon's cannon awoke knowledge of Egypt to new life, her religion proved the hardest task for the scholars who strove to decipher her inscriptions and papyri (pp. 8–9). Yet despite all difficulties which still remain, we venture to hope that our survey, unprejudiced and unbiassed, has shown that though the Egyptians can in no wise furnish us edification or be compared with the philosophic Greeks and Indians, or even with the more systematic Babylonians, the extremely primitive character of their faith makes it a most valuable and indispensable source of information for those who wish to study the origin and the growth of religion.

NOTES

EGYPTIAN

Introduction

1. For a collection of monotheistic expressions, which often, however, are only fallacious, see Pierret, *Mythologie*, viii; Brugsch, *Religion*, p. 96; Budge, *Gods*, pp. 120 ff. For the real approaches to monotheism, cf. Ch. XIII.

2. "Der ägyptische Fetischdienst und Götterglaube," in *Zeitschrift für Ethnologie*, x. 153–82 (1878). He had a predecessor in the work of the famous French scholar, C. de Brosses, *Du culte des dieux fétiches*, Paris, 1760.

3. If these factors were Asiatics who entered Egypt in considerable numbers, we could understand that such conquerors or immigrants would leave the religion of the natives absolutely untouched, as is shown by repeated parallels in the later history of Egypt. This explanation for the rapid development of Egypt is, however, at present merely a hypothesis which lacks confirmation from the monuments.

4. In similar fashion the costume of the kings affords reminiscences of primitive times, e. g. in such adornments as the long tail tied to their girdles, or the barbarous crowns.

Chapter I

1. See G. Maspero, *The Dawn of Civilization*, London, 1894, p. 121. Generally speaking, all serpents were supposed to embody spirits (pp. 166–67) or the one mentioned in the present connexion might be regarded as a manifestation of the harvest-goddess Renenutet (p. 66).

2. In many instances the phrase "souls of a city" is used instead of "its gods," especially for some of the very oldest cities, as for the two most ancient capitals, Buto and Hierakonpolis (Pe-Dep and Nekhen). It seems to be an archaic expression which was used with special reverence, or possibly it had a more general meaning than "gods." *Pyr.* 561 substitutes the word *ka* for "the souls of Pe," i. e. a word which is more distinctly used of defunct souls. Otherwise the divine nature of all departed souls is not so clear as in other animistic religions (cf. pp. 15–17).

3. Each Egyptian nome also had one or two tabus of its own. Thus in one place honey was the local "abomination," while in others a special piece of meat, such as the liver or even the hind quarters of all cattle, was tabu. In many places the head or the blood is mentioned as forbidden; but since both of these seem to have been avoided throughout Egypt, this may merely imply that the prohibition was more strictly observed in certain places, and the same statement probably holds true of some sexual sins mentioned in the lists of the nome tabus. Many prohibitions must have originated from tabus of holiness, as that of hurting a sheep, which was forbidden in one district; certainly the abhorrence of the hawk, recorded in one locality, does not denote its uncleanness, especially as the bird was sacred in all parts of Egypt. Other instances, as those in connexion with the hippopotamus, gazelle, etc., however, are to be understood as the consequences of curses. "Making light in daytime" is also declared to have been a local sin. The whole subject is thus far involved in much obscurity.

4. The religion of Babylonia likewise shows unmistakable evidences of an original animistic basis, although it was earlier adapted to cosmic theories and better systematized than was the religion of Egypt. Scholars have often tried to find traces of totemism in the symbols of the gods, the cities, and the districts of Egypt. Such an interpretation is especially tempting when these emblems, carried on a standard as the coat of arms of the nomes, represent an animal or a plant. The only statement which we can positively make is that the Egyptians in historic times were not conscious of a totemistic explanation of these symbols. Their application was divine or local, never tribal like the totemistic symbols of primitive peoples. The interpretation of totemism in general is at present in a state of discussion and uncertainty.

5. Such triads were the rule in Babylonia as well. It is quite wrong to call the Egyptian or Babylonian triad a trinity in the Christian sense.

6. Sometimes the Theban triad was Amon, Amonet, and Mut. In this instance the minor male god Khôns(u), who usually took the place here occupied by Amonet, was set aside to avoid exceeding the traditional number three.

7. This is always the meaning of the orthography in the Old Empire; it was only at a later period that the name was held to signify "Master of the West" (i. e. the region of the dead, *amentet*) or "the One before his (!) Westerners" (*Pyr.* 285). On the assimilation of Khent(i)-amentiu to Osiris see p. 98.

8. It is quite improbable that awe of pronouncing the sacrosanct name caused it to fall into desuetude. We do not find such fear in

the historic period in Egypt, where the divine name was used (and abused) in direct proportion to its sanctity. On the other hand, the names of certain ancient gods seem to have disappeared at a very early time. Thus the crocodile with an ostrich-feather, which once was worshipped in Denderah, remained on the standard of the nome, but its name was so completely lost that later it was held to symbolize the conquest of Sêth (here boldly identified with Sobk) by Horus (in this instance explained as symbolized by the feather; see Mariette, *Dendérah*, iii. 78). A divine name rendered in three contradictory ways (*Pyr.* 1017, 1719, etc.), so that we must conclude that it was unfamiliar to scholars as early as 3000 B. C., may have many parallels in names of doubtful occurrence or reading in the earliest hieroglyphic inscriptions.

9. Mariette, *Les Mastaba*, p. 112; Lepsius, *Denkmäler*, iii. 279 (near Memphis?).

CHAPTER II

1. On his later *rôle* in the Osiris-myth as son, re-embodiment, and avenger of Osiris see pp. 102, 113, 115–18, where the now popular theory is criticized that the winged disk of Edfu is the earliest form of Horus (p. 101).

2. This interpretation is evidently based on an etymological connexion with the root *khoper*, "to become, to be formed." This etymology leads also to an explanation of the name as "the One who Forms Himself, the Self-Begotten," as the sun-god later was called. For the earliest orthography, Kheprer, see *Pyr.* 1210, 2079.

3. A localization of Khepri at Heliopolis is scarcely original, for Atum(u) was the earlier solarized god of this place.

4. Some texts seem to understand the two *sekhnui* of the sun to be gangways, or something of the sort. *Pyr.* 337, for example, says, "Throw down the two gangways (*sekhnui*) of the sky for the sun-god that he may sail thereon toward the (eastern) horizon." Then their number is doubled, and they are located at the four cardinal points (see *Pyr.* 464), "These four clean gangways are laid down for Osiris when he comes forth to the sky, sailing to the cool place." Later their name is transferred to the four pillars of heaven. The original meaning of the word seems very soon to have become odscure. In the earliest pictures (Petrie, *Royal Tombs*, ii, Plates X–XI) it is clearly a mat hanging from the prow of the solar ship.

5. Very late art even tries to make it a curtain of beads or an ornament symbolizing the rays of the sun (e. g. Bénédite, *Philae*, Plate XLIII); or it may appear as a black tablet adorned with stars (*Ani Papyrus*).

6. *Pyr.* 1209. The numerical symbolism is interesting.

7. Later this expression loses its original force, so that all the righteous dead are expected to join the elect who sail in the boat of the sun (p. 26).

8. Bonomi and Sharpe, *Oimenepthah*, Plate XI.

9. These wars belong more properly to the later mythology; see p. 106.

10. The earlier idea was that during the night the bark of the sun was drawn by jackals "in the mountain to a hidden place" (*Harris Magic Papyrus*, 5). This and the idea of the "jackal (lakes)" (*Pyr.* 1164, 1457), or "jackal field(s)," into which the sun descends, seem to date from the time when the dog or jackal Anudis (already possibly identified with Ophoïs) was the only ruler of the nether world (see pp. 98, 110–11). Cf. the jackals at "the lake of life" (Bonomi and Sharpe, *Oimenepthah*, Plate VIII). The rope around the neck of such jackal-gods seems to refer to their towing of the solar ship.

11. Later, by a misreading, the "flaming island," or "island of flames," is interpreted as the "lake of flames" or the "canal of flames." The former becomes the place of torment for the wicked; while the latter is evolved into that portion of the subterranean water-way where the sun battles with its diabolical adversary 'Apop (pp. 104–06). Theologians also seek to distinguish other parts of the ocean where the sun sets or rises, e. g. the "lakes of growing [or of Khepri?], of Ḥeqet, and of Sokari" (Virey, *Tombeau de Rekhmara*, Plate XXIV). Four lakes (ib. Plate XXVII) refer to the four sources of the Nile as the birthplace of the sun (p. 46).

12. Or Mese(n)ktet; cf. P. Lacau, in *RT* xxv. 152 (1903), on the doubtful pronunciation of this name.

13. This is a strange feature, since Heliopolis, the place of worship of this latter local form of the sun, was situated at the eastern frontier of the Delta, so that we should expect him to represent the morning appearance. It is possible that Atum was the earliest solarization of a local god in Lower Egypt, so that he could represent the old sun, quite as Rê' did in some of the later myths (see the following Note). On the original sacred animal of Atum see p. 165.

14. See the myths recounting why the gods withdrew from earth (pp. 76–79). It is for this reason that very late texts equate Rê' with the feeble and dethroned Kronos of Classical mythology.

15. The special name given to this ram-headed form, Ef, Euf, cannot yet be definitely explained. Later the sun, again like Khnûm, is often represented with four rams' heads, probably on the analogy of the four mythological sources or subterranean branches of the Nile.

16. These numbers can be traced to the divisions of the month by seven and fourteen, which fit both the solar and the lunar chronology.

17. See E. Lefébure, *Le Mythe osirien*, i. *Les Yeux d'Horus*, Paris, 1874.

18. For a picture of the sun-god sitting on his stairs and with a single eye instead of a head see Mariette, *Dendérah*, iv. 78.

19. It is difficult to determine the extent to which the Asiatic concept of the planet Venus as a daughter of the sun (pp. 54, 101) and the femininity of the sun in certain Asiatic languages and religious systems may have affected the Egyptian development in this regard.

20. It is possible that the "female sun," Rê'et, or "Rê'et of the two countries" (*Ra't taui*), originated from these individualizations of the solar eye; yet it may have been merely the tendency to divide gods, especially those of cosmic character, into a male divinity and his female consort, as we find Amon(u)-Amonet, Anup(u)-Anupet, etc. At all events, the divinity Rê'et, who was worshipped as a minor deity at Heliopolis and some other places, is usually human-headed and is treated as analogous to the celestial goddesses, as is shown by her head-dress of horns and the solar disk; sometimes she is also analogous to the lion-headed Tefênet.

21. The original meaning of this symbolism was sometimes confused by the fact that Sêth came from the "golden city" of Ombos.

22. *Pyr.* 391; similarly 1178. The two obelisks in heaven were also called "the two marks, or signs [i. e. limits], of power" (*sekhmui*), a phrase which the later Egyptians did not understand and interpreted mechanically as "two sceptres" (W. Spiegelberg, in *RT* xxvi. 163 [1904]).

23. On the divine descent and worship of all kings see pp. 170–71.

24. W. von Bissing, in *RT* xxiv. 167 (1902).

25. "The great (cosmic) source" in Heliopolis (*Pyr.* 810).

26. See the three hawks from Pe-Dep (Buto) and the three jackals from Nekhen (Hierakonpolis), these latter animals from the "Hawk City" forming a strange contradiction to its name (Lepsius, *Denkmäler*, iv. 26, 77, 87, etc.).

27. For the name of these baboons, Hetu (feminine Hetet; cf. Heţet, *Pyr.* 505), see H. Schäfer, in *ÄZ* xxxi. 117 (1893), and Lanzone, *Dizionario*, p. 505. The sacred *qefden* (or *benti*) monkeys seem to be little different. Female marmosets surround the morning star (*Pyr.* 286). Regarding the four baboons of Tḥout, especially as the judges and guardians of condemned souls, see p. 180.

CHAPTER III

1. The moon as the father of the heavenly god (*Pyr.* 1104) is an isolated thought.

2. Thus he ought to correspond to the planet Mercury in the mythologies of other nations (see Note 63, on Sebgu). Phoenician mythology borrowed his name, under the form Taaut, as the inventor of writing.

3. Later the baboon form of Thout was called "Esden," as at Denderah; but this appellation seems to be merely a copyist's corruption of Esdes, the name of a god who is mentioned together with Thout as a wise counsellor and judge (for a collection of some early passages concerning Esdes see Erman, *Gespräch eines Lebensmüden mit seiner Seele*, p. 28), the two being subsequently blended. Esdes is represented as having the head of a wolf or jackal (Mariette, *Dendérah*, iv. 21; cf. also Champollion, *Notices*, i. 417, Lepsius, *Denkmäler*, i. 100, Dümichen, *Patuamenap*, iii. 28). It is possible that he was an earlier god of some necropolis who once wavered between identification with Thout and with Anubis, both being judges of the dead. If we were certain that he originally had a baboon's shape, we should assume that he was the god who transferred it to Thout.

4. Even as early as this period Khônsu is sometimes identified with the clerk Thout (Erman, *Gespräch*, p. 27).

5. Thus at Ombos Khôns appears as the son of the solarized Sobk and of Ḥat-ḥôr, the sky.

6. The symbol of the double bull has the value *khens* (e. g. *Pyr.* 416 as a constellation connected with hunting, as also on the "Hunter's Palette") and likewise seems to appear among constellations on the magic wands (p. 208). For the other symbol see on Dua, Ch. VII, Note 21.

7. For these female pillars see Mariette, *Dendérah*, ii. 55; De Morgan, *Ombos*, i. 254. For other interpretations of the four pillars of heaven see p. 44 on Shu with the pillars, p. 39 on Ḥat-ḥôr's tresses in the same function, Ch. II, Note 4, on the later name of the four pillars, and pp. 39, 111–13 on the sons or tresses of Horus. There were various other concepts of heaven which were less popular. Thus from the frequent idea of a ladder leading to the height of heaven (*Pyr.* 472, etc.) was developed the thought that heaven itself is a great ladder (ib. 479), corresponding to the great stairway of the sun in other texts. Many of these ideas are not yet clearly understood. The concept of several superimposed heavens (as in Fig. 47) is rare; but *Pyr.* 514, "he has united the heavens," and *Pyr.* 279, 541, "the

two heavens," may refer to the opposed skies of the upper and lower world.

8. *Pyr.* 1433, etc. For the two pillars as parallel to this idea see pp. 30–31 and Ch. II, Note 22.

9. *Pyr.* 1216.

10. The oldest texts speak more frequently of the heavenly wild bull, despite the Egyptian gender of the word *pêt;* and this also seems to explain why so many gods (especially deities of a celestial character) appear in the form of a black bull, since black and blue were felt to be the same colour. In *Pyr.* 470, for instance, mention is made of the heavenly bull with four horns, one for each cardinal point. Accordingly in earlier tradition Osiris often has the form of a bull. Thus the whole conception seems to be borrowed from countries farther north, where the lowing of heaven, i. e. thunder was more common than in Egypt.

11. The later Egyptian theological interpretation of this name as "the (celestial) house of Horus," i. e. the goddess who includes the sun-god in his wanderings, is philologically impossible. Originally the term can have meant nothing more than "temple with a face," i.e. with the skull of a cow nailed over its entrance to ward off evil spirits. The head of the cow or ox as a religious symbol throughout the ancient world may be traced partly to the Egyptian personification of the sky and partly to earlier Asiatic motives. Later the primary signification was no longer understood in most countries outside Egypt, and the head of the cow or bull became a mere ornament, although the "bucranium" still seems to have been used preferably for religious decoration over the whole ancient world (see E. Lefèbure, "Le Bucrâne," in *Sphinx*, x. 67–129 [1906]).

12. The "green ray" above the horizon has been used as an explanation by modern scholars, but the daily rise and death of the sun in the green ocean would seem to furnish a more natural interpretation. The Egyptians, however, were scarcely conscious of this origin of "the green." We again find the idea of the green bed of the sun in the story of Isis and the young sun in the green jungles of the Delta (pp. 115–16), in "Horus on his green" (ib.), and probably also in "the malachite lake(s)" in which the gods are sometimes said to dwell (*Pyr.* 1784, etc.). Malachite powder falls from the stars (*Pyr.* 567), just as the blue lapis lazuli is celestial in origin (ib. 513). Whether the goddess Ḥat-ḥôr as the patroness of the malachite mines on the Sinaïtic peninsula (and of a "Malachite City," Mefkat, in Egypt) is intentionally thus identified with the green colour is less certain, because Ḥat-ḥôr also rules over all foreign countries. On the other hand, the metal peculiar to the Asiatic Queen of Heaven (Astarte, etc.) is copper, from which the green colour of the ancient

Orientals was derived; but thus far we do not know whether this explanation was primary or secondary. We are equally unable to explain why the stars which cover the body of the heavenly cow in Egypt usually have four rays, while all other stars are depicted with five. Four is the special celestial or cosmic number (see e. g. Note 7, on the pillars of heaven).

13. When a leopard's skin forms the garment of the goddess (Mariette, *Dendérah*, iii. 40), she is assimilated to the goddess of fate.

14. Cf., in this connexion, Pharaoh's dream of the seven cows proceeding from the floods and plants of the Nile to indicate the nature of the coming harvest (Genesis xli).

15. See Brugsch, *Religion*, p. 318, Mariette, *Dendérah*, iii. 59, 76, Lepsius, *Denkmäler*, iv. 26, etc.

16. The reading Bat is furnished by *Pyr.* 1096, where her symbol is clearly a cow's head on a standard, differing from Ḥat-ḥôr's symbol only by the strong inward curve of the horns. The statement that Bat had "a double face" (ib.) is thus far unique.

17. The pronunciation of this name is very uncertain; it might also be read Nuet, Neyet, or Nunet, or in some other way containing two *n*'s. If the name of the ocean was Nûn or Nûnu, we should expect Nûnet, provided that the connexion of the goddess with the ocean was not merely an etymological play upon words, which is quite possible. Thus we retain a conventional error as pronunciation. For the equally doubtful pronunciation of Nuu or Nûn see *infra*, Note 38.

18. The earliest form of the name seems to have been Gêbeb (K. Sethe, in *ÄZ* xliii. 147 [1906]). For the reading Gebk (based on the Greek transcription Κηβκις) see W. Spiegelberg, in *ÄZ* xlvi. 141–42 (1910), but cf. Note 63. The form Qêb is here followed in harmony with the Greek transliterations Κοιβις, Κηβ, etc. Seb, the reading of the early Egyptologists, is erroneous.

19. He cackles at night before he lays this egg (*Harris Magic Papyrus*, vii. 7). The ordinary laws of sex, of course, do not apply to the gods. See also p. 71 on the symbol of the egg.

20. Thus as early as *Pyr.* 1464, etc. He is also master of snakes in *Pyr.* 439 and master of magic, ib. 477.

21. Qêb and Aker are mentioned together as early as *Pyr.* 796, 1014, 1713.

22. The Babylonian Nergal, the god of the lower world, is a single lion, but he may be, to a certain extent, parallel. Later we often find Aker with two differentiated heads or as a single lion, as when, for example in the accompanying picture (Lepsius, *Denkmäler*, iii. 266), Nut, bearing the sun in the form of a scarab, bends over

him as over her usual husband Qêb. Again, the source-god Khnûm stands on the back of a lion, which thus represents the depths of the earth (Mariette, *Dendérah*, iv. 80, etc.).

23. Champollion, *Notices*, ii. 584, 507.

24. See pp. 104–06. The thought that the underworld was a huge serpent, or that it

FIG. 221. NUT, AKER, AND KHEPRI

was encircled by one (an idea that may have been derived from the similar representation of the ocean), seems to be still later and more vague.

25. The pronunciation is not quite certain; it may be Shôu. The Greek renderings, Σως, Σωσος, Σωσις, seem to presuppose also a pronunciation Shôshu, but this may be based on an artificial etymology from *ashesh*, "to spit out," to which allusion is made e. g. in the creation-myth (*Pyr.* 1071, etc.; cf. p. 69). The lion-shaped rain-spouts of the temples perhaps represent Shu, although the later Egyptians were no longer conscious of this fact, but called them simply "storm-spouts" (*shen'*, Lepsius, *Denkmäler*, iv. 67, etc.).

26. When Shu is compared to the midday sun, this seems to mean that the sun is most under his power at noon, when the widest aerial space separates the sun from the earth. This idea, perhaps combined with an etymology from the verb *showi*, "to be dry," has led some Egyptologists to compare Shu to the (dry?) heat, the (drying?) air; but in his prevalent function as a god of air and wind he is often called the master of the cooling air-currents (cf. Fig. 71). Whether another etymology, from *shuo* (or *shuy*?), "to be empty, to empty," is the original reason for his identification with Ḥeḥ, "the empty space," or is only a secondary etymological paronomasia like so many of the forced etymologies of Egyptian theology (see Note 30 on Tefênet), is fully as doubtful. His earliest cosmic function seems to have been solar (and is still so, for example, in *Orbiney Papyrus*, v. 7); yielding to more recent sun-gods, he had early to assume the inferior *rôle* of carrying these deities.

FIG. 222. SHU WITH FOUR FEATHERS

27. The transition may frequently be seen in pictures which, as in Naville, *Deir el Bahari*, Plate XLVI, represent "Shu, the son of the sun," with four feathers. Cosmic explanations of this number easily suggest themselves (see Notes 7, 10, Ch. II, Note 15, Ch. V, Notes 27, 67).

28. This name is not to be pronounced Tefnut, Tefnuet, and consequently is not to be connected with the sky-goddess Nut.

29. At first she aids Shu in holding the sky (*Pyr.* 228, 1443, 1691, etc.), a function which the later Egyptians no longer mentioned.

30. An etymological connexion with *tof*, "to spit," seemed possible only to the paronomasiac mind of the Egyptian scribes (cf. Note 26 on the name of Shu), although this play on words appears as early as *Pyr.* 1652. Nevertheless they did not interpret it of her cosmic function, but of her creation by the sun-god. The conclusion of early Egyptologists that she denoted the dew rests on an erroneous etymology of her name ("spittle of Nut"), which is not supported by Egyptian texts (see Note 28 on the lack of a connexion with the name Nut).

31. This, however, does not seem to be a very ancient expression. The name is subsequently confused with an old god Ruruti (?), who is mentioned side by side with Atum (*Pyr.* 447 [like his wife?], 696, 2081, 2086; see also A. Erman, in *ÄZ* xxxviii. 25 [1900]).

32. Ḥaʻpi is not androgynous, as Egyptologists usually state; see p. 46 on his two wives. The pendulous breast recurs on many Egyptian representations of fat men; and the obesity of Ḥaʻpi (Greek pronunciation Ὦφι or Ὧφι; cf. the Κρῶφι and Μῶφι of Herodotus, ii. 28; the earliest orthography is simply Ḥp) symbolizes the fertility which is brought by the life-giving river.

33. These are usually differentiated into the plant-hieroglyphs for "north" and "south" in conformity with the traditional conception of Egypt as "the two countries," or kingdoms. Another explanation of the double Nile, according to its Egyptian or Nubian course, can also be applied to this distinction.

34. Cf. Genesis ii.

35. See e. g. Griffith, *Siut*, Plate XVII, 42, and *passim*. Four Niles are mentioned in Mariette, *Dendérah*, iv. 81.

36. See Lanzone, *Dizionario*, Plate XIV, and Borchardt, *Saʼḥu-rēʻ*, Plates XXIX–XXX (whence our Fig. 41 is drawn).

37. *Pyr.* 1229.

38. The pronunciation is quite uncertain, and it is difficult to say how the late (but excellent) tradition Nûn can be reconciled with the earlier orthography, which looks like Niu or Nuu. Later connexions with *n(y[?])ny*, "to be weak, inert, lazy," might seem to harmonize both traditions, but are apparently mere etymological plays on words, such as have been discussed in Notes 26, 30.

39. *Pyr.* 1691, etc.

40. *Pyr.* 1040.

41. Cf. praises of Nuu's fertility (Champollion, *Notices*, i. 731).

42. Champollion, *Notices*, ii. 429. Did the idea come from Asia?

43. Champollion, *Notices*, ii. 423.

44. The artist who copied this picture from early models evidently did not understand the two "mysterious gods" who appear behind Nuu, one representing the sun and the other carrying a strange symbol. In the latter we now see the divinity who figures among the birth-deities and for his symbol carries a milk-vessel on his head (Naville, *Deir el Bahari*, Plate LIII; in Gayet, *Louxor*, Plate LXVIII, significantly enough, a figure of the Nile takes its place). We might think that this is no new god, but merely the cataract-deity Khnûm, whose hieroglyph (a pitcher with one handle) later artists may not have recognized. In the old birth-temples he would thus appear as the creator of the king (p. 51). It is, however, possible that here we have an earlier god of the deep. Cf. *Pyr.* 123, 559, 565, where Ageb ("the Cool One"), an earlier name for the abyss, seems to be addressed as "water-furnisher (of the gods)." His name is there written with a similar jar, unless this is an earlier orthography for Nuu, which later was imperfectly understood (cf. *Pyr.* 1565).

FIG. 223. AGEB, THE WATERY DEPTH

45. See Lepsius, "Über die Götter der vier Elemente," in *ABAW*, 1856, pp. 181–234, who did not yet understand the true meaning of these gods. They were very popular in magic as being the most mysterious forces imaginable. We cannot yet say whether their strange shoes, which resemble a jackal's head, connect them with the jackals who draw the ship of the sun (Ch. II, Note 10), etc.

46. Because of the difficulty of the latter idea some monuments substituted the vaguer names Emen and Emenet ("the Hidden," as in *Pyr.* 446), terms which have no connexion with Amon; occasionally these other names replace the third pair in the ogdoad. A sarcophagus in the Metropolitan Museum of Art, New York, has for the consort of Niu a variant Hemset ("the Sitting, Resting Force"), and for that of Emen the primeval cow-form of the sky, Ehet, Ahet (p. 40). Heh(u) is understood by some texts to mean "flood" (or "rain-water"?). The earliest tradition knows only the first two pairs (e. g. Lanzone, *Domicile des ésprits*, v). On the system of dividing every principle into a male and female person cf. Ch. II, Note 20; it seems to symbolize the creative activity of the differentiated forces of nature.

47. See Mariette, *Dendérah*, iv. 76. The accompanying title, "father of the gods," may be a trace of the original interpretation as the ocean. Yet the earth-god Qêb also sometimes bears this title,

and it is certain that the latest period tried to find him in this unusual representation.

48. This conception of spontaneous creation was too profound for some priests, who gave gross interpretations to it, telling how the god "became enamoured with himself" or with his shadow, or polluted himself, such imaginings being found as early as *Pyr.* 1248 (cf. also the hymn of creation on p. 69). A more philosophical speculative text says, "the soul (i. e. apparition, incarnation) of Nuu is the sun-god," i. e. the sun is only a part of primitive matter (*Destruction of Men*, ed. É. Naville, l. 86). See pp. 219–20 for this pantheistic idea.

49. See *Hieroglyphic Texts . . . in the British Museum*, ii. 5, 6, etc., and Mariette, *Dendérah*, ii. 37.

50. e. g. *Hieroglyphic Texts . . . in the British Museum*, ii. 14 (Twelfth Dynasty). Both deities appear as masters of the necropolis of Abydos, etc.

51. This belief was entertained even before the New Empire (cf. *Westcar Papyrus*, x. 14, *Book of the Dead*, xxx). For the "double," or *ka*, see p. 174.

52. See *Pyr.* 1183–85 for the symbol of the feelers, which seem to furnish the etymology (from *sekhen*, "to meet, to touch"? cf. Ch. II, Note 4). The name of the goddess is written with the sign of the two birth-bricks (e. g. Mariette, *Dendérah*, iv. 27, 29, etc.) or with the bed (Budge, *Book of the Dead*, Plate III). As a birth-goddess she is sometimes identified with Êpet-Tuêris (Mariette, *loc. cit.*).

53. The exact form is doubtful; only the consonants S-*kh*-*t* are quite certain.

54. Borchardt, *Sa'ḥu-rēʿ*, ii. 19.

55. Similarly the name of Nut is often written with the hieroglyphic sign for "heaven" turned upside down, thus denoting the heaven of the underworld (p. 41).

56. She may once have been another personification of the seven Pleiades (cf. p. 40) or a single star which was rarely seen above the horizon. On the question whether the eight-rayed star of the Semitic Queen of Heaven is to be compared, since the shaft supporting the star of Sekhait might be counted as the eighth ray, see the present writer's notes in *MVG* ix. 170 (1904). Cf. also the seven-rayed star as a hieroglyph (Quibell, *Hierakonpolis*, Plates XXVIc, XXIX). For another symbolism of the stellar rays see Note 12.

57. In the Greek period Sekhait was, accordingly, identified with one of the Muses, though a more accurate parallel would be the Sibyl. She seems to be the Selene of Plutarch (*De Iside et Osiride*, xii), whom he describes as the mistress of time, although the femininity of the moon is quite foreign to Egyptian theology (pp. 32–34).

In this capacity, according to him, she yields to the wise moon-god one seventieth of the year (i. e. the five epagomenal days) for the birth of the great gods. Plutarch or his source seems to have mistaken the horns of Sekhait for the lunar crescent.

58. This identification is found as early as *Pyr.* 268, etc. For assimilation with Ḥat-ḥôr see Note 13.

59. This is not her original name, as is often erroneously supposed, but is merely an epithet which replaces it.

60. e. g. *Pyr.* 1207, where he is called "Horus of the Star-Abode" (i. e. abode of the dead, the underworld) and "god of the ocean" (*Pyr.* 1719, etc.). It is not quite certain whether "the single star" means the evening star as distinguished from the morning star. In the Roman period the planet Venus was represented with two male heads, this being, perhaps, an allusion to the double nature of the star (Brugsch, *Thesaurus*, p. 68) or to that of Orion, its parallel among the constellations.

61. A tradition (*Pyr.* 820) speaks of "the *duat*-star who has born Orion," but this may be a mistake for *duat*, "nether world, lower firmament." *Pyr.* 929, 1204, are obscure allusions to the birth of or by the morning star. In some later cosmic pictures the female figure carrying a star on her head and standing before the sun in his morning boat evidently meant Venus. The later Egyptians copied this without comprehending it and interpreted the figure as representing the hour of sunrise, a misunderstanding which proves that the original of these pictures goes back to a much older time. In other pictures, as that of two goddesses conceiving from the blood of Osiris (Fig. 118), it is difficult to decide, for Isis-Sothis could be meant, not the female morning star.

62. *Pyr.* 362, 488, 1455, etc.

63. Sebg(u)'s name is also written Sebga, Sebagu, early Coptic Sūkê (F. Ll. Griffith, in *ÄZ* xxxviii. 77 [1900]). The explanation of his association with Sêth seems to go back to the early attribution of a dangerous character to the planet Mercury. In Champollion, *Notices,* i. 452 = Lepsius, *Denkmäler,* iii. 206, "Sebeg who is in the wells(?)" appears as a dread guardian of the underworld, while in the *Book of the Dead,* cxxxvi A, his staircase is said to be at the sky. The explanation of this change of interpretation may be found in certain very obscure old texts (P. Lacau, in *RT* xxvi. 225–28 [1904]), where the dead fear "the pen and the inkstand of Gebga." It is probable that this name Gebga is a corruption of Sebga, so that Mercury really appears here like the Asiatic secretary of the gods, the deity of judgement, corresponding to the Egyptian Thout. This

FIG. 224. "SEBEG IN THE WELLS"

Gebga is there once called "the son of (the sun-god) Atumu," and at another time he is associated with the goddess of justice, so that we are told that he can send the soul either to the lake of flames (i.e. hell) or to the fields of the blessed (P. Lacau, in *RT* xxvi. 227 [1904]). It is not likely that the earth-god Qêb was meant here; variants of his name, like the Greek variant Κηβκις (Note 18), may be derived from the texts to which we have just referred.

64. *Pyr.* 749, 1144; cf. p. 26. The planets likewise are divine messengers (*Pyr.* 491).

65. ib. 1187.

66. If this name connects her with the god Sopd(u), who is usually called "the master of the east," we may infer that the Egyptians were not conscious of this association (to which allusion appears to be made only in *Pyr.* 1534), though it seems plausible because of the similar head-dress, etc., of both divinities.

67. She appears thus in Mariette, *Dendérah*, iv. 80, as well. This association may be based either on earlier tradition or on a late, but erroneous, etymology of the Greek pronunciation Σωθις, re-adapted to Egyptian *sat* (older form *saṭ*), "to shoot." The position assigned to the two spouses in the picture given in the text (De Morgan, *Ombos*, p. 250, Rosellini, *Monumenti del culto*, p. 78) tempts us to regard them as counterparts who interchange places like various consorts in universal mythology, especially constellations who descend alternately into the lower world. Though it could be possible that, as Lepsius assumed (*Denkmäler*, iv. 49), we here have merely a correcting superposition of one picture over another, yet the same detail occurs on the oldest Sothis-Orion group described by G. Daressy, in *Annales du service des antiquités de l'Égypte*, i. 80 (1900); it seems, therefore, to have been intentional.

68. *Pyr.* 965.

69. ib. 959. The south is here the lower world, as on p. 46, etc.

70. "Orion, the father of the gods" (*Pyr. W.* 516 = *T.* 328). As early as *Pyr. M.* 67 Orion is identified with Osiris and is connected with the fatal vine. The most important star of Orion is that on his shoulder (*Pyr.* 882, 1480, etc.). It is remarkable that the peculiar turban or frontal ribbon of the Asiatic types of Orion (cf. on Reshpu, p. 155), which often ornaments or blinds him, appears on the oldest Egyptian representation of him (G. Daressy, *Annales du service des antiquités de l'Égypte*, i. 80 [1900]). Cf. the mysterious reference to the fillet, e. g. "of the single star" (*Pyr.* 1048) or "on the head of the sun" (*Pyr. N.* 37, etc.). When the *Book of the Dead*, xxiii, speaks of a goddess as "the female Orion" or "the companion of Orion (*saḥet*) in the midst of the spirits (Ch. I, Note 2) of Heliopolis," the allusion is as yet inexplicable.

71. After Lepsius, *Denkmäler*, iii. 170.

72. See the *Book of That Which is in the Lower World*, reproduced by Budge, *Egyptian Heaven and Hell*, i. 58. This explains the strange pictures of the *Book of the Dead*, xvii (manuscript *Da*, etc.). It is possible that a remarkable representation (Rosellini, *Monumenti del culto*, p. 78, De Morgan, *Ombos*, i. 250) gives in two figures of Orion, drawn athwart each other, a hint of the changing or antagonistic nature of the twins, unless, as Lepsius (*Denkmäler*, iv. 49) assumes, we have merely a corrected picture. See, however, Note 67 for a similar instance.

73. This is indistinctly considered in *Pyr.* 925 and perhaps also in 2120. Cf. Note 70 on his fillet. In *Pyr.* 1201 he is called "the gate-keeper of Osiris." The names Nuru (1183), Ḥeqrer (1222), and Hezhez (1737), given to the ferryman, cannot yet be explained. *Pyr.* 493 seems to ascribe to him two faces, one looking forward, and the other backward.

74. See *Book of the Dead*, xvii. 63 (?). The passages cliii. 8, 25; clxx. 6, are obscure.

75. Thus *Pyr. W.* 511; *Pyr. T.* 332–34; Mariette, *Dendérah*, iv. 7, 16; *Book of the Dead*, xvii. 63; De Morgan, *Ombos*, p. 68. In *Pyr. P.* 707, he seems to give water and wine; *Pyr. T.* 41 connects him with a "vine-city," probably because of the hieroglyph for "press," just as his function of butcher may be derived from a forced etymology of *seshem* ("butcher's steel").

76. See G. Daressy, in *Annales du service des antiquités de l'Égypte*, i. 85 (1900), where the word is written Sebshesen, etc. The name of the goddess was discovered by P. Lacau (*RT* xxiv. 198 [1902]; cf. also É. Naville, in *ÄZ* xlvii. 56 [1910]). It was so unfamiliar to scribes of the Fifth Dynasty, and even earlier, that they doubted whether it was not merely the same as Sekhmet (hence the meaningless repetition in *Pyr.* 390 = *Book of the Dead*, clxxiv. 8). It is possible that her lion's head comes simply from this identification with Sekhmet, yet we must not forget that Shesmu also appears to be leontocephalous. She seems to be a companion to the deity who is called "the Horus of Shesmet" (*Pyr.* 449, etc.), although this may be an adaptation of the ancient Shesmu to the worship of Horus which prevailed later. At all events it is certain that when the decanal circle was established in the prehistoric period, the names Shesmu and Shesemtet must have been compared, though later the connexion became unintelligible, except in the Greek decanal list, where both are called Σεσμη.

77. The decanal lists mention a number of other forgotten stellar gods whose names are incredibly mutilated. Thus we know little about the eighteenth, Semdet(i), who had the head of some animal

(Lepsius, *Denkmäler*, iii. 270, etc.) and who appeared both in the northern and in the southern sky (G. Daressy, in *RT* xxi. 3 [1899], and *Annales du service des antiquités de l'Égypte*, i. 80 [1900]). None of these gods played a part in mythology, for the decanal system, originating in a very early period, soon became largely unintelligible. The "four sons of Horus" do not appear regularly among the decans (see pp. 111–13). Brugsch (*Thesaurus*, p. 179) claimed to have discovered a different decanal system, which would seem to have been purely local.

78. This constellation is also called "the Club Stars" (*Pyr.* 458, etc.). The number seven, which was generally unlucky to the Egyptian mind, recurs in the Pleiades, which are the constellation of fate (p. 40). The group of "the many stars" does not seem to be identical with the latter constellation.

79. She is called Epi in *Pyr.* 381 (cf. Epit in Lepsius, *Denkmäler*, iv. 34, etc.), and in Greek she once appears as T-υφις (Brugsch, *Thesaurus*, p. 735). Locally she was also named Sheput (perhaps to be read Eput), and sometimes also Riret ("Sow"), because a sow occasionally serves as her symbol instead of a hippopotamus. Since she often leans on a peculiar piece of wood (for which the hieroglyph for "talisman" was later substituted), she seems to be termed "the great landing-stick" (*menet*) in *Pyr.* 794, etc., where she likewise reappears as divine nurse (perhaps also *Pyr.* 658?).

80. He is called Dua-'Anu as early as *Pyr.* 1098; i. e. he is identified with the morning star (who equals Horus) and is connected with the "four sons of Horus." Accordingly his picture is sometimes called simply Dua ("Morning Star").

81. See J. Krall, "Ueber den ägyptischen Gott Bes," in *Jahrbuch der kunsthistorischen Sammlungen des allerhöchsten Kaiserhauses*, ix. 72–95 (1889), and also A. Grenfell, in *PSBA* xxiv. 21 (1902). The earliest mention of this god seems to be *Pyr.* 1768, which speaks of "the tail of Bês" (as stellar?).

82. When Plutarch (*De Iside et Osiride*, xix) calls Thuêris the wife of Typhon-Sêth, he evidently confuses the wicked Sêth with the ugly, but benevolent, Bês.

83. It is uncertain whether the reason for this mode of representation was that the full effect of his grinning face might frighten evil spirits away (cf. J. E. Harrison, "Gorgon," in *Encyclopædia of Religion and Ethics*, vi. 330–32), or whether it rested on a very archaic delineation.

84. For Bu-gemet ("Place of Finding") as the birth-place of the sun cf. p. 86 on the myth of the loss of the eye of the sun; for Bu-gemet as the birth-place of Osiris see Champollion, *Notices*, i. 172, etc.

NOTES 265

85. The first scarab after A. Grenfell, the second in the possession of the author.

86. The Egyptian kings, who at a very early time repeatedly sent expeditions to remote parts of Africa for obtaining a member of the dwarf tribes, stated that they were impelled not only by curiosity, but also by religious zeal, to have the dwarf "for the sacred dances." Possibly a personage wearing a mask (?) like Bês, and regarded, it would seem, as coming from Wawa (i. e. Central Nubia near the Second Cataract), appears in sacred dances and ceremonies (Naville, *Festival Hall*, Plate XV). "The dwarf of the sacred dances who amuses the divine heart" (*Pyr.* 1189) seems to be placed in the sky. We might suppose that the myths of Bês were reproduced in these religious performances and that these legends were actually connected with the interior of Africa. Another trace of this is possibly found in the idea (which seems to have found its way into other mythologies as well) that dwarfs are the best goldsmiths, since the interior of Africa furnished both dwarfs and gold. Diodorus (i. 18; cf. R. Pietschmann, in *ÄZ* xxxi. 73 [1893]) speaks of hairy Satyrs meeting Bacchus (i.e. Osiris) in Ethiopia with music, and mention is also made of Bês-like gods (*haitiu*) who, together with the baboons of the sun (p. 32), dance and play on musical instruments before solar gods coming from the east or south (cf. H. Junker, "Der Auszug der Hathor-Tefnut aus Nubien," in *ABAW*, 1911, pp. 45, 86). We have, however, no unmistakable connexion of these mythical ideas with the earthly dwarfs of Africa.

87. e. g. Lepsius, *Denkmäler*, Text, i. 100; cf. also Borchardt, *Saʾḥu-rēʿ*, Plate XXII.

88. e. g. Quibell, The *Ramesseum*, Plate III. For dwarf-like gods of the earliest period see, perhaps, Fig. 2, (*f*). This type occurs repeatedly (Quibell, *Hierakonpolis*, i. Plates XI, XVIII).

89. e. g., cf. Sopd, p. 149.

90. Herodotus, iii. 37. For Ptaḥ-Bês as the cosmic universe and for a magic hymn to a great god who is both dwarf and giant see p. 222. In very late times remarkable combinations of the two dwarf types, Bês and Khepri-Sokari, are found in which one of them carries the other on his shoulders, probably to express their close association.

91. Concerning him see von Bergmann, *Buch vom Durchwandeln*, p. 44, where proof is found that he was originally a local god, like most deities who were placed among the stars. The statement in Mariette, *Dendérah*, iv. 32, no. 1, is based on a misunderstanding.

92. See G. Daressy, in *RT* xxi. 3 (1899), on his stellar character and cf. *Pyr.* 452.

93. 1019, 1094, 1152, 1250.

94. For the Egyptian names of the zodiacal signs see W. Spiegelberg, in *ÄZ* xlviii. 146 (1911). Representations of them are always intermingled with some old pictures of decanal stars, etc., as also in Fig. 56.

95. Some pictures of the winds are collected by Brugsch, *Thesaurus*, p. 847.

96. Brugsch, *Thesaurus*, p. 736.

97. ib. 28–31.

98. Renenutet was also understood as a "Nurse-Goddess" who cared for the young gods and watched the growth of men. Possibly this was originally a distinct personality in human form, later confused with the harvest-serpent (p. 16). In this capacity she and Meskhenet (p. 52) watch the beginning of the second life in the realm of Osiris (Budge, *Book of the Dead*, Plate III; cf. *supra*, p. 52). The four harvest-goddesses (Mariette, *Dendérah*, iii. 75) seem to be parallel to the four genii at the birth of Osiris (pp. 52, 95). In *Pyr.* 302 Renenutet is identified with the asp on the head of the sun-god.

99. De Morgan, *Ombos*, no. 65.

100. Cf. p. 135 on Khnemtet.

101. See p. 44 for the old, irregular identification of Ḥeka with Shu.

102. Borchardt, *Saʾḥu-rēʿ*, Plate XXX. There are more personifications of this kind, such as the gods "Eternity" and "Endless Time" (Neḥeḥ, Zet); cf. von Bergmann, *Buch vom Durchwandeln*, line 26. "Abundance" may likewise be feminine as Baʿḥet (*Pyr.* 555). Personifications of cities and districts are usually feminine.

CHAPTER IV

1. See E. A. W. Budge, "The Hieratic Papyrus of Nesi-Amsu," in *Archæologia*, lii. 393–608 (1890); the original may now be found in the same scholar's *Facsimiles of Hieratic Papyri in the British Museum*, p. 14, Plate XII.

2. See Ch. II, Note 2, for the play on this name, "the One Forming, Becoming," which is here considerably elaborated.

3. i. e. my word (or thought) began the differentiation of living beings.

4. Hardly "(nor) the reptiles," etc., since the following line shows them already in existence. A variant text of this line reads, "I am he who was formed as the forms of Khepri."

5. Variant: "I created many other forms of the forming one" (Khepri; cf. Note 2).

6. See Ch. III, Notes 25, 30, for the etymological paronomasias on these two names.

7. Variant: "I used my mouth for (pronouncing) my own name, which was magical" (Budge, in *Archæologia*, lii. 558 [1890]).

8. One of the many confusing repetitions of the same word seems to be omitted.

9. Or, "libidinem excitavi."

10. Cf. Ch. III, Note 48, on this fancy (or crude lack of fancy) which, however, is very old and widely known.

11. The manuscript is corrupt here, but some obscure word meaning "kept them in rest," "kept them back," is implied. Possibly this word was *s-nyny*, with a play on the name Nuu (cf. Ch. III, Note 38).

12. The manuscript is again corrupt.

13. Or, "after I became a god."

14. The meaning is, apparently, "after I had replaced my eye." If this hypothesis is correct, the subsequent story of the disappointment of the eye on its return would belong to another myth; otherwise, the restoration of Shu and Tefênet to their father, the sun-god, would be meant. In Egyptian theology "members" denote the various manifestations of the same divine force (cf. p. 28).

15. This verse cannot be translated, or, rather, reconstructed with certainty.

16. "In them" evidently means "in the plants" (a term of uncertain signification). Cf. *Book of the Dead*, lxxviii. 15, on the creation of the first beings "which Atumu himself had created, which he formed from the plants (and ?) his eye."

17. The symbolism of the plants seems to be an analogy to the green plants which surround the heavenly beings at their rising; see pp. 38, 116. A variant of the same papyrus (Budge, in *Archæologia*, lii. 561 [1890]) goes so far as to make these plants and the primeval reptiles come from the tears shed from the divine eye (pp. 30, 70).

18. Thus the creation of man can also be connected once more with the source-god (later the potter) Khnûm, who was subsequently regarded as the special creator of the human race (see p. 51). For the myth of the loss of the sun's eye in the realm of Khnûm see pp. 89–90. We may here note that frequently (e. g. Mariette, *Dendêrah*, iii. 77; *Book of the Dead*, lii) we find a theological division of mankind into three or four classes; but until we understand the names of these categories with certainty, we cannot say whether they refer to the creation or to the present cosmic order. *Pe'tiu*, the name of one of these classes, means "nobles," but the explanation of *rekh(i)tiu* as "the knowing ones, the wise," is very uncertain, and one name, *henmemtiu*, often applied to celestial beings in the Pyramid Texts, is quite obscure. The fourth name ordinarily means "men."

19. Mariette, *Dendérah*, iii. Plate LXXVIII.

20. This expression seems to mean "in development," "in primitive shape." Cf. also Note 14.

21. The seeming indication of a basis on which the heavenly cow stands probably was in origin an indication of the ocean.

22. clxxv. 16 ff.; cf. also É. Naville, in *PSBA* xxvi. 81–83 (1904).

23. The manuscript refers this to Sêth as being in the boat, but the original seems to have been, "from those who are in the boat," i. e. the guardians of the monster were chosen from the companions of the sun-god (p. 26).

24. i. e. the celestial beings; see p. 41.

25. Or, perhaps, "an order of Atum is given to Thout."

26. *Destruction of Men*, first copied by É. Naville, in *TSBA* iv. 1–19 (1876) (cf. also ib. viii. 412–20 [1885]), and later by von Bergmann, *Hieroglyphische Inschriften*, Plates LXXV–LXXVII.

27. The words in brackets fill the lacunae in the original text.

28. Ms., "my god"(?).

29. This and the following imperative are in the masculine singular, so that we must suspect that the original address was to Thout, the divine messenger.

30. i. e. they shall not abandon their plan.

31. The epithets of Nuu and Rê' have here been confused, but we try to separate them again. On the expression *rekhtiu* for a class or generation of men see Note 18.

32. Or, "of it" (i. e. of the eye). We should, however, expect "before thee." It was, it would seem, not the brilliant manifestation of the sun by day, but its appearance by night, that was to pursue the evil-doers to their lairs.

33. Or, perhaps, "may it go as Hat-hôr."

34. Or, "fear" (?).

35. Or, "cakes"(?). The word recurs in l. 18.

36. This sentence, which is in part obscure, both concludes the preceding section by an etymology of a divine name and, in the manner of a title, introduces the following story.

37. An Ethiopian fruit which could be brought only from the southern frontier.

38. Apparently a goddess. We have here an allusion to the name of the city On (Heliopolis; p. 31) as meaning "great stone," i. e. either "monument" or "millstone."

39. Of the company of the gods? We should expect "her (i. e. of the destroying goddess) time."

40. If this is correctly understood, it means the coolest part of the night just preceding sunrise, the best time for working.

41. Emu at the western frontier of the Delta, famous for the local worship of Ḥat-ḥôr.

42. *Timæus*, p. 22, etc.; cf. H. Usener, *Die Sintflutsagen*, Bonn, 1899, p. 39.

43. The statement of *Sallier Papyrus*, IV. ii. 3, that on the night of the twenty-fifth day of the month Thout "Sekhmet went to the eastern mountain to strike the companions of Sêth," seems to allude to the same event, though in a secondary association with the Osiris-myth. Sekhmet is frequently mentioned as a flaming destroyer (p. 87).

44. Or, "pain" (= disgust?). The text is obscure.

45. Thus better than "is not . . . a failure" of the text.

46. This passage is very obscure.

47. The command to Shu to put himself under the heavenly cow Nut and to support her with his hands seems to have dropped out; but cf. the description as repeated below.

48. i. e. forgiven.

49. See p. 48 for this name of the aerial space, which is often identified with Shu, the air, as on p. 44 and in Fig. 71, as well as in this passage, though rather indistinctly. In *Destruction of Men*, ed. É. Naville, l. 86, Ḥeḥ is equated with Shu and Knûm, as is also the case *infra*, p. 89.

50. The meaning of this section was first elucidated correctly by E. Lefébure, in *ÄZ* xxi. 32 (1883).

51. The text is here corrected on the analogy of the following line.

52. i. e. the formulae for repressing and avoiding them.

53. Originally *ḥn'-y*, "with me"(?).

54. Or, "hole"(?).

55. This may also mean, "I shall rise on the sky," implying a removal from them.

56. Ḥeka; see pp. 44, 133.

57. This may also refer to their magic forces.

58. From a papyrus of about the thirteenth century B.C., preserved in the museum at Turin. The text is edited by Pleyte and Rossi, *Papyrus de Turin*, Plates CXXXI ff. (reprinted by Möller, *Hieratische Lesestücke*, ii. Plates XXIX ff.); the first translation and correct mythological interpretation are due to E. Lefébure, in *ÄZ* xxi. 27 (1883). The original division into verses (indicated by dots of red ink in the papyrus) has been followed here, except in a few instances, although it does not always seem to agree with the rules for logical parallelism. The biting of the sun-god Atumu by some monster (*Pyr.* 425) does not seem to be analogous.

59. We should expect "to whom an age means a year."

60. i. e. neither men nor gods.

61. This does not fit the preceding introduction; originally the connexion must have been different.

62. Or, "the world of men" (Lefébure).

63. i. e. [she thought:] "Could she not be?" We have adopted Lefébure's correction of the manuscript, which reads, "she was not able (to be)."

64. Manuscript, "land (of the) goddess." Möller (*loc. cit.*) proposed to divide, "mistress of the land. The goddess thought," etc.; but this has the difficulty that, according to the story, Isis is not yet a goddess.

65. Manuscript, "crew," as though he were in his ship (?).

66. This is apparently the meaning, although the manuscript is mutilated at this point.

67. Or, "concealed on the way" (?) or, "blocking the way" (?). The word is mutilated in the text.

68. i. e. Egypt, not the entire world. In l. 2 and Plate CXXXIII, l. 1, the land of Egypt also seems to be meant, not the earth.

69. The italicized words seem to have been erroneously transposed in the manuscript.

70. Correct the manuscript to *psḥ*.

71. The sun-god, breathing heavily and painfully, emits his flames.

72. Possibly an epithet of the sun-god. For the cosmic tree as a cedar see pp. 36, 115. After *emi*, "being in," the manuscript has an obscure and superfluous sign.

73. Literally, "moved, pushed."

74. Literally, "found his mouth."

75. Omitted in the manuscript.

76. Literally, "he established his heart."

77. Manuscript, "Khepri," a meaningless reading, though of theological interest; cf. pp. 25, 68.

78. If the manuscript reading is correct, we should translate, "my heart hath (now) noticed it, (but) mine eyes have not seen it."

79. "The Horus of Praises," i. e. the praise-worthy (cf. Ch. V, Note 28).

80. Or, "power (of) magic."

81. This may also be read as a question: "Is it fire? Is it water?" See, however, the repetition below.

82. The younger generations of gods who form the transition to mankind (pp. 69, 120).

83. We should expect, "my heart."

84. Manuscript, *shed* = old *ushed*, a remarkable archaism.

85. Manuscript, "bound together."

86. i. e. on the earth. The mention of the mountains must have been different in the original form.

87. This may also refer to the sun-god, "who became (was formed) in the great flood." For this Great Flood (*Meḥt-uêr*) as the name of a goddess see p. 39, and for the sun-god as "bull of his mother" see p. 38.

88. The manuscript (perhaps correctly) understands this as "the one who created the first life."

89. Or, referring the secrecy only to the horizon, "made the heaven and the secrets of the double horizon."

90. Literally, "the force." It must be noted that all gods are here treated as manifestations of the same force (cf. p. 28 and Note 14).

91. Manuscript, "palaces" (?).

92. i. e. at noontime. On the different manifestations of the sun see pp. 27–28.

93. Alluding to the belief that a man's personality and the memory of it live only as long as his name is in use.

94. Manuscript, "behold ye."

95. Is this the god Bebon (see p. 131), or has the word *baba* its ordinary signification of "hole, cave, cave of a spring, spring"?

96. The text is corrupt; perhaps we should read *sa'[r]t*, "wisdom."

97. The text is again corrupt, but seems to continue to allude to the revolt against the sun-god as described in myth No. III.

98. Or, "proxy."

99. Corrupt text.

100. A word later used for the foreigners coming from the north, such as the Greeks. Why the moon has this special function is very obscure. It is not probable that it is an allusion to the dark rain-clouds coming from the north in winter.

101. See H. Junker, "Der Auszug der Hathor-Tefnut aus Nubien," in *ABAW*, 1911, and W. Spiegelberg, in *SBAW*, 1915, p. 876.

102. See Ch. III, Note 84, on this place where young solar and stellar gods "are found."

103. Shu may here be compared with the warlike An-ḥôret (Onuris), as is often the case; see pp. 44, 143–44.

104. Junker, p. 54.

105. Cf. Ch. V, Note 28, for a similar form of Horus. The combination of gods in this passage is not clear.

106. *Sallier Papyrus*, IV. xxiv. 2, has an obscure reference to it: "The sun's eye (literally, "the Intact One"; cf. pp. 30, 91), the mistress who is in the sky as . . . to seeking (that which?) stood before, which was among the wicked ones, for (?) their . . . in the Delta." We cannot make much out of this version, which may possibly be connected with the story of the fall of mankind.

107. *Pyr.* 698.

108. *Pyr.* 1091, 660, etc.

109. ib. 195, etc. Cf. *Pyr.* 1040: "It was not the fear which arose for (? ḥr) the eye of Horus" (before the world was created). *Pyr.* 1147, however, speaks of "the eye of Horus, stronger than men and gods."

110. ib. 2090.

111. *Pyr. P.* 455.

112. *Pyr.* 1832. Hence the ferry of the underworld is called "the eye (i. e. the best activity) of Khnûm" (*Pyr.* 1227–28). Cf. likewise the restoration of "the eye of Khnûm" (*Pyr.* 1769) by the ferryman "who looks backward" (p. 58). For Khnûm cf. pp. 50, 135.

113. *Book of the Dead*, ed. Lepsius, ch. cxlix; Mariette, *Dendérah*, iv. 80, etc.

114. Attempts were, however, also made to localize this place at Heliopolis (*Pyr.* 2050), in the sacred well of that city (p. 31).

115. H. Junker and G. Möller, in *ÄZ* xlviii. 100–06 (1911). The texts are very obscure, and the scribes seem hopelessly to confuse the solar and lunar myths. We should expect the seventh day (cf. also the fourteen souls — i. e. manifestations — of the sun-god), though this number may intentionally have been avoided as unlucky (as it appears in Asiatic systems also) by the substitution of the astronomically meaningless number six. The sixth day and the middle of the month are mentioned as festivals as early as *Pyr.* 716, etc.

116. The explanation of the Nile flood in summer and of vegetation runs remarkably parallel to the well-known Babylonian myth of the descent of the goddess Ishtar to the lower world and of her return to the upper earth when she is needed there. Unfortunately the interpretation of the Nile's water which has been mentioned above, p. 90, seems to be a somewhat secondary explanation of the myth of the solar eye. Cf. also the pig in the sun's eye as described on pp. 124–25, and the Vatican Magic Papyrus, iii. 8: "When the sun was blind (and) saw (not), the goddess Nut opened the way to the divinities." See Ch. V, Note 28, on the "blind (?) Horus."

CHAPTER V

1. We must remember that the strictly localized, non-cosmic gods of the primitive period could develop very little mythology (p. 20).

2. The exact Egyptian pronunciation of the name is uncertain. If it was, as is usually assumed, Usir(i) (perhaps for an original Wesir[i]), the connexion with the name of his wife Isis, which is otherwise so plausible, becomes very forced (cf. p. 98). Paronomasias associating his name with that of the sun-god Rê' are as old

NOTES 273

as the Nineteenth Dynasty. The name looks very non-Egyptian, and it may be an old misreading of hieroglyphic symbols which had become unintelligible.

3. It is not certain whether the pillar as the hieroglyph of the city may not have been the earlier conception, and whether the deity may not merely have been called "the one of Dêd(u)" (cf. pp. 20–21 for such names of divinities). Later times may have reversed this relation of city and god. What the pillar represents is wholly obscure; it is neither a Nilometer, nor the backbone of Osiris. It may have been merely an old architectural experiment without any original religious meaning. Its frequent repetition simply means "Dêdi, the (god) of Dêd." In *Pyr.* 288 an old scholar registers the names Zedu, Zedet, Zedut for the city.

4. See Ch. III, Note 10. The identifications with the sacred bulls of 'Memphis (the Apis), Heliopolis (the Mnevis), and Hermonthis (the Buchis) are, however, much later; and the ancient ram (or goat?) of Mendes, called "the soul of Dêd(u)," proves that no consistency whatever exists in the incarnations of Osiris.

5. See Brugsch, *Religion*, p. 615, and *Book of the Dead*, cxlii. 5 (where Osiris is at the same time equated with Orion).

6. The exact date of the concept of Osiris as floating in a chest (cf. Fig. 76 and Plate II), is uncertain. For other ideas associated with the ship Argo see pp. 57–58.

7. A rare identification with Qêb seems to occur in Lanzone, *Dizionario*, Plate CLVII.

8. Plutarch (*De Iside et Osiride*, xxxvii) mentions a special flower which was sacred to him and which seems to have formed his crown (cf. also Petrie, *Athribis*, Plate XLI). Diodorus (i. 17) ascribes the ivy to him; for the vine connected with him as the Egyptian Dionysos see pp. 36, 113.

9. *Pyr.* 589, etc.

10. e. g. in the late monument given by Mariette, *Les Mastaba*, p. 448. A frequent prayer for the dead in the Eighteenth Dynasty is, "may he drink the water at the source of the river!" This water comes directly from Osiris or is a part of him; consequently it makes man one with the god.

11. Greek Leyden Papyrus, lxxv; cf. Brugsch, *Thesaurus*, p. 735.

12. The four birth-genii of Osiris-Horus, who are united here as elsewhere, are explained as Tefênet, Nut, Isis, and Nephthys (Mariette, *Dendérah*, iv. 43), or, better, as Nebt-meret (i. e. Muit-Nekhbet or Meret ?), Neith, Heqet, and Nephthys (Lepsius, *Denkmäler*, iv. 82); elsewhere as Isis, Nephthys, Meskhenet, and Heqet (cf. the parallel in *Westcar Papyrus*, ix. 23), and Isis, Nephthys, Neith, and Selqet (*Pyr.* 606).

13. See the god rolled up, Figs. 46, 47, which the later Egyptians probably misunderstood. For Osiris rolled together see Champollion, *Notices*, ii. 511, 601–02, 618; variants of the picture given in our text may be found ib. ii. 541, 614.

14. Sometimes Osiris is represented as green, which is often nothing but a discoloured blue; and blue, according to Oriental ideas, is merely another hue of black (cf. Ch. III, Note 10); see, however, Petrie, *Athribis*, p. 12, Budge, *Book of the Dead*, Plate IV, 20, etc., for unquestionable green colouring, which may hint at his life in sprouting plants.

15. Cf. p. 35 on the idea underlying this detail.

16. The earliest term for his realm, *Duat* (or *Daet*; latest traditional pronunciation in Greek letters Tηι), really means "Rising Abode of the Stars," and its localization, therefore, varies. The word is best translated "underworld" because we have no corresponding phrase and because, as a matter of fact, the later Egyptian conception closely corresponds with this rendering as denoting the place where the stars go to rest.

17. The old standard of the nome, a basket on a pole ornamented with feathers, did not represent this relic, as the priests later claimed; see e. g. Petrie, *Royal Tombs*, ii. 19, for the original form. The name of this old fetish was *ṭeni*, "the lifted (symbol)," whence came the name of the city *Ṭin*, the Greek This (*Pyr.* 627).

18. This identification is found as early as *Pyr.* 1256.

19. Greek writers claimed that the name and the picture of Serapis came from the Greek city of Sinope on the Euxine Sea, and as a matter of fact this god was worshipped in Egypt chiefly under the Greek representation of Zeus (cf. Plate II, 3, and pp. 239, 242). Nevertheless the Greek origin of Serapis is a disputed point, and the Egyptian etymology of his name which we have given appears as official at an early time under the Ptolemies.

20. This is suggested by the hieroglyphic orthography of both names and by parallel paronomasias on names of mythological consorts in other countries. According to the traditional pronunciations of these Egyptian names, Usir (Wesiri? see Note 2) and Êset (rarely written Aset; H. Grapow, in *ÄZ* xlvi. 108 [1910]), this connexion would appear to us an artificial play on words, and clearly betrays a poor imitation of a foreign mythological idea.

21. See Lanzone, *Dizionario*, Plate CLI, where Nut is shown with the knot hieroglyph of Isis, and cf. p. 99.

22. The confusion of the two different meanings of the feather hieroglyph, or at least the clear interpretation of the feather-bearing personage as "Justice," does not appear to be traceable to the earliest texts. It seems to begin with *Pyr.* 744, which says that "Justice

before the sun-god on that day of the new year" delights the world. For its development see *Book of the Dead*, lxv. 12, where we read that the solar deity "lives (i.e. feeds) on Justice." The source of the confusion can be found in such euphemisms as *Pyr*. 1208, 1230, where the region of death, whether on earth or in the depths of earth or sky, is termed "the beautiful one, the daughter of the great god." In *Pyr*. 282 "her beautiful tresses" plainly associate her with the sky, Ḥat-ḥôr (p. 39). The extensive worship of Maʿet ("Justice") at the court of the Ancient Empire has nothing to do with this misinterpretation of "the West." "Justice" there appears as the principle which governs state and dynasty.

23. We must, however, again remind the reader that this interesting development is quite secondary. Later ages were still correct in their interpretation of the arms stretched from the western mountains, or from the symbol of the west, to receive the dead, though they did not invariably understand the parallel meaning of the arms stretching from the sky to the sun. Sometimes they rightly explained these mysterious arms as "the embracer of the sun, the mistress of the west," but sometimes they also regarded them as a special deity, "the Embracer" (Ḥapet). We cannot yet explain with certainty why this alleged new divinity received a reptile's head and was associated with a great serpent (at the top of a flight of stairs; cf. pp. 42, 104, on the earth-god?) which separates Osiris from this world; possibly it may be connected with the dragon ʿApop. Similar goddesses are easily associated with a serpent, either in a bad sense (as on p. 80) or in a good sense, as when the "double justice" holds serpents (Fig. 95).

24. For Nephthys as a doublet of Isis as mistress of the west see p. 110.

25. For such pictures see *Book of the Dead*, xvii.

26. In the Græco-Roman period the *rôle* of Venus-Astarte as mistress of the sea and protectress of navigation was, therefore, given to Isis (cf. Ch. III, Note 61).

27. Cf. Lepsius, *Denkmäler*, iii. 36 b. The Horus of Hierakonpolis is contrasted with Sêth in *Pyr*. 2011, etc. We may note that at Hierakonpolis the principal representation of the god was an ancient effigy of such clumsiness that the feet were not indicated. Like everything dating from the prehistoric period, this statue was considered the most sacred of all, and its imperfections were carefully preserved in copies. Throughout Egypt we find such rude hawk-figures which remind us of a mummied and bandaged bird (see Fig. 153, representing Sopd); it is possible that they are all derived from the hawk-god of Hierakonpolis. The special name, *ʿakhom*, given to this peculiar hawk-form is not yet intelligible. Old texts speak of

four Horuses (see Breasted, *Development*, p. 155, etc.), and the same idea recurs in a four-faced god (*Pyr.* 1207), apparently symbolizing at first the four cardinal points of the sky, but later applied to the four planets or the four sources of the Nile, etc. The four Horuses are then variously localized in Egypt, and being also called "sons of Horus," are identified with the four sons of Osiris-Horus, for whom see pp. 111–13.

28. Some local forms of Horus diverge from the hawk-shape, such as the lion-headed "Horus of Mesen(?)" or "the fine Horus" (De Morgan, *Ombos*, no. 48) or Har-tehen ("Bright Horus"), who sometimes has a serpent's head (Lepsius, *Denkmäler*, iii. 35), and whose name is erroneously explained (see Naville, *Festival Hall*, Plate VII) as Har-tehenu ("Horus of the Libyans"). Many of these gods were evidently quite independent in origin, but were identified with Horus when he became the principal deity. Very late speculation produced the strangely varying "Horus in Three Hundred" (the number probably symbolizes the year), who was sometimes depicted as composed of parts of a lion, ichneumon, crocodile, and hippopotamus. Some of the local forms of Horus are the following: Har-akhti ("Horus of the Horizon") was worshipped at Heliopolis and was the most popular form after the Horus of Edfu. His name was sometimes interpreted as "Horus of the Two Horizons" (east and west), so that he was occasionally pictured as a double-headed god. This is also the explanation of the "resplendent" double-headed god in Champollion, *Notices*, i. 452, etc. On this name for the planet Mars, see p. 54. Later a similar god, whose name in Greek was Ἁρμαχις (i. e. Har-em-akhet, or "Horus in the Horizon"?), was worshipped at the Great Sphinx. Har-merti ("Horus with Two Eyes," i. e. sun and moon?) was adored at Athribis. Har-shuti ("Horus with Two Feathers"). Har-hekenu ("Horus of Praises,"

i. e. praiseworthy) often has a lion's body and also appears as astral (see p. 81). Har-sam-taui ("Horus the Uniter of Both Countries") is mentioned especially at Denderah(?). Har-khent(i)-khet(?) was worshipped at Athribis or Xoïs; on this deity, who is once represented with a crocodile's head, see A. Wiedemann, in *PSBA* xxiii. 272 (1901). Har-khent(i)-merti(?) ("Horus before the Two Eyes") received honour at Panopolis (*Pyr.* 1670, 2015).

FIG. 225.
"HORUS OF THE
TWO HORIZONS"

Later, strangely enough, the name (beginning with *Pyr.* 771?) was altered into "Horus in Front (of the one) Without Eyes," as if through some reminiscence of the blind, eclipsed sun-god (pp. 29, 85 ff.). When he is depicted as an ichneumon (Champollion, *Notices*, ii. 513), we may trace a similar thought, leading to identification with Atum as the evening sun (see p. 165 and Fig. 11 on his original animal form). The development of the name is not yet clear. On Horus in connexion with the planets — e. g. "Horus the Opener of Secrets" (or, "the Resplendent" [*upesh*]) = Jupiter; "the Red Horus" = Mars; and "Horus the Bull" = Saturn — see pp. 54–55; on a development as master of the lower world, not only like Osiris, but even as ruler of hell, see Ch. X, Note 21.

29. Accordingly "Qêb told Horus, 'Go where thy father swam!'" (i. e. take his place; A. Erman, in *SBAW*, 1911, p. 926). We therefore find "Horus in the ocean" (*Pyr.* 1505) and as "the star traversing the ocean" (*Pyr.* 1508). Thus both Horus and Osiris are born from the waters of the deep (pp. 95, 116). For the occasional confusion of Horus and Osiris as both represented in the constellation Orion, see p. 57, etc.

30. *Pyr.* 204, 370, etc. This "gold city" must not be confused with the more southern city which the Greeks also called Ombos.

31. The later Egyptian pronunciation must have been something like Sêt(e)kh. The name is written Sut(e)kh (pronounced Sôtekh) about 1400 B. C.; the earliest orthography also permits S(o)tesh. The final aspirate of the Greek transliteration is an attempt to represent the Egyptian *kh*. The transcription Σηθ, found once in Greek, would imply a dialectic pronunciation Sêeth. Whether the rare orthography Suti had its origin in a misreading or in an intentional mutilation for superstitious reasons is matter of doubt.

32. All male and some female deities carry a sceptre which bears his head, as stated on p. 12 (see Petrie, *Royal Tombs*, ii. 23, etc., and cf. our Fig. 30, etc.), although this detail does not seem to have been recognized by the later Egyptian artists. Consequently at some prehistoric period he must once have been the principal god of the entire pantheon, and he was accordingly worshipped at various places, e. g. as nome-god in the eleventh nome of Upper Egypt and also in the Delta.

33. After 1600 B. C. the Egyptians compared it more frequently to a red (i. e. wild) ass; later it was also regarded in rare instances as an antelope with straight horns. It is possible that it was likened to a boar as well, and that the whole religious prejudice of Asia and Africa against pork goes back to this identification (see pp. 124–25 on the beginning of this idea in the myth which tells how a black hog penetrated into the eye of Horus, perhaps at eclipses). Egyptologists and naturalists have sought to find in Sêth's animal the greyhound, jerboa, okapi, oryx, giraffe, or ant-eater, but none of these identifications agrees with the oldest pictures. The Egyptians called it "the *sha*-animal" and as late as 2000 B. C. they believed that it was

still to be found in the desert, which, however, they peopled with so many fabulous beings that this does not prove much for zoologists. Later the tail is often treated like an arrow (L. Borchardt, in *ÄZ* xlvi. 90 [1910], where the body seems striped from head to tail). In Naville, *Festival Hall*, Plate II, it erroneously looks as if it has three tails; and in Borchardt, *Sa'ḥu-rē*, Plate XLVIII, its skin is yellow.

34. This he showed even at his birth, when, according to Plutarch (*De Iside et Osiride*, xii), he broke through the side of his mother, Nut. Mythological fancy could thus attribute to him various moral weaknesses and perverse inclinations, which led him to pursue the youthful Horus and in punishment for which, according to a myth traceable to nearly 2000 B. c., he lost his manhood (Griffith, *Petrie Papyri*, Plate IV).

35. Accordingly iron was later regarded as the sacred metal of Sêth — "Typhon's bone" (*Pyr.* 393, 530 seems to mean rocks rather than metals). That Sêth became a god of the Asiatics was not so much due to their warlike character or their red hair (although both traits contributed to this patronage) as to the building of the stronghold and capital Auaris in the eastern Delta by the Hyksos kings, the Asiatic conquerors of Egypt, who found him there as the old local god and accordingly gave special honour to him. This accidental connexion with the Asiatics caused him to be compared to Ba'al, the Syrian god of heaven, and gave rise to the wide-spread slander that the Jews (and later the Christians) worshipped an ass, the latter idea receiving additional support in Egypt from the similarity of the Egyptian word for "ass," *iô'*, to the ordinary Hebrew pronunciation of Jehovah's name, Yāhū, Yāhô (see pp. 208–09). Later the crocodile, the hippopotamus, the turtle, and the griffin also became "Typhonic" animals belonging to Sêth.

36. Petrograd papyrus of "The Shipwrecked Sailor," ll. 32, 57, etc. The idea occurs as early as *Pyr.* 298, 326, where rain is associated with Sêth; ib. 289, "the heavenly cow (Meḥt-uêret) is between the two fighters." In *Pyr.* 418 Sêth is identified with the celestial bull (contrary to Ch. III, Note 10), probably because of his lowing.

37. Accordingly it is possible that originally the testicles of Sêth, which were torn from him, were found in the belemnites.

38. Or, 'Aapop, once 'Aapopi (Bonomi and Sharpe, *Oimenepthah*, p. 3). The name is derived from '*op*, "to fly," the reduplicated form signifying "to move as in flight" (i. e. swiftly). Old texts frequently state that 'Apop had legs which were cut off in the battle (see the hymn given on pp. 127–28). As a result there are many tales concerning serpents with two or with many legs.

39. The god Aker (pp. 42–43) acts as his gaoler, holding him fast

and confining him in his prison (*Harris Magic Papyrus*, v. 9); in another text "Qêb holds him down(?), (standing) on his back" (A. Erman, in *ÄZ* xxxviii. 20 [1900]; cf. Fig. 36).

40. The Egyptian text which accompanies this representation is in still greater error as to its meaning since it places the scene in heaven. All these pictures are from the sarcophagus of Sethos I (ed. J. Bonomi and S. Sharpe, *The Alabaster Sarcophagus of Oimenepthah I, King of Egypt*, London, 1864).

41. See Dümichen, *Patuamenap*, Plate XV.

42. Sometimes, by error, these heads are five in number, thus paralleling the five sons of Osiris, of whom there are, properly speaking, only four. For the origin of this change cf. Figs. 101–02.

43. Later we find, e. g., interesting connexions of Osiris with a great serpent which has a single (sometimes human) head. In the lower world or in the sky the god encircles or guards or carries this monster (Lanzone, *Dizionario*, Plates CLIX, CLXII [?], CXCIX, CCVIII–CCXI; in Plate CCLVII the serpent is bound by Horus). These ideas again try to harmonize the old (Osirian) and the later (Satanic) idea of the abyss (cf. Note 23). The placing of 'Apop near the source of the Nile was the easier because as early as *Pyr.* 489 the serpent Neheb-kau was thought to block the way there at the side of the goddess Selqet, or a serpent Qerery (*Pyr.* 1229) with the monstrous "Swallower" (p. 179), who watched this entrance to the lower world. In these old passages, however, the underlying idea was still unlike that of the 'Apop-myth.

44. *Book of the Dead*, xxxix, etc.

45. Bonomi and Sharpe, *Oimenepthah*, Plate IX.

46. ch. xl.

47. Or, "harpoon"? cf. Note 101 concerning this weapon, on which various traditions existed. It is probable that the last verse confuses Sêth with Horus.

48. A. Erman, in *ÄZ* xxxviii. 20 (1900).

49. A. Erman, ib. xxxi. 121 (1893).

50. Figs. 107–08 are from Bonomi and Sharpe, *Oimenepthah*, Plate XII, and Champollion, *Notices*, ii. 521.

51. The *Book of the Gates*, from which this picture has been taken, goes on to vary the idea of the infernal monster, describing it as having one body and eight heads, under each of which is a pair of human legs to justify the name Shemti, i. e. "the One who Walks" (as a variant of the name 'Apop, "Moving Swiftly"; see Note 38); or it appears as an even more complicated monster. In each instance gods of the lower world (once Khnûm and "Horus in the underworld") keep it down.

52. The net is drawn by Horus and Khnûm (in allusion to the

Cataract region in which the struggle usually takes place; see pp. 104–05); or sometimes by the "Book-Goddess" (Fate; see pp. 52–54). The genii of pictures like Fig. 109 bear distinct nets (e. g. Champollion, *Notices*, ii. 520, etc.).

53. The etymology is uncertain, but possibly the name is to be explained as Neki ("the Harmful One").

54. For the confusion of Sêth with the serpent Neḥa-ḥor see p. 141. In the New Empire, when Sêth was still honoured as a real god, his name began occasionally to be avoided by euphemisms. Thus Setkhuy (Sethos) I ("He who Belongs to Sêth") changes his name to "the Osirian" or "He who Belongs to Isis" in his funerary inscriptions or in places where Osiris is not to be offended. The last king bearing Sêth's name belongs to the Twentieth Dynasty, about 1200 B. C. The interesting evolution of this god into a Satan is due to the influence of the Babylonian myth of Tiãmat.

55. Sêth's Greek name, Τυφων, has been derived by some scholars from the Semitic word for "north" (cf. Hebrew *ṣāfôn*), supposed to designate Charles's Wain as "the northern constellation." According to an older view, this constellation, here called "the Great Club," battles against Sêth (Budge, in *Archæologia*, lii. 548 [1890]).

56. Nebt-ḥôt's name is scarcely derived from Ḥôt (better Ḥôit), "the Temple (City)," the capital of the seventh nome of Upper Egypt, for the goddess worshipped there seems to have been Hat-ḥôr and not to have been compared with Nephthys until later, on the basis of the similarity of the name of the city of Ḥôt (cf. on Hat-ḥôr, Ch. III, Note 11). At Antaiopolis, in the tenth nome (cf. p. 130 and Note 101), Nephthys was a neighbour of Sêth, and their union would become intelligible from this proximity if we were not compelled to assume the northern Ombos as Sêth's original seat of worship.

57. Once (Mariette, *Dendérah*, iv. 81) she appears, strangely enough, with the head of a crane or ibis, like her sister Isis.

58. See also pp. 100–01 on Isis and Nephthys as becoming the feather-wearing "double justice," though originally they were the two divinities of the west, the region of the dead. By calling Nephthys Τελευτή ("End") Plutarch (*De Iside et Osiride* xii, lix) likewise makes her the sterner side of Fate. On the other hand, his identifications of Nephthys with Aphrodite (= Isis-Hat-ḥôr?) and with Nike ("Victory"; perhaps because of the wings on the later representations of her, cf. e. g. *Mythology of All Races*, Boston, 1916, i. Plate LIX; later, however, all Egyptian goddesses appear as winged) are meaningless. A Greek papyrus (cf. p. 95) identifies Ἡσενεφυς (i. e. Isis-Nephthys) with the springtime, but this is obviously a

confusion of the foreign conception of Adonis as the god of spring
with the Egyptian idea of inundation. According to *Pyr.* 489, Sêth
has two wives, the Teti-(y?)êb, and from this obscure name seems
to be derived the idea (*Pyr.* 1521) that Neith also was his spouse.
All this is perhaps explicable as due to misreadings of the name
Nephthys.

59. Perhaps this is the reason why she is called Menkhet ("the
Kind One").

60. The god of this seventeenth nome and its capital, the city of
Saka, was later identified with Anubis, and under this name he appears as the ·brother and rival of his neighbour
Bati in the *Tale of the Two Brothers*, although the
earliest inscribed monuments (Petrie, *Royal Tombs*,
i. 30) seem to distinguish between Anubis and the
jackal (?) with a feather (confused in *Pyr.* 896?).
Probably the "Anubis of Saka" originally had a
name of his own, just as he had his own hieroglyphic symbol (cf. *Pyr.* 1995). A local form of
Anubis is "the one before his chapel."

FIG. 226.
THE JACKAL(?) WITH
A FEATHER

61. Possibly, however, this *rôle* of guide (whence the Greeks
termed him Ἑρμανουβις, after Hermes, the *psychopompos*, or guide
of the dead; cf. *Mythology of All Races*, Boston, 1916, i. 194) is secondary and is derived from his identification (which may be as early
as *Pyr.* 1287) with the (standing) wolf Up-uaut ("Opener of the
Ways"; 'Οφοϊς in Greek transcription) of Assiut and Saïs, on whom
see p. 144. The Greeks (Diodorus, i. 18) speak of a dog-god Μακεδων
as companion of Osiris, which suggests some misunderstanding of
Ophoïs (W. von Bissing, in *RT* xxvii. 250 [1905]); but the Hellenic
name remains enigmatic.

62. The present writer has suggested (*OL* xiii. 433 [1910]) that
this symbol was first transferred to Osiris or to his myth (possibly
associating the skin with the vine of Osiris, pp. 36, 113). So, for
example, the Asianic myth of Marsyas (cf. *Mythology of All Races*,
Boston, 1916, i. 181), which is closely connected with that of Osiris,
derives the river (originally the Nile) from the bleeding of a sus-
pended divine skin. At all events this skin-symbol is constantly
represented before Osiris (see Petrie, *Royal Tombs*, ii. 11, where the
skin-symbol may interchange with Anubis, though it seems to be
distinguished in Petrie, *Abydos*, ii. 2). The title Emi-uet ("the One
[in the city of (?)] Uet"), given to this symbol, was interpreted,
somewhat later, to mean "the Embalmer" and thus was transferred
to Anubis. Did the symbol originally designate "the one (hidden)
in the skin, the one wrapped up"?

63. In this latter case the genii are called the grandchildren of

Osiris (*Pyr.* 1983). On the interchange of Osiris and Horus see p. 102, etc.; on the four Horuses cf. Note 67.

64. *Pyr.* 1228, 1483, 2078, 1141. Accordingly they are near the ferryman of the lower world (*Pyr.* 1222), who can be found in the constellation Argo and may be explained as Osiris (p. 57).

65. *Book of the Dead*, cxiii.

66. From Dümichen, *Patuamenap*, Plate XV.

67. *Pyr.* 436, 418 (?). Thus they correspond to the four pillars of the sky (p. 35). Their tresses indicate youth (pp. 34, 193), or they themselves thus become another interpretation of Ḥat-ḥôr's blue-black celestial tresses (p. 39). We again recognize these four celestial gods in many allusions, e. g. as four long-haired youths in the east, watching the birth of the sun-god and preparing his ship for his daily course (*Pyr.* 1205), or sitting there in the shadow of the chapel (?) of Qati (*Pyr.* 1105). Or, they dwell in the south, "on the water of the lower world" (*Kenset; Pyr.* 1141), where they guard the blessed against storms (*Pyr.* 1207). Thus they are at the same time celestial and protect the souls against the subterranean serpent Neḥ-ebkau (*Pyr.* 340). They are also called "four spirits of Horus" (*Pyr.* 1092). By another blending of the celestial and abysmal localization (*Pyr.* 2078) their abode is in the south, the region of the lower world, and there they hold the heavenly ladder. When they are localized in the city of Pe, a quarter of Buto, the ancient capital of the Delta, they are confused with the hawk-headed "souls of Pe" (Ch. II, Note 26). The four-headed god of the lower world (*Pyr.* 1207; cf. Note 27 on the four-headed Horus) seems to be compared with them because his faces likewise "dispel storms"; originally, like them, he may have represented the four subterranean rivers as well (see Figs. 101, 103, 115). It would seem that, in similar fashion, the four male gods with crocodiles' heads (cf. Sobk, p. 148) who assist at royal births (Naville, *Deir el Bahari*, Plate LI) are merely another representation of the sons of Horus as bringing Osiris (the Nile) to life.

68. A. M. Blackman, in *ÄZ* xlvii. 117 (1910).

69. Lepsius, *Denkmäler*, iii. 137.

70. On these days see p. 57 and Ch. III, Note 57. According to *Pyr.* 1961, they were "the birthdays of the gods," i. e. of the most prominent among them.

71. On the birth of Osiris from the ocean see p. 94, etc. His identity with Horus receives additional proof, e. g., in the fact that Osiris also had "two nurses" (*Pyr.* 313). Nephthys is called the sister of Horus in the *Harris Magic Papyrus*, etc., and Sêth is often regarded as his brother (pp. 103, 114), etc.

72. Connexion with music is frequent in the myths outside of Egypt, but cannot be proved in the hieroglyphs.

73. Plutarch's idea (*De Iside et Osiride*, xiii) that Osiris preached humanitarian views over the whole world is absolutely non-Egyptian and probably shows some indirect influence of Christianity.

74. *Pyr.* 972, etc.

75. Seventy-two as a cosmic number ordinarily expresses the circle of heaven, the number of half-decades (p. 57) which constitute a year. The original meaning was, therefore, that for a whole year Osiris regularly vanished until he reappeared in some phenomenon of nature, this being, according to the version which Plutarch chiefly follows, the swelling of the Nile (pp. 94–95).

76. This *motif*, which is unknown elsewhere, seems to point to Ethiopia as the region or type of the lower world. Comparing the Greek form of the myth of Adonis (see *Mythology of All Races*, Boston, 1916, i. 198), we should think of Nephthys as the rival of Isis and perhaps should regard it as a later variant under Asiatic influence; see, however, p. 87 on two rival goddesses, one of whom came from the depths. The name Aso is thus far unexplained.

77. See pp. 63–64 on the dwarf divinities connected with the young sun and p. 32 on the parallel animal companions, who are here confused by Plutarch.

78. The number has its parallel in the days of the half month or the fourteen souls of the sun, and in the fourteen fragments of the solar eye (pp. 28, 90). Originally the stars were probably regarded as the scattered and reunited fragments of the sun.

79. On the winged deities of later times see Note 58. It is, however, possible to find here the bird-form of the mourning Isis.

80. According to some versions, only the virile organ was lost, being eaten by a fish [or by three kinds of fish, if we follow Plutarch] which was, therefore, considered unclean. This is a variant of the *motif* of death because of sinful love (see p. 119).

81. The Egyptian mind felt no difficulty in duplicating relics, as when, for example, the head of Osiris, the seat of his life, was worshipped both at Abydos (p. 98) and at Memphis. The localization of the worship of other relics shows many similar contradictions. The appearance of the legs at the frontiers of the Delta betrays the conception of Osiris as the Nile, particularly as the Egyptian word for "leg" also means "branch of a river."

82. See p. 36 and Fig. 84 on Osiris in the celestial tree, and cf. K. Sethe, in *ÄZ* xlvii. 72 (1910), where the vine, sycamore, acacia, and other trees are also mentioned (cf. p. 36).

83. That she might not confer immortality by her milk, a detail which contradicts the fire-story.

84. This detail of the fire around Isis, which has not yet been found in Egypt, seems to be the Asiatic *motif* of the Queen of Heaven

surrounded by flames, although the most mysterious gods of the later Egyptian magicians are likewise described as encircled with fire, and the ancient gods draw their magic wisdom from "the island of (i. e. surrounded by?) flames" (*Pyr.* 506; cf. p. 202 and Ch. II, Note 11). In other respects the prince whom Isis nursed in Syria seems to be her own son (i. e. Osiris-Horus) as worshipped by the Phoenicians at Byblos under the name of Tammuz-Adonis. Evidently some later Egyptian priests were unwilling to accord full recognition to the Asiatic parallels. For the Greek analogue of Demeter and Demophon see *Mythology of All Races*, Boston, 1916, i. 228.

85. It will be noted that the question constantly recurs (although more or less effaced in the tradition) why Osiris and (through him) mankind lost immortality. Plutarch (*De Iside et Osiride*, xvii) interpolates a hopelessly confused story of an alleged prince Maneros, who was killed by the angry glance of Isis; he derives this from the Egyptian convivial Maneros-song about the brevity of earthly existence, thus instinctively reverting to the problem why human life is so short. The reason for this is here ascribed to Isis and her Asiatic double, Astarte (pp. 155–56); cf. also p. 119.

86. For the pillar of Osiris, which the Phoenicians seem to have imitated, see pp. 92–93.

87. A calendric hint (see Note 78 on the number fourteen); cf. also p. 94 on the predominantly lunar character of the festivals of Osiris.

88. "The (goddess of the) sky conceived by wine" (*Pyr.* 1082), etc. (cf. p. 36).

89. For the green place of the birth or death of the solar god see pp. 35, 38.

90. On Êpet-Tuêris and Bês as helpers in earlier mythology see pp. 60–62.

91. See pp. 57–58 on the star Canopus, the steersman of Argo, and the possible interchange of Orion and Argo.

92. See Note 75 for a parallel explanation of the yearly interval.

93. The more original form of the legend must be that, as in the Asiatic parallels, Pamyles did not know the divine nature of the babe. From this announcement the gay and wanton festival of the Pamylia had its origin. As yet, however, we have no Egyptian evidence either for Pamyles or for the Pamylia. The Asiatic versions that the finder of the infant was a shepherd or husbandman are less clear in Egypt (see, however, Note 111). In Asia the water-carrier is Aquarius, who corresponds in Egypt to the Nile-god, because Osiris himself is connected with the swelling Nile (pp. 94–95), and because the new inundation brings Osiris. On other primeval

gods who are similarly represented as floating in embryon form in a chest in the abyss see p. 71; and the young Horus is also shown sitting in a chest (e. g. Rosellini, *Monumenti del culto*, p. 18, etc.).

94. Hence Pharaoh's daughter, who found Moses in the Nile and brought him up, is called Θερμουθις by Josephus (*Antiquities*, II. ix. 5–7). In the Greek period the name Menuthias ("Island of the Nurse") was given to a mythical island in the south as being the abode of the divine nurse, and later this was identified with Madagascar as the most remote island in the south, i. e. the lower world. Renenutet may be understood to nurse Horus in her double capacity of goddess of harvest and of educator (p. 66).

95. See pp. 210–11 for a magic text containing a similar story. It is perhaps a variant of the myth which tells how the sun-god was bitten by a serpent (see pp. 79–83). The *rôle* of Isis seems simply to be reversed.

96. This may be a recollection that "the great Horus" was an old form of this deity which remained independent of the Osiris-myth. As an older god he was sometimes even called "father of Osiris" when he was associated with the latter or regarded as his equal.

97. See p. 110 and cf., as a variant, Fig. 118, where both sisters receive the fertilizing blood of Osiris to bear posthumous offspring.

98. Perhaps implying that he was deprived of his mother, particularly as the myth of the dying goddess (pp. 100–01) would later furnish a basis for such a theory.

99. *Pyr.* 1214.

100. The word here translated "avenger" is also interpreted as "the one who shakes," "awakens," or "takes care of."

101. The word *deb*, "hippopotamus," can also mean "bear," and in Phoenicia the enemy of the young nature-god is a bear or a boar. Although the Egyptians understood *deb* to denote "hippopotamus," they also substituted various other animals for it (see Note 35). In later times Horus sometimes appears fighting from a chariot drawn by griffins or dragons, and in the Roman period he even fights

FIG. 227.
THE HARPOON OF HORUS

from horseback. For the winged disk of Edfu see p. 101. Horus fights with a harpoon which has a strange, often practically impossible head (H. Schäfer, in *ÄZ* xli. 69 [1904]). Originally it must have had three points (Lepsius, *Denkmäler*, iv. 35), this hypothesis being confirmed by paronomasias in the texts, e. g. "the weapon (which marks) thirty" (*Pyr. P.* 424, 1212, etc.), i. e. possessing three hooks, since a hook is a sign for "ten" (and represents a month?).

Unfortunately the word can be confused with one for "battle-ax" (see Note 47). Even in pre-Osirian mythology the sun-god wields a harpoon with hooks at both ends (⟨══════⟩ ; *Pyr. P.* 1212). We can thus see that Egyptian art originally had in mind the strange weapon carried by the Babylonian god of light, the short spear with three points at both ends which the Greeks interpreted as the thunderbolt of Zeus or the trident of Poseidon. When a serpent winds around the head of the spear, this symbolizes the fiery rays of the sun (p. 26, etc.). On the net as a weapon in this fight see p. 109. It is not yet clear why Diodorus (i. 21) places the struggle near Antaiopolis; the battle had many localizations.

102. For these "Typhonic" animals see Note 35 and Fig. 214. In later times Sêth himself very often appears as a crocodile (see Fig. 122).

103. This may be a reversion to the myth mentioned in Note 62 regarding the skin of the celestial divinity which is found in the symbol standing before Osiris; on the confusion of this legend with the myth of 'Apop, see pp. 127–28.

104. See pp. 104–06. The converse of this, i. e. the eschatological interpretation, has not yet been demonstrated in Egyptian mythology, where thus far we have no evidence of eschatological speculations, although some theories on this subject probably existed.

105. Sothis is the sister of Orion (*Pyr.* 363 [1707]) and the "beloved daughter" of Osiris (*Pyr.* 965; an obscurer hint is found ib. 632); when Osiris is identified with Horus, she becomes his mother.

106. e.g. the *Tale of the Two Brothers*, the *Haunted Prince*, and the myth in which Isis overcomes the sun-god by her magic (cf. pp. 79–84). It is quite true that all of these, especially the *Tale of the Two Brothers*, in which a woman, fair, faithless, and cruel, persecutes the Osirian hero, being both his daughter, seducer, and mother, are strongly influenced by Asiatic *motifs*, but the most characteristic feature, the remorseful self-emasculation of Osiris or the sun-god Rê‘, is as old as the *Book of the Dead*, xvii. 29; i.e. it dates from the Middle Empire. A variant of this myth is found in the *Harris Magic Papyrus*, vii. 8, which is translated on p. 125. Here Horus (i. e. the young Osiris) violates his mother Isis, whose tears at this outrage make the Nile overflow, while its water is filled with the fish said to have arisen when the *virilia* of Osiris were thrown into it, evidently by himself in remorse for his sin; elsewhere these fish devour them (Note 80). For a reverse variant, in which Horus beheads his mother for some sin, see pp. 118, 126. The present writer has shown (*OL* v. 348 [1902]) that in a magic text (A. Erman, *Zaubersprüche*, pp. 2, 7) we find an allusion to a wicked daughter of Osiris, coming from Asia or Nubia (cf. Note 76), "who made bricks

[the text should be corrected to read, 'wove a garment'] for him,"
these works of her fingers evidently being poisoned or otherwise
fatal. It is not yet clear why "she said of her father, 'May he
live on *za'es*-herbs and honey.'" In a story which strangely
confuses Osiris and Mykerinos, the builder of the Pyramids, Herodotus (ii. 129–33) seems to regard Isis as the daughter of his hero,
whose death she causes. Cf. also the opposition of Osiris-Horus
and Sothis in Fig. 55, and see Note 85 on woman as the reason
why man forfeited immortality or failed to attain it; pp. 99–100
on Isis as united with the goddess of the region of the dead; and
p. 118 on her saving Sêth and thus battling with the powers of light.

107. See the myths given on pp. 73 ff.

108. The Historical Papyrus of Turin enumerates the earthly
reigns of Qêb, Osiris, Sêth, Horus, Thout, the queen Justice, and
Horus (the younger? cf. p. 117). The reasons for this sequence
are plain from the Osiris-myth.

109. For this jubilee see F. Ll. Griffith, in *ÄZ* xxxviii. 71 ff. (1900).

110. For the myth of Adonis see *Mythology of All Races*, Boston,
1916, i. 198–99, and Note 112. That Byblos is really the Phoenician
city and not, as has been alleged, merely an erroneous interpretation
of the Greek word βύβλος, "papyrus" (referring to the papyrus thickets in the Delta; p. 116), is directly asserted, at least by later texts,
as when Osiris is termed "bull of Byblos" (Lanzone, *Dizionario*,
p. 751). The goddess of Byblos was much worshipped in Egypt
from about 2000 B. c. onward (cf. p. 154). On the other hand, when
Osiris is said to dwell in the Oases (*Book of the Dead*, cxlii), this
merely characterizes him as lord of the west, the desert, and the
region of the dead.

111. Thus the killing of Adonis by the boar looks as though it
had been borrowed from a later explanation of Sêth in animal form
(see Note 33 on his sacred animal); in other words, Syria appears
to have derived it from Egypt. Thus the pillar worshipped at Byblos (p. 154) seems to be simply the Egyptian symbol of Dêd. On
the other hand, the Egyptian parallels to the "Gardens of Adonis,"
the images of Osiris made of sprouting grain to symbolize resurrection, cannot be traced before 1600 B.C., although it is in Egypt that
we find Osiris most clearly connected with the tree or plant of life
(p. 94, etc.). Tammuz as a shepherd has only rare parallels in Egypt,
e. g. in the *Tale of the Two Brothers*, which is manifestly Asiatized
(cf. Note 106), and in Orion watching over calves (*Pyr.* 1533, 1183);
but the *rôle* of Osiris as a neat-herd seems originally to have associated him with the celestial cow, a thought which is not logically
expressed anywhere in Asia. The *Tale of the Two Brothers* appears,
indeed, to regard the younger, dying brother, Bati-Osiris (see Notes

60, 106, and pp. 131–32), as the shepherd, although it does not distinctly state that the elder of the pair, Anubis (i. e. the predecessor of Osiris as the god of the dead, and consequently the fosterer of him or of his double, Horus; cf. p. 102), is the tiller of the soil as contrasted with the shepherd. In the Leyden-London Gnostic Papyrus (vi. 2, 7; xiv. 28; cf. also De Morgan, *Ombos*, nos. 66, 114) Anubis appears as a neat-herd, though this may merely have been derived later from the canine form of the deity. On the other hand, Osiris as patron of agriculture (p. 113), and especially of the vine, harmonizes with the myth of Adonis. Thus shepherd and field-labourer seem to interchange freely in Egypt. In Asia the idea of the god in the floating chest or ship (Note 29, etc.) is much more richly developed, while the rivalry of the hero's two wives (perhaps the upper and lower sky or world) is obscured in Egypt (Note 76). The high, conical head-dress of Osiris reminds us of that of the Syrian gods (p. 156) and seems quite distinctly to betray his Asiatic character.

112. The very scanty Babylonian material on this subject now has been most completely gathered by H. Zimmern, "Der babylonische Gott Tamūz," in *Abhandlungen der königlichen sächsischen Gesellschaft der Wissenschaften*, xxvii. 701–38 (1909). For a full discussion of analogues in other mythologies see Sir J. G. Frazer, *The Dying God* (2nd ed., London, 1911).

CHAPTER VI

1. Berlin papyrus of the Greek period, first translated by P. J. de Horrack, *Les Lamentations d'Isis et de Nephthys*, Paris, 1866. It claims to contain the words which restore Osiris to life and "place Horus on his father's throne." On Osiris as "the one before the west" see pp. 21, 98.

2. The fourth month.

3. Or, "the Heliopolitan" (?). In early times, it is true, Osiris was not prominent at Heliopolis (but see p. 98). Others regard this name as an allusion to the square pillars against which the figures of Osiris usually lean. This pillar has nothing to do with the round pillar of Dêd (pp. 92–93).

4. For this title of Osiris see p. 97.

5. Page iv of the papyrus.

6. Or, "thou shinest" (?).

7. i. e. manifestation; see p. 160 on this original etymology of the word for "soul," and cf. Ch. IV, Note 90.

8. Page v of the papyrus.

9. *Book of the Dead*, cxii.

10. i. e. represented on a flower or plant, and, according to p. 50,

often as a child. Here also "the green" probably meant originally the ocean (Ch. III, Note 12); our text vainly tries to explain this expression, which had become unintelligible. "Horus, the lord of the four greens" (*Pyr.* 457), clearly refers to his birth in the four lakes or sources of the Nile.

11. *Harris Magic Papyrus*, vii. 8.

12. We should expect "on the (dry) bottom," or "on the bank."

13. *Her*, misplaced four words before.

14. Or, "again" (?).

15. Thus Brugsch, *Religion*, p. 724; less probably, "Sothis."

16. From the calendar of lucky and unlucky days in the *Sallier Papyrus*, IV. ii. 6, now in the British Museum (cf. Ch. XII, Note 7). This very important text seems to be an awkward schoolboy's copy, like so many of the most interesting Egyptian manuscripts; hence it is often unintelligible.

FIG. 228. "HORUS ON HIS GREEN"

17. The first month of the Egyptian calendar.

18. The name means "the place containing weapons," "the arsenal," so that the combat is localized near this city of the eastern frontier of the Delta, not far from Heliopolis. On the hippopotamus-shape, so contradictory to the use of weapons, see pp. 107, 118.

19. We are tempted to read "her metal." Otherwise Isis would appear not only as the sorceress (p. 80), but also as Fate (p. 53).

20. Lacuna in the text.

21. The negative is omitted in the manuscript. Sêth refers to his former passion for Osiris (cf. Ch. V, Note 34).

22. Literally, "turning the back to speaking."

23. The phrase is obscure, but perhaps alludes to a renewal of the combat in the sky.

24. Corrupted in the manuscript for "fixing a cow's head in its place."

25. *De Iside et Osiride*, xix–xx.

26. Budge, in *Archæologia*, lii. 542 (1890); see p. 68 for the very late manuscript from which the text is taken.

27. Manuscript, "goddess."

28. The children of the sun-god, created by him as has been described on pp. 68–69.

29. Or, "as my limbs" (?).

30. Thus after the analogy of other texts rather than "piercing."

31. i. e. Sekhmet; cf. p. 75 for a play on this name, and pp. 29–30 for the sun as female.

32. Manuscript, "thou hast" (?).

33. i. e. the sun, which he had swallowed (cf. p. 106).

34. Thus he is described as lying bound in the depths of the dry

land; or, by a repetition of ideas (Budge, in *Archæologia*, lii. 562 [1890]), he is guarded by Aker (cf. p. 43).

35. More literally, "I made his teeth jagged" (?).

36. A variant adds, "nor his neighbours," probably to be corrected to "tribe," i.e. his kin.

37. Literally, "archive."

38. Budge, in *Archæologia*, lii. 555 (1890).

CHAPTER VII

1. This list includes most gods of any real importance; the intentional exclusions are a few names whose reading is too uncertain (for some of these cf. Ch. I, Note 8), some dubious Græco-Roman traditions, and most demons and astral beings who are rarely mentioned and for whom we cannot prove an actual cult. Sacred animals and foreign deities will be considered in special chapters, although some divinities who occasionally appear in animal form cannot here be overlooked. A few references to names previously mentioned add details.

2. K. Piehl, in *ÄZ* xix. 18 (1881).

3. See p. 21 for this rare instance of dissimilation of one god into two.

4. See p. 164. Connexion with the constellation Aries through the solarization of Amon is possible for the latest period, though the hieroglyphs nowhere state it. For the different ram-headed forms of the solar god see Ch. II, Note 15. Later the solarized Amon also appears as the solar hawk (p. 24), usually with a human head (very rarely as a crocodile). For a strange local form of Amon see G. Daressy, in *Annales du service des antiquités de l'Égypte*, ix. 64 (1908).

5. W. Spiegelberg, in *ÄZ* xlix. 127 (1911).

6. She is thus confused with Mut (Naville, *Shrine of Saft el Henneh*, Plate II).

7. Gayet, *Louxor*, Plate IX, etc.

8. *Pyr.* 182, 220, 614, 1833, and Brugsch, *Dictionnaire géographique*, p. 130; in the latter passage 'Anezti is localized in the eastern Delta.

9. See K. Sethe and A. H. Gardiner, in *ÄZ* xlvii. 49 (1910).

10. See W. Golenischeff, in *ÄZ* xx. 125 (1882), where his sacred plant (like ivy?) is also depicted.

11. e.g. Naville, *Shrine of Saft el Henneh*, Plate VI.

12. Mariette, *Dendérah*, iv. 81, *Pyr.* 556, Lacau, *Sarcophages*, p. 226. Her name, "the Flaming One" (cf. *aseb*, "flaming," as applied to male gods in *Book of the Dead*, lxix), may refer to her serpent's form.

13. For this deity see Ch. VIII, Note 1. He is scarcely identical with the special patron of the old king Per-eb-sen (Petrie, *Royal Tombs*, i. Plate XIX, ii. Plates XXI–XXIII), a god who usually has a hawk's head and a name with many variants which possibly is to be read "the One of the Horus-Lake."

14. *Pyr. W.* 644 ff. The Pyramid Texts generally write Babi (*Pyr.* 568) or Baibu; and the query arises whether the "Babui with red ears and striped loins" (*Pyr.* 604), i.e. a striped hyena, is identical. Even in these earliest texts the god seems to belong to the realm of magic. Later his name is etymologically connected with *baba*, "hole, cave," as is possibly the case on p. 84.

15. lxiii. His great sexual power also harmonizes with his Osirian character (Schack-Schackenburg, *Buch von den zwei Wegen*, xvi. 9). In *Pyr.* 419 Babi is associated with Chemmis (i.e. a comparison with the ithyphallic Mîn? cf. p. 138).

16. xvii, cxxv, and ed. Lepsius, xxx.

17. See É. Naville, in *ÄZ* xliii. 77 (1906), who identifies him with Bat (pp. 40–41) and accordingly endeavours to see in him a double-faced bull, like the one represented in Fig. 2 (*d*). A trace of a Baiti as Osiris may be found in *Book of the Dead*, cxlii. 14, but the Horus-Baiti of *Pyr.* 580, 767, and "the two souls" (*baiui*) in human form of *Pyr.* 1314 and Borchardt, *Sa'ḥu-rē'*, Plate XIX, seem to be different.

18. In the *Book of the Gates* (Bonomi and Sharpe, *Oimenepthah*, Plate XII) a monstrous serpent of the underworld is called Biṭ(!), Bita, and is already confused with Sêth-'Apop. The fact that on his two heads he wears the crown of Upper Egypt again connects Bati with Babi and strengthens the suspicion that the two names were confused at an early date. Cf., perhaps, Fig. 2 (*e*), which would well explain the mingling of a bull-deity and a serpent-god. Naville (*Festival Hall*, Plate X) records the orthography Batbat (*sic*) beside Bat. It is uncertain whether a monkey-shaped genius Eb'ebta, Ebta, Ebi(?)u belongs here.

19. *Vice versa*, both appear as vultures (De Morgan, *Ombos*, no. 329). Originally Buto seems to have presided only over that quarter of her city which was called Pe(y). "The Goddess of Pe" (Peyet) and "the One of Dep" (Depet) (Naville, *Festival Hall*, Plate VII) may be differentiations or divinities who earlier were distinct. Is the leontocephalous Uazet (Naville, *Shrine of Saft el Henneh*, Plate VI) a rare form of Buto?

20. The oldest pronunciation was Zedet (*Pyr.* 1100), and Zedut is found even in Mariette, *Dendérah*, i. 6 e, as contrasted with ii. 27. Cf. Ch. V, Note 3.

21. The pronunciation Dua(u) is given by *Pyr.* 480, 994, 1155, and the connexion with Herakleopolis by Naville, *Festival Hall*,

Plate IX, where the symbol looks more like a nose. The comparison of Mariette, *Dendérah*, iv. 21 and 32, now proves beyond doubt that the reading Khônsu for the symbol (p. 34) is a later error for the correct "Herakleopolitan."

22. Petrie, *Royal Tombs*, i. Plate X, Borchardt, *Sa'ḥu-rē'*, Plate XIX (where the god appears in human shape), Mariette, *Les Mastaba*, p. 366, etc. For the pronunciation cf. *Pyr.* 631, where possibly we should read "the Divine Worshipper," so that assimilation with the morning star would be complete even there. The divine symbol, of course, has only a very remote resemblance to a bearded chin; it must have been an old unintelligible sculpture, like the pillar of Osiris (pp. 92–93).

23. *Pyr.* 1428, 2042.

24. ib. 632, 1428.

25. Petrie, *Royal Tombs*, ii. Plate V.

26. *Pyr.* 198, etc.

27. See H. Junker, "Der Auszug der Hathor-Tefnut aus Nubien," in *ABAW*, 1911, p. 37, for material regarding him. The comparison with Shu also rests on the myth given on pp. 86–90.

28. The name may likewise mean "Mistress of the Northland" (Emḥit).

29. Mariette, *Dendérah*, iii. 36.

30. *Pyr.* 288.

31. ib. 1013, etc.

32. Naville, *Shrine of Saft el Henneh*, Plate V.

33. The form Ḥeqit appears in *Book of the Dead*, ed. Lepsius, cxlii. 5.

34. "Ḥesat bore the celestial bull" (*Pyr.* 2080).

35. This is now proved for Isis-Ḥesat; see Petrie and Mackay, *Heliopolis, Kafr Ammar, and Shurafa*, Plates XLI ff. Even by the time of the later Egyptians the name seems often to have been misread Ḥetmet (cf. the following Note).

36. Lepsius, *Denkmäler*, iv. 65. The serpent Ḥetmet (Mariette, *Dendérah*, iii. 75), or Ḥetmut (*Pyr.* 485), seems to be distinct (cf. the preceding Note).

37. *Pyr.* 1210, where she is called "daughter of Qêb," apparently associated even then with Isis. Is she identical with "the great maiden (*ḥunet*) in Heliopolis" (*Pyr.* 728, 809, etc.)?

38. He was perhaps localized at or near Akhmîn (see Lacau, *Sarcophages*, p. 17). He is mentioned in *Pyr.* 1603 and appears in Memphis (L. Borchardt, in *ÄZ* xlii. 83 [1905]). His name was misread An-mutef by Egyptian scribes themselves, and in Mariette, *Dendérah*, iii. 36, the disfigured form Mer-mut-f is found.

39. In *Pyr.* 1226 the soul of the dead is endangered by Kenemti,

a demon in the form of a bird or of a leopard, or wearing a leopard's skin. Once more we see how many forgotten gods were embodied in the decanal stars (pp. 57, 59).

40. This is our provisional reading of the divine name, meaning "the One from the Mountainous, Foreign, Country" (Naville, *Deir el Bahari*, Plate LXIII, Lanzone, *Dizionario*, p. 995, etc.), so long as its exact pronunciation is uncertain. The name is now read Aḥu by many scholars, but the orthography Ḥa (*Pyr. M.* 1013 [= Horus], 699, etc.), Ḥat (*Pyr.* 1284; cf. also Naville, *Festival Hall*, Plate XII) points at least to a pronunciation Aḥuti.

41. *Book of the Dead*, ed. Lepsius, i. 21, etc.

42. So also von Bergmann, *Buch vom Durchwandeln*, l. 70, where she is confused with the birth-goddess Ḥeqet.

43. The Greek form of this divine name is based on the (later?) pronunciation Khnûv, which is implied also in the Ethiopian hiero-glyphic orthography Knûfi (Lepsius, *Denkmäler*, v. 39) and Khnf; the Κνηφ of Plutarch (*De Iside et Osiride*, xxi) is problematic. On Khnûm's wife (at Esneh?) see Ḥeqet (pp. 50–52, 133–34); on his two wives at Elephantine see p. 20; on his connexion with the abyss and the lower world and on his later function as creator see pp. 50–52.

44. Cf. p. 106. That her symbol was usually connected with the hieroglyph *shems*, "to follow," as shown in our illustration (taken from Petrie, *Royal Tombs*, ii. Plate VII, where a different representation is also found), is confirmed by *Pyr. M.* 608 = *Pyr. N.* 1213, *Pyr.* 280, 1212. Her localization in the twelfth nome of Upper Egypt (*Pyr.* 1258) is questionable, and the site of her temple, "the House of Life" (*Pyr.* 440, etc.), is unknown.

45. *Pyr.* 1440.

46. Mariette, *Monuments divers*, p. 46.

47. Mehit with a human head and two high feathers in Mariette, *Dendérah*, iv. 29, seems to be a different deity.

48. *Book of the Dead*, clxxx.

49. Mariette, *Dendérah*, iv. 29. The name is written Menḥiu in *Book of the Dead*, xvii. 59, ed. Lepsius (Menḥu, ed. Budge); the old manuscripts, however, read Amon or Ḥemen.

50. *Book of the Dead*, xci, see also cxlii, V. 26, Mariette, *Dendérah*, iv. 6, 15, De Morgan, *Ombos*, no. 112, von Bergmann, *Buch vom Durchwandeln*, l. 71.

51. In this capacity she equals Muut, Muit (p. 46), and it is even possible that her name was so read.

52. Naville, *Shrine of Saft el Henneh*, Plate IV.

53. Mariette, *Dendérah*, ii. 66, Lepsius, *Denkmäler*, iv. 26, 74, De Morgan, *Ombos*, no. 963.

294   EGYPTIAN MYTHOLOGY

54. A. Erman, in *ÄZ* xxxviii. 20 (1900).

55. His name is also written Mnrui(?). The Greek transcription Μανδουλις suggests that the ordinary orthography is abridged. A Greek inscription from Kalabsheh, in Nubia, edited by H. Gauthier, in *Annales du service des antiquités de l'Égypte*, x. 68 ff. [1910], seems to connect him with an otherwise unknown goddess Breith.

56. The name was formerly misread Khem, Amsi, etc.

57. Our picture (after Mariette, *Dendérah*, i. 23) seems to indicate that later the mysterious rite was interpreted partly as a pilgrimage to the god's chapel on a high rock and partly as a symbolic striving after wealth and honour from the divinity. The earliest representations of the ceremony, however (Müller, *Egyptological Researches*, i. Plate XLII, Gayet, *Louxor*, Plate X), contain no such speculations and do not even connect it with the ascent to Mîn's chapel.

58. For these statues see J. Capart, *Les Débuts de l'art en Égypte*, Brussels, 1904, p. 217.

59. Thus he appears on a relief of the Middle Empire in the Metropolitan Museum of Art, New York. Cf. also his variant, the blue Amon (p. 129); for the confusion of black and blue see Ch. III, Note 10.

60. Cf. Note 15 and Ch. V, Notes 80, 106. Hence Mîn is also "the beloved one" (*Pyr.* 953) and later becomes associated with Qedesh-Astarte (p. 156).

61. Perhaps this interpretation was aided by a misunderstanding of the representation of his sacred trees as ears of grain.

62. In *Pyr.* 1378 he flies to heaven, i.e. is already identified with the solar hawk.

63. So Naville, *Shrine of Saft el Henneh*, Plate II. Once he is represented with a strange animal head (Lanzone, *Dizionario*, p. 386). His lion's head seems to be derived from that of his mother, Sekhmet.

64. *Pyr.* 1146 (cf. ib. 483?).

65. This identification with 'Apop occurs as early as *Harris Magic Papyrus*, v. 7.

66. Mariette, *Dendérah*, iii. 69, Lanzone, *Dizionario*, Plate CLXXIV.

67. This unusual pronunciation of the feminine termination as -*th* is a local and possibly non-Egyptian archaism, parallel to the long preservation of the feminine ending -*t* of 'Anuqet in the semi-Egyptian region near the First Cataract.

68. With these weapons she drives evil spirits away from sleepers (G. Daressy, in *Annales du service des antiquités de l'Égypte*, x. 177 ([1910]).

69. Even in the Middle Empire the sign was entirely disfigured (De Morgan, *Fouilles à Dahchour*, p. 104), and this was the case as

early as *Pyr.* 489. For later misinterpretations see Mariette, *Den-dérah*, iv. 4, etc.

70. The famous statement of Plutarch (*De Iside et Osiride*, ix) regarding an alleged mysterious inscription, "None hath ever lifted my garment," seems to be nothing more than a fanciful misinterpretation of references to her good fabrics for the burial of Osiris (see Pierret, *Études égyptologiques*, p. 45, Budge, *Gods*, p. 460, etc.).

71. She was also called "the great wild cow" and at the same time "long-haired" (*Pyr.* 728, 2003, etc.). She was likewise worshipped at some neighbouring places, above all at Fa'get (Fa'giet) and Herakleopolis Magna.

72. Naville, *Festival Hall*, Plate IX. At This-Abydos Ophoïs seems to have been known in the early period principally as the wolf(?)-god of the necropolis. For his name "the One Before the Westerners" and for his change of character see pp. 21, 98. A local form, "Ophoïs from his Tamarisk," is mentioned in *Pyr.* 126, etc.

73. The vulture-goddess Pekhat (*Book of the Dead*, ed. Lepsius, clxiv. 12) is probably to be distinguished from this divinity.

74. In this colour we are tempted to see a non-Egyptian characteristic, for usually only women (who are less exposed to the sun than are men) and some foreigners are painted yellow. The yellow skin of Ḥeka, the god of magic (Borchardt, *Sa'ḥu-rēʿ*, Plate XX), and sometimes of Thout, suggests, however, other explanations for this feature, seeming to indicate a retired, reflective nature, scholarship, and wisdom, in that he stays diligently in his workship.

75. This epithet is found as early as *Pyr.* 560.

76. Hence "Ptaḥ, resting on justice, satisfied with justice," sometimes appears as the god who watches over oaths; cf. p. 234 for texts referring to this function. Osiris often stands on a similar pedestal, a like explanation being given (p. 97).

77. "Ptaḥ opens the mouth (of the dead) with his stylus of metal" (Virey, *Tombeau de Rekhmara*, p. 168), i.e. to restore his speech. In this capacity he may perhaps already be confused with Sokari, and as a potter, probably, with Nuu-Khnûm. For the ceremony cf. p. 181.

78. Was the situation of Memphis near the great division of the Nile one of the reasons for this identification, or was it, rather, Ptaḥ's claim to be the oldest of all the gods, like Nuu?

79. See pp. 220–22 for the later, pantheistic conception of Ptaḥ as the god of the universe; for his later son, I-m-ḥotep, see p. 171, and on his late association with Astarte see Ch. VIII, Note 9.

80. *Pyr.* 468, 1180, 1348, 2153.

81. Mariette, *Dendérah*, iv. 55, etc.

82. "The two maidens" as mothers of Osiris (*Book of the Dead*,

cxlii. 14) seem to mean Isis and Nephthys as a later interpretation and have no association with Triphis. The earliest orthography of Repit's name (e.g. K. Piehl, in *ÄZ* xix. 18 [1881]) appears to connect it with a word *repit*, "statue in a small chapel," so that all the etymologies cited above would be secondary.

83. The form Seṭit occurs in *Pyr.* 1116.

84. Louvre C 15, etc. (ed. A. Gayet, *Musée du Louvre: Stèles de la douzième dynastie*, Paris, 1889).

85. *Pyr.* 1575, etc.

86. Formerly the name was erroneously read Sekhet, Pakht, etc. The vocalization Sokhmet is unsafe.

87. *Pyr.* 606, 1375, etc.

88. Cf. pp. 104, 157, Ch. V, Note 43. See also *Pyr.* 1274, etc., Petrie, *Gizeh and Rifeh*, Plate XIII f, etc.

89. *Pyr.* 489.

90. Naville, *Festival Hall*, Plate VIII.

91. If the orthography in *Pyr.* 1139, 1751, is really to be read Semtet, she would seem to be "the goddess of the necropolis," this word being written Semit in Petrie, *Gizeh and Rifeh*, Plate IX, though elsewhere in the Ancient Empire it appears as St.

92. Cf. Naville, *Shrine of Saft el Henneh*, Plate II.

93. ib.

94. Lanzone, *Dizionario*, p. 1170, Plate XV.

95. The name is written with an arm holding a sceptre (*Pyr. P.* 662) or a child (*Pyr. M.* 773), which seems to confirm the fact that the later orthography Shenet is identical. It is doubtful whether *Pyr.* 444, 681, 689 characterize her as a serpent (for the serpent as an emblem of all goddesses see p. 166). For Shenṭet's identification with Isis see Lanzone, *Dizionario*, p. 1178, and *Book of the Dead*, ed. Lepsius, cxlii. 17. The temple of (Per-)Shentit (von Bergmann, *Buch vom Durchwandeln*, l. 54, Mariette, *Dendérah*, iv. 35) was probably the one in Abydos (Lanzone, *op. cit.* p. 729).

96. Naville, *Shrine of Saft el Henneh*, Plate VI.

97. *Pyr.* 1196, 2013.

98. Earlier orthographies were Sbek, Sbeuk; in the Fayûm a late local form was called Petesuchos ("Gift of Sobk"). In *Pyr.* 507 Sobk wears a green feather.

99. The origin of this seems to be that the Pharaohs of the Twelfth Dynasty built their residence in the Fayûm. Thus the Sobk of the city of Shedet became the official god of all Egypt and was necessarily solarized, this being evident as early as the "Hymns to the Diadem of the Pharaoh" (ed. A. Erman, in *ABAW*, 1911, p. 24, etc.). Accordingly he has "the solar eye of Sobk on his head" (*Book of the Dead*, cxxv, *ad fin.*), and this solarization was furthered by

the clerical error (or change) in the manuscripts of the *Book of the Dead* which altered Sobk's home Ba'eru into Bekhu, i.e. the mountain of sunrise. Later he was also compared on rare occasions to the earth-god Qêb, but the reason for this is quite obscure.

100. This was the case in the city of Apis in the Delta, even at a time which regarded the crocodile as "Typhonic" (p. 107). A (late?) female form, Sobket, had to be compared with Sobk's wife or mother, Neith, and must be distinguished from an earlier leontocephalous goddess Seqbet (*Book of the Dead*, ed. Lepsius, cxliv. V).

101. *Pyr.* 445, etc.

102. This is as early as *Pyr. W.* 211, which mentions "Horus in his sledge-bark"; cf. *Pyr. T.* 270 and *Pyr.* 1429 for the explanation of his bark as solar; in *Pyr.* 1824 Sokar is already the solarized Osiris.

103. A. Erman, in *ÄZ* xxxviii. 29–30 (1900) (Twentieth Dynasty).

104. Sop is clearly one with the god Sepa (*Book of the Dead*, xvii; identified with Osiris?). In the same text, lxix. 6, 8, where he may be identified with Anubis, Sop's name is written with the sign of the centipede (*Pyr. M.* 763, etc.), which later scribes mistook for a backbone, etc. The latest spelling was S'ep (von Bergmann, *Buch vom Durchwandeln*, l. 49). It is uncertain whether he was worshipped in Ḥebet (see G. Maspero, "Mémoire sur quelques papyrus du Louvre," in *Notices et extraits des manuscrits de la Bibliothèque Nationale*, xxiv. 24 [1883]). Manetho blended Joseph and Moses into one personality, substituting Osiris for Hebrew Yô = Yahveh (regarded as the first component of Joseph's name), and thus reconstructing the name as half Egyptian and half Hebrew. In his association of Sop's name with Heliopolis he is supported by "Atum of Sep(a)" (*Book of the Dead*, cxxv).

105. For this god see É. Naville, *The Shrine of Saft el Henneh and the Land of Goshen*, London, 1887. The Asiatized picture given in the text (taken from Borchardt, *Sa'ḥu-rē'*, i. Plate V) is the oldest known. His sacred *kesbet*-tree or *kesbet*-trees (*Pyr.* 1476, etc.) were subsequently mistaken for sycamores (*nubs*), whence the later name of his city.

106. Dümichen, *Patuamenap*, Plate XV. The site of her city, Tatet, Taitet (*Pyr.* 737, 1642, 1794, etc.), is unknown.

107. *Pyr.* 290.

108. Thus A. Wiedemann, in *PSBA* xxiii. 272 (1901).

109. Her name is not to be read Bast(et), as many Egyptologists still think.

110. With greater correctness we might write this name Weng(i), and so the following names, Wert, Wesret, etc.; but cf. the preface on the popularization of transliteration. For Ung see *Pyr.* 607, 952.

111. Naville, *Shrine of Saft el Henneh*, Plate VI.
112. *Pyr. W.* 329.
113. Petrie, *Athribis*, Plate XVIII.
114. *Pyr.* 650 (619), 1153.
115. ib. 631, etc.
116. ib. 662.
117. ib. 994, 1476.
118. ib. 131, 1537.
119. Ahmed Bey Kamal, in *Annales du service des antiquités de l'Égypte*, xiii. 170 (1913).

CHAPTER VIII

1. Foreign countries in general were thought to be under the protection of Ḥat-ḥôr, the goddess of heaven; and for this reason we find her especially in Nubia, on the coast of the Red Sea, in the Sinaitic Peninsula (Ch. III, Note 12), and as the goddess of the Libyans (Champollion, *Notices*, ii. 208). It is not safe to call divinities of frontier districts foreign gods, because they are sometimes said to be masters of the alien countries adjoining; thus Neith of Saïs has no trace of a Libyan origin or character (p. 142), neither is Mîn of Koptos (pp. 137–39) really a Troglodyte god, although they are called respectively "mistress of the Libyans" and "master of the Troglodytes." In like manner the deity "Ash, the lord of the Libyans," who introduces these barbarians by the side of the goddesses of the west (Borchardt, *Saʾḥu-rēʿ*, Plate I; cf. p. 131), is still an Egyptian divinity. See also on Sopd and Khasti, pp. 149, 134.

2. Manifest Asiatic tendencies are found even in the Pyramid Texts; see e. g. p. 104 on the approximately datable adoption of the myth of the cosmic serpent; Ch. III, Note 70, on the blind Orion-type; p. 109 on the spear of the celestial god; p. 58 on the double Orion, etc.; and, above all, p. 120 on the great difficulty of deciding exactly which details of the Osiris-myth were native to Egypt and which were received from abroad, although it is probable that it had its roots in the myth of the dying god from countries east and north of Egypt (p. 120). The tendency to make all goddesses celestial runs remarkably parallel with Asiatic theology and leads us to the prehistoric age.

3. For the raised foot of the running Orion see p. 57. We have already found (pp. 80–83) another reason for the lifted foot of the walking sun-god or of his representative at night, Orion, in a version which makes Isis-Virgo wickedly use the serpent against the god, thus showing the same Asiatic *motifs* inverted.

4. On the general problem of relationship, especially between the Egyptian and the Babylonian religions, see A. Jeremias, *Die Panbabylonisten, der alte Orient und die ägyptische Religion*, Leipzig, 1907. This very suggestive little study, however, contains some comparisons which are quite strained. While it is a great step in advance no longer to consider the Egyptian religion as an isolated growth, the claims of some zealous "pan-Babylonians" to treat it as nothing but a mechanical reproduction of Babylonian beliefs are erroneous. See pp. 56–57 for the remarkable fact that not even the astronomical basis of the major part of the Babylonian religion was reproduced in earlier Egypt, which had an astronomy that was widely different. It is only in the Græco-Roman period that we find many mechanical copies of Babylonian doctrines, e. g. in astrology or magic (see p. 200).

5. For fuller information on these deities see Müller, *Asien und Europa*, p. 309.

6. This cap, plaited of rushes, is the characteristic head-dress of most Asiatic gods. We have already noted (Ch. V, Note 111) that its regular occurrence with Osiris, as originally a divinity of Lower Egypt, where this type of crown would be unsuitable, may be a bond of union between Osiris and Asia.

7. Like Orion as well. For this ribbon see Ch. III, Note 70.

8. See W. Spiegelberg, in *Zeitschrift für Assyriologie*, xiii. 120 (1898).

9. From this most famous temple of hers she is called "daughter of Ptaḥ" in fragments of a strange tale (W. Spiegelberg, in *PSBA* xxiv. 49 [1902]), in which, after wandering between Egypt and Syria, she appears sitting naked on the sea-shore like the Greek Aphrodite or the Asiatic "daughter of the sea" (i. e. Astarte).

10. The lion's head in Fig. 160 shows Astarte confused with the warlike Sekhmet, her neighbour in Memphis (pp. 146–47; so also De Morgan, *Ombos*, no. 208?). For the double nature of Astarte cf. likewise on 'Anat (p. 156).

11. This is an astral myth: Virgo stands on Leo, holding Spica and Hydra, which recurs in the legends telling how Isis conquered the sun-god by a serpent (pp. 79–83) or aided him (cf. p. 153). Egyptian mythology could also consider it as a reversion of an Egyptian mythological idea (see pp. 29, 88 on the asp as a lost member of the solar deity).

12. The name also seems to be written Dedunti. It is rather strange that the ancient hieroglyph is not clearly recognized in *Pyr.* 803, 994, 1718, and this would appear to militate against reading this divine name in the appellation of King Menenrê', Dedun(?)-em-sa(u)-f. Manetho read this Μεθουσουφις, i. e. with the god-name

Meḥti. It is possible that we have here a confusion of Egyptian divinities whose names were written similarly, or that Dedun, when transferred to Egypt, assumed different local designations.

13. Quibell, *Hierakonpolis*, Plates XIX (with emblems of war and conquest), XXXIV. In like manner both names occur in the tomb of Menes (Petrie, *Royal Tombs*, i. Plate III). Dedun is mentioned among Egyptian gods (Quibell, *op. cit.* i. Plate XXVI c), as is Selqet alone (ib. Plates XVII, XVIII, etc.); both are shown on other prehistoric vessels (Petrie, *Diospolis Parva*, Plate XVI).

FIG. 229. SYMBOL OF SELQET AS THE CONQUEROR

14. The theory that Bês was an East African or Arabian deity must, however, now be abandoned; cf. p. 62.

CHAPTER IX

1. This subject has been treated especially by A. Wiedemann in various essays (see the literature cited in his *Religion of the Ancient Egyptians*, London, 1897, p. 172) and in his *Tierkult der alten Aegypter*, Leipzig, 1912. The most complete treatise is by T. Hopfner, *Tierkult der alten Aegypter*, Vienna, 1913.

2. Êpet, originally a mixed form, appears as a hippopotamus only in more recent times (p. 59). The association of this animal with Sêth belongs to the very latest period (p. 118 and Ch. V, Note 35).

3. See Ch. IV, Note 90, on this real meaning of the ordinary word for "soul."

4. For the earliest examples of such mixed representations of deities see Petrie, *Royal Tombs*, ii. Plates XXI ff. (from the First Dynasty ?); cf. also the confused description of the goddess Nekhbet (Ch. VII, Note 71). A remarkable attempt of a very advanced Egyptian thinker to explain the origin of the sacred animals in his own peculiar way has been mentioned on p. 85; this shows the difficulty which that remnant of antiquity began to present.

5. In the Græco-Roman period he was called Serapis, i.e. Osor-ḥap (see p. 98 for this etymology). Sometimes he seems to have been confused with Ḥepi, a son of Osiris-Horus (p. 112), as in *Pyr.* 1313. For the etymology "the Runner" see the orthography in Mariette, *Les Mastaba*, p. 183.

6. There is a tradition, though of questionable authority, that the priests drowned the Apis when he reached the age of twenty-five years. This drowning would again imply the explanation as the Nile and Osiris.

7. Seventy is a characteristic cosmic number; cf. Ch. V, Note 75, on the more exact number seventy-two as expressing the circle of the year.

8. A cattle owner is denounced for having ill-treated a calf with sacred marks (a Mnevis) and his mother (W. Spiegelberg, in *ÄZ* xxix. 82 [1891]).

9. Hence the bull appears on the Roman coins of the nome of Her-monthis; see p. 139 on the original form of Monṭu.

10. Ahmed Bey Kamal, in *Annales du service des antiquités de l'Égypte*, v. 198 (1904).

11. The black colour of most of these sacred animals seems to confirm the suspicion that the celestial bull or cow was soon sought in them (see Ch. III, Note 10, for the identity of black and blue), although in general the beginning of their worship must have been much earlier than this cosmic interpretation (p. 160).

12. This designation seems to show that the fusion of the pillar-god of Busiris (p. 92) and of the Mendes-"spirit" was earlier than the explanation of the former as the dying god Osiris.

13. See p. 28 and Lanzone, *Dizionario*, Plate LXVII, 2 (which also proves that the Egyptians did not take the word $b(a)i$ to mean "ram," but "soul"). The Stele of Mendes (cf. É. Naville, *Ahnas el Medineh*, London, 1894, pp. 20–21) and the Hibeh Hymn (l. 27; see p. 221 for this text from the Persian period) identify this god with "the living soul" of Shu, Qêb, Osiris, Rê', etc., i.e. pantheistically with the entire world (cf. the underlying idea of the four elements, p. 66, and perhaps likewise the deity with the four rams' heads, ib.).

14. It might be supposed that the race of sheep with wide-spreading horns could, when it had later become extinct, be misunderstood as goats in the old pictures, or that a goat was substituted when these sheep had disappeared, or that for superstitious reasons the goat was not called by its correct designation; but none of these explanations is convincing. That the Greeks were not wrong is shown by Lanzone, *Dizionario*, Plate LXVII, 1, where a goat appears with the inscription "the divine soul (or, "ram"?), the chief of the gods" (cf. also the designation of the universal god as *hai* ["buck"] in the Hibeh Hymn, l. 27). Mummies of goats, both male and female, have been found in Upper Egypt as well.

15. See Mariette, *Dendérah*, iv. 80, Naville, *Shrine of Saft el Henneh*, Plate VI.

16. See the present writer's remarks on this name (first explained by Lefébure) in *MVG*, xvii. 290 (1913). The best picture, reproduced in Fig. 172, is taken from Naville, *Shrine of Saft el Henneh*, Plate VII.

17. The name means "the shining one," perhaps because of its

white feathers (cf. the paronomasia in *Pyr.* 1652). This explains why at Heliopolis it could be interpreted as a symbol of light.

18. These tales begin with Herodotus, ii. 73.

19. On the goose of Amon see p. 129; on the goose later attributed to Qêb p. 42; on the ibis of Thout pp. 33–34; on the hawk or falcon of Horus p. 101. All these birds, however, had little prominence; cf. pp. 167–68.

20. XVII. i. 38 (= pp. 811–12, ed. Casaubon).

21. Mariette, *Dendérah*, iii. 28, 29, etc. A picture (ib. iv. 25) also shows us, it is true, four lions as traditional guardians of the temple and represents them as being fed, but these were scarcely living animals.

22. XVII. i. 22 (= p. 803, ed. Casaubon).

23. In similar fashion cosmic types like the bull and the hawk may have taken the place of other animals in this period (see p. 160 and Note 11).

24. See F. Preisigke and W. Spiegelberg, *Die Prinz Joachim Ostraka*, Strassburg, 1914, for documents of the inspection of such "tombs of gods," and cf. W. Spiegelberg, in *Report on Some Excavations in the Necropolis of Thebes*, London, 1908, pp. 19 ff. On the inability of the masses to distinguish between "divine" and "sacred" see p. 161.

25. See Ch. I, Note 3, on the difficulty of separating these underlying ideas.

26. Cf. e.g. Newberry and Griffith, *Beni Hasan*, ii. Plate XIII, as to what strange creatures hunters expected to see in the desert.

27. For the divinity of the kings see especially A. Moret, *Du caractère religieux de la royauté pharaonique*, Paris, 1902, and S. A. B. Mercer, in *Journal of the Society of Oriental Research*, i. 10 (1917) (where references to the general literature are given).

28. Naville, *Deir el Bahari*, Plate LI (with an alternating synonym for *ka*), etc.

29. Temples at Deir el-Baḥri, Luxor, Edfu (ed. Naville, Gayet, and Chassinat respectively), etc. The theory of divine incarnation which artists and poets describe on these monuments—with an excess of detail for modern taste — is that the sun-god (Amon), attracted by the charms of the queen and falling in love with her, approaches her by filling the Pharaoh with his soul. The child born of such a union is, therefore, the offspring of the god as well as of the king.

30. U. Wilcken, in *ÄZ* xlii. 111 (1905).

31. The statement that he came from Kochome, i.e. "the City of the Black Bull," or from Athribis looks like a later theory derived from the name of his father (= Apis) in an effort to explain his divinity.

32. Lepsius, *Denkmäler*, iv. 73, etc. Such cults seem to have flourished especially in Nubia.

CHAPTER X

1. For special studies of this subject see A. Wiedemann, *The Ancient Egyptian Doctrine of the Immortality of the Soul*, English tr., London, 1895, E. A. W. Budge, *Egyptian Ideas of the Future Life*, London, 1908, G. A. Reisner, *The Egyptian Conception of Immortality*, London, 1912.

2. Possibly, however, this custom may have been understood as equipment for becoming a "follower of the sun-god," a member of his crew (pp. 26, 55).

3. That *ka* is merely an earlier and more carefully chosen word for "soul" is evident from the interchange of both terms, e.g. in cases of divine incarnation in animals (p. 165) and men (p. 170). The original etymology of the word is disputed. The higher meaning attributed to the term *ka* is also revealed in the prevailing idea that in form it is a double of man's personality (cf. Fig. 180). As another word for "soul" the term *ikh* is found as early as *Pyr.* 403, etc.

4. Since cremation was believed to involve the complete annihilation of personality, it was feared as endangering the very existence of the soul (see A. Erman, *Gespräch eines Lebensmüden mit seiner Seele*, Berlin, 1896); drowning, on the contrary, made one like Osiris and was a blessed death (F. Ll. Griffith, in *ÄZ* xlvi. 132 [1910]).

5. This must not be mistaken, as it often is, for the Indian doctrine of transmigration of souls. It is most obviously a survival of the primitive animism described in Ch. I. Animals have no soul unless a human or divine soul temporarily makes its abode in them.

6. If we correctly understand the numerous invocations against "dead, male or female," such lurking spirits were feared and seem to have been considered the cause of illness. A papyrus contains a curious letter written by a widower to his deceased wife (tr. G. Maspero, in *JA* VII. xv. 371–82 [1880]), enumerating all the kindness which he had shown her in her lifetime and at her burial and begging her to leave him in peace; it does not state whether disturbing dreams were meant or whether illness was attributed to her.

7. The Egyptian title is *The Book of Coming Forth by Day* (i. e. with the morning sun). It is wholly erroneous to call it the "Bible of the Egyptians"; although it is a rich mine of information, it does not seek to formulate the creed. The text, ultimately codified after 700 B.C., was first edited by R. Lepsius (Leipzig, 1842) and better by E. Naville (Berlin, 1886); it has been translated into English by

Lepage Renouf (London, 1904) and E. A. W. Budge (London, 1901).
Smaller works (in part imitations and extracts) of this kind are *The
Book of Respiration* (ed. H. K. Brugsch, *Saï An Sinsin*, Berlin, 1851),
The Book "That my Name may Flourish" (ed. J. Lieblein, Leipzig,
1895), *The Book of Wandering through Eternity* (ed. E. von Bergmann, Vienna, 1877), *The Rituals of Embalmment* (ed. G. Maspero,
in "Mémoire sur quelques papyrus du Louvre," in *Notices et extraits
des manuscrits de la Bibliothèque Nationale*, xxiv. 14–51 [1883]), *The
Rituals of Funerary Offerings* (ed. E. Schiaparelli, Turin, 1881–90),
etc.   Forerunners of the *Book of the Dead* — apart from the Pyramid Texts, our oldest Egyptian religious documents — are such works
as *The Book of the Two Ways* (ed. H. Schack-Schackenburg, Leipzig,
1903; better ed. P. Lacau, in *RT* xxix. 143–50 [1907]).

8. This number corresponds to that of the nomes in Egypt
(pp. 17–18), whence the manuscripts make unsatisfactory attempts
to localize all judges in these nomes.   Does the number survive in
the Ethiopic Liturgy, where the priest, after saying the Kyrie thrice,
repeats it secretly forty-two times (S. A. B. Mercer, *The Ethiopic
Liturgy*, Milwaukee, 1915, p. 360)?

9. Originally they were for the most part evil demons, as is obvious in the case of Neheb-kau, the "Overthrower of Souls" (p. 141),
who later cannot entirely deny his evil source (cf. Ch. V, Notes
43, 54).

10. This may perhaps show that originally, as we have suggested
(pp. 33–34), they were two distinct gods.

11. *Pyr.* 1112, etc.

12. In the early texts the "fields of sacrifices (? *Pyr.* 471 has the
variant, "of those at rest"), of sprouts (*earu*), of altars, of malachite"
(pp. 55, 97, Ch. III, Note 12), etc., were originally green pleasure-
places in heaven, with lakes and canals depicted in the stars (p. 55);
they were not yet fields for toil.   Cf. also Ch. II, Note 10, for the
"jackal lake."   The "lakes of the (female) worshippers" (*duaut*; *Pyr.
P.* 245) are confused with such designations as "underworld (*duat*;
Ch. V, Note 16) lakes," etc.   "Lake" is rather synonymous with
"field" in this celestial sense.   Thus we have, for example, a
"nurse(ry?) lake" (*Pyr.* 343, etc.) beside a "lake of the green plant"
(*khat*, ib.; possibly the earlier reading for *khaut*, "altars"), a "lake
of plenty" (ib. 1228), etc.

13. This seems to be a later etymology for the earlier orthography
shawabtiu ("procurers of food").

14. The earlier period was especially anxious that the departed
might enjoy sexual pleasure and be protected against sexual weakness.   The figures of alleged "dolls" deposited in the graves simply
meant concubines for the dead.

15. *Pyr.* 950 more modestly describes how they bail out this ship.

16. lxxx, lxxxii.

17. The rarer expressions occur as early as *Pyr.* 392, 1679; "servants of the god" are mentioned in *Pyr.* 754, "followers of Osiris" in *Pyr.* 749, 1803, "followers of Ophoïs" in *Pyr.* 928, 1245, "followers (from) the celestial abode" in *Pyr.* 306.

18. The watch-dog of Osiris has this name as early as *Pyr.* 1229, where the scene of the judgement is laid near the source of the Nile (Ch. V, Note 43). In Bonomi and Sharpe, *Oimenepthah*, Plate V, he seems to be confused with the pig or sow which sometimes symbolizes the condemned sinner (p. 180).

19. This stands in contrast to the belief that drowning confers a blessed immortality (see Note 4).

20. These four baboons (cf. Fig. 186) interchange with the four sons of Osiris-Horus in the *Book of the Dead*, cliii A and B, showing once more that, as we have proved above, the scene is where the Nile comes from the lower world in the south.

21. The idea of such a hell does not develop until the New Empire, and then under influences which are not yet determined. The most detailed accounts of the underworld, heaven, and hell are found in two collections which enjoyed a certain popularity between 1500 and 1000 B.C.: the *Book of That Which is in the Other World* and the *Book of the Gates*. The principal purpose of these collections of ancient pictures, which were often misinterpreted, was to describe the nocturnal course of the sun through the realm of the dead. Originally, as we have stated (Ch. II, Note 11), the "island of flames" was not a hell; and the *Book of the Gates*, making it the abode of blessed souls who live on its bread and green herbs, seems to revert to the conception of the fields and islands which the stars form in the sky (see Bonomi and Sharpe, *Oimenepthah*, Plate XIV). Other texts, such as Lacau, *Sarcophages*, p. 225, likewise represent the island as a place of bliss.

FIG. 230. SOULS IN THE ISLAND OF FLAMES AMONG FLOWERS AND FOOD

A "god of cauldrons" (Ketuiti), usually pictured with the head of a cat (cf. p. 106?) and once with that of an ox (cf. on Nuu, p. 47?), is partially recognized as master of hell from the Eighteenth Dynasty. Curiously enough, Horus, the god of light, is more frequently regarded as the ruler of the place of torture. An inscription at the beginning of the Roman period (Lepsius, *Auswahl der wichtigsten Urkunden des ägyptischen Alterthums*, Plate XVI, etc.) states that all the dead, even the good, must go to the same Hades. "The west is a land of sleep and darkness" where all souls slumber in torpor and oblivion, and yet (in direct contradiction to this view) they are in misery, longing in vain even for a drink of water and regretting that they have not enjoyed more pleasure during their earthly life. This is not, however, to be considered as an expression of old Egyptian doctrine, but represents foreign thought, especially Greek.

22. Thus far this is merely a hypothesis. As a survival of the same idea, even in the New Empire, we occasionally find the genitals of mummies cut off and wrapped with the mummy (cf. Ch. V, Note 106, for the origin of this practice from the Osiris-myth). It is uncertain why the skin was sometimes removed from the soles of the feet, nor do we know whether a religious explanation was given to the gilding of parts of the mummy (such as the face and the tips of the fingers) in the later period.

23. As in many other lands, objects deposited with the dead were often broken to "kill" them and thus to send them with the soul of the departed, e.g. literary papyri for his entertainment were frequently torn in pieces. As a security for gaining eternal life in the New Empire the burial customs of the blessed earliest ancestors (Ch. XI, Note 23) were imitated, at least symbolically or in pictures. Thus we find allusions to the prehistoric custom of sewing the body in a skin, or a little pyramid of stone seems to have put the departed in the status of the early kings who rested in real pyramids, etc.

CHAPTER XI

1. cxxv, introduction.

2. Variant: who guard the sins (variant: the lower world); further variant: who live on truth and abhor wrong. This passage affords an excellent example of the way in which scholars struggled with the texts, which were often obscure and corrupt.

3. Cf. p. 29 for this interpretation of the two eyes, which here appear in an exceptional way as guardians of righteousness.

4. This song existed in various recensions and was claimed to have been popular before 2000 B.C., being found in the funerary temple of one of the Antef kings of the Eleventh Dynasty. For the most complete discussion of it see the present writer's *Liebespoesie der alten Aegypter*, p. 29; cf. also Breasted, *Development*, p. 182.

5. The oldest of these moral writings is the famous Prisse Papyrus, first translated by F. Chabas in his *Études sur le papyrus Prisse*, Paris, 1887 (cf. B. G. Gunn, *The Instructions of Ptahhotep*, London, 1908). This prosaic and utilitarian text, which still remains very obscure, claims to date from the time of the Third and Fourth Dynasties. The exhortations of the wise Ani (Chabas, *Les Maximes d'Ani*, Châlon-sur-Saône, 1876), written during the New Empire, have much higher literary and ethical value (see pp. 232–33).

6. Scenes of drunkenness are commemorated as good jokes even in tombs. It is significant that the name of King Psammetichus means "the mixer," i. e. the inventor of new mixed drinks (*p-sa-n-metk*).

7. Especially cxxv. So far as the text, which is badly corrupted in the manuscripts, can be understood, the best English translation of this important document is by F. Ll. Griffith, in *Library of the World's Best Literature*, pp. 5320–22.

8. See Renouf, *Religion of Ancient Egypt*, pp. 73 ff.; Breasted, *Development*, pp. 165 ff.

9. This interesting text was mixed by mistake with ritual formulae for the king (*Pyr. P.* 164, etc.).

10. See *Mythology of All Races*, Boston, 1916, i. 195.

11. The picture is drawn from Naville, *Festival Hall*, Plate IX. See, further, Mariette, *Dendérah*, iii. Plate LXIII, where we learn that the smaller pillars were often covered with vestments to make them look like statues. W. Spiegelberg has shown (*RT* xxv. 184 [1903]) that the name of these monuments was "sticks" (i. e., probably, "poles"). Our picture confirms the frequency of horned skulls (for the meaning of which see p. 37) on the earliest of these pillars. Obelisks and such emblems are connected in *Pyr.* 1178.

12. For one of very unusual character see Naville, *The Eleventh Dynasty Temple at Deir el Bahari*, London, 1894–1908.

13. The repetition of these festivals at intervals much shorter than thirty years, like their curious name, which is now usually interpreted as "festival of the tail" (?), is not yet intelligible. Petrie (*Royal Tombs*, i. Plates VII, VIII) has shown that the earlier name was different ("festival of opening" [?]), and that the oldest buildings which commemorated this festival were rather simple, as in the accompanying illustration. The first of the elaborate structures of later times was found by Naville and is described in his *Festival Hall of Osorkon II*, London, 1892.

FIG. 231. THE EARLIEST CONSTRUCTION COMMEMORATING A "FESTIVAL OF THE TAIL"

14. On the orders of the Egyptian priesthood see W. Otto, *Priester und Tempel im hellenistischen Aegypten*, Leipzig, 1905. This work refers, of course, only to the latest period.

15. ii. 35.

16. ib. 92.

17. See A. Wiedemann, in *PSBA* xxiii. 263 (1901), A. Erman, in *ÄZ* xxxviii. 53 (1901), and several writers in *ÄZ* xxxix. (1902). The vessels described by Wiedemann (*op. cit.*, pp. 271 ff.) are, however, water-clocks for regulating the hours of worship. The whole problem

of these purifications is still obscure, for the Greek writers gave different explanations to the ceremony, confusing the symbolism of lustration, a sign of presence, and the registering or dropping of monetary gifts in brass boxes.

18. The application of this earlier Egyptian cosmetic usage to the deities produced the large ornamented palettes carved from

slate, on which the green paint for the eyes of the gods was mixed in prehistoric and earliest dynastic times. Even sacred (and sacrificial ?) animals sometimes had their eyes decorated in this manner (Borchardt, *Sa'ḥu-rē'*, Plate XLVII). The priestess who thus adorns the cow (which symbolizes Ḥat-ḥôr, according to a picture given in *ÄZ* xxxviii. Plate V [1901])

FIG. 232.   A PRIESTESS PAINTING THE EYES OF A SACRED COW

wears only a cord around her loins, so that she represents a goddess and accordingly enacts some mythological scene (to which *Pyr. W.* 421, etc., allude?).

19. From Louvre C 15 (ed. A. Gayet, *Musée du Louvre: Stèles de la douzième dynastie*, Paris, 1889).

20. See Petrograd Papyrus I (*Tale of the Shipwrecked Sailor*), l. 145, for an instance of such a sacrifice to an absent god. The burning of whole oxen is represented in connexion with the human sacrifices to be discussed below.

21. H. Junker, in *ÄZ* xlviii. 69 (1911). The representations of the king as a conqueror do not, however, refer to human sacrifice.

22. *De Iside et Osiride*, lxxiii, etc. An altar for human sacrifice found at Edfu is described by A. E. P. Weigall, in *Annales du service des antiquités de l'Égypte*, viii. 45 (1907). The pictures given in our text all belong to the funeral sacrifices and may, therefore, have a different aim (cf. Ch. X, Note 23, for the possibility that the sole object in killing slaves was to send them with the soul of their master); but they permit a certain conclusion about human sacrifice in divine cults.

23. See G. Maspero, in *Mémoires publiés par les membres de la mission archéologique française au Caire*, v. 452 (1894), and Griffith, in Tylor, *Tomb of Paheri*, large ed., text of Plate VIII, where, however, we find no consideration of the fact that the Egyptians of the sixteenth century B.C. no longer understood these representations, but confused the ceremony of interring the dead in the fashion of the blessed prehistoric ancestors — in a crouching position and sewn in a skin — with similar burials of human sacrifices. This has been

noted in part by Davies (*Five Theban Tombs*, p. 9), who also reproduces (Plate VIII) the sacrifice of Nubian slaves given in our text (Fig. 210). In our older picture (drawn from Petrie, *Royal Tombs*, ii. Plate III) the peculiar wooden sledge on which the sacrifice is drawn to the grave appears in an unusual form. Cf. Fig. 210, where this sledge is carefully buried after it has been used.

24. See K. Sethe, in *ÄZ* xliv. 30–35 (1907).

25. The most important of these are the demotic papyrus at Paris, at first erroneously interpreted as a chronicle (now edited by W. Spiegelberg, in his *Demotische Studien*, vii, Leipzig, 1914), and a prophecy in a papyrus at Petrograd. A Leyden papyrus (ed. A. Gardiner, *Admonitions of an Egyptian Sage*, Leipzig, 1909) is not prophetic.

CHAPTER XII

1. The fullest collection of material on Egyptian magic is contained in A. Erman's *Egyptian Religion*. In many works usages and texts are treated as magical which should rather be classified as purely religious.

2. See p. 171. For his magical book see G. Maspero, "Mémoire sur quelques papyrus du Louvre," in *Notices et extraits des manuscrits de la Bibliothèque Nationale*, xxiv. 58 (1883).

3. Until the Roman period this was never uttered as a wish — "may he go!" — for to the mind of the earlier Egyptians this would have deprived the sentence of its efficacy. It must be stated as a fact, and then it will become a fact. On the magic effect connected with such religious texts see Breasted, *Development*, p. 94.

4. Every number is sacred because the cosmic system reveals them all, but especial value attaches to 4, 9, (14,) 18, 27, 42, 110. The number seven is usually unlucky (cf. pp. 40, 59 on constellations of seven stars), although, on the other hand, it appears in the fourteen souls of the sun-god (see pp. 28, 170), etc. It is only in the latest period that three becomes especially sacred. For the dread forty-two judges of the departed see p. 176.

5. The most famous text on this theme, telling how the princess of an alleged Asiatic country called Bekhten was healed by a statue of Khônsu (translated by Maspero, *Contes populaires de l'Égypte ancienne*, 3rd ed., Paris, 1906, pp. 161–67), is a pious forgery; but there are historical analogues of such expeditions, such as the sending of the idol of the Ishtar of Nineveh from Mesopotamia to Egypt to cure the illness of Amen-ḥotep III.

6. The hieroglyph for "talisman" (*sa*,) seems to represent a cord with numerous magic loops (cf. on Neith, p. 142). For a papyrus on the magic properties of gems see Spiegel-

berg, *Demotische Papyrus aus den königlichen Museen von Berlin*, p. 29. The symbol of the open hand, so popular in the Orient to this day, already appears among the amulets which cannot be traced back to a religious idea.

7. The longest calendar of this nature is contained in Sallier Papyrus IV and has been translated by F. Chabas (*Le Calendrier des jours fastes et nefastes*, Châlon-sur-Saône, 1870). It shows very little agreement with other texts of this character (see e.g. Budge, *Facsimiles of Egyptian Hieratic Papyri in the British Museum*, p. 41; cf. also Ch. VI, Note 16). The priests must have disagreed widely regarding these calendric systems.

8. Cf. p. 185 and Ch. I, Note 3, on this occupation, which easily assumed a religious significance.

9. See especially the astrological handbook discussed by Spiegelberg, *op. cit.*, p. 28.

10. For a collection of such passages see H. Grapow, in *ÄZ* xlix. 48 (1911).

11. *Pyr. W.* 496 = *T* 319.

12. Explained in later times as "they fight among themselves," but perhaps originally meaning "they fall like rain."

13. i.e. Aker (see pp. 42–43); variant: "of those who live in the depths of the earth, the folk of Aker."

14. Originally "my soul," revealing the fact that primarily the entire hymn used the first person, thus increasing its magic character.

15. See Ch. II, Note 11, and Ch. X, Note 21, for the varying ideas of this place.

16. A play on the similar words meaning "message, messenger" and "locks on the top of the head."

17. Variant: "upon the colours"; but the text is corrupt. Perhaps we should read "Shesmet" (cf. p. 59 for this goddess, who was soon forgotten).

18. The word for "hunting" is *khensu*. Whether we here have an allusion to Khônsu (cf. p. 34) is uncertain; for the "knife-bearers" as powerful (and usually hostile) demons see pp. 175, 180.

19. See p. 58 for this butcher and cook; this seems to corroborate the suspicion that originally Shesmet was mentioned above (Note 17).

20. The greatest sidereal gods (see pp. 54 ff., 178).

21. i.e. as fuel, because they are too tough to be eaten.

22. i.e. as his servants (so Breasted, *Development*, p. 128), but perhaps the meaning is, rather, "they are under his spell" (so that without difficulty he can choose the fattest).

23. The word also means "nourishment, fullness." A later, but meaningless, variant has "his dignities, sign of nobility."

24. See pp. 173–74. The possibility that we here have a poetic treatment of the *motif* of the moon which grows every month by swallowing the stars, or of Saturn, etc., who devours his children, as A.
Jeremias holds in his *Die Panbabylonisten, der alte Orient und die
ägyptische Religion* (Leipzig, 1907), following C. P. Tiele's explanation
of the myth of Kronos (cf. *Mythology of All Races*, Boston, 1916, i. 6–
7), is very remote and in any case would not have been understood
by the scribes who copied this old text and expanded it.

25. See Müller, *Liebespoesie der alten Ägypter*, p. 17, where a girl
in love declares that she will defy bastinados to keep her philtre.
The "Negative Confession" (p. 185), however, enumerates this usage
among the most heinous sins.

26. This remarkable manuscript, dating from the third century
A. D., and thus constituting the latest product of pagan Egyptian
literature, has been translated by F. Ll. Griffith and H. Thompson
(*The Demotic Magical Papyrus of London and Leiden*, London, 1904),
where other material of this kind is also mentioned.

27. Westcar Papyrus, ed. A. Erman, *Die Märchen des Papyrus
Westcar*, Berlin, 1890 (see also Petrie, *Egyptian Tales*, i. 9 ff., and
Maspero, *Les Contes populaires de l'Égypte ancienne*, 3rd ed.,
Paris, 1906, pp. 25 ff.).

28. See Griffith, *Stories of the High Priests of Memphis*, p. 103 (also
translated in the books mentioned in the preceding Note).

29. Cf. W. H. Worrell, "Ink, Oil and Mirror Gazing Ceremonies
in Modern Egypt," in *Journal of the American Oriental Society*,
xxxvi. 37–53 (1917).

30. See pp. 63, 207 for their selection of gods. The inscription given
by Daressy, *Textes et dessins magiques*, p. 46, calls them "these gods
who come choosing protection for N. N." Such objects have been
found chiefly in tombs and are discussed by F. Legge, in *PSBA*
xxvii. 130–52, 297–303 (1905), xxviii. 159–70 (1906), and M. A.
Murray, ib. xxviii. 33–43 (1906).

31. Griffith and Thompson, *op. cit.* Plate XX, ll. 28 ff., text,
p. 133. It contains many non-Egyptian elements (see Notes 32, 44).

32. Mutilations of Hebrew Yô (= YHVH) S̩ebhāôth ("Jehovah
of Hosts ").

33. i.e. "I am he."

34. i.e. he possesses sun and moon.

35. Griffith and Thompson, *op. cit.* Plate XIX, ll. 33 ff., text,
p. 127.

36. *Heber* ("angel"?).

37. Literally, "the one great in secrecy."

38. The word *beḥen* ("to bark") is recognizable, so that we might
translate more freely "lord of barking."

39. Perhaps an allusion to the four sons of Horus or Osiris (see pp. 111–13) and also to Anubis.

40. Coptic *kolch*, "to bend."

41. Literally, "put down."

42. The meaning is, "Let this dog-bite be as ineffective as the attempts of the powers of darkness to swallow the sun" (pp. 79, 106).

43. An allusion to the burning pain of the wound, yet seeming at the same time to refer to a cosmic conflagration. In this event it is one of the few suggestions of eschatological or cosmogonic conflagration, concepts which often blend with each other (cf. Ch. V, Note 104).

44. Cf. Note 32. Here we have an interesting variant, *ab-iaho*, "Father of Jehovah," i. e. the one who preceded even the eternal god.

45. See p. 117. The legend is given in the Metternich Stele (ed. W. Golenisheff, Leipzig, 1877), Verso A, ll. 48 ff.

46. i. e. a man of good birth and breeding knows how to obey.

47. This "crocodile city" is not the Psoïs of Upper Egypt.

48. Literally, "women of husbands."

49. These four verses about the fire seem to be incongruous; their insertion is perhaps due to the fact that the original text may have stated that the sting burned like fire.

50. The text also states (l. 67) that the poor woman was rewarded for her kindness: "She (i. e. Isis) filled the house of the poor woman with victuals (?), because she had opened the door of her house, unlike the rich one, who remained grieved." This part of the legend, however, is not essential for the sorcerer, who mentions it only in passing.

51. For other myths used as magic incantations see pp. 79–83, 125–26, 127–28.

Chapter XIII

1. For the human figures which, at the commencement of the historic period, began partly to replace the animal bodies, so that strangely blended figures were the result, see pp. 160–61.

2. Cf., for example, pp. 58, 165 for such errors or uncertainties.

3. On the antiquity of the artistic expression of this tendency in the composite, half-human figures of deities see p. 161.

4. For the cosmic system underlying this grouping see pp. 49–50.

5. For the ennead see G. Maspero, in *RHR*, xxv. 1–48 (1892).

6. See e. g. *Pyr.* 2009, where Atum is identified with Osiris.

7. ch. clxii.

8. *Book of the Dead*, ed. Naville, xvii. 6 ff.

9. *Destruction of Men*, ed. É. Naville, in *TSBA* iv. 1–19 (1876), viii. 412–20 (1885), l. 85; cf. also pp. 73–79, 84–85 for this collection of myths. This part is younger than the other stories taken from that collection.

10. See Ch. VII, Note 99, for this land of sunrise. The fiend is usually sought in the south (cf. pp. 104–05, etc.).

11. Noticed by Renouf, *Religion of Ancient Egypt*, p. 229, copied completely by J. H. Breasted, in *ÄZ* xxxix. 39–54 (1901) (cf. the same scholar, "The First Philosopher," in *The Monist*, xii. 321–36 [1902]), and more elaborately discussed by A. Erman, in *SBAW*, 1911, pp. 925–50. In part it is still unintelligible. Its age must not be overrated; the religious thought is not that of the Pyramid Age.

12. The argumentation is as follows: the primeval flood, manifested on earth in the ocean (Nuu) and — to obtain a creative pair (cf. p. 48) — in Nekhbet as the female Nile (p. 46), is simply a revelation of the Memphitic god of beginnings. The sun in his Heliopolitan designation must take second place after the principle of water, which shows itself in every part of the creation. In other respects the Heliopolitan system, adapted to the Memphitic idea of cosmic beginnings, is followed. The confusion of male and female divinities was a step which was rather rare and daring in the earlier period.

13. The remainder of the document is concerned with the traditions of the Osiris-myth in a more conservative fashion.

14. See also p. 66 for his incarnation, Mendes, as the cosmic god of all four elements.

15. Text given by Brugsch, *Religion*, p. 515. The Pyramid Texts (2067) cannot yet rise above the concept of a god who upholds the sky and stands on the earth.

16. A. Erman, in *ÄZ* xxxviii. 30 (1900). In earlier times Osiris is not yet clearly understood as the deity of all nature, although he recurs in all its changing forms (pp. 93–96).

17. Brugsch, *Reise nach der grossen Oase Khargeh*, Plate XXVII; extracts are translated by Renouf, *Religion of Ancient Egypt*, p. 240.

18. Translated by Budge, *Gods*, i. 339.

19. *Harris Magic Papyrus*, viii. 9 ff.

20. Perhaps to be corrected to read "dwarf of gold." An abnormal stature may appear either as dwarfish or as gigantic (p. 61).

21. See pp. 92–93 for this form of Busiris-Dêdu.

22. A corrupted name, possibly also to be read "Maga" (p. 111).

23. This would seem to explain "Heliopolitan" as the title of Osiris (Ch. VI, Note 3).

24. The manuscript confuses two similar words meaning "hut" (i.e. cabin) and "ship."

25. More exactly, "long-tailed monkey, marmoset."

26. Probably corrupted and to be restored, "quenched (*'akhem*) only by the abyss."

27. Or "of Triphis"; cf. p. 146, and the corresponding Note, according to which allusion might be made to the earliest meaning of the name, "Goddess in a Shrine."

28. See *Mythology of All Races*, Boston, 1916, i. 29–30.

29. *Harris Magic Papyrus*, vii. 6.

30. Cf. p. 27 and Ch. V, Note 84, on the island of flames as a possible basis of this idea.

31. The exact vocalization is doubtful, and the pronunciation Ikhnaton in particular is quite uncertain.

32. For earlier traces of such amalgamation cf. the myth given on pp. 80–83 and the old commentaries cited on pp. 219–20. It is true that the tendency does not find its clearest expression until after the heretic king, but, as we have repeatedly shown, it can be traced long before him.

33. The best edition of the original text is by Davies, *Rock Tombs of El Amarna*, vi. Plate XXVII. J. H. Breasted, *De hymnis in solem sub Amenophide IV conceptis*, Berlin, 1894, was the first to occupy himself with this important inscription, which has since found many translators, but still presents a number of difficulties. Despite the opinion of some scholars, the hymn cannot have been composed by the King himself (see Note 44).

34. By implication this also means "growing."

35. Perhaps the more correct translation of *red* is "growth."

36. From the following words the text erroneously adds "it from."

37. i. e. is predestined (cf. p. 52 for the older idea of predestination).

38. i.e. the colour, the complexion of the various human races. In earlier tradition likewise Horus is the patron of these races; in other words, the sun burned them to different hues.

39. This might also mean "weary (because) of them" (thus Griffith, in Davies, *Rock Tombs of El Amarna*, vi. 30), but an allusion to the myth of the sun's withdrawal from earth (see pp. 76–79) does not seem to be in harmony with the jubilant tone of the hymn. The passage remains obscure.

40. Correct the text to *tekheb*.

41. The verb is omitted.

42. Correct the text to *her*.

43. Literally "nurse."

44. These lines show that the author of the hymn was not the monarch himself (cf. Note 33), but a courtier of the reforming

NOTES 315

Pharaoh. He now understands the divine nature of the sun since his gracious sovereign has instructed him in the new wisdom.

45. Literally "for thy limbs."

46. A conjectural translation which implies several corrections of the text.

47. Text, "them."

48. Or, perhaps, "from" (cf. the parallel expression in Ch. V, Note 22).

49. For the longest of these see Davies, *Rock Tombs of El Amarna*, iv. Plate XXXIII; it is translated by Griffith, ib. vi. 28.

50. This tendency in Egyptian literature is set forth by A. Erman, *Religion*, pp. 98 ff., and in *SBAW*, 1911, p. 1086. Unfortunately we cannot determine how far this change in literary style corresponded to a true religious awakening.

51. Mariette, *Les Papyrus égyptiens du musée de Boulaq*, Plate XVII; see also Chabas, *Maximes d'Ani*, p. 91; and cf. Ch. XI, Note 5.

52. Apparently alluding to the deity in his quiet and secluded sanctuary, where he should not be disturbed more than is absolutely necessary.

53. Possibly meaning "thoughts," or, perhaps, "its words," referring to the heart.

54. *Sallier Papyrus*, I. viii. 4.

55. Literally, "the one who findeth his mouth."

56. A. Erman, in *SBAW*, 1911, p. 1089.

57. Plate XVI; Chabas, *Maximes d'Ani*, p. 31.

58. Literally "repeat."

59. A. Erman, in *SBAW*, 1911, p. 1102, after G. Maspero, in *RT* iv. 143 (1883).

60. ib.

61. i.e. in a question of property?

62. A. Erman, in *SBAW*, 1911, p. 1101. Note how in all these inscriptions a public confession of the sin is considered necessary.

63. Or, perhaps, "it."

64. A. Erman, in *SBAW*, 1911, p. 1109.

65. *Anastasi Papyrus*, II. x. 5 ff.

66. Thus the corrected manuscript after the present writer's collation of the original in London.

67. Literally "belly."

68. i.e. without brain, stupid.

69. The last verses, which are very obscure, may be understood of helpless wandering in a circle. "My time" may perhaps mean the time for returning home to the fold, following the simile of the ox.

70. See Müller, *Egyptological Researches*, ii. 149.

71. Mariette, *Les Papyrus égyptiens du musée de Boulaq*, No. 17 (Plates XI ff.); the text in question has been especially studied by E. Grébaut, "Hymne à Ammon-Ra," in *Revue archéologique*, new series, xxv. 384–97 (1873).

72. This part of the hymn was originally in praise of Mîn (see pp. 129, 137–39), as is also shown by the stele Louvre C 30.

73. The name of some sanctuary is missing. Cf. the pictures of chapels of Mîn given on p. 138.

74. Cf. pp. 138, 129 for the use of this ribbon with Mîn and Amon.

75. i.e. of Buto and Nekhbet; see p. 132.

76. i.e. the king.

77. An important passage for showing that the monstrous enemy of the sun is the ocean (p. 106).

78. Literally "colour" (cf. Note 38).

79. The paronomasia of the original is untranslatable in English; the Egyptian terms here used for "knowledge" and "wisdom" also mean "satisfaction" and "abundance" (see p. 67).

80. The manuscript has "heareth."

81. This word also means "beauty."

82. Correct the manuscript to *saneḥem* and *khnems*.

83. Cf. p. 225 for the image of the solar disk, "who sendeth forth his arms" (cf. p. 227).

84. See the examples given on pp. 114, 119, 126.

85. A monkey also appears as the solar archer, being perhaps confused with Thout (Rosellini, *Monumenti del culto*, Plate XLII). For the Greek view of life after death entering into an Egyptian inscription see Ch. X, Note 21.

86. A similar view is expressed as early as the Homeric poems, as when *Iliad*, i. 423, speaks of "the blameless Ethiopians" (cf. also *Odyssey*, i. 22 ff., *Iliad*, xxiii. 205–07).

87. Cf. Legge, *Forerunners and Rivals of Christianity*, ch. ii.

88. See W. M. Flinders Petrie, *Personal Religion in Egypt before Christianity*, London, 1909; G. R. S. Mead, *Fragments of a Faith Forgotten*, London, 1900, and *Thrice-Greatest Hermes*, 3 vols. London, 1906; R. Reitzenstein, *Poimandres*, Leipzig, 1904.

BIBLIOGRAPHY

EGYPTIAN

BY THE EDITOR

I. ABBREVIATIONS

ABAW . . Abhandlungen der Berliner Akademie der Wissen-
schaften.
AR . . . . Archiv für Religionswissenschaft.
ÄZ . . . Zeitschrift für ägyptische Sprache und Altertumskunde.
JA . . . . Journal asiatique.
MVG . . Mitteilungen der vorderasiatischen Gesellschaft.
OL . . . . Orientalistische Literaturzeitung.
PSBA . . Proceedings of the Society of Biblical Archæology.
Pyr. . . . Pyramid Texts (ed. K. Sethe).
Pyr. M. . Texts of the Pyramid of Mri-n-rê' I.
Pyr. N. . . Texts of the Pyramid of Nfr-k'-r' Pipi II.
Pyr. P. . . Texts of the Pyramid of Pipi.
Pyr. T. . Texts of the Pyramid of Tti.
Pyr. W. . Texts of the Pyramid of Wn-is.
RHR . . . Revue de l'histoire des religions.
RP . . . Records of the Past.
RT . . . Recueil de travaux relatifs à la philologie et à l'arché-
ologie égyptiennes et assyriennes.
SBAW . . Sitzungsberichte der Berliner Akademie der Wissen-
schaften.
TSBA . . Transactions of the Society of Biblical Archæology.

II. BIBLIOGRAPHY

AHMED BEY KAMAL, "Les Idoles arabes et les divinités égyptiennes,"
in *RT* xxiv. 11–24 (1902).
AKMAR, E., *Le Papyrus magique Harris*. Upsala, 1916.
AMÉLINEAU, A., "Un Tombeau égyptien," in *RHR* xxiii. 137–73
(1891).
—— *Essai sur l'évolution historique et philosophique des idées
morales dans l'Égypte ancienne*. Paris, 1895.
—— "Du rôle des serpents dans les croyances religieuses de
l'Égypte," in *RHR* li. 335–60 (1905), lii. 1–32 (1905).

Amélineau, A., "Le Culte des rois préhistoriques d'Abydos sous l'ancien empire égyptien," in *JA* X. vii. 233–72 (1906).

——— *Prolegomènes à l'étude de la religion égyptienne.* Paris, 1907.

Ani Papyrus. See Budge, E. A. W.

Anonymous, *Select Papyri in the Hieratic Character from the Collections of the British Museum.* 2 vols. London, 1841–60.

——— *Hieroglyphic Texts from Égyptian Stelae, etc., in the British Museum.* 5 vols. London, 1911–14.

Baillet, J., *Introduction à l'étude des idées morales dans l'Égypte antique.* Paris, 1912.

Bénédite, G., *Description et histoire de l'île de Philæ.* 2 vols. Paris, 1893–95.

Benson, M., and Gourlay, J., *The Temple of Mut in Asher.* London, 1899.

Bergmann, E. von, *Das Buch vom Durchwandeln der Ewigkeit.* Vienna, 1877.

——— *Hieroglyphische Inschriften gesammelt während einer im Winter, 1877, 78 unternommenen Reise in Aegypten.* Vienna, 1879.

Birch, S., "On the Shade or Shadow of the Dead," in *TSBA* viii. 386–97 (1885).

Blackman, A. M., "The Nubian God Arsenuphis as Osiris," in *PSBA* xxxii. 33–36 (1910).

Bonomi, J., and Sharpe, S., *The Alabaster Sarcophagus of Oimenepthah I, King of Egypt.* London, 1864.

Book of That Which is in the Lower World. See Budge, E. A. W., *Egyptian Heaven and Hell.*

Book of the Dead. See Budge, E. A. W.; Lepsius, C. R.; Naville, É.; Renouf, Sir P. le Page, and Naville, É.

Book of the Gates. See Budge, E. A. W., *Egyptian Heaven and Hell.*

Borchardt, L., *Das Grabdenkmal des Königs Saʾḥu-rēʿ.* 2 vols. Leipzig, 1910–13.

Breasted, J.H., *De hymnis in solem sub rege Amenophide IV conceptis.* Berlin, 1894.

——— *Ancient Records of Egypt.* 5 vols. Chicago, 1906–07.

——— *Development of Religion and Thought in Ancient Egypt.* New York, 1912.

Brooksbank, F. H., *Stories of Egyptian Gods and Heroes.* New York, 1914.

BRUGSCH, H. K., *Saï An Sinsin sive liber metempsychosis veterum Ægyptiorum.* Berlin, 1851.

—— *Reise nach der grossen Oase El Khargeh.* Leipzig, 1878.

—— *Dictionnaire géographique de l'ancienne Égypte.* Leipzig, 1879–80.

—— "Das Osiris-Mysterium von Tentyra," in *ÄZ* xix. 77–111 (1881).

—— *Thesaurus inscriptionum Ægypticarum.* 6 vols. Leipzig, 1883–91.

—— *Religion und Mythologie der alten Ägypter.* 2 vols. Leipzig, 1885–88. 2nd ed. Leipzig, 1891.

BRUGSCH, H. K., and DÜMICHEN, J., *Recueil de monuments égyptiens* 4 vols. Leipzig, 1862–85.

BUDGE, E. A. W., "The Hieratic Papyrus of Nesi-Amsu," in *Archæologia*, lii. 393–608 (1890).

—— *The Mummy.* Cambridge, 1893.

—— *Papyrus of Ani.* 2 vols. London, 1894–95.

—— *The Book of the Dead.* 3 vols. London, 1898.

—— *Egyptian Magic.* London, 1899.

—— *Egyptian Religion.* London, 1900.

—— *Egyptian Ideas of the Future Life.* 2nd ed. London, 1900.

—— *The Gods of the Egyptians.* 2 vols. London, 1904.

—— *The Egyptian Heaven and Hell.* 3 vols. London, 1906.

—— *The Book of Opening the Mouth.* 2 vols. London, 1909.

—— *The Liturgy of Funerary Offerings.* London, 1909.

—— *Facsimiles of Egyptian Hieratic Papyri in the British Museum.* London, 1910.

—— *Osiris and the Egyptian Resurrection.* 2 vols. London, 1911.

—— *Greenfield Papyrus.* London, 1912.

—— *Legends of the Gods.* London, 1912.

CAPART, J., "La Fête de frapper les anou," in *Actes du premier congrès international d'histoire des religions*, ii. 1–26. Paris, 1902. (Also in *RHR* xliii. 249–74 [1901].)

CHABAS, F., *Le Papyrus magique Harris.* Châlon-sur-Saône, 1860. English translation in *RP* x. 137–58.

—— "Horus sur les crocodiles," in *ÄZ* vi. 99–106 (1868).

—— *Le Calendrier des jours fastes et néfastes.* Châlon-sur-Saône, 1870.

CHABAS, F., *Les Maximes du scribe Ani.* Châlon-sur-Saône, 1876.

CHAMPOLLION, J. F., *Panthéon égyptien.* Paris, 1825.

—— *Monuments de l'Égypte et de la Nubie.* 4 vols. Paris, 1835–45.

—— *Notices déscriptives conformes aux notices autographes rédigées sur les lieux.* (Ed. J. J. Champollion Figeac, É. de Rougé, and G. Maspero.) 2 vols. Paris, 1844–79.

CHASSINAT, E., "Le Livre de protéger la barque divine," in *RT* xvi. 105–22 (1894).

—— *Le Temple d'Edfou.* 2 vols. Paris, 1897.

—— "Les νέκυες de Manéthon et la troisième ennéade héliopolitaine," in *RT* xix. 23–31 (1897).

CUMONT, F., *Oriental Religions in Roman Paganism.* Chicago, 1911.

DARESSY, G., "Une ancienne liste des décans égyptiens," in *Annales du service des antiquités de l'Égypte,* i. 79–90 (1900).

—— *Textes et dessins magiques.* Cairo, 1903.

—— "Hymne à Khnoum," in *RT* xxvii. 82–93, 187–93 (1905).

—— *Statues de divinités.* 2 vols. Cairo, 1905–06.

—— "Une Nouvelle Forme d'Amon," in *Annales du service des antiquités de l'Égypte,* ix. 64–69 (1908).

—— "Litanies d'Amon du temple du Louxor," in *RT* xxxii. 62–69 (1910).

—— "Thouéris et Meskhenit," in *RT* xxxiv. 189–93 (1912).

DAVIES, N. DE G., *The Mastaba of Ptahhetep and Akhethep at Saqqareh.* 2 vols. London, 1900–01.

—— *The Rock Tombs of Deir el Gebrâwi.* 2 vols. London, 1902.

—— *The Rock Tombs of El Amarna.* 6 vols. London, 1903–08.

—— *Five Theban Tombs.* London, 1913.

DE MORGAN, J., *De la frontière de Nubie à Kom Ombos.* 3 vols. Vienna, 1894–1909.

—— *Fouilles à Dahchour.* Paris, 1895.

DESTRUCTION OF MEN. See NAVILLE, É.

DÜMICHEN, J., *Altägyptische Tempelinschriften.* Leipzig, 1867.

—— *Der Grabpalast des Patuamenap.* 3 vols. Leipzig, 1884–85.

EBERS, G., *Ägypten und die Bücher Moses.* Leipzig, 1868.

ERMAN, A., *Die Märchen des Papyrus Westcar.* Berlin, 1890.

—— "Der Zauberpapyrus des Vatikan," in *ÄZ* xxxi. 119–24 (1893).

—— "Gespräch eines Lebensmüden mit seiner Seele," in *ABAW,* 1896, no. 2.

—— "Zaubersprüche für Mutter und Kind," in *ABAW,* 1901, no. 1.

ERMAN, A., *Hieratische Papyrus aus den königlichen Museen zu Berlin.* 5 vols. Leipzig, 1901–11.

——— *Die altägyptische Religion.* 2nd ed. Berlin, 1909. English translation, *Handbook of Egyptian Religion.* London, 1907.

——— "Hymnen an das Diadem der Pharaonen," in *ABAW*, 1911, no. 2.

——— "Ein Denkmal memphitischer Theologie," in *SBAW*, 1911, pp. 916–50.

ERMONI, V., *Religion de l'Égypte ancienne.* Paris, 1910.

FOUCART, G., "Sur le culte des statues funéraires dans l'ancienne Égypte," in *RHR* xliv. 40–61, 337–69 (1901).

——— "Recherches sur les cultes d'Héliopolis," in *Sphinx*, x. 160–225 (1906).

GARDINER, A. H., "Egypt: Ancient Religion," in *Encyclopædia Britannica*, 11th ed., ix. 48–57.

——— *Admonitions of an Egyptian Sage.* Leipzig, 1909.

GARSTANG, J., *Burial Customs of Ancient Egypt.* London, 1907.

GAUTHIER, H., "La Déesse Triphis," in *Bulletin de l'Institut français de l'archéologie orientale*, iii. 165–81 (1903).

GAUTIER, J. É., and JÉQUIER, G., *Mémoire sur les fouilles de Licht.* Cairo, 1902.

GAYET, A., *Musée du Louvre: Stèles de la douzième dynastie.* 2 vols. Paris, 1886.

——— *Le Temple de Louxor.* Paris, 1894.

GOLENISHEFF, W., *Die Metternichstele.* Leipzig, 1877.

GOODWIN, C. W., "Translation of an Egyptian Hymn to Amen," in *TSBA* ii. 250–63 (1873).

GRAPOW, H., "Bedrohungen der Götter durch den Verstorbenen," in *ÄZ* xlix. 48–54 (1911).

GRÉBAUT, E., *Hymne à Ammon-Ra.* Paris, 1874.

——— "Des deux yeux du disque solaire," in *RT* i. 72–87, 112–31 (1880).

GRENFELL, ALICE, "The Iconography of Bes and of Phœnician Bes-Hand Scarabs," in *PSBA* xxiv. 21–40 (1902).

——— "Amuletic Scarabs, etc., for the Deceased," in *RT* xxx. 105–20 (1908).

GRIFFITH, F. LL., *The Inscriptions of Siut and Dêr Rîfeh.* London, 1889.

——— *The Petrie Papyri: Hieratic Papyri from Kahun and Gurob.* London, 1898.

GRIFFITH, F. LL., *Stories of the High Priests of Memphis*. Oxford, 1900.

—— "Herodotus II. 90. Apotheosis by Drowning," in *ÄZ* xlvi. 132–34 (1909).

GRIFFITH, F. LL., and THOMPSON, H., *The Demotic Magical Papyrus of London and Leiden*. London, 1904.

GSELL, S., "Les Cultes égyptiens dans le nord-ouest de l'Afrique sous l'empire romain," in *RHR* lix. 149–59 (1909).

GUIEYSSE, P., "Hymne au Nil," in *RT* xiii. 1–26 (1890). English translation in *RP*, new series, iii. 48–54.

GUIMET, É., "Les Âmes égyptiennes," in *RHR* lxviii. 1–17 (1913).

HARRIS MAGIC PAPYRUS. See AKMAR, E., and CHABAS, F.

HERODOTUS. See WIEDEMANN, A.

HISTORICAL PAPYRUS OF TURIN. See PLEYTE, W., and ROSSI, F.

HOMMEL, F., "Zum babylonischen Ursprung der ägyptischen Kultur," in *Memnon*, i. 80–85, 207–10 (1907).

HOPFNER, T., *Tierkult der alten Aegypter*. Vienna, 1913.

HORRACK, P. J. D', *Le Lamentations d'Isis et de Nephthys*. Paris, 1866. English translation in *RP* ii. 119–26.

—— *Le Livre des respirations*. Paris, 1877. English translation in *RP* iv. 121–28.

JABLONSKI, P. E., *Pantheon Ægypticum*. 3 vols. Frankfort, 1750–52.

JACOBY, A., and SPIEGELBERG, W., "Der Frosch als Symbol der Auferstehung bei den Aegyptern," in *Sphinx*, vii. 215–28 (1903).

JÉQUIER, G., *Le Livre de ce qu'il y a dans l'Hadès*. Paris, 1894.

—— *Le Papyrus Prisse et ses variantes*. Paris, 1911.

JEREMIAS, A., *Die Panbabylonisten, der alte Orient und die ägyptische Religion*. Leipzig, 1907.

JOUBIN, A., "Scène d'initiation aux mystères d'Isis sur un relief crétois," in *RT* xvi. 162–66 (1894).

JUNKER, H., *Die Stundenwachen in den Osirismysterien*. Vienna, 1910.

—— "Die Schlacht- und Brandopfer und ihre Symbolik im Tempelkult der Spätzeit," in *ÄZ* xlviii. 69–77 (1910).

—— "Die sechs Teile des Horusauges und der 'sechste Tag,'" in *ÄZ* xlviii. 101–06 (1910).

—— "Der Auszug der Hathor-Tefnut aus Nubien," in *ABAW*, 1911, Anhang, no. 3.

KEES, H., "Eine Liste memphitischer Götter im Tempel von Abydos," in *RT* xxxvii. 57–76 (1915).

KING, L. W., and HALL, H. R., *Egypt and Western Asia in the Light of Recent Discoveries*. London, 1907.

KNIGHT, A. E., *Amentet: An Account of the Gods, Amulets, and Scarabs of the Ancient Egyptians*. London, 1915.

KRISTENSEN, W. B., *Ägypternes forestillinger om livet efter döden*. Copenhagen, 1896.

LACAU, P., *Sarcophages antérieurs au nouvel empire*. 2 vols. Cairo, 1904–06.

—— *Textes religieux égyptiens*. Paris, 1910.

LAFAYE, G., *Histoire du culte des divinités d'Alexandrie, Sérapis, Isis, Harpocrate et Anubis, hors de l'Égypte*. Paris, 1884.

LANGE, H. O., "Die Aegypter," in P. D. Chantepie de la Saussaye, *Lehrbuch der Religionsgeschichte*, i. 172–245. 3rd ed. Tübingen, 1905.

LANZONE, R. V., *Le Domicile des esprits*. Paris, 1879.

—— *Dizionario di mitologia egizia*. Turin, 1881–86.

LEFÉBURE, E., *Le Mythe osirien*. 2 vols. Paris, 1874–75.

—— "L'Étude de la religion égyptienne," in *RHR* xiv. 26–48 (1886).

—— "L'Œuf dans la religion égyptienne," in *RHR* xvi. 16–25 (1887).

—— *Rites égyptiens*. Paris, 1890.

—— "L'Animal typhonien," in *Sphinx*, ii. 63–74 (1898).

—— "Le Sacrifice humain d'après les rites de Busiris et d'Abydos," in *Sphinx*, iii. 129–64 (1900).

—— "Le Paradis égyptien," in *Sphinx*, iii. 191–222 (1900).

—— "Khem et Ammon," in *Sphinx*, iv. 164–70 (1901).

—— "L'Arbre sacré d'Héliopolis," in *Sphinx*, v. 1–22, 65–88 (1902).

—— "Osiris à Byblos," in *Sphinx*, v. 210–20 (1902), vi. 1–14 (1903).

—— "Le Vase divinatoire," in *Sphinx*, vi. 61–85 (1903).

—— "Les Dieux du type rat dans le culte égyptien," in *Sphinx*, vi. 189–205 (1903), vii. 25–56 (1903).

—— "La Vertu du sacrifice funéraire," in *Sphinx*, vii. 185–209 (1903), viii. 1–51 (1904).

—— "Le Bucrâne," in *Sphinx*, x. 67–129 (1906).

—— "The Book of Hades," in *RP* x. 79–134, xii. 3–35.

LEGGE, F., "Magic Ivories of the Middle Empire," in *PSBA* xxvii. 130–52, 297–303 (1905), xxviii. 159–70 (1906).

1#

LEGGE, F., "The Greek Worship of Serapis and Isis," in *PSBA* xxxvi. 79–99 (1914).

—— *Forerunners and Rivals of Christianity*, ch. ii. 2 vols. Cambridge, 1915.

LEMM, O. VON, *Studien zum Ritualbuch des Amondienstes*. Leipzig, 1882.

LEPSIUS, C. R., *Das Todtenbuch der Aegypter*. Leipzig, 1842.

—— *Auswahl der wichtigsten Urkunden des ägyptischen Alterthums*. Leipzig, 1842.

—— *Denkmäler aus Ägypten und Äthiopien*. 12 vols. Berlin, 1849–56. (Revised edition by É. Naville, L. Borchardt, and K. Sethe. 6 vols. Leipzig, 1897–1913).

—— "Ueber den ersten ägyptischen Götterkreis und seine geschichtlich-mythologische Entstehung," in *ABAW*, 1851, pp. 157–214.

—— "Ueber die Götter der vier Elemente," in *ABAW*, 1856, pp. 181–234.

LEYDEN-LONDON GNOSTIC PAPYRUS. See GRIFFITH, F. LL., and THOMPSON, H.

LEYDEN PAPYRUS. See PLEYTE, W.

LIEBLEIN, J., *Gammelaegyptisk Religion*. 2 vols. Christiania, 1883–85. English summary in his *Egyptian Religion*. Christiania, 1884.

—— *Le Livre égyptien . . . Que mon nom fleurisse*. Leipzig, 1895.

LORET, V., "Les Fêtes d'Osiris au mois de Khoiak," in *RT* iii. 43–57 (1882), iv. 21–33 (1883), v. 85–103 (1884).

—— "L'Emblème hiéroglyphique de la vie," in *Sphinx*, v. 138–47 (1902).

—— "Horus-le-faucon," in *Bulletin de l'Institut français de l'archéologie orientale*, iii. 1–24 (1903).

MAHLER, E., "Notes on the Funeral Statuettes of the Ancient Egyptians, Commonly Called Ushabti Figures," in *PSBA* xxxiv. 146–51 (1912).

—— "The Jackal-Gods on Ancient Egyptian Monuments," in *PSBA* xxxvi. 143–64 (1914).

MALLET, D., *Le Culte de Neit à Sais*. Paris, 1888.

—— "Hymn to Osiris on the Stele of Amon-em-ha," in *RP*, new series, iv. 14–23.

MANETHO, ed. C. Müller, *Fragmenta historicorum Græcorum*, ii. 511–616. Paris, 1848.

MARIETTE, A. E., *Abydos*. 3 vols. Paris, 1869–80.

——— *Dendérah*. 4 vols. Paris, 1870–74.

——— *Les Papyrus égyptiens du musée de Boulaq*. 3 vols. Paris, 1871–76.

——— *Monuments diverses recueillis en Égypte et en Nubie*. 2 vols. Paris, 1872–89.

——— "Identification des dieux d'Hérodote avec les dieux égyptiens," in *Revue archéologique*, III. iv. 343–50 (1884).

——— *Les Mastaba de l'ancien empire*. Paris, 1889.

MASPERO, G., "Egyptian Documents relating to the Statues of the Dead," in *TSBA* vii. 6–36 (1882).

——— "Mémoire sur quelques papyrus du Louvre," in *Notices et extraits des manuscrits de la Bibliothèque Nationale*, xxiv. 1–123 (1883).

——— "Sur l'ennéade," in *RHR* xxv. 1–48 (1892).

——— *Études de mythologie et d'archéologie égyptiennes*. 7 vols. Paris, 1893–1900.

——— "La Table d'offrandes des tombeaux égyptiens," in *RHR* xxxv. 275–330 (1897), xxxvi. 1–19 (1897).

——— *Les Contes populaires de l'Égypte ancienne*. 4th ed. Paris, 1911. English translation. London, 1915.

——— "Le Ka des Égyptiens est-il un génie ou un double?" in *Memnon*, vi. 125–46 (1913).

MEAD, G. R. S., *Fragments of a Faith Forgotten*. London, 1900.

——— *Thrice-Greatest Hermes*. 3 vols. London, 1906.

MEYER, E. *Set-Typhon*. Leipzig, 1875.

———"Die Entwickelung der Kulte von Abydos und die sogenannten Schackalsgötter," in *ÄZ* xli. 97–107 (1904).

MÖLLER, G., *Hieratische Lesestücke*. 3 parts. Leipzig, 1909–10.

——— *Die beiden Totenpapyrus Rhind*. Leipzig, 1913.

MOORE, G. F., *History of Religions*, chh. viii–ix. Edinburgh, 1913.

MORET, A., *Du caractère religieuse de la royauté pharaonique*. Paris, 1902.

——— *Le Ritual du culte divin journalier en Égypte*. Paris, 1902.

——— *La Magie dans l'Égypte ancienne*. Paris, 1907.

——— "Du sacrifice en Égypte," in *RHR* lvii. 81–101 (1908).

——— *Mystères égyptiens*. Paris, 1913.

——— "Le Ka des Égyptiens est-il un ancien totem?" in *RHR* lxvii. 181–91 (1913).

MÜLLER, W. MAX, *Asien und Europa nach altägyptischen Denkmälern.* Leipzig, 1893.

—— *Die Liebespoesie der alten Ägypter.* Leipzig, 1899.

—— "Der Gott Proteus in Memphis," in *OL* vi. 99–101 (1903).

—— *Egyptological Researches.* 2 vols. Washington, 1906–10.

—— "Der Anspruch auf göttliche Inkarnation in den Pharaonennamen," in *OL* xii. 1–5 (1909).

—— "Marsyas," in *OL* xvi. 433–36 (1913).

MURRAY, MARGARET A., "The Astrological Character of the Egyptian Magical Wands," in *PSBA* xxviii. 33–43 (1906).

—— "The Cult of the Drowned in Egypt," in *ÄZ* li. 127–35 (1913).

NAVILLE, É., *La Litanie du soleil.* 2 vols. Leipzig, 1875.

—— "La Destruction des hommes par les dieux," in *TSBA* iv. 1–19 (1876), viii. 412–20 (1885). English translation in *RP* vi. 105–12.

—— "The Litany of Ra," in *RP* viii. 103–28.

—— *Das ägyptische Todtenbuch.* Berlin, 1886.

—— *The Shrine of Saft el Henneh and the Land of Goshen.* London, 1888.

—— *The Festival Hall of Osorkon II.* London, 1892.

—— *The Eleventh Dynasty Temple at Deir el Bahari.* 7 vols. London, 1894–1908.

—— *La Religion des anciens Égyptiens.* Paris, 1906. English translation, *The Old Egyptian Faith.* London, 1909.

NESI-AMSU. See BUDGE, E. A W.

NEWBERRY, P. E., and GRIFFITH, F. LL., *Beni Hasan.* 4 vols. London, 1893–1900.

ORELLI, C. VON, "Religion der alten Ägypter," in *Allgemeine Religionsgeschichte,* i. 122–81. 2nd ed. Bonn, 1911–13.

OTTO, W., *Priester und Tempel im hellenistischen Ägypten.* Leipzig, 1905.

PARISOTTI, A., *Ricerche sul culto di Iside e Serapide.* Rome, 1888.

PETERSEN, E., "Die Serapislegende," in *AR* xiii. 47–74 (1910).

PETRIE, W. M. F., *Tanis.* 2 vols. London, 1885–88.

—— *Egyptian Tales.* 2 vols. London, 1895.

—— *Religion and Conscience in Ancient Egypt.* London, 1898.

—— *Royal Tombs.* 2 vols. London, 1900–01.

—— *Diospolis Parva.* London, 1901.

—— *Abydos.* 3 vols. London, 1902–04.

—— *Religion of Ancient Egypt.* London, 1906.

PETRIE, W. M. F., *Gizeh and Rifeh*. London, 1907.
—— *Athribis*. London, 1908.
—— *Personal Religion in Egypt Before Christianity*. London, 1909.
—— *Memphis*. 6 vols. London, 1909-15.
PETRIE, W. M. F., and MACKAY, E., *Heliopolis, Kafr Ammar, and Shurafa*. London, 1915.
PIERRET, P., *Études égyptologiques*. Paris, 1873.
—— *Essai sur la mythologie égyptienne*. Paris, 1879.
—— *Le Panthéon égyptien*. Paris, 1881.
—— *Le Livre des morts des anciens Égyptiens*. 2nd ed. Paris, 1907.
—— *Les Interpretations de la religion égyptienne*. Paris, 1912.
PIETSCHMANN, R., "Der ägyptische Fetischdienst und Götterglaube," in *Zeitschrift für Ethnologie*, x. 153–82 (1878).
PLEYTE, W., *Set dans la barque du soleil*. Leyden, 1865.
—— *Étude sur un rouleau magique du musée de Leyde*. Leyden, 1866.
—— "La Couronne de la justification," in *Actes du sixième congrès international des orientalistes*, iv. 1–30. Leyden, 1885.
PLEYTE, W., and ROSSI, F., *Papyrus de Turin*. 2 vols. Leyden, 1869–76.
PLUTARCH, *De Iside et Osiride*. Ed. and tr. G. Parthey. Berlin, 1850.
PREISIGKE, F., and SPIEGELBERG, W., *Die Prinz Joachim Ostraka*. Strassburg, 1914.
QUIBELL, J. E., *The Ramesseum*. London, 1898.
—— *Hierakonpolis*. 2 vols. London, 1900–02.
RAVISI, TEXTOR DE, "L'Âme et le corps d'après la théogonie égyptienne," in *Congrès provincial des orientalistes français, Égyptologie*, pp. 171–420. Paris, 1880.
READ, F. W., "Egyptian Calendars of Lucky and Unlucky Days," in *PSBA* xxxviii. 19–26, 60–69 (1916).
READ, F. W., and BRYANT, A. C., "A Mythological Text from Memphis," in *PSBA* xxiii. 160–87 (1901), xxiv. 206–16 (1902).
REISNER, G. A., *Amulets*. Cairo, 1907.
—— *The Egyptian Conception of Immortality*. London, 1912.
REITZENSTEIN, R., *Poimandres*. Leipzig, 1904.
RENOUF, SIR P. LE PAGE, *Lectures on the Origin and Growth of Religion as Illustrated by the Religion of Ancient Egypt*. London, 1880.
—— "Egyptian Mythology, Particularly with Reference to Mist and Cloud," in *TSBA* viii. 198–229 (1885).
—— "The Myth of Osiris Unnefer," in *TSBA* ix. 281–94 (1893).

Renouf, Sir P. le Page, and Naville, É., *The Egyptian Book of the Dead.* London, 1904.

Robiou, F., "La Religion de l'ancienne Égypte et les influences étrangères," in *Congrès scientifique international des Catholiques,* i. 22–60. Paris, 1889.

Roeder, G., "Sothis und Satis," in *ÄZ* xlv. 22–30 (1908).

—— "Der Name und das Tier des Gottes Set," in *ÄZ* l. 84–86 (1912).

—— "Das ägyptische Pantheon," in *AR* xv. 59–98 (1912).

—— "Die ägyptischen 'Sargtexte' und das Totenbuch," in *AR* xvi. 66–85 (1913).

Rosellini, I., *Monumenti del culto.* 2 vols. Pisa, 1882–84. (Part iii of his *Monumenti dell' Egitto e della Nubia.*)

Rusch, A., *De Serapide et Iside in Græcia cultis.* Berlin, 1906.

Sallier Papyrus. See Anonymous, *Select Papyri.*

Sayce, A. H., *The Religions of Ancient Egypt and Babylonia.* Edinburgh, 1902.

Schack-Schackenburg, H., *Buch von den zwei Wegen.* Leipzig, 1903.

Schäfer, H., *Die Mysterien des Osiris in Abydos.* Leipzig, 1904.

Schencke, W., *Amon-Re.* Christiania, 1904.

Schiaparelli, E., *Il Libro dei funerali dei antichi Egiziani.* 2 vols. and atlas. Turin, 1881–90.

Sethe, K., *Die altägyptischen Pyramidtexte.* 2 vols. Leipzig, 1908–10.

—— "Der Name der Göttin Neith," in *ÄZ* xliii. 144–47 (1906).

—— "Der Name des Gottes Kꜣ𝛽," in *ÄZ* xliii. 147–49 (1906).

—— "Der Name des Gottes Suchos," in *ÄZ* l. 80–83 (1912).

Sethe, K., and Schäfer, H., *Urkunden des ägyptischen Altertums.* 10 vols. Leipzig, 1903–09.

Sourdille, C., *Hérodote et la religion de l'Égypte.* Paris, 1910.

Spence, L., *Myths and Legends of Ancient Egypt.* London, 1915.

Spiegelberg, W., *Demotische Papyrus aus den königlichen Museen von Berlin.* Leipzig, 1902.

—— "Ein ägyptisches Verzeichnis der Planeten und Tierkreisbilder," in *OL* v. 6–9 (1902).

—— "Der Stabkultus bei den Ægyptern," in *RT* xxv. 184–90 (1903).

—— *Aegyptologische Randglossen zum Alten Testament.* Strassburg, 1904.

—— *Die demotischen Denkmäler.* 2 vols. Leipzig, 1904–08.

BIBLIOGRAPHY 33¹

SPIEGELBERG, W., "Der ägyptische Mythus vom Sonnenauge in einem demotischen Papyrus der römischen Kaiserzeit," in *SBAW*, 1915, pp. 876–95.

STEINDORFF, G., *The Religion of the Early Egyptians*. New York, 1903.

—— "Der Ka und die Grabstatuen," in *ÄZ* xlviii. 152–59 (1910).

STERN, L., "Ein Hymnus an Amon-Rā," in *ÄZ* xi. 74–81, 125–27 (1873).

STRAUSS UND TORNEY, V. VON, *Der altägyptische Götterglaube*. 2 vols. Heidelberg, 1889–91.

TIELE, C. P., *Vergelijkende Geschiedenis der egyptische en mesopotamische Godsdiensten*. 2 vols. Amsterdam, 1869–72. English translation of i, *History of the Egyptian Religion*. London, 1882.

—— *Geschiedenis van den Godsdienst in de Oudheid*. 2 vols. Amsterdam, 1895–1901.

TYLOR, J. J., *The Tomb of Paheri at El Kab*. London, 1894.

VATICAN MAGIC PAPYRUS. See ERMAN, A.

VIREY, P., *Études sur le Papyrus Prisse, le Livre de Kaqimna et Leçons de Ptah-hotep*. Paris, 1887.

—— "Le Tombeau de Rekhmara," in *Mémoires publiés par les membres de la mission archéologique française au Caire*, v. 1–195 (1894).

—— *La Religion de l'ancienne Égypte*. Paris, 1910.

WESTCAR PAPYRUS. See ERMAN, A.

WIEDEMANN, A., "Die Phönix-Sage im alten Aegypten," in *ÄZ* xvi. 89–106 (1878).

—— "Maa déesse de la vérité et son rôle dans le panthéon égyptien," in *Annales du Musée Guimet*, x. 561–73 (1887).

—— *Die Religion der alten Ägypter*. Münster, 1890. English translation. London, 1897.

—— *Herodot's zweites Buch mit sachlichen Erläuterungen*. Leipzig, 1890.

—— *The Ancient Egyptian Doctrine of the Immortality of the Soul*. London, 1895.

—— *Die Todten und ihre Reiche im Glauben der alten Ägypter*. Leipzig, 1900. English translation, *The Realms of the Egyptian Dead*. London, 1901.

—— "Religion of Egypt," in *Dictionary of the Bible*, extra volume, pp. 176–97. Edinburgh, 1904.

—— *Magie und Zauberei im alten Ägypten*. Leipzig, 1905.

WIEDEMANN, A., *Die Amulette der alten Aegypter*. Leipzig, 1910.
—— *Tierkult der alten Aegypter*. Leipzig, 1912.
WILKINSON, J. G., *Manners and Customs of the Ancient Egyptians*. 3 vols. London, 1837.
WRESZINSKI, W., "Tagewählerei im alten Ägypten," in *AR* xvi. 86–100 (1913).
ZIMMERMANN, F., *Die ägyptische Religion nach der Darstellung der Kirchenschriftsteller und der ägyptischen Denkmäler*. Paderborn, 1912.

III. PRINCIPAL ARTICLES ON EGYPTIAN RELIGION IN THE ENCYCLOPÆDIA OF RELIGION AND ETHICS (VOLS. I–IX)

BAIKIE, J., "Confession (Egyptian)," iii. 827–29.
—— "Creed (Egyptian)," iv. 242–44.
—— "Hymns (Egyptian)," vii. 38–40.
—— "Images and Idols (Egyptian)," vii. 131–33.
—— "Literature (Egyptian)," viii. 92–95.
—— "Manetho," viii. 393–94.
—— "Music (Egyptian)," ix. 33–36.
—— "Nature (Egyptian)," ix. 217–20.
FOUCART, G., "Body (Egyptian)," ii. 763–68.
—— "Calendar (Egyptian)," iii. 91–105.
—— "Children (Egyptian)," iii. 532–39.
—— "Circumcision (Egyptian)," iii. 670–77.
—— "Conscience (Egyptian)," iv. 34–37.
—— "Demons and Spirits (Egyptian)," iv. 584–90.
—— "Disease and Medicine (Egyptian)," iv. 749–53.
—— "Divination (Egyptian)," iv. 792–96.
—— "Dreams and Sleep (Egyptian)," v. 34–37.
—— "Dualism (Egyptian)," v. 104–07.
—— "Festivals and Fasts (Egyptian)," v. 853–57.
—— "Inheritance (Egyptian)," vii. 299–302.
—— "King (Egyptian)," vii. 711–15.
—— "Names (Egyptian)," ix. 151–55.
GARDINER, A. H., "Ethics and Morality (Egyptian)," v. 475–85.
—— "Life and Death (Egyptian)," viii. 19–25.

GARDINER, A. H., "Magic (Egyptian)," viii. 262–69.

—— "Personification (Egyptian)," ix. 787–92.

—— "Philosophy (Egyptian)," ix. 857–59.

GRIFFITH, F. LL., "Altar (Egyptian)," i. 342.

—— "Atheism (Egyptian)," ii. 184.

—— "Birth (Egyptian)," ii. 646–47.

—— "Crimes and Punishments (Egyptian)," iv. 272–73.

—— "Law (Egyptian)," vii. 846–47.

—— "Marriage (Egyptian)," viii. 443–44.

HALL, H. R., "Ancestor-Worship and Cult of the Dead (Egyptian),"
  i. 440–43.

—— "Death and Disposal of the Dead (Egyptian)," iv. 458–64.

—— "Expiation and Atonement (Egyptian)," v. 650–51.

—— "Family (Egyptian)," v. 733–35.

—— "Fate (Egyptian)," v. 785–86.

MILNE, J. G., "Græco-Egyptian Religion," vi. 374–84.

MORET, A., "Mysteries (Egyptian)," ix. 74–77.

NAVILLE, É., "Charms and Amulets (Egyptian)," iii. 430–33.

PETRIE, W. M. F., "Architecture (Egyptian)," i. 722–26.

—— "Art (Egyptian)," i. 862–63.

—— "Communion with Deity (Egyptian)," iii. 760–62.

—— "Cosmogony and Cosmology (Egyptian)," iv. 144–45.

—— "Egyptian Religion," v. 236–50.

SETHE, K., "Heroes and Hero-Gods (Egyptian)," vi. 647–52.

SHOWERMAN, G., "Isis," vii. 434–37.

STOCK, ST. G., "Hermes Trismegistos," vi. 626–29.

WIEDEMANN, A., "God (Egyptian)," vi. 274–79.

—— "Incarnation (Egyptian)," vii. 188–92.

A CATALOG OF SELECTED
DOVER BOOKS
IN ALL FIELDS OF INTEREST

A CATALOG OF SELECTED DOVER
BOOKS IN ALL FIELDS OF INTEREST

CONCERNING THE SPIRITUAL IN ART, Wassily Kandinsky. Pioneering work by father of abstract art. Thoughts on color theory, nature of art. Analysis of earlier masters. 12 illustrations. 80pp. of text. 5⅜ x 8½.   0-486-23411-8

CELTIC ART: The Methods of Construction, George Bain. Simple geometric techniques for making Celtic interlacements, spirals, Kells-type initials, animals, humans, etc. Over 500 illustrations. 160pp. 9 x 12. (Available in U.S. only.)   0-486-22923-8

AN ATLAS OF ANATOMY FOR ARTISTS, Fritz Schider. Most thorough reference work on art anatomy in the world. Hundreds of illustrations, including selections from works by Vesalius, Leonardo, Goya, Ingres, Michelangelo, others. 593 illustrations. 192pp. 7⅛ x 10¼.   0-486-20241-0

CELTIC HAND STROKE-BY-STROKE (Irish Half-Uncial from "The Book of Kells"): An Arthur Baker Calligraphy Manual, Arthur Baker. Complete guide to creating each letter of the alphabet in distinctive Celtic manner. Covers hand position, strokes, pens, inks, paper, more. Illustrated. 48pp. 8¼ x 11.   0-486-24336-2

EASY ORIGAMI, John Montroll. Charming collection of 32 projects (hat, cup, pelican, piano, swan, many more) specially designed for the novice origami hobbyist. Clearly illustrated easy-to-follow instructions insure that even beginning papercrafters will achieve successful results. 48pp. 8¼ x 11.   0-486-27298-2

BLOOMINGDALE'S ILLUSTRATED 1886 CATALOG: Fashions, Dry Goods and Housewares, Bloomingdale Brothers. Famed merchants' extremely rare catalog depicting about 1,700 products: clothing, housewares, firearms, dry goods, jewelry, more. Invaluable for dating, identifying vintage items. Also, copyright-free graphics for artists, designers. Co-published with Henry Ford Museum & Greenfield Village. 160pp. 8¼ x 11.   0-486-25780-0

THE ART OF WORLDLY WISDOM, Baltasar Gracian. "Think with the few and speak with the many," "Friends are a second existence," and "Be able to forget" are among this 1637 volume's 300 pithy maxims. A perfect source of mental and spiritual refreshment, it can be opened at random and appreciated either in brief or at length. 128pp. 5⅜ x 8½.   0-486-44034-6

JOHNSON'S DICTIONARY: A Modern Selection, Samuel Johnson (E. L. McAdam and George Milne, eds.). This modern version reduces the original 1755 edition's 2,300 pages of definitions and literary examples to a more manageable length, retaining the verbal pleasure and historical curiosity of the original. 480pp. 5⁹⁄₁₆ x 8¼.   0-486-44089-3

ADVENTURES OF HUCKLEBERRY FINN, Mark Twain, Illustrated by E. W. Kemble. A work of eternal richness and complexity, a source of ongoing critical debate, and a literary landmark, Twain's 1885 masterpiece about a barefoot boy's journey of self-discovery has enthralled readers around the world. This handsome clothbound reproduction of the first edition features all 174 of the original black-and-white illustrations. 368pp. 5⅜ x 8½.   0-486-44322-1

CATALOG OF DOVER BOOKS

STICKLEY CRAFTSMAN FURNITURE CATALOGS, Gustav Stickley and L. & J. G. Stickley. Beautiful, functional furniture in two authentic catalogs from 1910. 594 illustrations, including 277 photos, show settles, rockers, armchairs, reclining chairs, bookcases, desks, tables. 183pp. 6½ x 9¼. 0-486-23838-5

AMERICAN LOCOMOTIVES IN HISTORIC PHOTOGRAPHS: 1858 to 1949, Ron Ziel (ed.). A rare collection of 126 meticulously detailed official photographs, called "builder portraits," of American locomotives that majestically chronicle the rise of steam locomotive power in America. Introduction. Detailed captions. xi+ 129pp. 9 x 12. 0-486-27393-8

AMERICA'S LIGHTHOUSES: An Illustrated History, Francis Ross Holland, Jr. Delightfully written, profusely illustrated fact-filled survey of over 200 American lighthouses since 1716. History, anecdotes, technological advances, more. 240pp. 8 x 10¾. 0-486-25576-X

TOWARDS A NEW ARCHITECTURE, Le Corbusier. Pioneering manifesto by founder of "International School." Technical and aesthetic theories, views of industry, economics, relation of form to function, "mass-production split" and much more. Profusely illustrated. 320pp. 6⅛ x 9¼. (Available in U.S. only.) 0-486-25023-7

HOW THE OTHER HALF LIVES, Jacob Riis. Famous journalistic record, exposing poverty and degradation of New York slums around 1900, by major social reformer. 100 striking and influential photographs. 233pp. 10 x 7⅞. 0-486-22012-5

FRUIT KEY AND TWIG KEY TO TREES AND SHRUBS, William M. Harlow. One of the handiest and most widely used identification aids. Fruit key covers 120 deciduous and evergreen species; twig key 160 deciduous species. Easily used. Over 300 photographs. 126pp. 5⅜ x 8½. 0-486-20511-8

COMMON BIRD SONGS, Dr. Donald J. Borror. Songs of 60 most common U.S. birds: robins, sparrows, cardinals, bluejays, finches, more–arranged in order of increasing complexity. Up to 9 variations of songs of each species.
Cassette and manual 0-486-99911-4

ORCHIDS AS HOUSE PLANTS, Rebecca Tyson Northen. Grow cattleyas and many other kinds of orchids–in a window, in a case, or under artificial light. 63 illustrations. 148pp. 5⅜ x 8½. 0-486-23261-1

MONSTER MAZES, Dave Phillips. Masterful mazes at four levels of difficulty. Avoid deadly perils and evil creatures to find magical treasures. Solutions for all 32 exciting illustrated puzzles. 48pp. 8¼ x 11. 0-486-26005-4

MOZART'S DON GIOVANNI (DOVER OPERA LIBRETTO SERIES), Wolfgang Amadeus Mozart. Introduced and translated by Ellen H. Bleiler. Standard Italian libretto, with complete English translation. Convenient and thoroughly portable–an ideal companion for reading along with a recording or the performance itself. Introduction. List of characters. Plot summary. 121pp. 5¼ x 8½. 0-486-24944-1

FRANK LLOYD WRIGHT'S DANA HOUSE, Donald Hoffmann. Pictorial essay of residential masterpiece with over 160 interior and exterior photos, plans, elevations, sketches and studies. 128pp. 9¼ x 10¾. 0-486-29120-0

THE CLARINET AND CLARINET PLAYING, David Pino. Lively, comprehensive work features suggestions about technique, musicianship, and musical interpretation, as well as guidelines for teaching, making your own reeds, and preparing for public performance. Includes an intriguing look at clarinet history. "A godsend," *The Clarinet,* Journal of the International Clarinet Society. Appendixes. 7 illus. 320pp. $5\frac{3}{8}$ x $8\frac{1}{2}$. 0-486-40270-3

HOLLYWOOD GLAMOR PORTRAITS, John Kobal (ed.). 145 photos from 1926-49. Harlow, Gable, Bogart, Bacall; 94 stars in all. Full background on photographers, technical aspects. 160pp. $8\frac{3}{8}$ x $11\frac{1}{4}$. 0-486-23352-9

THE RAVEN AND OTHER FAVORITE POEMS, Edgar Allan Poe. Over 40 of the author's most memorable poems: "The Bells," "Ulalume," "Israfel," "To Helen," "The Conqueror Worm," "Eldorado," "Annabel Lee," many more. Alphabetic lists of titles and first lines. 64pp. $5\frac{3}{16}$ x $8\frac{1}{4}$. 0-486-26685-0

PERSONAL MEMOIRS OF U. S. GRANT, Ulysses Simpson Grant. Intelligent, deeply moving firsthand account of Civil War campaigns, considered by many the finest military memoirs ever written. Includes letters, historic photographs, maps and more. 528pp. $6\frac{1}{8}$ x $9\frac{1}{4}$. 0-486-28587-1

POE ILLUSTRATED: Art by Doré, Dulac, Rackham and Others, selected and edited by Jeff A. Menges. More than 100 compelling illustrations, in brilliant color and crisp black-and-white, include scenes from "The Raven," "The Pit and the Pendulum," "The Gold-Bug," and other stories and poems. 96pp. $8\frac{3}{8}$ x 11. 0-486-45746-X

RUSSIAN STORIES/RUSSKIE RASSKAZY: A Dual-Language Book, edited by Gleb Struve. Twelve tales by such masters as Chekhov, Tolstoy, Dostoevsky, Pushkin, others. Excellent word-for-word English translations on facing pages, plus teaching and study aids, Russian/English vocabulary, biographical/critical introductions, more. 416pp. $5\frac{3}{8}$ x $8\frac{1}{2}$. 0-486-26244-8

PHILADELPHIA THEN AND NOW: 60 Sites Photographed in the Past and Present, Kenneth Finkel and Susan Oyama. Rare photographs of City Hall, Logan Square, Independence Hall, Betsy Ross House, other landmarks juxtaposed with contemporary views. Captures changing face of historic city. Introduction. Captions. 128pp. $8\frac{1}{4}$ x 11. 0-486-25790-8

NORTH AMERICAN INDIAN LIFE: Customs and Traditions of 23 Tribes, Elsie Clews Parsons (ed.). 27 fictionalized essays by noted anthropologists examine religion, customs, government, additional facets of life among the Winnebago, Crow, Zuni, Eskimo, other tribes. 480pp. $6\frac{1}{8}$ x $9\frac{1}{4}$. 0-486-27377-6

TECHNICAL MANUAL AND DICTIONARY OF CLASSICAL BALLET, Gail Grant. Defines, explains, comments on steps, movements, poses and concepts. 15-page pictorial section. Basic book for student, viewer. 127pp. $5\frac{3}{8}$ x $8\frac{1}{2}$. 0-486-21843-0

THE MALE AND FEMALE FIGURE IN MOTION: 60 Classic Photographic Sequences, Eadweard Muybridge. 60 true-action photographs of men and women walking, running, climbing, bending, turning, etc., reproduced from a rare 19th-century masterpiece. vi + 121pp. 9 x 12. 0-486-24745-7

CATALOG OF DOVER BOOKS

ANIMALS: 1,419 Copyright-Free Illustrations of Mammals, Birds, Fish, Insects, etc., Jim Harter (ed.). Clear wood engravings present, in extremely lifelike poses, over 1,000 species of animals. One of the most extensive pictorial sourcebooks of its kind. Captions. Index. 284pp. 9 x 12. 0-486-23766-4

1001 QUESTIONS ANSWERED ABOUT THE SEASHORE, N. J. Berrill and Jacquelyn Berrill. Queries answered about dolphins, sea snails, sponges, starfish, fishes, shore birds, many others. Covers appearance, breeding, growth, feeding, much more. 305pp. 5¼ x 8¼. 0-486-23366-9

ATTRACTING BIRDS TO YOUR YARD, William J. Weber. Easy-to-follow guide offers advice on how to attract the greatest diversity of birds: birdhouses, feeders, water and waterers, much more. 96pp. 5³⁄₁₆ x 8¼. 0-486-28927-3

MEDICINAL AND OTHER USES OF NORTH AMERICAN PLANTS: A Historical Survey with Special Reference to the Eastern Indian Tribes, Charlotte Erichsen-Brown. Chronological historical citations document 500 years of usage of plants, trees, shrubs native to eastern Canada, northeastern U.S. Also complete identifying information. 343 illustrations. 544pp. 6½ x 9¼. 0-486-25951-X

STORYBOOK MAZES, Dave Phillips. 23 stories and mazes on two-page spreads: Wizard of Oz, Treasure Island, Robin Hood, etc. Solutions. 64pp. 8¼ x 11.
0-486-23628-5

AMERICAN NEGRO SONGS: 230 Folk Songs and Spirituals, Religious and Secular, John W. Work. This authoritative study traces the African influences of songs sung and played by black Americans at work, in church, and as entertainment. The author discusses the lyric significance of such songs as "Swing Low, Sweet Chariot," "John Henry," and others and offers the words and music for 230 songs. Bibliography. Index of Song Titles. 272pp. 6½ x 9¼. 0-486-40271-1

MOVIE-STAR PORTRAITS OF THE FORTIES, John Kobal (ed.). 163 glamor, studio photos of 106 stars of the 1940s: Rita Hayworth, Ava Gardner, Marlon Brando, Clark Gable, many more. 176pp. 8⅜ x 11¼. 0-486-23546-7

YEKL and THE IMPORTED BRIDEGROOM AND OTHER STORIES OF YIDDISH NEW YORK, Abraham Cahan. Film Hester Street based on *Yekl* (1896). Novel, other stories among first about Jewish immigrants on N.Y.'s East Side. 240pp. 5⅜ x 8½. 0-486-22427-9

SELECTED POEMS, Walt Whitman. Generous sampling from *Leaves of Grass*. Twenty-four poems include "I Hear America Singing," "Song of the Open Road," "I Sing the Body Electric," "When Lilacs Last in the Dooryard Bloom'd," "O Captain! My Captain!"—all reprinted from an authoritative edition. Lists of titles and first lines. 128pp. 5³⁄₁₆ x 8¼. 0-486-26878-0

SONGS OF EXPERIENCE: Facsimile Reproduction with 26 Plates in Full Color, William Blake. 26 full-color plates from a rare 1826 edition. Includes "The Tyger," "London," "Holy Thursday," and other poems. Printed text of poems. 48pp. 5¼ x 7.
0-486-24636-1

THE BEST TALES OF HOFFMANN, E. T. A. Hoffmann. 10 of Hoffmann's most important stories: "Nutcracker and the King of Mice," "The Golden Flowerpot," etc. 458pp. 5⅜ x 8½. 0-486-21793-0

THE BOOK OF TEA, Kakuzo Okakura. Minor classic of the Orient: entertaining, charming explanation, interpretation of traditional Japanese culture in terms of tea ceremony. 94pp. 5⅜ x 8½. 0-486-20070-1

CATALOG OF DOVER BOOKS

FRENCH STORIES/CONTES FRANÇAIS: A Dual-Language Book, Wallace Fowlie. Ten stories by French masters, Voltaire to Camus: "Micromegas" by Voltaire; "The Atheist's Mass" by Balzac; "Minuet" by de Maupassant; "The Guest" by Camus, six more. Excellent English translations on facing pages. Also French-English vocabulary list, exercises, more. 352pp. 5⅜ x 8½. 0-486-26443-2

CHICAGO AT THE TURN OF THE CENTURY IN PHOTOGRAPHS: 122 Historic Views from the Collections of the Chicago Historical Society, Larry A. Viskochil. Rare large-format prints offer detailed views of City Hall, State Street, the Loop, Hull House, Union Station, many other landmarks, circa 1904-1913. Introduction. Captions. Maps. 144pp. 9⅜ x 12¼. 0-486-24656-6

OLD BROOKLYN IN EARLY PHOTOGRAPHS, 1865–1929, William Lee Younger. Luna Park, Gravesend race track, construction of Grand Army Plaza, moving of Hotel Brighton, etc. 157 previously unpublished photographs. 165pp. 8⅞ x 11¾. 0-486-23587-4

THE MYTHS OF THE NORTH AMERICAN INDIANS, Lewis Spence. Rich anthology of the myths and legends of the Algonquins, Iroquois, Pawnees and Sioux, prefaced by an extensive historical and ethnological commentary. 36 illustrations. 480pp. 5⅜ x 8½. 0-486-25967-6

AN ENCYCLOPEDIA OF BATTLES: Accounts of Over 1,560 Battles from 1479 B.C. to the Present, David Eggenberger. Essential details of every major battle in recorded history from the first battle of Megiddo in 1479 B.C. to Grenada in 1984. List of Battle Maps. New Appendix covering the years 1967–1984. Index. 99 illustrations. 544pp. 6½ x 9¼. 0-486-24913-1

SAILING ALONE AROUND THE WORLD, Captain Joshua Slocum. First man to sail around the world, alone, in small boat. One of the great feats of seamanship told in delightful manner. 67 illustrations. 294pp. 5⅜ x 8½. 0-486-20326-3

ANARCHISM AND OTHER ESSAYS, Emma Goldman. Powerful, penetrating, prophetic essays on direct action, role of minorities, prison reform, puritan hypocrisy, violence, etc. 271pp. 5⅜ x 8½. 0-486-22484-8

MYTHS OF THE HINDUS AND BUDDHISTS, Ananda K. Coomaraswamy and Sister Nivedita. Great stories of the epics; deeds of Krishna, Shiva, taken from puranas, Vedas, folk tales; etc. 32 illustrations. 400pp. 5⅜ x 8½. 0-486-21759-0

MY BONDAGE AND MY FREEDOM, Frederick Douglass. Born a slave, Douglass became outspoken force in antislavery movement. The best of Douglass' autobiographies. Graphic description of slave life. 464pp. 5⅜ x 8½. 0-486-22457-0

FOLLOWING THE EQUATOR: A Journey Around the World, Mark Twain. Fascinating humorous account of 1897 voyage to Hawaii, Australia, India, New Zealand, etc. Ironic, bemused reports on peoples, customs, climate, flora and fauna, politics, much more. 197 illustrations. 720pp. 5⅜ x 8½. 0-486-26113-1

GREAT SPEECHES BY AMERICAN WOMEN, edited by James Daley. Here are 21 legendary speeches from the country's most inspirational female voices, including Sojourner Truth, Susan B. Anthony, Eleanor Roosevelt, Hillary Rodham Clinton, Nancy Pelosi, and many others. 192pp. 5³⁄₁₆ x 8¼. 0-486-46141-6

THE MYTHS OF GREECE AND ROME, H. A. Guerber. A classic of mythology, generously illustrated, long prized for its simple, graphic, accurate retelling of the principal myths of Greece and Rome, and for its commentary on their origins and significance. With 64 illustrations by Michelangelo, Raphael, Titian, Rubens, Canova, Bernini and others. 480pp. 5⅜ x 8½. 0-486-27584-1

CATALOG OF DOVER BOOKS

PSYCHOLOGY OF MUSIC, Carl E. Seashore. Classic work discusses music as a medium from psychological viewpoint. Clear treatment of physical acoustics, auditory apparatus, sound perception, development of musical skills, nature of musical feeling, host of other topics. 88 figures. 408pp. 5⅜ x 8½.   0-486-21851-1

LIFE IN ANCIENT EGYPT, Adolf Erman. Fullest, most thorough, detailed older account with much not in more recent books, domestic life, religion, magic, medicine, commerce, much more. Many illustrations reproduce tomb paintings, carvings, hieroglyphs, etc. 597pp. 5⅜ x 8½.   0-486-22632-8

SUNDIALS, Their Theory and Construction, Albert Waugh. Far and away the best, most thorough coverage of ideas, mathematics concerned, types, construction, adjusting anywhere. Simple, nontechnical treatment allows even children to build several of these dials. Over 100 illustrations. 230pp. 5⅜ x 8½.   0-486-22947-5

GREAT SPEECHES BY AFRICAN AMERICANS: Frederick Douglass, Sojourner Truth, Dr. Martin Luther King, Jr., Barack Obama, and Others, edited by James Daley. Tracing the struggle for freedom and civil rights across two centuries, this anthology comprises speeches by Martin Luther King, Jr., Marcus Garvey, Malcolm X, Barack Obama, and many other influential figures. 160pp. 5³⁄₁₆ x 8¼.
0-486-44761-8

OLD-TIME VIGNETTES IN FULL COLOR, Carol Belanger Grafton (ed.). Over 390 charming, often sentimental illustrations, selected from archives of Victorian graphics—pretty women posing, children playing, food, flowers, kittens and puppies, smiling cherubs, birds and butterflies, much more. All copyright-free. 48pp. 9¼ x 12¼.
0-486-27269-9

PERSPECTIVE FOR ARTISTS, Rex Vicat Cole. Depth, perspective of sky and sea, shadows, much more, not usually covered. 391 diagrams, 81 reproductions of drawings and paintings. 279pp. 5⅜ x 8½.   0-486-22487-2

DRAWING THE LIVING FIGURE, Joseph Sheppard. Innovative approach to artistic anatomy focuses on specifics of surface anatomy, rather than muscles and bones. Over 170 drawings of live models in front, back and side views, and in widely varying poses. Accompanying diagrams. 177 illustrations. Introduction. Index. 144pp. 8⅜ x11¼.   0-486-26723-7

GOTHIC AND OLD ENGLISH ALPHABETS: 100 Complete Fonts, Dan X. Solo. Add power, elegance to posters, signs, other graphics with 100 stunning copyright-free alphabets: Blackstone, Dolbey, Germania, 97 more—including many lower-case, numerals, punctuation marks. 104pp. 8⅛ x 11.   0-486-24695-7

THE BOOK OF WOOD CARVING, Charles Marshall Sayers. Finest book for beginners discusses fundamentals and offers 34 designs. "Absolutely first rate . . . well thought out and well executed."–E. J. Tangerman. 118pp. 7¾ x 10⅝. 0-486-23654-4

ILLUSTRATED CATALOG OF CIVIL WAR MILITARY GOODS: Union Army Weapons, Insignia, Uniform Accessories, and Other Equipment, Schuyler, Hartley, and Graham. Rare, profusely illustrated 1846 catalog includes Union Army uniform and dress regulations, arms and ammunition, coats, insignia, flags, swords, rifles, etc. 226 illustrations. 160pp. 9 x 12.   0-486-24939-5

WOMEN'S FASHIONS OF THE EARLY 1900s: An Unabridged Republication of "New York Fashions, 1909," National Cloak & Suit Co. Rare catalog of mail-order fashions documents women's and children's clothing styles shortly after the turn of the century. Captions offer full descriptions, prices. Invaluable resource for fashion, costume historians. Approximately 725 illustrations. 128pp. 8⅜ x 11¼.   0-486-27276-1

HOW TO DO BEADWORK, Mary White. Fundamental book on craft from simple projects to five-bead chains and woven works. 106 illustrations. 142pp. 5⅜ x 8.
0-486-20697-1

THE 1912 AND 1915 GUSTAV STICKLEY FURNITURE CATALOGS, Gustav Stickley. With over 200 detailed illustrations and descriptions, these two catalogs are essential reading and reference materials and identification guides for Stickley furniture. Captions cite materials, dimensions and prices. 112pp. 6½ x 9¼. 0-486-26676-1

SIX GREAT DIALOGUES: Apology, Crito, Phaedo, Phaedrus, Symposium, The Republic, Plato, translated by Benjamin Jowett. Plato's Dialogues rank among Western civilization's most important and influential philosophical works. These 6 selections of his major works explore a broad range of enduringly relevant issues. Authoritative Jowett translations. 480pp. 5³⁄₁₆ x 8¼.   0-486-45465-7

DEMONOLATRY: An Account of the Historical Practice of Witchcraft, Nicolas Remy, edited with an Introduction and Notes by Montague Summers, translated by E. A. Ashwin. This extremely influential 1595 study was frequently cited at witchcraft trials. In addition to lurid details of satanic pacts and sexual perversity, it presents the particulars of numerous court cases. 240pp. 6½ x 9¼.   0-486-46137-8

VICTORIAN FASHIONS AND COSTUMES FROM HARPER'S BAZAAR, 1867–1898, Stella Blum (ed.). Day costumes, evening wear, sports clothes, shoes, hats, other accessories in over 1,000 detailed engravings. 320pp. 9⅜ x 12¼.
0-486-22990-4

THE LONG ISLAND RAIL ROAD IN EARLY PHOTOGRAPHS, Ron Ziel. Over 220 rare photos, informative text document origin (1844) and development of rail service on Long Island. Vintage views of early trains, locomotives, stations, passengers, crews, much more. Captions. 8⅞ x 11¾.   0-486-26301-0

VOYAGE OF THE LIBERDADE, Joshua Slocum. Great 19th-century mariner's thrilling, first-hand account of the wreck of his ship off South America, the 35-foot boat he built from the wreckage, and its remarkable voyage home. 128pp. 5⅜ x 8½.
0-486-40022-0

TEN BOOKS ON ARCHITECTURE, Vitruvius. The most important book ever written on architecture. Early Roman aesthetics, technology, classical orders, site selection, all other aspects. Morgan translation. 331pp. 5⅜ x 8½.   0-486-20645-9

THE HUMAN FIGURE IN MOTION, Eadweard Muybridge. More than 4,500 stopped-action photos, in action series, showing undraped men, women, children jumping, lying down, throwing, sitting, wrestling, carrying, etc. 390pp. 7⅞ x 10⅝.
0-486-20204-6 Clothbd.

TREES OF THE EASTERN AND CENTRAL UNITED STATES AND CANADA, William M. Harlow. Best one-volume guide to 140 trees. Full descriptions, woodlore, range, etc. Over 600 illustrations. Handy size. 288pp. 4½ x 6⅜.   0-486-20395-6

MY FIRST BOOK OF TCHAIKOVSKY: Favorite Pieces in Easy Piano Arrangements, edited by David Dutkanicz. These special arrangements of favorite Tchaikovsky themes are ideal for beginner pianists, child or adult. Contents include themes from "The Nutcracker," "March Slav," Symphonies Nos. 5 and 6, "Swan Lake," "Sleeping Beauty," and more. 48pp. 8¼ x 11.   0-486-46416-4

BIG BOOK OF MAZES AND LABYRINTHS, Walter Shepherd. 50 mazes and labyrinths in all–classical, solid, ripple, and more–in one great volume. Perfect inexpensive puzzler for clever youngsters. Full solutions. 112pp. 8⅛ x 11. 0-486-22951-3

PIANO TUNING, J. Cree Fischer. Clearest, best book for beginner, amateur. Simple repairs, raising dropped notes, tuning by easy method of flattened fifths. No previous skills needed. 4 illustrations. 201pp. 5⅜ x 8½.   0-486-23267-0

HINTS TO SINGERS, Lillian Nordica. Selecting the right teacher, developing confidence, overcoming stage fright, and many other important skills receive thoughtful discussion in this indispensible guide, written by a world-famous diva of four decades' experience. 96pp. $5\frac{3}{8}$ x $8\frac{1}{2}$. 0-486-40094-8

THE COMPLETE NONSENSE OF EDWARD LEAR, Edward Lear. All nonsense limericks, zany alphabets, Owl and Pussycat, songs, nonsense botany, etc., illustrated by Lear. Total of 320pp. $5\frac{3}{8}$ x $8\frac{1}{2}$. (Available in U.S. only.) 0-486-20167-8

VICTORIAN PARLOUR POETRY: An Annotated Anthology, Michael R. Turner. 117 gems by Longfellow, Tennyson, Browning, many lesser-known poets. "The Village Blacksmith," "Curfew Must Not Ring Tonight," "Only a Baby Small," dozens more, often difficult to find elsewhere. Index of poets, titles, first lines. xxiii + 325pp. $5\frac{5}{8}$ x $8\frac{1}{4}$. 0-486-27044-0

DUBLINERS, James Joyce. Fifteen stories offer vivid, tightly focused observations of the lives of Dublin's poorer classes. At least one, "The Dead," is considered a masterpiece. Reprinted complete and unabridged from standard edition. 160pp. $5\frac{3}{16}$ x $8\frac{1}{4}$. 0-486-26870-5

THE LITTLE RED SCHOOLHOUSE, Eric Sloane. Harkening back to a time when the three Rs stood for reading, 'riting, and religion, Sloane's sketchbook explores the history of early American schools. Includes marvelous illustrations of one-room New England schoolhouses, desks, and benches. 48pp. $8\frac{1}{4}$ x 11. 0-486-45604-8

THE BOOK OF THE SACRED MAGIC OF ABRAMELIN THE MAGE, translated by S. MacGregor Mathers. Medieval manuscript of ceremonial magic. Basic document in Aleister Crowley, Golden Dawn groups. 268pp. $5\frac{3}{8}$ x $8\frac{1}{2}$. 0-486-23211-5

THE BATTLES THAT CHANGED HISTORY, Fletcher Pratt. Eminent historian profiles 16 crucial conflicts, ancient to modern, that changed the course of civilization. 352pp. $5\frac{3}{8}$ x $8\frac{1}{2}$. 0-486-41129-X

NEW RUSSIAN-ENGLISH AND ENGLISH-RUSSIAN DICTIONARY, M. A. O'Brien. This is a remarkably handy Russian dictionary, containing a surprising amount of information, including over 70,000 entries. 366pp. $4\frac{1}{2}$ x $6\frac{1}{8}$. 0-486-20208-9

NEW YORK IN THE FORTIES, Andreas Feininger. 162 brilliant photographs by the well-known photographer, formerly with *Life* magazine. Commuters, shoppers, Times Square at night, much else from city at its peak. Captions by John von Hartz. 181pp. $9\frac{1}{4}$ x $10\frac{3}{4}$. 0-486-23585-8

INDIAN SIGN LANGUAGE, William Tomkins. Over 525 signs developed by Sioux and other tribes. Written instructions and diagrams. Also 290 pictographs. 111pp. $6\frac{1}{8}$ x $9\frac{1}{4}$. 0-486-22029-X

ANATOMY: A Complete Guide for Artists, Joseph Sheppard. A master of figure drawing shows artists how to render human anatomy convincingly. Over 460 illustrations. 224pp. $8\frac{3}{8}$ x $11\frac{1}{4}$. 0-486-27279-6

MEDIEVAL CALLIGRAPHY: Its History and Technique, Marc Drogin. Spirited history, comprehensive instruction manual covers 13 styles (ca. 4th century through 15th). Excellent photographs; directions for duplicating medieval techniques with modern tools. 224pp. $8\frac{3}{8}$ x $11\frac{1}{4}$. 0-486-26142-5

CATALOG OF DOVER BOOKS

DRIED FLOWERS: How to Prepare Them, Sarah Whitlock and Martha Rankin. Complete instructions on how to use silica gel, meal and borax, perlite aggregate, sand and borax, glycerine and water to create attractive permanent flower arrangements. 12 illustrations. 32pp. 5⅜ x 8½. 0-486-21802-3

EASY-TO-MAKE BIRD FEEDERS FOR WOODWORKERS, Scott D. Campbell. Detailed, simple-to-use guide for designing, constructing, caring for and using feeders. Text, illustrations for 12 classic and contemporary designs. 96pp. 5⅜ x 8½. 0-486-25847-5

THE COMPLETE BOOK OF BIRDHOUSE CONSTRUCTION FOR WOOD-WORKERS, Scott D. Campbell. Detailed instructions, illustrations, tables. Also data on bird habitat and instinct patterns. Bibliography. 3 tables. 63 illustrations in 15 figures. 48pp. 5¼ x 8½. 0-486-24407-5

SCOTTISH WONDER TALES FROM MYTH AND LEGEND, Donald A. Mackenzie. 16 lively tales tell of giants rumbling down mountainsides, of a magic wand that turns stone pillars into warriors, of gods and goddesses, evil hags, powerful forces and more. 240pp. 5⅜ x 8½. 0-486-29677-6

THE HISTORY OF UNDERCLOTHES, C. Willett Cunnington and Phyllis Cunnington. Fascinating, well-documented survey covering six centuries of English undergarments, enhanced with over 100 illustrations: 12th-century laced-up bodice, footed long drawers (1795), 19th-century bustles, l9th-century corsets for men, Victorian "bust improvers," much more. 272pp. 5⅜ x 8¼. 0-486-27124-2

FIRST FRENCH READER: A Beginner's Dual-Language Book, edited and translated by Stanley Appelbaum. This anthology introduces fifty legendary writers—Voltaire, Balzac, Baudelaire, Proust, more—through passages from The Red and the Black, Les Misérables, Madame Bovary, and other classics. Original French text plus English translation on facing pages. 240pp. 5⅜ x 8½. 0-486-46178-5

WILBUR AND ORVILLE: A Biography of the Wright Brothers, Fred Howard. Definitive, crisply written study tells the full story of the brothers' lives and work. A vividly written biography, unparalleled in scope and color, that also captures the spirit of an extraordinary era. 560pp. 6⅛ x 9¼. 0-486-40297-5

THE ARTS OF THE SAILOR: Knotting, Splicing and Ropework, Hervey Garrett Smith. Indispensable shipboard reference covers tools, basic knots and useful hitches; handsewing and canvas work, more. Over 100 illustrations. Delightful reading for sea lovers. 256pp. 5⅜ x 8½. 0-486-26440-8

FRANK LLOYD WRIGHT'S FALLINGWATER: The House and Its History, Second, Revised Edition, Donald Hoffmann. A total revision—both in text and illustrations—of the standard document on Fallingwater, the boldest, most personal architectural statement of Wright's mature years, updated with valuable new material from the recently opened Frank Lloyd Wright Archives. "Fascinating"—The New York Times. 116 illustrations. 128pp. 9¼ x 10¾. 0-486-27430-6

PHOTOGRAPHIC SKETCHBOOK OF THE CIVIL WAR, Alexander Gardner. 100 photos taken on field during the Civil War. Famous shots of Manassas Harper's Ferry, Lincoln, Richmond, slave pens, etc. 244pp. 10⅝ x 8¼. 0-486-22731-6

FIVE ACRES AND INDEPENDENCE, Maurice G. Kains. Great back-to-the-land classic explains basics of self-sufficient farming. The one book to get. 95 illustrations. 397pp. 5⅜ x 8½. 0-486-20974-1

CATALOG OF DOVER BOOKS

A MODERN HERBAL, Margaret Grieve. Much the fullest, most exact, most useful compilation of herbal material. Gigantic alphabetical encyclopedia, from aconite to zedoary, gives botanical information, medical properties, folklore, economic uses, much else. Indispensable to serious reader. 161 illustrations. 888pp. 6½ x 9¼. 2-vol. set. (Available in U.S. only.)   Vol. I: 0-486-22798-7   Vol. II: 0-486-22799-5

HIDDEN TREASURE MAZE BOOK, Dave Phillips. Solve 34 challenging mazes accompanied by heroic tales of adventure. Evil dragons, people-eating plants, bloodthirsty giants, many more dangerous adversaries lurk at every twist and turn. 34 mazes, stories, solutions. 48pp. 8¼ x 11.   0-486-24566-7

LETTERS OF W. A. MOZART, Wolfgang A. Mozart. Remarkable letters show bawdy wit, humor, imagination, musical insights, contemporary musical world; includes some letters from Leopold Mozart. 276pp. 5⅜ x 8½.   0-486-22859-2

BASIC PRINCIPLES OF CLASSICAL BALLET, Agrippina Vaganova. Great Russian theoretician, teacher explains methods for teaching classical ballet. 118 illustrations. 175pp. 5⅜ x 8½.   0-486-22036-2

THE JUMPING FROG, Mark Twain. Revenge edition. The original story of The Celebrated Jumping Frog of Calaveras County, a hapless French translation, and Twain's hilarious "retranslation" from the French. 12 illustrations. 66pp. 5⅜ x 8½.
                                                               0-486-22686-7

BEST REMEMBERED POEMS, Martin Gardner (ed.). The 126 poems in this superb collection of 19th- and 20th-century British and American verse range from Shelley's "To a Skylark" to the impassioned "Renascence" of Edna St. Vincent Millay and to Edward Lear's whimsical "The Owl and the Pussycat." 224pp. 5⅜ x 8½.
                                                               0-486-27165-X

COMPLETE SONNETS, William Shakespeare. Over 150 exquisite poems deal with love, friendship, the tyranny of time, beauty's evanescence, death and other themes in language of remarkable power, precision and beauty. Glossary of archaic terms. 80pp. 5³⁄₁₆ x 8¼.   0-486-26686-9

HISTORIC HOMES OF THE AMERICAN PRESIDENTS, Second, Revised Edition, Irvin Haas. A traveler's guide to American Presidential homes, most open to the public, depicting and describing homes occupied by every American President from George Washington to George Bush. With visiting hours, admission charges, travel routes. 175 photographs. Index. 160pp. 8¼ x 11.   0-486-26751-2

THE WIT AND HUMOR OF OSCAR WILDE, Alvin Redman (ed.). More than 1,000 ripostes, paradoxes, wisecracks: Work is the curse of the drinking classes; I can resist everything except temptation; etc. 258pp. 5⅜ x 8½.   0-486-20602-5

SHAKESPEARE LEXICON AND QUOTATION DICTIONARY, Alexander Schmidt. Full definitions, locations, shades of meaning in every word in plays and poems. More than 50,000 exact quotations. 1,485pp. 6½ x 9¼. 2-vol. set.
                        Vol. 1: 0-486-22726-X   Vol. 2: 0-486-22727-8

SELECTED POEMS, Emily Dickinson. Over 100 best-known, best-loved poems by one of America's foremost poets, reprinted from authoritative early editions. No comparable edition at this price. Index of first lines. 64pp. 5³⁄₁₆ x 8¼. 0-486-26466-1

THE INSIDIOUS DR. FU-MANCHU, Sax Rohmer. The first of the popular mystery series introduces a pair of English detectives to their archnemesis, the diabolical Dr. Fu-Manchu. Flavorful atmosphere, fast-paced action, and colorful characters enliven this classic of the genre. 208pp. 5³⁄₁₆ x 8¼.   0-486-29898-1

CATALOG OF DOVER BOOKS

THE MALLEUS MALEFICARUM OF KRAMER AND SPRENGER, translated by Montague Summers. Full text of most important witchhunter's "bible," used by both Catholics and Protestants. 278pp. 6⅝ x 10. 0-486-22802-9

SPANISH STORIES/CUENTOS ESPAÑOLES: A Dual-Language Book, Angel Flores (ed.). Unique format offers 13 great stories in Spanish by Cervantes, Borges, others. Faithful English translations on facing pages. 352pp. 5⅜ x 8½.
0-486-25399-6

GARDEN CITY, LONG ISLAND, IN EARLY PHOTOGRAPHS, 1869–1919, Mildred H. Smith. Handsome treasury of 118 vintage pictures, accompanied by carefully researched captions, document the Garden City Hotel fire (1899), the Vanderbilt Cup Race (1908), the first airmail flight departing from the Nassau Boulevard Aerodrome (1911), and much more. 96pp. 8⅞ x 11¾. 0-486-40669-5

OLD QUEENS, N.Y., IN EARLY PHOTOGRAPHS, Vincent F. Seyfried and William Asadorian. Over 160 rare photographs of Maspeth, Jamaica, Jackson Heights, and other areas. Vintage views of DeWitt Clinton mansion, 1939 World's Fair and more. Captions. 192pp. 8⅞ x 11. 0-486-26358-4

CAPTURED BY THE INDIANS: 15 Firsthand Accounts, 1750-1870, Frederick Drimmer. Astounding true historical accounts of grisly torture, bloody conflicts, relentless pursuits, miraculous escapes and more, by people who lived to tell the tale. 384pp. 5⅜ x 8½. 0-486-24901-8

THE WORLD'S GREAT SPEECHES (Fourth Enlarged Edition), Lewis Copeland, Lawrence W. Lamm, and Stephen J. McKenna. Nearly 300 speeches provide public speakers with a wealth of updated quotes and inspiration–from Pericles' funeral oration and William Jennings Bryan's "Cross of Gold Speech" to Malcolm X's powerful words on the Black Revolution and Earl of Spenser's tribute to his sister, Diana, Princess of Wales. 944pp. 5⅜ x 8⅜. 0-486-40903-1

THE BOOK OF THE SWORD, Sir Richard F. Burton. Great Victorian scholar/adventurer's eloquent, erudite history of the "queen of weapons"–from prehistory to early Roman Empire. Evolution and development of early swords, variations (sabre, broadsword, cutlass, scimitar, etc.), much more. 336pp. 6⅛ x 9¼.
0-486-25434-8

AUTOBIOGRAPHY: The Story of My Experiments with Truth, Mohandas K. Gandhi. Boyhood, legal studies, purification, the growth of the Satyagraha (nonviolent protest) movement. Critical, inspiring work of the man responsible for the freedom of India. 480pp. 5⅜ x 8½. (Available in U.S. only.) 0-486-24593-4

CELTIC MYTHS AND LEGENDS, T. W. Rolleston. Masterful retelling of Irish and Welsh stories and tales. Cuchulain, King Arthur, Deirdre, the Grail, many more. First paperback edition. 58 full-page illustrations. 512pp. 5⅜ x 8½. 0-486-26507-2

THE PRINCIPLES OF PSYCHOLOGY, William James. Famous long course complete, unabridged. Stream of thought, time perception, memory, experimental methods; great work decades ahead of its time. 94 figures. 1,391pp. 5⅜ x 8½. 2-vol. set.
Vol. I: 0-486-20381-6   Vol. II: 0-486-20382-4

THE WORLD AS WILL AND REPRESENTATION, Arthur Schopenhauer. Definitive English translation of Schopenhauer's life work, correcting more than 1,000 errors, omissions in earlier translations. Translated by E. F. J. Payne. Total of 1,269pp. 5⅜ x 8½. 2-vol. set.   Vol. 1: 0-486-21761-2   Vol. 2: 0-486-21762-0

CATALOG OF DOVER BOOKS

MAGIC AND MYSTERY IN TIBET, Madame Alexandra David-Neel. Experiences among lamas, magicians, sages, sorcerers, Bonpa wizards. A true psychic discovery. 32 illustrations. 321pp. 5⅜ x 8½. (Available in U.S. only.) 0-486-22682-4

THE EGYPTIAN BOOK OF THE DEAD, E. A. Wallis Budge. Complete reproduction of Ani's papyrus, finest ever found. Full hieroglyphic text, interlinear transliteration, word-for-word translation, smooth translation. 533pp. 6½ x 9¼.
0-486-21866-X

HISTORIC COSTUME IN PICTURES, Braun & Schneider. Over 1,450 costumed figures in clearly detailed engravings—from dawn of civilization to end of 19th century. Captions. Many folk costumes. 256pp. 8⅜ x 11¾. 0-486-23150-X

MATHEMATICS FOR THE NONMATHEMATICIAN, Morris Kline. Detailed, college-level treatment of mathematics in cultural and historical context, with numerous exercises. Recommended Reading Lists. Tables. Numerous figures. 641pp. 5⅜ x 8½. 0-486-24823-2

PROBABILISTIC METHODS IN THE THEORY OF STRUCTURES, Isaac Elishakoff. Well-written introduction covers the elements of the theory of probability from two or more random variables, the reliability of such multivariable structures, the theory of random function, Monte Carlo methods of treating problems incapable of exact solution, and more. Examples. 502pp. 5⅜ x 8½. 0-486-40691-1

THE RIME OF THE ANCIENT MARINER, Gustave Doré, S. T. Coleridge. Doré's finest work; 34 plates capture moods, subtleties of poem. Flawless full-size reproductions printed on facing pages with authoritative text of poem. "Beautiful. Simply beautiful."–Publisher's Weekly. 77pp. 9¼ x 12. 0-486-22305-1

SCULPTURE: Principles and Practice, Louis Slobodkin. Step-by-step approach to clay, plaster, metals, stone; classical and modern. 253 drawings, photos. 255pp. 8⅛ x 11. 0-486-22960-2

THE INFLUENCE OF SEA POWER UPON HISTORY, 1660–1783, A. T. Mahan. Influential classic of naval history and tactics still used as text in war colleges. First paperback edition. 4 maps. 24 battle plans. 640pp. 5⅜ x 8½. 0-486-25509-3

THE STORY OF THE TITANIC AS TOLD BY ITS SURVIVORS, Jack Winocour (ed.). What it was really like. Panic, despair, shocking inefficiency, and a little heroism. More thrilling than any fictional account. 26 illustrations. 320pp. 5⅜ x 8½.
0-486-20610-6

ONE TWO THREE . . . INFINITY: Facts and Speculations of Science, George Gamow. Great physicist's fascinating, readable overview of contemporary science: number theory, relativity, fourth dimension, entropy, genes, atomic structure, much more. 128 illustrations. Index. 352pp. 5⅜ x 8½. 0-486-25664-2

DALÍ ON MODERN ART: The Cuckolds of Antiquated Modern Art, Salvador Dalí. Influential painter skewers modern art and its practitioners. Outrageous evaluations of Picasso, Cézanne, Turner, more. 15 renderings of paintings discussed. 44 calligraphic decorations by Dalí. 96pp. 5⅜ x 8½. (Available in U.S. only.) 0-486-29220-7

ANTIQUE PLAYING CARDS: A Pictorial History, Henry René D'Allemagne. Over 900 elaborate, decorative images from rare playing cards (14th–20th centuries): Bacchus, death, dancing dogs, hunting scenes, royal coats of arms, players cheating, much more. 96pp. 9¼ x 12¼. 0-486-29265-7

MAKING FURNITURE MASTERPIECES: 30 Projects with Measured Drawings, Franklin H. Gottshall. Step-by-step instructions, illustrations for constructing handsome, useful pieces, among them a Sheraton desk, Chippendale chair, Spanish desk, Queen Anne table and a William and Mary dressing mirror. 224pp. 8⅛ x 11¼.
0-486-29338-6

NORTH AMERICAN INDIAN DESIGNS FOR ARTISTS AND CRAFTSPEOPLE, Eva Wilson. Over 360 authentic copyright-free designs adapted from Navajo blankets, Hopi pottery, Sioux buffalo hides, more. Geometrics, symbolic figures, plant and animal motifs, etc. 128pp. 8⅜ x 11. (Not for sale in the United Kingdom.)   0-486-25341-4

THE FOSSIL BOOK: A Record of Prehistoric Life, Patricia V. Rich et al. Profusely illustrated definitive guide covers everything from single-celled organisms and dinosaurs to birds and mammals and the interplay between climate and man. Over 1,500 illustrations. 760pp. 7½ x 10⅛.   0-486-29371-8

VICTORIAN ARCHITECTURAL DETAILS: Designs for Over 700 Stairs, Mantels, Doors, Windows, Cornices, Porches, and Other Decorative Elements, A. J. Bicknell & Company. Everything from dormer windows and piazzas to balconies and gable ornaments. Also includes elevations and floor plans for handsome, private residences and commercial structures. 80pp. 9⅜ x 12¼.   0-486-44015-X

WESTERN ISLAMIC ARCHITECTURE: A Concise Introduction, John D. Hoag. Profusely illustrated critical appraisal compares and contrasts Islamic mosques and palaces—from Spain and Egypt to other areas in the Middle East. 139 illustrations. 128pp. 6 x 9.   0-486-43760-4

CHINESE ARCHITECTURE: A Pictorial History, Liang Ssu-ch'eng. More than 240 rare photographs and drawings depict temples, pagodas, tombs, bridges, and imperial palaces comprising much of China's architectural heritage. 152 halftones, 94 diagrams. 232pp. 10¾ x 9⅞.   0-486-43999-2

THE RENAISSANCE: Studies in Art and Poetry, Walter Pater. One of the most talked-about books of the 19th century, *The Renaissance* combines scholarship and philosophy in an innovative work of cultural criticism that examines the achievements of Botticelli, Leonardo, Michelangelo, and other artists. "The holy writ of beauty."–Oscar Wilde. 160pp. 5⅜ x 8½.   0-486-44025-7

A TREATISE ON PAINTING, Leonardo da Vinci. The great Renaissance artist's practical advice on drawing and painting techniques covers anatomy, perspective, composition, light and shadow, and color. A classic of art instruction, it features 48 drawings by Nicholas Poussin and Leon Battista Alberti. 192pp. 5⅜ x 8½.
0-486-44155-5

THE ESSENTIAL JEFFERSON, Thomas Jefferson, edited by John Dewey. This extraordinary primer offers a superb survey of Jeffersonian thought. It features writings on political and economic philosophy, morals and religion, intellectual freedom and progress, education, secession, slavery, and more. 176pp. 5⅜ x 8½.
0-486-46599-3

WASHINGTON IRVING'S RIP VAN WINKLE, Illustrated by Arthur Rackham. Lovely prints that established artist as a leading illustrator of the time and forever etched into the popular imagination a classic of Catskill lore. 51 full-color plates. 80pp. 8⅜ x 11.   0-486-44242-X

HENSCHE ON PAINTING, John W. Robichaux. Basic painting philosophy and methodology of a great teacher, as expounded in his famous classes and workshops on Cape Cod. 7 illustrations in color on covers. 80pp. 5⅜ x 8½.   0-486-43728-0

LIGHT AND SHADE: A Classic Approach to Three-Dimensional Drawing, Mrs. Mary P. Merrifield. Handy reference clearly demonstrates principles of light and shade by revealing effects of common daylight, sunshine, and candle or artificial light on geometrical solids. 13 plates. 64pp. 5⅜ x 8½. 0-486-44143-1

ASTROLOGY AND ASTRONOMY: A Pictorial Archive of Signs and Symbols, Ernst and Johanna Lehner. Treasure trove of stories, lore, and myth, accompanied by more than 300 rare illustrations of planets, the Milky Way, signs of the zodiac, comets, meteors, and other astronomical phenomena. 192pp. 8⅜ x 11. 0-486-43981-X

JEWELRY MAKING: Techniques for Metal, Tim McCreight. Easy-to-follow instructions and carefully executed illustrations describe tools and techniques, use of gems and enamels, wire inlay, casting, and other topics. 72 line illustrations and diagrams. 176pp. 8¼ x 10⅞. 0-486-44043-5

MAKING BIRDHOUSES: Easy and Advanced Projects, Gladstone Califf. Easy-to-follow instructions include diagrams for everything from a one-room house for bluebirds to a forty-two-room structure for purple martins. 56 plates; 4 figures. 80pp. 8¾ x 6⅜. 0-486-44183-0

LITTLE BOOK OF LOG CABINS: How to Build and Furnish Them, William S. Wicks. Handy how-to manual, with instructions and illustrations for building cabins in the Adirondack style, fireplaces, stairways, furniture, beamed ceilings, and more. 102 line drawings. 96pp. 8¾ x 6⅜. 0-486-44259-4

THE SEASONS OF AMERICA PAST, Eric Sloane. From "sugaring time" and strawberry picking to Indian summer and fall harvest, a whole year's activities described in charming prose and enhanced with 79 of the author's own illustrations. 160pp. 8¼ x 11. 0-486-44220-9

THE METROPOLIS OF TOMORROW, Hugh Ferriss. Generous, prophetic vision of the metropolis of the future, as perceived in 1929. Powerful illustrations of towering structures, wide avenues, and rooftop parks–all features in many of today's modern cities. 59 illustrations. 144pp. 8¼ x 11. 0-486-43727-2

THE PATH TO ROME, Hilaire Belloc. This 1902 memoir abounds in lively vignettes from a vanished time, recounting a pilgrimage on foot across the Alps and Apennines in order to "see all Europe which the Christian Faith has saved." 77 of the author's original line drawings complement his sparkling prose. 272pp. 5⅜ x 8½. 0-486-44001-X

THE HISTORY OF RASSELAS: Prince of Abissinia, Samuel Johnson. Distinguished English writer attacks eighteenth-century optimism and man's unrealistic estimates of what life has to offer. 112pp. 5⅜ x 8½. 0-486-44094-X

A VOYAGE TO ARCTURUS, David Lindsay. A brilliant flight of pure fancy, where wild creatures crowd the fantastic landscape and demented torturers dominate victims with their bizarre mental powers. 272pp. 5⅜ x 8½. 0-486-44198-9

Paperbound unless otherwise indicated. Available at your book dealer, online at **www.doverpublications.com**, or by writing to Dept. GI, Dover Publications, Inc., 31 East 2nd Street, Mineola, NY 11501. For current price information or for free catalogs (please indicate field of interest), write to Dover Publications or log on to **www.doverpublications.com** and see every Dover book in print. Dover publishes more than 400 books each year on science, elementary and advanced mathematics, biology, music, art, literary history, social sciences, and other areas.